FROM ABORTION
TO PEDERASTY

FROM ABORTION TO PEDERASTY

Addressing Difficult Topics in the Classics Classroom

EDITED BY
Nancy Sorkin Rabinowitz
AND **Fiona McHardy**

 THE OHIO STATE UNIVERSITY PRESS · COLUMBUS

Copyright © 2014 by The Ohio State University.
All rights reserved.

Library of Congress Cataloging-in-Publication Data available online.

ISBN-13: 978-0-8142-1261-5 (cloth : alk. paper)
ISBN-13: 978-0-8142-9365-2 (cd-rom)

Cover design by Juliet Williams
Text design by Juliet Williams
Type set in Adobe Garamond Pro
Printed by Thomson-Shore, Inc.

♾ The paper used in this publication meets the minimum requirements of the American National Standard for Information Sciences—Permanence of Paper for Printed Library Materials. ANSI Z39.48–1992.

9 8 7 6 5 4 3 2 1

CONTENTS

List of Illustrations   vii

Editors' Preface   ix

INTRODUCTION · Difficult and Sensitive Discussions
             NANCY SORKIN RABINOWITZ   1

CHAPTER 1 · Near Death Experiences: Greek Art and Archaeology beyond the Grave
             TYLER JO SMITH AND CARRIE L. SULOSKY WEAVER   13

CHAPTER 2 · Raising Lazarus: Death in the Classics Classroom
             MARGARET E. BUTLER   39

CHAPTER 3 · Teaching about Disability in Today's Classics Classroom
             LISA TRENTIN   53

CHAPTER 4 · Teaching Ancient Medicine: The Issues of Abortion
             PATTY BAKER, HELEN KING, AND LAURENCE TOTELIN   71

CHAPTER 5 · The "Whole-University Approach" to the Pedagogy of Domestic Violence
             SUSAN DEACY AND FIONA MCHARDY   92

CHAPTER 6 · Teaching Uncomfortable Subjects: When Religious Beliefs Get in the Way
             POLYXENI STROLONGA   107

CHAPTER 7 · Too Sexy for South Africa?: Teaching Aristophanes' *Lysistrata* in the Land of the Rainbow Nation
 SUZANNE SHARLAND   119

CHAPTER 8 · Pedagogy and Pornography in the Classics Classroom
 GENEVIEVE LIVELEY   139

CHAPTER 9 · Challenges in Teaching Sexual Violence and Rape: A Male Perspective
 SANJAYA THAKUR   152

CHAPTER 10 · Talking Rape in the Classics Classroom: Further Thoughts
 SHARON L. JAMES   171

CHAPTER 11 · Teaching the Uncomfortable Subject of Slavery
 PAGE DUBOIS   187

CHAPTER 12 · Teaching Ancient Comedy: Joking About Race, Ethnicity, and Slavery
 BARBARA GOLD   199

CHAPTER 13 · Difficult Dialogues about a Difficult Dialogue: Plato's *Symposium* and Its Gay Tradition
 NIKOLAI ENDRES   212

CHAPTER 14 · A World Away from Ours: Homoeroticism in the Classics Classroom
 WALTER DUVALL PENROSE, JR.   227

CHAPTER 15 · Queering Catullus in the Classroom: The Ethics of Teaching Poem 63
 MAXINE LEWIS   248

Bibliography   267
Contributors   295
Index   298

ILLUSTRATIONS

FIGURE 1.1	Drawing of burial from the heroön at Lefkandi. 10th c. BCE	14
FIGURE 1.2	Athenian red-figure loutrophoros. c. 430 BCE	23
FIGURE 1.3	South Italian funerary relief. c. 325–300 BCE	25
FIGURE 1.4	Detail of Klazomenian sarcophagus. Late 6th c. BCE	29
FIGURE 1.5	Reconstructed grave from Rhitsona (no. 145), Boeotia. First half of 6th c. BCE	35
FIGURE 4.1	Egyptian image depicting circumcision	81
FIGURE 4.2	Roman vaginal specula	82
FIGURE 4.3	Roman fetal hook with reconstructed drawing	83
FIGURE 4.4	Equipment used for a gynecological examination. Modern speculum on the right.	84

EDITORS' PREFACE

AS THE Introduction makes clear, this volume grows out of a series of conversations on pedagogy in the Classics. We want to thank all of those who participated in electronic and face-to-face conversations between the panel on pedagogy at the University of Michigan Feminism and Classics Conference in 2008 and the present publication. Their interest in questions of how to teach difficult topics was an inspiration.

INTRODUCTION

Difficult and Sensitive Discussions[1]

NANCY SORKIN RABINOWITZ

THIS VOLUME had its beginnings at the fifth Feminism and Classics conference, held at the University of Michigan in spring of 2008. At that time, Sharon James organized a panel on the topic of pedagogy with some of her graduate students. Her paper, which was published in *Cloelia* (2008), focused on teaching texts that depict rape, and she described an incident that had taken place years earlier when she was teaching a large, lecture-style mythology course. She realized that deep problems can emerge in the process of addressing such texts, especially if, as in her case, both the rape survivor and the assailant are in the room (on teaching Ovid, see Kahn 2004). In the discussion that followed her paper, participants took up the question of what we as a group of feminist scholars might do about the problem of rape. Some were so moved by the topic that we organized a round table discussion entitled "Teaching Rape Texts in Classical Literature: Activism, Pedagogy, and the American University" at the next annual meeting of the American Philological Association (APA). The open format of that event allowed us to identify others interested in the problem and to keep the issue of teaching rape on the agenda of the Women's Classical Caucus. Internationally, we took the conversation to the British Classical Association with a roundtable discussion in Glasgow in 2009.

---

1. I would like to thank Eugene O'Connor for his vision and encouragement, the anonymous reviewers for their help and suggestions, and Fiona McHardy and Corinne Bancroft for their careful reading and commentary.

As a result of the email correspondence, in the fall of 2009 members of the Women's Classical Caucus began the process of expanding the dialogue to include other topics that seemed to be as important and as difficult to discuss. Thus arose a panel entitled "How to Manage Difficult Conversations in Classics Classrooms" at the Classics Association of the Atlantic States. Finally, the proximate cause and kernel of this current volume was an APA panel in 2011 called "Teaching Difficult Subjects in the Classics Classroom." In this collection of essays, we address potentially politically divisive topics such as race, sexual orientation, and abortion, as well as those topics that might arouse emotional as well as political anxiety, such as rape, sex, and death. We recognize that these categories overlap and intersect; for instance, rape and sexuality are closely related to current political debates.

The conversations we have been having within Classics should be placed in the context of two larger discourses both nationally and internationally. First, scholars have noticed the "crisis in the Humanities" for at least fifty years—J. H. Plumb edited a book with that title in 1964—and perhaps even as long ago as Aristophanes' attacks on Socrates. In the 1990s the conservatives in the academy mocked the "politically correct" left wing for its insistence on changing the curriculum; William Cain analyzes Gerald Graff's argument that theories that denied "'that poetry asserts anything or makes propositional truth claims' had worsened the plight of humanists, who had defined themselves in a manner that separated them from 'the everyday demands of objectivity and public reality.' . . . If humanists shunned making claims for the knowledge that the arts offer, . . . then they could hardly complain, Graff stated, when their activities were regarded as ornamental and, at bottom, trivial" (Cain 1994: xxiii, citing Graff 1970: xiv).[2] There has been a shift in nomenclature, the term "culture wars" and talk of political correctness have ebbed, but much remains the same (Cartledge 1998: 17).

Indeed, the attacks have intensified with the corporatization of the academy, by which I mean the involvement of corporations in every aspect of the schools, including: the big-business of testing, the privatization of education, the dominance in universities of attitudes borrowed from business board rooms. In this context, the Humanities and the liberal arts seem useless; the fundamentally anti-intellectual arguments from the corporatization of the academy (Clegg and David 2008; Tuchman 2009; Schrecker 2010: esp. chapters 6, 7) are accompanied by demands for direct lines from education to employment, assessment to demonstrate the value of the lib-

---

2. See Gubar and Kamholtz (1993) for a summary of the impact of those wars, though more on English departments than on Classics.

eral arts (with talk in the faculty of the need to show "value added"). The cuts in Humanities departments' staff and funding are clear evidence of the effects of this situation.³ In an article about English literary study, Mark Eaton has this to say: "Ironically, the justification for reading literature is articulated more and more frequently in terms of a set of skills rather than a body of knowledge. English departments are now heavily invested in teaching writing, and many students encounter literary texts only in writing courses" (Eaton 2001: 313). In January of 2012, President Barack Obama unveiled his new education thinking; his plan "calls for linking federal aid not only to net price increases but to whether colleges provide 'good value' to students—a 'quality education and training that prepares graduates to obtain employment and repay their loans'" (Nelson 2012). This demand is very chilling—especially given the problems in the global economy.

Second, the liberation movements of the 60s, with their accompanying attention to racial diversity in the student body, also led to the demand for more relevant courses. As a result, the curriculum has been a site of cultural and political contestation.⁴ The Classics in particular have been attacked from the left, as being not only a mausoleum of dead white male authors but also for the discipline's role as the gate keeper to the halls of power—keeping women and people of color out (though this has been less and less true since 1950; see Cartledge 1998; Hardwick and Stray 2008: 1–11; Stray 1998; duBois 2010a). The function of Classics, as defined and critiqued by Seth Schein, "to legitimate a social order and a set of institutions, beliefs, and values that are commonly associated with western civilization and 'our' western cultural heritage" (Schein 2008: 75), and its role as a status marker, have exacerbated our problems (Stray 1998: 40). The Classical curriculum's double role in European culture, subjecting students to discipline while promising to elevate them in society, was also prominent in colonial education (Goff and Simpson 2007; Hardwick and Gillespie 2007; Greenwood 2010). Furthermore, Classics' philological method has also tended to insulate the field from developments in critical theory taking place elsewhere in the Humanities.

What happens to Classics in the case of the movement for curricular change? Yun Lee Too concludes the introduction to *Power and Pedagogy*

---

3. See for example the cuts in language departments at SUNY Albany and the challenges to the Classics degree at Royal Holloway (Jaschik 2010; Higgins 2011).

4. The relationship of liberation movements to curriculum and pedagogic innovation is discussed by Sleeter and McLaren (1995) and in particular the ways in which the language of diversity and multiculturalism moved "multicultural education away from social struggles and redefined it to mean the celebration of ethnic foods and festivals" (Sleeter and McLaren 1995: 12).

(1998: 15) with the claim that "Classics can be displaced from its position as an 'elite' subject that excludes many groups (women, minorities, older students) and reinstated as a more democratic and plural subject which may help to authorize less empowered groups." There are many ways to approach this task (Knox 1994a; 1994b; duBois 2001; 2010a). As early as 1989, Shelley Haley was studying the role of a classical education for African American men and women as it related to a possible future for the field (Haley 1989; on women, see Haley 1993). In an address at the American Philological Association, Emily Greenwood, author of *Afro-Greeks,* argued that the ancient canon still carries cultural capital for today's students. Cartledge favors a "comparative, interdisciplinary approach" (Cartledge 1998: 26); he also raises the issue of cultural capital in a different sort of way. He argues that Classics can begin to do cultural studies instead of positioning itself against such approaches to the material from Greece and Rome (Cartledge 1998: 27). In her recent book, *Out of Athens,* Page duBois argues for expanding the Greeks geographically and critically to take account of changes in history: "Classics itself can often seem closed off both to the present, to tracings of its survival and resurgence, and to its connections with a very early global network" (duBois 2010a: 25 cf. Richlin 1993; Rose 2001: 291–97 esp. summarizes the debate and emphasizes teaching the ancient as strange). And there is the approach of multicultural Classics—the ancient world was not white, and it is not modern Europe (Greenwood 2010: 2), and we do not need to teach it as if it were. Thus, we can change the content and the emphasis that is included under the heading of "Classics." Scholars in the field of reception studies have recently tried to address this challenge by attending to the role of Classics globally in post-colonial writing and in African-American literature (see Goff 2005; Rankine 2006; Goff and Simpson 2007; Hardwick and Gillespie 2007; Greenwood 2009; 2010; Cook and Tatum 2010).

Such approaches to our discipline can help to make clear its continuing relevance and thus the benefit of Classics to students.[5] Though not all women and students of color will necessarily be interested in these topics, an open discussion of these issues can make Classics attractive (Haley 1989; McCoskey 1999: 553). To be sure, the presentation of the actual multiculturalism of the ancient world won't address the specific issues of concern to today's students; as Chew argues, saying: "But classicists' assertion of the inherent and prior 'multiculturalism' of the classical world is limited in that

---

5. See the Paedagogus section on "Classics and Colonialism" in *Classical World* (2003) 96.4: 409–33. See Graff (1992) on the ways that the academy can benefit by addressing the conflicts at stake in the culture wars.

it does not address the texts and the issues that concern scholars of ethnic, African-American, Asian American, Chicano, Latin American, and Native American studies, the 'multiculturalists.' Multicultural or ethnic literatures are believed to speak to the experience of these groups with an immediacy that literature by long-dead white male Western writers cannot" (Chew 1997: 59). While there is not a necessary conflict between the two curricula, the college or university can't teach everything, and students have a limited number of courses they can take. Within these constraints, we can attempt to make the connections. Sally McEwen (2003) points out that by teaching in the college's diversity curriculum, she learned lessons applicable to her teaching in Classics.

Discussions of pedagogy on U.S. college campuses have to a large extent emerged from the pressure to change the curriculum following the Black Power and women's liberation movements, as well as more recently gay and lesbian liberation and disability activism (see Sleeter and McLaren 1995: 5–32 for a summary). While not all faculty members agreed that anything needed to change, in Women's Studies the curriculum itself generated heightened awareness of the importance not only of the material covered but also of the methods of teaching. Feminist theory and critical pedagogy assume that knowledge(s) are situated and grounded in experience; feminism in particular pays special attention to the personal, noting the inadequacy of attending only to the public domain; finally, it is politically committed, viewing teaching as a means of making change and producing an alternate reality to the hegemonic vision (summarized in Weiler 1988).

Attending only to gender as a factor of analysis was itself critiqued early in the 80s by women of color; since that time, feminism has sought to put forth a complex analysis that addresses race and class as they intersect with gender. Amie Macdonald and Susan Sanchez-Casal argue for a realist view of identity and an anti-racist pedagogy that takes into account "the complex networks of privilege and oppression that structure all of our identities" (Macdonald and Sanchez-Casal 2002: 5). They further argue that the emphasis on difference does not mean that there can be no objective knowledge: "it is only from within the examination of difference that we can reach for theory-mediated objectivity" (Macdonald and Sanchez-Casal 2002: 7). But if students simply take one course to fill a requirement—either a special diversity course, or a course in Women's Studies, Latino Studies, or Africana Studies—it will not have a truly liberatory effect. Furthermore, such a requirement carries its own risks, for instance, of ghettoization, with issues of diversity and minority politics confined to programs that are taken by self-selecting groups of students. Change comes slowly over time, if at all, and requires multiple approaches. Therefore, it is very important that students have opportunities *across the curriculum* to learn how to engage with the differences that may be present in a text and in the classroom.[6]

For quite some time feminists within the academy have been trying to educate colleagues about the fact the traditional curriculum was, to put it bluntly, sexist; even introductory Latin and Greek language text books can be exclusionary. In the developing fields, particular attention was drawn to the effect of the examples given in text books. Hoover, for instance, comments about Latin textbooks that there is "an assumed audience for textbooks that excludes ethnic, racial, and gender diversity. But the representation of women is disturbing" (Hoover 2000: 58).

How do we change our teaching to take account of the different students in our classrooms? As Too, one of the editors of *Pedagogy and Power*, puts it, pedagogy was formerly "a dirty little secret, the fearsome and demeaned professional impropriety" (1998: 5, n. 14, citing Tompkins 1990: 655 and Miller 1995: 155), but it has acquired more importance in the wake of these challenges to the demographics and the curriculum in Classics as well as in other disciplines. There is a realization that we must address what happens when we change the object studied and the subjects who are studying. Henry Giroux, a philosopher of education, argues that "What is at stake here is not simply the issue of bad teaching but the broader refusal to take seriously the categories of meaning, experience, and voice that students use to make sense of themselves and the world around them" (Giroux 1992: 125). In fact there is a question about how much we can allow our students to speak in "their own voice" in class (Kahn 2005: 1–7), esp. given the requirements of the disciplines that we have been trained in. As we think about pedagogy, we may recognize other ways to liberate the Classics from the past (on approach, see Chew 1997: 56; Eaton 2001; Benton 2003: 247–48; McEwen 2003).

Given its origins in the discourse around rape, it is not surprising that this volume is grounded in feminist pedagogy. In their classic text, *The Feminist Classroom*, Maher and Tetreault point out several key elements in the change in teaching methods: demographics, struggle for egalitarian and inclusive knowledge, and epistemological revolutions (Maher and Tetreault 2001: 2). Feminism's emphasis on perspective in knowledge formation—that is, knowledge is partial and deriving from one's position (Maher

---

6. The recent work on race in antiquity by Denise McCoskey (2012) is a good example of a sophisticated way to approach these topics.

and Tetreault 2001: 2–3)—has been crucial. Feminists were searching for a new method, one related to the liberal and radical pedagogies of John Dewey and Paulo Freire, but "unique" in "its attention to the particular needs of women students and its grounding in feminist theory as the basis for its multidimensional and positional view of the construction of classroom knowledge" (Maher and Tetreault 2001: 2). Thus, feminist pedagogy starts with an acknowledgment that researchers and teachers are personally involved.

That position is fundamentally at odds with the precepts of philology and history in Classics, of empiricism in archaeology, and the epistemologies of many other disciplines. Some of us would claim that it has been harder to dislodge the assumed truth of those practices and ideologies in Classics (and archaeology [see Brown 1993]) than in more modern disciplines. One's sense of the pressing nature of demographic changes, cited above, will also depend in part on where one is located—what kind of college or university, and what discipline. As Barbara Gold notes in her essay in this volume, "Classics may be seen as a hiding place" for the kind of white male student that Maher and Tetreault (2001: 1) cite: "If you're born and you have your choice of what you wanted to be, white and male would probably be the choice, because that's the best thing to be." Classicists are familiar with this way of thinking:

> But Hermippus, in his *Lives,* refers to Thales the story which is told by some of Socrates, namely, that he used to say that there were three blessings for which he was grateful to Fortune: "first that I was born a man and not a brute; next, that I was born a man and not a woman; and thirdly, a Greek and not a barbarian." (Diogenes Laertius *Life of Thales,* I. 34)

And to return to an earlier point, the field may not draw many students of color. Though historically Classics was important to the members of the black intelligentsia and those aspiring to its ranks (see above, p. 3; Haley 1993; Ronnick 2006: 2–6), more recently it has not traditionally been the academic home for students of color, who, in my experience, tend to elect more apparently relevant fields such as sociology, Africana Studies, or Communications. Those of us adopting these new methods may come up against quite a few problems—which will differ depending on one's position (tenured to temporary to adjunct) and institution. It is important to note that most Ph.D. programs include no specific instruction about teaching practices; we learn by sitting in class and then by doing. When teaching is done as a way of getting a fellowship while the candidate is also taking courses or writing a dissertation, there is not a lot of time and space for careful consideration of what is going on in the classroom. In addition, in Classics in particular, as in other foreign language departments, there is pressure to cover the material because there is always a great deal of content to be transmitted so that a student can successfully progress to the next level (Hoover 2000: 56–57).[7]

As we prepared this volume, our email headers reflected other underlying issues; specifically, we alternated between the terms "difficult conversations," or "difficult dialogues," on the one hand, and "sensitive" or "uncomfortable" subjects on the other. The title was the last thing to be decided on! This question of what to call what we are doing arises from a deeper issue: What makes something difficult or sensitive? Are they synonyms? Some of the difficulty stems from geographical location. In the United States, there is a specific connotation to "difficult dialogues." In 2006, for instance, the "difficult dialogues initiative" of the National Resource Center announced its purpose of "promoting civic engagement, academic freedom and pluralism in higher education. The Center seeks to foster constructive dialogue about some of society's most contentious issues, including: race, religion, sexual orientation, and conflicts in the Middle East. We provide training and other resources to enable faculty, staff and students to more effectively address these issues in the classroom and across the campus" (www.difficultdialogues.org). The motivation for the program seems to be that some issues themselves are contentious. But is it really the issues that are contentious or the people that make them so, because they have different points of view? Programs like that one arose in the context of the push for multiculturalism in the curriculum and in the student body; this particular initiative was an acknowledgement that in the United States we often avoid certain conversations that we need to have. The topics most needing consideration are also the most difficult to discuss because people have deeply held personal and religious opinions about them. Since the right wing has made moral issues the center of their platform, these are also divisive topics politically. The commitment to addressing politically volatile topics, such as race and disability, may actually raise problems for classroom discussion depending on who is in the room. That is, discussing race in a racially mixed classroom, or disability when people display various levels of able-bodiedness, can present challenges to the professor.

In the United Kingdom there has been a recent emphasis on how to teach sensitive subjects, by which we mean those that are difficult to bring

---

7. Paolo Freire in *Pedagogy of the Oppressed* (1970) argues that even languages do not have to be taught in the traditional way, and indeed language instruction has been changed considerably.

up in a classroom for fear that we will upset someone, for instance, someone who has experienced death in the family quite recently (see *CUCD Bulletin* 2012, www.rhul.ac.uk/Classics/CUCD/Bulletin2012.pdf). The term "sensitive" may also conjure up the image of fragility or touchiness, and that has indeed been the case in the political correctness debates. Dinesh D'Souza (1991) sounds that note, as does Hentoff (1992: 55). These critics imply that all speech should be allowed, and that the questions raised about language in the classroom are stifling to the very debate we should be encouraging (Ayim 1996: 201). As Ayim replies, however, "So long as racist, sexist, and homophobic slurs, for example, are not merely tolerated, but zealously protected in the name of freedom of expression, people of color, women of all colors, and gay and lesbian people will continue to be gagged in the very form that prides itself on fostering freedom of expression" (Ayim 1996: 206). She concludes her essay with this inspiring statement: "If we want, like Charles Sanders Peirce (1931–1958), to insist that scholarship 'not block the way of inquiry' (p. 56, vol. 1, paragraph 1.135) on such important issues, we must begin by not reducing them to matters of etiquette, but by acknowledging their profound impact on all of us" (Ayim 1996: 214).

What is our pedagogical responsibility in the face of these discussions? The essays in this volume take as their assumption that something more than hurt feelings is at stake in our classrooms and offices; that students' ability to attend to the material and what they perceive in the material is influenced by their life experiences; therefore, students' experiences outside the classroom are relevant factors in their learning. Furthermore, the essays are grounded in the commitment to address these issues instead of ignoring them. This volume is not limited to those topics typically conjured up by the term "politically correct" or even "sensitive subjects," however. Once you take into account the feelings of the student as reader, concepts like death itself become relevant to our discussion. For instance, when I was teaching a survey of world literature, I realized that many of the books dealt with death, and even suicide; I then found out that a student in the class had lost both his parents recently—one to suicide. That information came after much of the discussion, so I did not change my teaching to accommodate this young man, but I did offer him the option of coming to talk to me and urged him to go to the counseling center.

The remarks I make here do not claim to be exhaustive but merely to point out the larger context behind the panels and this volume. The titles alluded to above, "How to Manage Difficult Conversations in Classics Classrooms" and "Teaching Sensitive Subjects in the Classics Classroom," make some interesting assumptions that need to be fleshed out;

they may even be in contradiction in the essays that follow. We noted in our workshop submission, for instance, that our intention was "to broaden the discussion," pointing out that "ancient texts raise a variety of issues—slavery, infanticide, adoption, abortion, rape—that may be difficult to discuss in a classroom where some students will have had personal experiences that might make them uncomfortable." What is the difference between managing difficult conversations and teaching difficult subjects? Managing implies that we have the conversations, but we don't want them to blow up in our faces, so we manage them, to a certain extent attempting to control where the conversation goes. Teaching sensitive subjects suggests that we should or will have to teach subjects that some consider sensitive or personal. Particularly in the Classics classroom, but also in the academy more generally, we have not been historically used to addressing such topics with an eye to the personal experience of the student (Gold). This volume aims to aid those of us engaged in such a pedagogical practice. We hope that the specific contributions will help our colleagues navigate the sometimes treacherous but also rewarding waters of the modern academy with its conflicting demands on us.

Page duBois challenges us to make students uncomfortable when they are complacent; her very valuable point must be set off against the problem that in so doing we might have unforeseen traumatic effects. Most of the essays suggest offering the students options for avoiding the difficult discussion or sensitive subject if they feel it is *too* difficult, but while we don't want to unduly upset a young person, don't we have an obligation to open their minds (Butler)? So if the issue is simply that abortion is against their religious beliefs, not that they have had a recent personal experience that still bothers them, should they be offered the option not to participate? Many of the authors suggest giving students other ways to participate—reading but perhaps not coming to class. King, Baker and Totelin offer this insight into one of the dangers in this area—students may disengage; their solution is "to communicate the subject in a mature and professional manner that does not cause the student to cease to engage due to feeling in some way 'offended.'"[8] Of course, it remains to be seen exactly what constitutes a "mature and professional manner."

Some of the essays discuss what is uncomfortable for the teacher, and why. First, is it our faculty discomfort that creates an uncomfortable situation for a student? Lisa Trentin admits to being relieved that her one dis-

---

8. The issue of 'offense' is a pedagogically interesting one; learning may come precisely by having one's core values challenged, but if this is taken too far then the learner may simply refuse to engage.

abled student accepted her invitation to miss class; she then wished she had been there. Can we find a middle ground between simply encouraging students to avoid the encounter and insisting that they just get thicker skins? That would seem to me to be the ideal.

Second, as I mentioned above, the identity of the instructor is relevant, as well as their position, and what kind of institution they teach at. For instance, men and women teaching rape will have somewhat different positions in the classroom (James, Thakur). Any faculty member, but mainly junior colleagues, may feel the threat of repercussions (Penrose, Baker et al.), especially in this era of consumerism in education, where complaints in teaching evaluations can have impact on professional careers. Classroom discussions on fraught topics like homophobia (Endres, Penrose) and abortion (Baker et al.), in particular, can have political implications. And they can lead to someone being reported to the authorities. Thus, there are pragmatic reasons for feeling uncomfortable. Tenure can help alleviate some of these anxieties but not all.

The essays that follow take different approaches and take up different areas of the curriculum, and they run the gamut. Meg Butler, Tyler Jo Smith and Carrie Sulosky Weaver centrally address the most universal topic in the volume: death. Their problem derives from courses that present information that is also unavoidable in Classics, especially archaeology; the subject matter might be challenging to students reluctant to face their own mortality, or to students who may still be grieving. The fact that death is taken up in three essays (Baker et al.; Smith and Sulosky Weaver; Butler) underlines that the domain we are entering with this volume is not strictly speaking formed by politics. As Butler points out, students decide themselves what is too difficult for them, and they may drop a course without even telling the professor (though this was not the case in her course). Young people, especially those with privilege, may feel that they are immortal and may find it a rude awakening to be told that they will assuredly die. With the topic of disability, Lisa Trentin moves us into an area that is more politically inflected, introducing the fear of "offending" someone in the class who might have a hidden disability. Authors Patty Baker, Helen King and Laurence Totelin move us further into the treacherous area of the loaded topic of abortion, which is often treated in courses on ancient medicine.

The volume takes on gender fully with the next set of essays. Susan Deacy and Fiona McHardy report on their teaching and research around domestic violence and in the end advocate strongly for an approach that trains students and faculty on how to address the problem when they are confronted with it. Religious institutions or the religious backgrounds of students make for their own complex environment, as Polyxeni Strolonga makes clear. Suzanne Sharland recounts specific problems in teaching Aristophanes in South Africa and asks what makes for these difficulties; Genevieve Liveley takes us into the area of sexually explicit representations of sexuality and specifically argues for the usefulness of pornography *because* it is transgressive. She enters into the debate on the appropriateness of pornography in the Classics classroom. All these essays participate in the larger conversation of what a faculty member should do—should we facilitate students' comfort to the extent of allowing them not to confront the issue at stake?

Two authors address rape, one male, Sanjaya Thakur, and one female, Sharon James, who here expands on her groundbreaking work on the topic (James 2008). Both shed light on what happens not only in the classroom but in the office. One emphasis here must be on making yourself conversant with the codes and resources at your institution and knowing the boundaries of one's role as professor. We are not counselors and should not try to fill that role.

Page duBois writes about ancient slavery and confronts the ways in which and reasons why her students do not find it an uncomfortable subject; she then points out that she views it as her duty to make it uncomfortable. Her point is an important one: if teaching is to open students' eyes, it will present a challenge. Consciousness-raising is uncomfortable by definition since in the process we have to give up the old ways of looking at things. Barbara Gold also discusses the fact that her course that touched on slavery was not difficult for a black student in her class; she analyzes the ways in which Classics may be a way into a discussion that might have been difficult or even traumatic in other settings.

Finally, we have a group of three essays that deal with the teaching of ancient sexuality and gender variance. Nikolai Endres and Walter Penrose address the topic in very different ways; Endres focuses on the ways in which Plato is used in the gay literary tradition to make Plato more accessible, while Penrose discusses how one can teach pederasty in Ancient Greek history in such a way as to contest homophobia in the classroom. Maxine Lewis uses Catullus 63 and the story of Attis to introduce transgender issues and language in the classroom.

Although each essay takes on specific subjects and different content areas and thus will be useful to those teaching those texts and periods, the editors hope that the questions we are addressing in this volume will also be of general pedagogical interest to any faculty member who is "sensitive" to students' needs.

Near Death Experiences
Greek Art and Archaeology beyond the Grave

TYLER JO SMITH AND
CARRIE L. SULOSKY WEAVER

DEATH CAN BE an uncomfortable subject.[1] Yet, much of what we know about ancient societies comes from funerary contexts, making discussions of death in the classroom unavoidable. When the subject is approached through a lens of mythology, or as a topic of philosophical debate, discourse is often dispassionate and detached (in fact, Socrates believed the study of philosophy to be strategic preparation for death).[2] However, when the subject of death is combined with tangible visual evidence, the anxiety quotient often escalates. When faced with disturbing scenes, such as the *prothesis* on a Greek vase, where mourners surround a corpse, tear at their dishevelled hair and lacerate their cheeks, or whenever one must confront the meaning of a macabre image, like those from Lefkandi (figure 1.1) that feature the skeletal remains of a bound woman, likely sacrificed to be buried with a man who was probably her husband, an obvious and predictable discomfort fills the classroom.[3] Such visual and material expressions of death force us to ponder our mortality and recall our own painful losses.

---

1. We are grateful to the editors for inviting our submission and for their helpful critiques. We also thank D. Weiss for his drawing of the burials from Lefkandi and Dr. A. C. Smith for providing a photograph of the burial from Rhitsona.
2. Plato (*Phaedo* 61c–69e).
3. Popham et al. (1993).

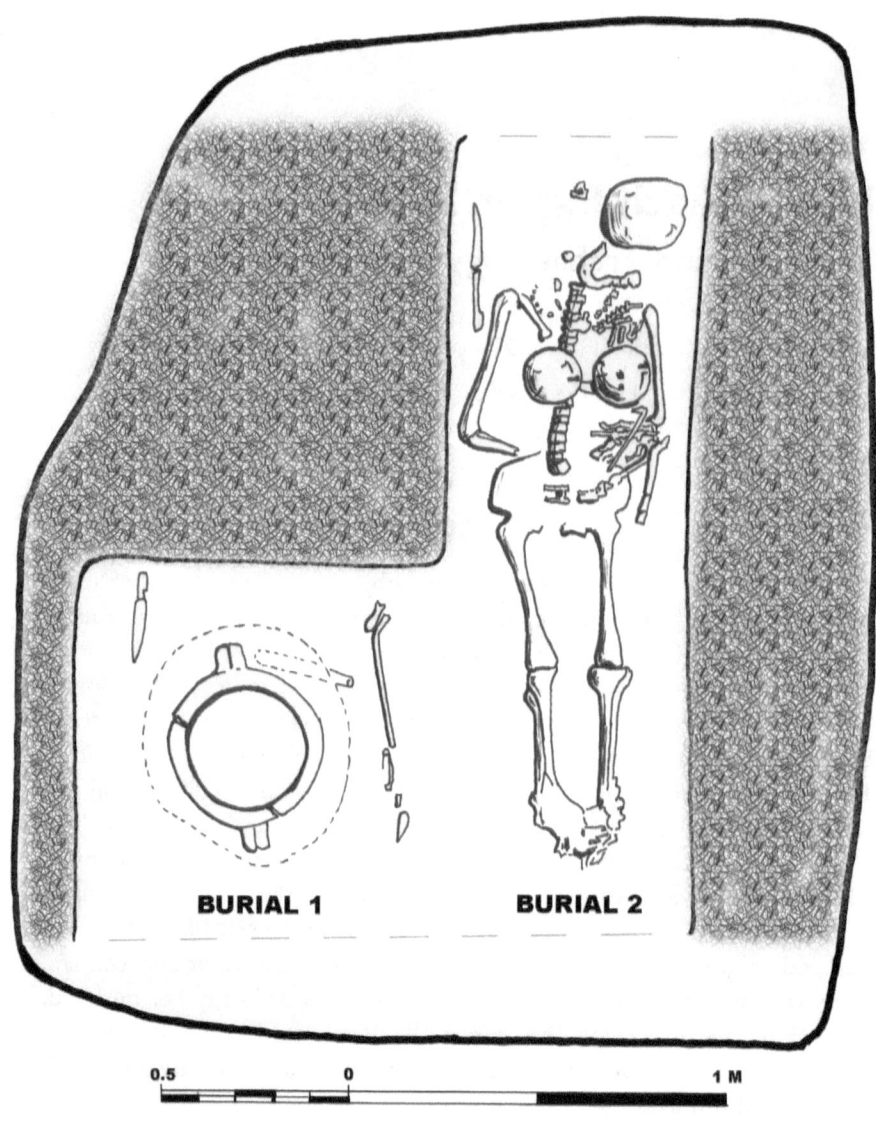

FIGURE 1.1 Drawing of burial from the heroön at Lefkandi. 10th c. BCE. Drawing: Dan Weiss (after Popham et al., *Lefkandi* II, pl. 13).

Death impacts all members of the university community. Although the typical student body is composed primarily of young adults, there is no reason to assume that undergraduates are not already grappling with issues of significant personal loss, or even suicide. Together with their professors, more mature students could be facing the decline of their aging parents. Furthermore, when the death of a peer occurs within a university setting, it is a tragedy that students, faculty, and higher administrations are not entirely equipped to deal with. The murder of one student at the hand of another, such as occurred at our own university, the University of Virginia, in April 2010, is a case in point. Other recent instances that have directly affected our community include the shootings of students and faculty at Virginia Tech on April 16, 2007, the abduction of Morgan Harrington and the grisly recovery of her remains on January 26, 2010, and the pain still felt over the terrorist attacks on September 11, 2001 (especially since many of our students have family employed at the Pentagon). Even historical deaths have the potential to upset members of a university community. The discovery of an African American cemetery on the University of Virginia's South Lawn sparked a flurry of public interest, much like the reaction prompted by the excavations of an African burial ground in New York City (1991–1992), albeit on a smaller scale.[4] After a period of public discussion and investigation, it was decided that the coffins would be unopened and reinterred, underscoring the fine line that archaeologists tread between scientific inquiry and 'desecration' in public opinion.[5]

As archaeologists we are acutely aware that our 'classroom' extends beyond the walls of the university. Much of our teaching takes place in museums, where we study objects recovered from burials or whose imagery is death-related, and on archaeological sites, where human remains are excavated and analyzed. In these disparate settings, we encounter students from different cultures and religious backgrounds, making it apparent to us that while death is ubiquitous, every person (including the instructor) enters the classroom with inherent biases. For example, for an Orthodox Christian, an observant Jew, or a Muslim, cremation is forbidden, and even ancient evidence of the practice might seem uncomfortable and unfamiliar.[6] By the same token, Myson's image of Creosus (first quarter of the 5th c. BCE) atop his funeral pyre, or Homer's description of Patroclus (*Iliad* 23.110–225)

---

4. La Roche and Blakey (1997).

5. Virginia press release "Out of the Shadows: Event to Commemorate Kitty Foster and Canada Community" *UVa Today* website. On the excavation and study of human remains, see Landau and Steele (1996); Scarre and Scarre (2006: 146–62, 181–218).

6. E.g., see Breck (1998: 277–82); Levine (2009: 107, 122); Jonker (2009: 152).

ablaze on his own, may seem like the stuff of myth, but to modern Hindus the burning of a body is sacred and signifies the release of the soul from its earthly existence.[7] Nevertheless, the classroom, wherever it may be, is a unique nexus where individuals of different beliefs and backgrounds converge in the spirit of learning and academic honesty. Although it is generally beneficial to have input from students with different perspectives, this boon can become a bane when uncomfortable subjects are the topic of discussion.

Regardless of academic discipline, many professors find it difficult to broach the topic of death. Two years after the untimely death of his wife, Jeffrey Berman, an English professor at State University of New York (Albany), devised a course called 'Love and Loss' which focused on the literature of bereavement and was intended to be cathartic for both teacher and student. To help his students understand their emotional reactions to death, Berman advocated self-disclosure and encouraged his students to write essays about their feelings and experiences. Intense classroom discussions and moving personal accounts caused Berman to conclude that there are:

> . . . expected and unexpected consequences of a loved one's death. Just as every death is different, so is every person's reaction to death different. Despite these differences, death usually comes as a shock to most of us, even when anticipated, and few can be prepared adequately for the pain and sorrow arising from loss.[8]

Reactions to death vary, and so do pedagogical approaches. In this chapter we present a multi-faceted method for teaching death in the classroom, beginning with contextualization. Separated by time and culture, modern people do not experience death in the same manner as the ancient Greeks. When students are equipped with a better understanding of the ancient Greek culture of death, it is hoped that they will gain objectivity and the ability to separate classroom material from personal events. Thus, in the first and second parts of this chapter, we hope to educate teachers and provide, as a reference, a sampling of the visual and material evidence for death that is most relevant and most frequently encountered in the Classics classroom. The first part presents depictions of corpses and funerals in Greek art, and how 'made to order' objects commemorate and memorialize the dead, while the second part explains why we excavate and study graves. Shifting

---

7. Boardman (1988: fig. 171). For Hindu beliefs regarding cremation, see Laungani (2009: esp. 61).

8. Berman (2009: 2).

the focus to the classroom, the third part suggests techniques for facilitating an open discussion of death meant to complement those discussed in Meg Butler's contribution to this volume. To cope with negative emotional responses, a series of student writing assignments are offered, such as journaling, wiki participation, and responding to writing prompts. Also, a framework for a classroom debate on the ethics of displaying human remains in museums is provided. The intention of this final exercise is to encourage students to think critically about both sides of a controversial issue and understand how material remains from the past can inform the present.

PART I: IMAGE AND OBJECT

Imaging Death

Death-related themes are well attested in ancient Greek art. Depictions of the dead or dying on the battlefield, suicides, and funerals appear on vases and sculptures made in the city of Athens and elsewhere. Such images are commonplace in courses on ancient art or Classical civilization, as well as those concerned with mythology or daily life. Important distinctions must be made by way of introduction: in general, vases are smaller, somewhat portable, and private while sculptures are larger in scale, heavy to transport, and displayed publicly. There are always exceptions to these broad patterns: depending on scale, material, date, and other factors, both vases and sculptures could be buried with the dead and/or mark a grave. Furthermore, vases and sculpture are by no means the only sources of evidence relevant here, but together they are the most abundant.

Greek artists employed specific conventions for portraying the dead. Many of the best examples are found in depictions of mythological figures on painted vases. The dead children of Niobe, killed by Apollo and Artemis, are strewn across an uneven landscape on a red-figure krater of c. 450 BCE.[9] Still clothed, arrows pierce their young bodies, and their frontal faces reveal the fully closed eyes of the departed. Unsurprisingly, Troy is a favorite setting for death, a place where we witness fallen warriors (e.g., Achilles, Hector, Sarpedon, Patroclus) again with eyes closed, arms and armor removed, and bodies nude or shrouded. Scenes depicting the dead Hector are among the most gruesome and disturbing, as Achilles prepares to drag his stripped and lifeless corpse around the walls of Troy; or those where

---

9. Boardman (1989: fig. 4.1).

Hector's old father, King Priam, ransoms the body of his slain son from Achilles.[10] Among the most cited examples is the krater on which a Lycian prince, Sarpedon, is being removed from the battlefield of Troy by Hypnos and Thanatos, personifications of 'sleep' and 'death.'[11] Again, the warrior is a full nude, who wears only his protective greaves. Blood spills from fresh wounds on his chest, abdomen and leg, and to increase dramatic effect, his body has been foreshortened by the artist, Euphronios. The presence of Hermes, in his role as divine escort of the souls of the dead to the Underworld, reinforces the finality of it all.

Suicide is sometimes shown by vase-painters and other artists, and such scenes often involve the dead, the dying, or the preparation for death. A well-known example decorates a black-figure amphora by Exekias (c. 540 BCE), who reveals a fully nude Ajax preparing to fall on the sword previously given to him by Hector.[12] The tension of the moment is quite pronounced as the isolated hero of Troy affixes his sword to a mount with total concentration. The scene is visible on other vases, such as a Corinthian black-figure cup of about 580 BCE, where Ajax has fallen onto the sharp weapon, forcing Odysseus, Agamemnon, and many others to confront the horror.[13] Fresh blood spurts from the wounds. We are sure the hero is already dead because his eyes are closed and, as in the previous example, he is fully nude, vulnerable, and stripped of his protective armor. A similar depiction of Ajax fallen on the sword decorates a metope from the Archaic temple of Hera at Paestum in southern Italy.[14] As in Exekias' version, Ajax's suffering is emphasized by his total seclusion. The story as an artistic motif is fairly widespread over a long period, also produced on a shield band relief, as a bronze figurine, on red-figure vases, and in gem engraving. How the Greeks felt about suicide is a matter of some debate, yet the Ajax story, known from art and literature (i.e., Sophocles' *Ajax*), is one of our best extant sources.[15]

Human sacrifice, although thinly attested in the archaeological record, is another theme harnessed by vase-painters who offer up mythological examples.[16] Iphigenia is dressed as a bride and led to a sacrificial altar.[17] Much more explicit is the portrayal of Polyxena having her throat cut by

---

10. Ibid. (figs. 203 and 241).
11. Woodford (1993: 76, fig. 68).
12. Homer (*Iliad* 7.355–6). Woodford (1993: 99, fig. 94).
13. Woodford (1993: 100, fig. 95).
14. Pedley (2006: 178, fig. 9, Paestum Museum).
15. Parker (1983: 42); Garland (2001: 95–9).
16. Hughes (1991).
17. Carpenter (1991: fig. 299).

Neoptolemus on a black-figure amphora made in Athens c. 560 BCE.[18] Like Sarpedon and Ajax, blood flows directly from her wound and drips dramatically onto a fire-burning altar and/or the tomb of Achilles below.[19] Related to such images are other epic-derived moments, where the altar, the object most obviously associated with animal sacrifice, is instead used to symbolize the fate of such tragic figures as Priam or his son Troilus. One of the most memorable and horrific scenes is the sack of Troy (*Ilioupersis*), such as one on a red-figure hydria of the Kleophrades Painter (c. 490 BCE), where the old king is seated on a blood-stained altar with a newly dead, still-armed soldier at his feet, while his dead grandson, the child Astyanax, is lying across his lap.[20] According to Homer (*Little Iliad*), the king was dragged from the altar where he sought refuge and, according to Euripides (*Trojan Women* 719ff) the little boy was thrown from the walls of Troy.[21] The painter here gives a synopsis of these events, replete with details and characters—the living, the dead, the fighting, the struggling to survive. The murder of Troilus by Achilles, like the suicide of Ajax, is shown at various stages: the ambush, the capture, and the killing. On a shield band relief dated to c. 580 from Olympia, Troilus is a nude figure being held above the altar by a fully armed Achilles.[22] A more explicit version decorates a black-figure amphora of slightly later date, where Achilles has beheaded the Trojan prince and prepares to hurl the head over the altar, using it as a weapon against the Trojans themselves.[23]

Prothesis and Ekphora

The artistic examples considered thus far have been largely concerned with the characters of ancient mythology and have focused on moments derived from the Homeric epics. If anything, they demonstrate the concerns of artists working throughout the Archaic and early Classical periods, and the types of subjects and themes that interested them: pain, suffering, and the horrors of war. However, a substantial amount of visual and material evidence related to death derives from an even longer and more prolific tradi-

---

18. Boardman (1974: fig. 57).
19. Cf. Euripides (*Hecuba*, 218ff). See Carpenter (1991: 19, and fig. 23, "a fire burns on an altar," and also a similar object on another vase of the same group, where the object (fig. 33) is identified as an "omphalos-shaped altar."
20. Boardman (1988: fig. 135).
21. Schefold (1992: 284–5).
22. Carpenter (1991: fig. 31).
23. Ibid. (fig. 33).

tion of iconography highlighting the ritual actions of mortals. Throughout the Geometric period (c. 1000–700 BCE), burials in the city of Athens were filled with geometric-styled pottery, employing standard decorative motifs on a range of available shapes. If we fast-forward to the last fifty years of this period, we discover overt examples of funerary iconography on funerary vases. Scenes of *prothesis* and *ekphora* have survived in enough quantity to catch more than a glimpse of the occasion.[24] Together they represent the first two 'acts' of what Garland has termed a three-act drama of Greek funerary ritual; the third act, the disposal of the body, is almost never shown, though notable exceptions are recognized on vases that show the body or the coffin being lowered into the ground.[25] The *prothesis*, or laying out of the dead body, is the subject chosen for decoration on the monumental Dipylon amphora, from a cemetery in Athens, and dated to c. 750 BCE. On one side of the vessel the dead person is laid out on a bier (*kline*), the shroud waiting to be dropped from above, and figures in mourning are all around. The mourning figures tear at their hair in a fashion well known in both literature and in art, and attested as early as the Late Bronze Age.[26] The mourning gesture, a demonstration of extreme distress, is also practiced by Geometric clay figurines, and in the Archaic period is witnessed again in vase-painting, plaques, and on sculpted clay figures.[27] In most instances and time periods, it is a gesture performed by women.

The *ekphora*, or funeral procession, sets the *prothesis* in motion by transporting the body (bier and all) to the final resting place. Such scenes have been associated by some scholars with the Homeric past, envisioned as the lavish funerals of heroic individuals, while others view them as scenes of contemporary events. A clay model of an *ekphora* from Vari in Attica, shows the mourners, no doubt fully mortal, decked out in long drapery, mounted atop a horse-drawn cart; surrounding the shrouded body on a bier, they tear at their hair.[28] Despite the rigid early Archaic style of this terracotta group, anyone familiar with the extreme emotional outpouring of attendees at a modern Greek or Middle Eastern funeral, can easily imagine their emotional outpouring, even hear their deafening lament.[29] Such open demonstrations of grief continue to be the subject of black-figure vase-paintings and plaques. On red-figure examples of the fifth and fourth centuries they

---

24. Garland (2001: 23–34), who notes the numbers of *prothesis* far exceed *ekphora*.
25. Ibid. (21) for the stages; Kurtz and Boardman (1971: figs. 36–7).
26. Bronze Age examples: Vermeule (1965: 123–48); Kurtz and Boardman (1971: 27–30).
27. Kurtz and Boardman (1971: figs. 11–16).
28. Ibid. (fig. 16).
29. On the 'voice' and 'speech' of objects, see Himmelmann (1998: 34–35); Steiner (2001: 30–32). For the funeral lament over time see Alexiou (2002).

come to be associated with the tragic stage and may even represent actual plays and performances.

Objects, Offerings, and Commemoration

An abundance of artistic and archaeological evidence concerned with death is found in objects that were purposefully made to be used during the funeral, deposited as offerings with the body, or both. Decorated pottery is again our largest form of evidence from Late Geometric through Classical times. As Boardman has pointed out, actual funeral scenes are rare, and "virtually all other vases found in graves were not designed for this purpose but their choice of shape was—to feed the thirsty dead, to carry sustenance for a journey to the other world, or for their service in purification rites, occasionally perhaps as a prized possession of the dead."[30] As already noted, certain vessels may have been used as grave-markers, such as the famous Dipylon amphora mentioned above. From the seventh century, the Orientalizing period, comes another version, a tall and slender amphora assigned to the Analatos Painter.[31] Though significantly smaller than the Dipylon amphora, the Analatos Painter's vase is rife with death symbolism. The decoration includes a chariot procession (perhaps an abbreviated *ekphora*), a row of male and female dancers, and sphinxes. Additional touches include the 'plastic' snakes attached to the rim of the vessel and its handles, and the 'fenestrated' handles indicating the vase was displayed (perhaps a gravemarker) rather than carried. Another highly decorated vase from the same period, an amphora by the Polyphemos Painter, diversifies the picture. The large vessel, standing nearly 4 ½ feet tall, was discovered at Eleusis. It contained the remains of a dead child. The fenestrated handles coupled with the scant decoration on the back of the vase are indications of display before burial. The figure decoration is derived from Homeric epic (blinding of Polyphemus) and mythology (Perseus escapes the gorgons). Although such stories might be numbered among the stock themes of Archaic art, the decapitated Medusa who flies through the decorated field lends a disturbing otherworldliness to the scene.[32]

There are other objects made by potters and painters that speak more emphatically to death and funerary ritual. Perhaps the best known are vessels intentionally made for specific funerary purposes. The lekythos, a

30. Boardman (1998: 264–65).
31. Ibid. (fig. 189).
32. Boardman (1998: fig. 208.1–2.)

container intended to hold the oil used to anoint the body, is the most numerous of this category. The large number of small black-figure versions discovered in the Marathon tumulus suggests that the funerary function of the lekythos was in place by 490 BCE.[33] However, at this date, the imagery on the vases has no clear link to funerary rituals or death-related mythology. By contrast, the series of white-ground lekythoi produced in Athens during the second half of the fifth century combine form, function, and decorative theme. The tall cylindrical vessels were obviously made for funerals, and most have been found deposited in the graves of the Athenian Kerameikos cemetery. Their decoration provides additional clues about their usage, as some provide representation of the shape itself positioned near the foot of the grave.[34] On some, women tend the grave, carrying baskets of garlands or other offerings; on others it is men who are present, at times demonstrating the typical mourning gestures. The grave-marker (stele) or tomb is sometimes visible, and the deceased may be shown as if still alive or as long dead. These decorated lekythoi are among our best visual evidence for attitudes, customs, and participants surrounding death at a certain place and time. Also, belonging to this category of made-to-order objects is another vessel called the loutrophoros. The elegant shape is connected to both weddings and funerals, and again provides a correspondence between form, function, and image (figure 1.2).[35] Although the shape first appears in early Archaic art and has clear funerary associations, some of the best examples are decorated in Athenian and South Italian red-figure and feature tragic mythological themes. The lekythos and the loutrophoros appear together on a sculpted marble relief from Athens dated to c. 380 BCE, suggesting the continued association of both shapes with the death and burial.[36]

Sculpture also plays a significant role in our understanding of Greek death. Kouros and kore statues of varying sizes have been associated with the dead, and could even serve as grave markers, as indicated by archaeological find spots or inscriptions.[37] The well-preserved marble statue of Phrasikleia (c. 550 BCE), discovered in 1972 buried in a pit alongside a kouros, brings to life the sad reality of her parting: "Marker of Phrasikleia. I shall ever be called maiden (kore), the gods allotted me this title in place of

---

33. Biers (1992: 19–20); Oakley (2004: 4–6).
34. Oakley (2004: 205–7, fig. 168).
35. Rehm (1994: 11–42) on the relationship between the rituals; Garland (2007: 75).
36. Knigge (1991: fig. 151b).
37. E.g., Boardman (1985: fig. 107, from Attica, and fig. 144, from Keos).

FIGURE 1.2 Athenian red-figure loutrophoros. c. 430 BCE. London, British Museum 1930.0417.1. © Trustees of the British Museum.

marriage."[38] Sculpted stelai and reliefs are another window into funerary rituals and perceptions of the dead. The stelai change their sizes, styles, and decorative motifs over time and in keeping with the trends of the Archaic through Hellenistic periods. Archaic examples from Athens and Attica carried sphinxes on the top, and often portrayed a single male kouros carved onto a tall narrow shaft. Classical and Hellenistic examples more often include women, family groups, and combine seated and standing figures (figure 1.3). Painted examples are less common, and those from Demetrias in northern Greece and Chersonesos on the Black Sea add significantly to the history of Hellenistic painting.[39] All in one way or another memorialize the dead, honoring them as members of a family and community. Sculpted relief plaques of the heroized dead partaking in the funerary banquet, such as one discovered near Athens and dated c. 400 BCE, depict the deceased reclining, and in this case holding a phiale, with his wife seated at his feet.[40] Such a vision of events lends credence to the idea that the dead were present at their own death-feast. Life and afterlife are celebrated with an ample supply of food and drink.

Having surveyed the iconographic and material evidence, it is useful also to consider student responses to such images of death and grieving. When a student is confronted with an image of the dead and mourners in a *prothesis* on a Geometric vase, or with a family group depicted on a sculpted stele that once marked a Classical grave, does he or she feel pity for or empathy with the artistic figures?[41] This question has no simple answer. For instance, the faceless silhouette figures represented on Geometric vases can elicit a variety of reactions. Arguably, all of the ancient figures in a *prothesis* scene seem distant and irrelevant to the modern viewer. As teachers of this material, it is our basic goal to bring the details of these and other figures into sharper focus. This can be achieved, first and foremost, through distinguishing mythical figures from mortal ones (where known) and by distinguishing the dead from the grieving in any given artwork. Often, the modern student viewer will react more strongly to a representation of grieving than to the image of a corpse; and this is especially the case once students are made aware of the painful mourning gestures (i.e., tearing hair, lacerating cheeks) they are witnessing.[42] Their disconcerted responses can in fact be palpable in the classroom, as was noted recently by Smith during a lecture in her

---

38. Boardman (1985: 73, fig. 108a).
39. Kurtz and Boardman (1971: 234–5, and fig. 62); Posamentir (2011).
40. Kurtz and Boardman (1971: 234); Garland (2001: 71, fig. 14); Larson (1995: 42–50).
41. Davies (2002: 200–3).
42. See Davies (2002: 50–51, 135–38) for a comparison with modern Greece; and note 29, above.

FIGURE 1.3 South Italian funerary relief. c. 325–300 BCE. New York, Metropolitan Museum of Art 29.54. © The Metropolitan Museum of Art. Image Source: Art Resource, NY.

Introduction to Classical Archaeology course when she showed a Mycenaean larnax (small coffin) with a row of mourning females.[43] Despite the fact that Greek art is highly conventional, the ancient images can conjure mental images of actual behaviors, actions, and pain—a possibility instructors should be prepared for.

---

43. See notes 26 and 27, above.

PART II: DEATH AND BURIAL

Like art and objects, burials are rich sources of archaeological information. Yet, burials alone require an inevitable encounter with human skeletal remains, while art and objects do not. Powerful and timeless, the skeleton is a ubiquitous symbol that has been associated with numerous concepts and caveats. But skeletons are more than skull and crossbones. Although it is commonly recognized as the personification of death, the skeleton has historically represented vanity, famine, and rebirth, and often served as a potent reminder of life's brevity and the concomitant need to partake of earthly pleasures.[44] In Classical Athens, the alleged bones of Theseus and other heroes were enshrined and treated as powerful talismans,[45] whereas in American popular culture, the image of the skeleton is employed—from horror films to Halloween—to evoke feelings of terror, dread, and danger. Thus, it is unsurprising that a student's conditioned first-response to human remains typically ranges from curiosity to discomfort and fright. However, emotional reactions can be alleviated by the contextual presentation of human bones and burials. When students are armed with additional information, human remains are stripped of their macabre mystique and transformed from objects of fear into respected remnants of the past.

Reading Graves

Ancient Greeks considered proper burial to be an absolute necessity. Without the requisite rites and rituals, the deceased were denied entrance to the Underworld, and their souls were condemned to forever wander the earth.[46] The significant personal risks endured by King Priam (*Iliad* 24.202–944) and Antigone (*Antigone* 21–257) illustrate that family members were willing to sacrifice their very lives in order to rescue their unburied loved ones from such an ignominious fate. Given its importance, it is not surprising that formal burial is a deeply symbolic act that is meticulously planned and carefully executed.[47] Bearing witness to this concept are the excavated cemeteries of the Athenian Keramikos, Corinth, and Samothrace, among others. Since burial is highly prescribed, each aspect of it is infused with

---

44. Dunbabin (1986).
45. Plutarch (*Kimon* 8; *Theseus* 6, 36); Mayor (2000: 104–26).
46. Johnston (1999: 9).
47. Parker Pearson (1999: 5–11).

meaning and bears the potential to reveal crucial information about the interred individual and the culture from which he/she derived. Looking beyond inscriptions and epigrams, which provide specific, if sometimes cryptic, information about the deceased, the other elements of a grave are also capable of unlocking its secrets. Beginning on the surface, the shape of a tomb is chosen intentionally. For instance, the tradition of depositing the dead in house-like structures is a widespread human practice as the tomb is generally viewed as the deceased's 'eternal home.'[48] Well-preserved examples of Greek house-shaped tombs can be found in Lycia, such as the painted chamber tomb at Kızılbel or the monumental arched tombs from Xanthos.[49] Furthermore, tombs that mimic Greek temples, especially popular in Anatolia during the Hellenistic period, exist throughout the Greek world, and were likely intended to heroize the deceased individual within the tomb (e.g., the so-called Tomb of Philip II and the Prince's Tomb at Vergina).[50] The orientation of the grave, the deceased itself, and the funerary monument are also significant. Late Minoan (c. 1450–1190 BCE) tombs from Armenoi, Crete were constructed to face either the rising of the sun or moon, whereas the dead in Anatolia (i.e., Phrygia, Lydia, Lycia) and Cyprus (c. 8th–4th c. BCE) were often positioned with their heads toward the entrance of the tomb.[51]

Grave markers and burial containers are typically linked to social status, gender, or age. Wooden markers, stelai, sculptures, vases, stones and built monuments have all marked the graves of Greeks at various points in history. Elites in Archaic Greece used the necropolis as an arena for the display of wealth through the erection of lavish, carved grave markers, specifically stelai or sculpture-in-the-round of the aforementioned types.[52] During the Geometric period, graves of Athenian males were marked by kraters, while those of females were denoted by amphorae. These vase shapes were purposely chosen. Kraters were associated with the male sphere because they were used to mix water and wine, and in later periods they were commonly present at the symposion. Amphorae, such as the famous Dipylon amphora, were associated with the domestic domain because they were storage vessels that commonly held olive oil or grain. Furthermore, late Classical and early Hellenistic gravestones at Chersonesos, a Greek colony in the Black Sea region, were strictly conventional, and without excep-

---

48. Parker Pearson (1999: 21–45).
49. Mellink (1998); Jenkins (2006: 151–85).
50. Fedak (1990: 66–74).
51. Papathanassiou et al. (1992) S43-S55A; Baughan (2009: 58).
52. Morris (1987: 151–54).

tion the shape of the stone indicated the gender of the individual buried beneath it.[53] Likewise, burial containers can also provide important information. The dead can be interred in any type of receptacle, and throughout the Mediterranean they are found in cooking pots, large vases (cf. Polyphemos amphora), clay tubs, wooden or lead coffins, monolithic stone or marble sarcophagi, terracotta sarcophagi, coffins made of roof tiles, natural geological depressions, or oftentimes buried without a container of any sort. Frequently, there is a correlation between cost of the receptacle and socio-economic status of the deceased; in other words, the more expensive and lavish the burial container, the higher the social status of the deceased individual. During the Archaic period, for example, elites from Syracuse preferred to be buried in monolithic limestone sarcophagi.[54] In the same period at Klazomenai in East Greece, prominent individuals chose painted terracotta sarcophagi (figure 1.4), which bore ornate decoration in obvious imitation of painted vases.[55] One, however, must be cautious when assigning socio-economic status based solely on burial containers, because individuals or families quite commonly invested considerable resources in their burial accoutrements to make themselves appear wealthier than they actually were (this practice, in fact, still takes place in Ghana).[56] In a later period, this self-aggrandizement was commonly practiced by Roman freedmen, who used the iconography and burial containers favored by Roman elites to symbolically elevate their social identity.[57] The most striking difference in burial treatment is witnessed when one compares the graves of children to those of adults. Children are quite commonly afforded differential burial treatment, with a notable exception being the Greek Black Sea colony of Nymphaion, where children were buried in the same manner as adults.[58] For example, when extramural burial is the rule for adults, children are often permitted to be buried inside the city walls, generally beneath the homes of their parents.[59] In the western Greek settlements, such as Kamarina and Syracuse, children who died in the seventh and sixth centuries BCE were often buried in pots (called *enchytrismoi*), while adults were buried in sarcophagi, tile-built graves, or graves dug into the natural rock.[60]

---

53. Posamentir (2007: 46) and note 38, above.
54. Frederiksen (1999: 247–48).
55. Boardman (1998: 148–49); Hürmüzlü (2004).
56. van der Geest (2000).
57. Petersen (2006: 45).
58. Petersen (2010: 250).
59. Parker Pearson (1999: 103).
60. Shepherd (2007: 97–8).

FIGURE 1.4 Detail of Klazomenian sarcophagus. Late 6th c. BCE. London, British Museum 96.6-15.1. © Trustees of the British Museum.

Within the grave, the arrangement of the body and grave goods (objects buried with the dead) are purposeful and symbolic. Bodies can be buried in a variety of positions, each culturally-specific and bearing meaning. Skeletons have been found lying on their backs (supine; cf. figure 1.1), on their bellies (prone), on their sides with their legs flexed (called flexed or contracted burials), and sometimes even sitting or standing. In the Greek west, burials in the supine position are interpreted as 'Greek,' whereas flexed burials are believed to belong to native Italic or Sikel individuals.[61] Prone burials are among some of the most interesting, because they are often classified as 'deviant' burials. A deviant burial is one that contains a person who was buried in an extraordinary manner for a specific reason, and usually these people were criminals, disabled, women who died in childbirth, children who died unbaptized, suicides, or supposed revenants (e.g., vampires), among others.[62] Two chilling examples of deviant burials were found in a cistern in the House of the Fourni on Delos (c. late 2nd c. or early 1st c. BCE). These individuals, both females, were apparently bound, ritually killed, and discarded in the cistern.[63] Just as body arrangement is capable of revealing cultural and social variations, the position of the arms, legs and grave goods can point to the presence of different groups within the same cemetery. Ellen Pader's multivariate statistical analysis of body position and grave good placement determined that smaller, distinct groups were discernable within the pagan Anglo-Saxon cemeteries (5th–6th centuries CE) of East Anglia.[64] Grave goods are additionally capable of indicating the wealth of the individual, such as the golden jewelry and masks found in shaft graves at Mycenae, their ethnicity (e.g., individuals in Greek cemeteries in the Black Sea region that were buried with precious metal objects and weapons are traditionally identified as Scythian), or their trade networks, like the bronze and faience bowls imported from the Near East and Egypt that were discovered in the ninth century BCE graves at Lefkandi.

What's in a Cemetery?

Like all cemeteries, the ancient Greek necropolis is an unwritten record of population dynamics. Consider this scenario: a man is born in a town. He raises a family there, watches as old friends move away and immigrants trickle in. The man dies and is buried in the local cemetery. In the cemetery

---

61. Shepherd (2005).
62. Murphy (2008: xii).
63. Charlier (2008).
64. Pader (1982); Parker Pearson (1999: 6).

there are hundreds of people like this man, and by studying their graves and skeletons, we are able to reconstruct the population that lived in the town. Just as the individual components of a grave are capable of revealing hidden secrets about the person buried inside, the skeleton itself yields additional information that is crucial to paleodemographic reconstruction, namely, the reconstruction of ancient human mortality, fertility, and migration.[65] From the skeleton, an osteologist, a specialist in the scientific analysis of human bones, can determine the biological sex, age, stature, state of health, and migratory status (i.e., was the individual born in the region or an immigrant) of the deceased individual.[66] When the data from each skeleton are analyzed, a more complete picture of the population emerges. Through a series of equations and models, derived ages and sexes are used to discern mortality patterns, such as age-specific mortality rates for males and females. Lawrence Angel, for example, calculated the average age at death in Classical mainland Greece to be 44.1 years for males and 36.8 years for females.[67] Skeletal evidence for disease is collated to determine what diseases were present and in what frequencies. The paleodemographic study of cemeteries can address an array of difficult archaeological questions, such as how environmental change impacted human populations, how (and if) population events (i.e., expansion, migration and colonization) coincided with cultural change, and how population structures were affected by communicable diseases.[68] For example, an examination of Late Bronze Age (c. 1300–1200 BCE) skeletons from Pylos revealed that many females were anemic and consistently exhibited poorer dental health than their male counterparts, which could be attributed to sex-based dietary differences or pregnancy, among other causes.[69] In Greek archaeology, such studies are increasing in number because they are essential to our understanding of ancient peoples and the societies in which they lived.

PART III: FROM CLASSROOM TO MUSEUM

Responding to Death

Having set the contextual stage, we now shift to the topic of strategies for teaching material pertaining to death and dying. As mentioned in the intro-

---

65. Chamberlain (2006).
66. See Roberts (2009) for methods osteologists use to gather data.
67. Bisel and Angel (1985).
68. Chamberlain (2006: 178).
69. Schepartz et al. (2009).

duction to this chapter and by Butler in her contribution to this volume, the topics typically covered in the Classics classroom can prove to be disturbing and uncomfortable for students. Take, for example, an incident that took place in Smith's Greek Religious Festivals class. While reading Euripides' *Bacchae* and discussing the cult of Dionysus, a student in the front row bolted from her seat and promptly left the room. She was visibly upset—her face was flushed and she appeared on the verge of tears. The next day, she arrived at Smith's office with a form to drop the class. Since it was late in the semester, Smith was perplexed by this development and asked the student why she had reached this decision. The student explained that the description of Pentheus' dismemberment at the hands of the Bacchants (*Bacchae* 990–1153) was distressing, and based on her religious beliefs, she felt that the material was inappropriate for the classroom and for her personally. Despite Smith's attempts to change her mind, this student ultimately stood by her decision to drop the class, illustrating that it is sometimes impossible to bridge the gap between strong personal emotions and objective academic discourse. There are, however, proven strategies that can be used to curtail the intensity of passionate reactions. Foremost, successful navigation of sensitive subjects relies heavily upon the teacher, and ground rules should be established before discussing any controversial topic with students. It is the role of the instructor to act as a facilitator, ensuring that the class maintains a positive and civil atmosphere. Negative thinking and strong emotions should be moderated, and when comments stray from the material under discussion, focus should be redirected to the topic-at-hand.[70] The overarching goal is to aid students in the cultivation of thoughts that are objective and analytical, rather than emotional and irrational. Thus, with the proper ambiance in place, students should be receptive to assignments, such as those presented below, that will achieve this aim. As a result of her experience, Smith now circulates an anonymous questionnaire on the first day of class, asking the students about their religious beliefs and practices, and any concerns they might have about the planned content. This preemptive strategy has made a huge difference toward getting students to think before they react, and has also cultivated a group dynamic (i.e., "we're all in this together") from the outset.

Although it can be initially distressing, writing about emotional experiences yields significant physical and mental health improvements.[71] Berman, teacher of the aforementioned 'Love and Loss' course, modeled his peda-

---

70. Yale Graduate Teaching Center, *Teaching Controversial Subjects* (2008).
71. Pennebaker (1997).

gogical approach on that premise. He found that " . . . college teachers can initiate awareness by encouraging students to write about their own experiences with loss."[72] Accordingly, from the moment the subject of death arises, students should be asked to journal their thoughts and feelings about death and related classroom material. In addition to journal entries, they could be periodically assigned to answer objective questions, such as "how do Greek burial practices differ from modern ones?," so that they have an opportunity to reflect on classroom material and also analyze their own encounters with present-day funerary rituals. Another possible assignment is a video prompt. The internet is replete with videos of the Great Tumulus at Vergina in northern Greece. This monument has been turned into a museum, with *dromos* (entrance corridor), "royal" and lesser tombs, offerings and other burial contents on view nearby. In this dimly lit, haunting public space, modern visitors are invited to enter the world of the ancient Greek dead, if only briefly. By watching the video tour, students are able to share in this experience, and upon the video's completion, they could be asked to respond to it in their journals. Overall, these writings are meant to be personal and private, but a forum to share them with the class should be made available. Some time could be set aside at the end of the class to read journal entries and writing assignments (either collectively or in small groups), or students could post their work and related comments to a classroom wiki (the benefits of which are discussed in depth in Butler's chapter). Inevitably, there are students who will prefer that their writing remain private, but it is, however, helpful for all to hear from those who wish to share. "Students who shared their essays on death," Berman found, "also learned from their classmates' experiences, thus experiencing the phenomenon of 'normalization.' Students discovered that their anger, sadness, confusion, and guilt are part of a process of grieving."[73]

In addition to journaling, Berman asks his students to write obituaries and eulogies. Obituary-writing is a technique that is touted by self-improvement advocates. Crafting one's own obituary allows writers to discern what is important in their lives and what they want their legacies to be.[74] Berman slightly modified this exercise and required his students to write obituaries for their classmates. Each student was asked to determine their own age-at-death and describe ten important life events (past, present or future) that they would include in their obituary. Students were then assigned partners. They exchanged the personal written information, interviewed each other

---

72. Berman (2009: 3).
73. Ibid. (13).
74. For an example of how self-help authors use the obituary exercise, see Brickley (2000: 126).

to fill in any remaining gaps, and then wrote their partner's obituary. The exercise was emotionally demanding for Berman's students, but it ultimately left them with a heightened self-awareness of death and a profound appreciation of life.[75] The format of Berman's eulogy assignment differed slightly from the obituary one, as students were asked to write a eulogy for a person, either living or dead, who was not a member of the class. Keeping in mind that the eulogy is usually the most important and personal component of the funeral, students were entreated to focus on the description of the special qualities of the deceased individual.[76] Although parents, grandparents, friends, and mentors are common subjects for the eulogy exercise, this assignment can be tailored specifically to the Classics classroom. For example, students could be asked to write eulogies for any of the myriad Homeric characters, a figure from Greek tragedy, a figure represented on a stele, or even the inhabitant of a grave. Regardless of the subject, students who wrote eulogies found that the exercise heightened their self-awareness of both death and life. However, when students wrote eulogies for close friends or relatives, they found that it was more personally significant. The writing was therapeutic because it helped them to confront and cope with painful emotions, actively reflect on the lives of deceased loved ones, and deeply appreciate those who are still living.[77]

Debating the Display of Human Remains

The ways in which museums display human remains vary throughout the world. Historically, skeletons were not displayed at all. Grave goods, instead, were prioritized and often separated from other ancient art exhibits, typically presented under categories such as 'death and afterlife,' 'daily life,' or 'religion.' Even today, in the newly renovated Ashmolean Museum at Oxford University, such marginalization has been taken to an extreme: a glass case crammed with lekythoi of all types, dates, and sizes stands alone in the Greek art display in a unique presentation of ritual and form. Another recent example can be found in the quiet and intimate space of the Ure Museum of Classical Archaeology at the University of Reading, where a reconstructed burial from Rhitsona (Boeotia) is shown with its pottery and other offerings (figure 1.5). Although present in the actual burial, the skull that was interred with these grave goods (or a replica of it) was not

---
75. Berman (2009: 42–43, 53–54).
76. Ibid. (60).
77. Ibid. (75–76).

FIGURE 1.5 Reconstructed grave from Rhitsona (no. 145), Boeotia. First half of the 6th c. BCE. Skull located in photograph on "east end." Ure Museum of Classical Archaeology, University of Reading. Photo: Amy C. Smith.

placed in the display case and is shown only in a photograph found on the visitor's right.[78]

Despite these notable exceptions, most modern western societies treat human remains as artifacts and display them in the same manner as other archaeological materials. Often, efforts are made to reconstruct graves in order to provide visitors with an understanding of how the individual components of a burial relate to one another (the Egyptian mummy 'Ginger' in the British Museum is a famous example, but this is also the manner in which ancient Greek skeletons are most frequently displayed). Some muse-

---

78. The arrangement is based on Ure (1934: 14–15, no. 145); and Ure (1927: 6).

ums, however, have reconceptualized the traditional presentation of human remains and developed new approaches that seek to preserve the educational value of the remains by exhibiting them in an informative, yet respectful, manner that allows them to retain their human dignity. For example, the Petrie Museum in London displayed Egyptian remains behind a shroud, ensuring that visitors would only see the remains if they so chose. Likewise, curators at the Turin Egyptian Museum placed an Egyptian mummy in a cloth-lined case where it could only be seen from above, again allowing visitors to decide their course of action.[79] Other museums use clear, informative signs to alert visitors about the potentially disturbing content of the exhibit before they enter. One such exhibit is the Museum of London's *London Bodies* (1998–1999), which used human remains to show how the physical appearance of Londoners has changed since prehistory.[80] Thus, whether visitors' objections to the display of human remains are caused by religious, cultural, or personal conflicts, museums are proactively responding to these concerns.

One proven technique of addressing the concerns surrounding the display of human remains is to conduct a classroom debate. Like writing exercises, debates are effective classroom tools because they actively engage students and expose them to both side of an issue. Furthermore, the nature of debate requires careful thought and mastery of content, so it is unsurprising that students generally profess to learn more through debates than lectures.[81] The following description is a debate prompt which highlights some of the controversial issues surrounding the display of human remains in museums. In advance, supply students with a copy of the prompt and ask them to prepare to defend their point of view (or alternatively, the opposing position). By requiring students to confront this difficult topic, the issue is transformed from an emotionally-charged subject into an object of academic inquiry and analysis. The debate can be arranged formally, where opposing and supporting arguments are heard, or it can be organized more loosely, where students are invited to respond to a series of provocative questions asked by the professor (potential discussion questions are provided below the prompt). Some options for formal organization are 'fishbowl debate,' where the class is divided into two groups, each assigned a position that must be collectively researched and argued; 'think-pair-share,' where students first individually think and makes notes, next they work in pairs to create lists of key issues for both sides, then join with another pair

---

79. Swain (2007: 162–63).
80. Ibid. (164–66).
81. Kennedy (2007).

to select a position and refine their arguments, and ultimately present their selected argument and conclusions to the class; 'Lincoln-Douglas debate,' which is limited to two students, each arguing an opposing viewpoint; 'meeting-house debate,' where small groups are created to give opening and closing arguments, while the rest of the class asks questions and offers comments in between; and 'problem-solving debate,' which requires two teams of four students: for each team, one speaker presents the historical and philosophical background of a subject, one explains why changes are or are not warranted, one proposes a well-reasoned solution and the final speaker summarizes the argument.[82]

Prompt

Human remains are important sources of information for archaeologists, but do they belong in museum exhibits and are they a valuable part of a museum's public educational mission? On the one hand, "it has been suggested that the presence of human remains in displays is one way of bringing the public into direct contact with past people and 'humanizing' displays and interpretations."[83] On the other hand, there is a vocal segment of the population that finds the display of human remains to be disturbing and unethical, as evidenced by the legal response to the call for the repatriation and reburial of the remains of Indigenous peoples (e.g., the Native American Graves Protection and Repatriation Act, or NAGPRA, that was enacted in the United States in 1990), the 2008 British legislation mandating the reburial of all archaeological skeletons two years after excavation, and the controversy surrounding the traveling exhibition *Body Worlds,* which uses plastinated cadavers to educate the public about anatomy, physiology, health, and disease.[84] Furthermore, there are outright restrictions on the exhibition of some skeletal collections. For example, the 92 sailors recovered from the shipwreck of Henry VIII's flagship, the *Mary Rose,* are strictly forbidden to be seen by the public.[85] Even among museum curatorial staff, there is the strong belief that human remains should be studied and then reburied. Perhaps most notable is Jack Lohman, current director of the Museum of London, who "has publicly stated that he would like the museum's entire human remains collection to be reburied."[86]

---

82. Ibid. (186–7).
83. Brooks and Rumsey (2007: 276–8); Swain (2007: 148).
84. Swain (2007: 152).
85. Brooks and Rumsey (2007: 283).
86. Ibid. (276).

By its very nature, debating yields no right or wrong answers, only critical thinking. Further topics for classroom debate might include:

- Is archaeological excavation desecration? Are archaeologists tomb robbers?
- Should special interest groups be permitted to rebury excavated skeletons? Even if they, arguably, are not their descendants? Should *all* excavated skeletons be reburied?
- What, in your opinion, is the best way to exhibit human remains and grave goods, especially when the grave goods are considered to be objects of art?
- What manners of display are acceptable and what are not?
- Are human remains educational?

In his book *Howards End,* E. M. Forster writes that, "Death destroys a man: the idea of Death saves him."[87] As students become more familiar with death through an in-depth understanding of the funerary beliefs and practices of the culture they are studying, active written reflection, and academic analysis, their strong emotional responses to death can be replaced with self-awareness and objectivity. It is hoped that the contextual framework and pedagogical techniques presented here will acquaint teachers and their students with the idea that death can serve as a learning-tool in the Classics classroom and in general. Put another way, a better grasp of disturbing or controversial material, such as painted images of suicide or a human skeleton, equips students with the emotional distance they need to perform more effectively in discussion, debates, or even on a written exam. Taken together, the art and archaeology of ancient Greece provide a window that aids not only in reconstructing the past, but also in plotting the present.

---

87. Forster (1921: 273).

Raising Lazarus
Death in the Classics Classroom

MARGARET E. BUTLER

"I DON'T THINK THIS IS THE BEST TOPIC FOR ME TO STUDY RIGHT NOW."

A student, one whom I taught only briefly, wrote this sentence, informing me via email that s/he was choosing to drop my course, the one with the enigmatic title "The Greek Way of Death." I did not choose the title, obviously a borrowing from Robert Garland's (2001) book of the same name, but the course material covers one of my research specialties: the anthropology, archaeology, and cultural history of death-ritual, especially with regard to the ancient Greek world. After ensuring that the student knew where to find appropriate counseling resources, I realized the student's statement was a good reminder for me that, at times, the course's subject matter was (pardon the pun) rather grave.

Uncomfortable subjects arise rather frequently in the Classics classroom, depending on the instructor's approach to the material. Like my peers, I have taught about war, politics, slavery, class warfare, sexuality, religion, and philosophy. Leading a discussion about the growth of Athenian military and political power can be uncomfortable when you have an ROTC or veteran student in the classroom, and partisan political debates are not infrequent. Similarly, whatever the course topic, I always have one student who asks something along the lines of, "Was Hippolytus gay?," thus necessitating a brief or not so brief introduction to ancient Greek attitudes toward sexuality and gender.

Death is perhaps a less controversial topic than others in this volume, but talking about it can make students very uncomfortable. One approach to handling this is to illustrate to students, using ancient material and modern theory, how death-ritual can be a celebration of life, as Tyler Jo Smith and Carrie Sulosky Weaver do in their chapter in this volume. The theoretical and methodological approaches to studying death-ritual, especially death as a celebration of life and identity, should be discussed in any course on death-ritual, accompanied by a selection of the extensive scholarship on this topic, as well as a basic introduction to ritual as a concept; Smith and Sulosky Weaver cover this material in their chapter, so I see little reason to repeat it here.[1] I am aided in my teaching by what I consider the good fortune to be teaching in New Orleans, home of above ground cemeteries, brass band funerals, and second lines, which are impromptu parades that follow the funeral cortege to and from the cemetery, singing solemn songs on the way there, and then launching into "When The Saints Go Marching In" afterwards, to celebrate the life of the deceased and his or her entrance into Heaven.

The flipside, of course, is the gut-wrenching poverty, creating high mortality rates from preventable diseases like Type II diabetes, and the horrific loss of life occurring during the breaching of the levees after Katrina. I find, however, that in my "death" course, there is a tricky balance to be struck between not unnecessarily upsetting students who may be dealing with life and death issues, such as a cancer diagnosis or the loss of a parent, and engaging those students who are really very isolated from what is, at least in many English-speaking countries, a sanitized and limited experience with dying, death, and death-ritual.

After talking about where striking this balance enters into the course, I spend the rest of this chapter presenting three pedagogical aids that I use in my "Greek Way of Death" course. The first is a required presentation on a

---

1. My personal favorite literature "stash" from which I choose and suggest readings each time I teach the course: Radcliffe-Brown (1922) and (1945); Childe (1945); Lévi-Strauss (1953); Leach (1954); Vallee (1955); Hertz (1960) [1907]; Van Gennep (1960) [1909]; Goody (1962); Douglas (1966); Ucko (1969); Saxe (1970); Binford (1971); Brown (1971); Curl (1972); Geertz (1974); Shennan (1975); Peebles and Kus (1977); Tainter (1978); Hodder (1979); Chapman and Randsborg (1981); Shils (1981); Bloch and Parry (1982); Pader (1982); Parker Pearson (1982); Shanks and Tilley (1982); Bradley (1982) and (1984); O'Shea (1984); Cohen (1985); Richards (1988); Cannon (1989); R. S. Watson (1990); Huntington and Metcalf (1991); Bell (1992); Morris (1992) and (1994); Durkheim (1995); Houby-Nielsen (1995); Turner (1995); Bell (1997); Kubler-Ross (1997); Parkes, Laungani, and Young (1997); Palavestra (1998); Olivier (1999); Parker Pearson (1999); Regis (1999); Tarlow (1999); Davies (2002); Shepherd (2005); Anderson (2006) [1983].

personal ritual, such as Thanksgiving dinner or a regular morning run. The second is the use of a course wiki to provide a "safe space" for discussion of difficult or troubling issues that arise in the course. The third aid is a very open-ended final essay question—"What did it mean to die well in ancient Greece?"—that gives the students a chance to choose if, how, and to what degree they wrestle with potentially upsetting issues like the existence of an afterlife or the legacy people leave behind. I find that these three activities help the students talk about the Greek material honestly and candidly, without the detachment they might otherwise feel or adopt in self-defense, as well as helping them reflect on how studying the Greek material helps them better understand the roles that dying, death, and death-ritual may play in their own lives. In sharing these pedagogical aids, I hope to help others in their efforts to engage with uncomfortable subjects in the Classics classroom.

DISTANCE AND DRAWING CLOSER TO DEATH

In teaching a course on death, I first have to deal with my own detachment from it, perhaps arising from being overfamiliar with certain aspects of death-ritual. My research uses burial data to fill in gaps in our social history that texts and other archaeological evidence cannot.[2] Given my upbringing, studying death-ritual in the ancient world seemed like a perfectly natural fit for me, especially since it has been an accepted practice in Classics for many decades. I have always associated death-ritual with my identity, and death-ritual has been a regular part of my life. My father sang me to sleep with old Irish and Southern songs about death, dying, wakes, and funerals. I saw open caskets from an early age and, as a child, attended far more funerals than weddings, joking with my cousins about how much fun our funeral "after-parties" were. My mother taught me how to meld the emotion, faith, and frankness of the Catholicism on her side with social norms and expectations for a "proper" Southern funeral.[3] My brothers and

---

2. I currently am finishing a book on death-ritual in ancient Macedon, entitled *The King's Canvas: The Transformation of Ancient Macedon*.

3. A humorous but often accurate take on Southern funerals can be found in *Being Dead Is No Excuse: The Official Southern Ladies' Guide to Hosting the Perfect Funeral* (Metcalfe and Hays 2005). My mother-in-law gave this to me as a joke gift after I assured her that I had been well raised in knowing how to put on a proper funeral. Sadly, as I was finishing final edits, my mother died rather unexpectedly, and she has been buried at the cemetery mentioned above. I can say with reasonable confidence that she is happy with the funeral we gave her, and my five-year-old son handled her death well, as a normal part of human existence—and these things give me great comfort.

I spent many childhood vacations being dragged to cemeteries across the Southern United States to "visit" our ancestors. My grandfather, director of alumni relations at a flagship state university, made a daily habit of reading obituary pages from newspapers across the state so that he could write condolence letters to the families of alumni. I have a drawing of my favorite hometown cemetery, a place I visited often in high school, on my dining room wall. I did not, however, acquire an intimate association with the process of dying until I watched a close family member die slowly of cancer over a three-year period. It was only when I saw, from my students' perspective, my perhaps gothic familiarity with death-ritual that I began to understand the broad spectrum of experiences with death, dying, and death-ritual that I was encountering in the classroom.

Obviously students who attend Tulane University and choose to take a course called "The Greek Way of Death" do not constitute a proxy for the "average" student; student populations vary widely. In any case, there is a very delicate balance to be struck, drawing some students in towards a more intimate knowledge of death, respecting other students' over-exposure or over-sensitivity, for various reasons, to death, and acknowledging how my own relationship with death, dying, and death-ritual may be affecting both my understanding and my teaching of the ancient Greek material.[4] I have taught the class and written about death while dealing with dying, death, and death-ritual in my own close family, and so just as that student who withdrew from the course surely had a good reason for doing so, there are times where I need to check my own emotions when deciding what personal experiences to share and what to hold back when teaching this course. I have chosen also to eschew discussing my personal religious faith and understanding of an afterlife, and students follow suit in class (although not after class or during office hours). This is a decision based primarily on context, and in another version of this course I could envision incorporating these matters into class discussion.

While aware of the fatalities in the 9/11 attacks, and somewhat cognizant that there are significant military and civilian casualties throughout the Middle East, most of my students were born after the horrors and morbid-

---

4. Research on discussions of death in the classroom, with few exceptions, largely focuses on primary and secondary rather than higher education. Examples regarding different levels of education include Barton and Crowder (1975); Knoll and Prull (1976; Keith and Ellis (1978); Barton, Crowder, and Flexner (1980); Lisman (1989); Gibson and Zaidman (1991); Hoffman (1994); and Mahon, Goldberg, and Washington (1999). A selection of other "death in the classroom" literature: Gaffney (1988) on the nursing classroom; Johnson (1995) on violence and the urban classroom; Rowling (1990) and Cullinan (1990) on the effect of the material on teachers; Bohm (1989) on discussions of the death penalty; Hagopian (2000) on veterans in the classroom.

ity of the emergence and spread of HIV and AIDS in the 1980s, just as I was born after the terrible images and stories that came out of Vietnam, and my parents were born immediately after the hell of the Second World War. Each generation has its own broad and significant associations with death. The explosion of the *Challenger* is one such association, but of course those deaths were unintentional. It was not until I taught my "death" course that I had cause to recall that in sixth grade, our teachers showed us live coverage of the first Gulf war. It now seems to me incredibly sick to show to children real bombings that, as portrayed on television, resembled popular video games of the 1970s, 1980s and early 1990s. We watched smart bombs strike UN coalition targets, our impressionable minds equating each little green video-game-like blip on the screen not with death and destruction but with cheer-worthy victory, like taking out a villain in an Atari or Nintendo game. Regardless of one's opinion on UN coalition war efforts in the Middle East, the dissociation of those little green lights and the destruction and in some cases deaths they represented is exactly the kind of conditioning that leads to a callousness toward death and a lack of humility about the taking of another person's life, however despicable the person.

In a typical semester teaching this course, a majority of my students have seen at least one (but rarely more) embalmed body, while only a small percentage have seen an unembalmed body. This same small percentage usually also has watched a close family member die over a short or extended span of time and are familiar with intimate aspects of death, such as the grey, ashen hue that often precedes it, and very generously, some of them choose to help me explain it to the class. The literature addressing death in the twentieth and twenty-first centuries shows us how medical advances, hospice care, cremation, improvements in sanitation, the development of vaccines, the growth of the funeral industry, and the demise of extended family households, at least in North America and the United Kingdom, all have contributed to a more medicalized and sanitized culture of dying.[5] Just as rarely, I get a student who grew up around violent crime, served in the military, or the extremely rare student who grew up, within or outside

---

5. Medicalization and sanitization of death well discussed in the following: Mitford (1963) Gorer (1965); Ariès (1975); Dempsey (1975); Lerner (1975); Lofland (1978); Farrell (1980); Cannadine (1981); Ragon (1983); Jordan (1984); Jackson (1989); Kearl (1989); Leaney (1989); Meyer (1989); Habenstein and Lamers (1990) [1955]; Walter (1991); Mellor and Shilling (1993); Walter (1995); Laderman (1996); Charmatz, Howarth, and Kellehear (1997); Mitford (2000); Parsons (2003); Olivere and Monroe (2004); Grainger (2005); Kaufman (2005); Parsons (2005); Gilbert (2006); Lambert (2006); Cullen (2007); Holwarth (2007); Kellehear (2007); DeSpelder and Strickland (2008); Green (2008); Harris (2008); Lee (2008); Nicosia (2009); Leming (2010); Smith (2010); Slocum and Carlson (2011); Tarlow (2011).

of the United States, facing poor health care, poverty, famine, and/or widespread outbreaks of diseases such as malaria and cholera.

Only a very few students admit to knowing someone who has at least attempted suicide; I use the term "admit," because this topic makes them the most uncomfortable of all death-related topics, and I am not inclined to press the issue beyond a brief and informal inquiry. Of all issues, this one also causes me the most discomfort, not only because suicide and suicide attempts have touched my close and extended family, but also because I worry that this is the topic that could trigger an attempt in an already severely depressed student, such as the one who chose to withdraw from my class. It is a very rare occasion indeed when I choose to share my personal experiences with suicidal friends and relatives, and I usually limit it to one phrase from a suicide note I read: *broken person*. Sharing this personal anecdote helps break the tension and get students to speak up about the reasons people commit suicide, and it opens the door for us to talk about honor, shame, and legacy, as we encounter them in Sophocles' *Ajax* and Euripides' *Hippolytus*.

Sophocles' *Ajax* is a difficult play for many students to digest; they do not know what to make of Ajax's suicide. Some think that ancient soldiers tend to fall on their swords as a matter of course, while others are absolutely appalled that anyone would contemplate suicide over a bunch of farm animals (and shepherds, as I often have to remind them), a few enemies, and an abstract concept of honor. In both cases, of course, the students are completely unable to relate to the Greek situation, and I do my best to give them the historical and cultural context they need for an understanding of Ajax's situation and decision. One of the exercises we do in conjunction with our discussion of the play is the translation of the basic plot and themes of Ajax into a film set in the current-day United States. One class found it easier to relate to Ajax's mental state and choice when they saw him as a young father and veteran of the recent and ongoing U.S. and British military operations in Afghanistan. Their Ajax suffered from PTSD, manifested most gruesomely in his killing the family dog. Confused, ashamed, and left largely unaided by VA psychiatric services, this modern-day Ajax then killed himself, only worsening his family's suffering. Although some of the parallels were a stretch, I think this exercise helped the students to take Ajax's situation and decision more seriously and to learn from Ajax's suffering, much as Odysseus did by the end of the play.[6]

---

6. For PTSD and the mentalities, words, actions, and events that caused it, see Jonathan Shay's *Achilles in Vietnam: Combat Trauma and the Undoing of Character* (1995) and *Odysseus in America: Combat Trauma and the Trials of Homecoming* (2003) and Peter Meineck (2009) on *Theater of War*.

It is difficult to decide whether or not to assign these plays in classes with ROTC students or members of the military or of military families. Presumably these students know that serving active military duty on enemy territory carries great risk with it, and while I have deep respect for the American military, some of the recruiting techniques give me pause. The student in the front row, however, may be paying for college with a military scholarship, requiring an established number of years in active service, and may become completely unnerved after a particular reading assignment. So is it good that s/he now knows the risks but perhaps bad that s/he may be talked out of a military career that might have been a good fit and the military deprived of a good recruit. The student in the back row may have a sibling or parent in active combat and might be too worried about his or her loved one to verbalize those personal parallels with ancient Greek examples.[7]

To note that death is "everywhere" in ancient Greece would be a bit foolish, given that death is the one human universal certainty, but I think it is fair to say that death, dying, and death-ritual are a frequent part of the Classics classroom, as Smith and Sulosky Weaver demonstrate in their chapter. Tragedy and epic, funeral orations and cemeteries, hero cults and mystery cults all have their place in courses on Greek literature, history, culture, and art and archaeology. Smith and Sulosky Weaver cover many of the essential facets of "Greek death" in their chapter, and I do not want to repeat that material here; suffice it to say, we read excerpts from the *Iliad* and *Odyssey*, many "standard" Greek tragedies, a few funeral orations (accompanied by excerpts from Loraux 1986), and some texts by Plato, accompanied by lectures on and discussions of evidence for the afterlife, the underworld, mystery cults, the material culture depicting death, and the archaeological remains of death-ritual and burials; the bibliography involved is too lengthy to list in this chapter.

I am honest about the course content up front, as well as the fact that we will be dealing with some tough issues—issues with which they might be dealing personally at the time of the course, and other issues that might be foreign at the beginning of the course but unexpectedly upsetting when

---

See also the websites "Theater of War" http://www.outsidethewirellc.com/projects/theater-of-war/overview, and "In Ancient Dramas, Vital Words for Today's Warriors" http://www.npr.org/templates/story/story.php?storyId=97413320.

7. For relevant news and examples, see, "Urban Tool in Recruiting by the Army: An Arcade" (2009 – http://www.nytimes.com/2009/01/05/us/05army.html?pagewanted=all); "$12 Million Army Video Game Recruitment Center to Close" (2010 –http://www.huffingtonpost.com/.../12-million-army-video-gam_b_618783.html); "America's Army" (http://www.huffingtonpost.com/.../12-million-army-video-gam_b_618783.html; and www.americasarmy.com).

encountered in class readings or discussions. Often I take an informal poll to see what experiences students have had with dying, death, and death-ritual; this also allows me to gauge whether any students seem particularly uncomfortable, indicating a possible problem they might be facing. If the class largely is unfamiliar with dying and death, outside of violent movies, video games, and the deaths of Harry Potter characters, I sometimes show films that can give them perspectives on different "ways" of dying, death, and mourning, as well as bringing them a little more face-to-face with death. My short list of helpful films (and this is just the tip of the iceberg) includes *Himalaya, The Snow Walker, The Descendants, Terms of Endearment, Cries and Whispers, Winter's Bone, The Stand, Moonstruck, The Tenth Man, Philadelphia, Into Thin Air: Death on Everest, My Life, Waking Life, Steel Magnolias, The Big Chill, The Family Stone, The Tree of Life, The Painted Veil, And the Band Played On, Departures, In America, Il Postino, Restrepo, Dead Man Walking, The Farm: Angola, USA, The Tree of Life, Zero Kelvin, The Seventh Seal, Meet Joe Black, Shadowlands, 127 Hours, The Grey, The Hunter, Beasts of the Southern Wild, Schindler's List, Death at a Funeral, Breaking the Waves, Dancer in the Dark, Melancholia, Dogville, The Sea, Gravity*, the miniseries version of *Angels in America*, a documentary about funerals in New Orleans, and the new show *The Walking Dead*.[8] These films show actual death, not pretty death, not fake and gory death, but actual grey, messy, stark dying and death and grappling with both from multiple points of view—sometimes with humor, sometimes with pathos, but always trapping the audience into facing the fear, uncertainty, risk, time, memory, loss, and emptiness associated with death and dying. The point of showing these films is to show the students that, although we all mourn and die, there are many attitudes and reactions to death and many faces of death, and the students' feelings about death, whatever they are, are legitimate. It is while they are finishing up their final papers, to be discussed below, that we look briefly at death-ritual in our own community of New Orleans, helping them to understand that for much of the world, death-ritual and legacy still are very much a part of life and must be respected as such.

To facilitate an open, healthy, and safe space for discussion, I have developed three pedagogical aids and assignments that are essential to the course experience, helping students engage with sometimes difficult, troubling, and emotionally charged course material. It is my hope that any classicist teaching an "uncomfortable" subject may find one or more of these aids and

---

8. I give all students a warning about movie content so those who are dealing with death-related situations can choose to skip class or arrive late on movie days.

assignments useful in creating an environment for constructive discussion of and engagement with difficult or sensitive issues.

TOOLS FOR CREATING A "SAFE SPACE"

I start each term by asking the students to present to the class a personal or family ritual that is an important part of their lives. I find that this assignment helps the students become comfortable with one another, especially during the question-and-answer session following each presentation, when students open up and are brutally honest about their lives. It also demonstrates to them the pervasiveness of ritual behavior in our lives, and thus it becomes easier for them to see death-ritual as one of many rituals they encounter. It is noteworthy that, to date, not a single student has chosen death-ritual for his or her ritual behavior presentation, and yet the assignment still paves the way for discussion of tough issues later in the course and helps the students feel comfortable discussing death with classmates they come to know at a more personal level.

I have two primary goals in mind with this assignment: 1) to teach them how to talk about ritual, especially what constitutes "meaning" in ritual, as well as class/race/identity issues that might be sensitive, and 2) to get them comfortable talking about their personal lives and how ritual functions in their lives. By starting with something more innocuous than death (things like high school pep rallies, Thanksgiving dinner, or morning runs), the students get to know and trust each other at a more personal level and create a "safe" space for discussion in the classroom. I request that students pick a ritual that they feel comfortable discussing with their classmates. They are required to describe the ritual or activities and scenarios that are integral parts of the ritual, as well as to outline specific associated practices and the roles of the participants. Each student must articulate why the activity qualifies as a ritual behavior and explain how it functions in his or her life: what it says about his or her family and friends, how it helps negotiate roles and relationships, and what it means to each student, to his or her beliefs and identity.

I ask students to create a wiki page in conjunction with this presentation. A wiki, for readers unfamiliar with it, is a webpage that is very easy for group members to edit; it requires no special knowledge of HTML or any other webpage-building language or skills. I use the free educational wiki space offered by Wikidot, as I find it easier to manipulate and to read than those wikis offered by course management systems like Blackboard and Moodle. My course wiki is a closed wiki, meaning that the only people who can read and edit it are group members who have accepted my invitation to join. Students thus are assured of relative privacy; their wiki pages and comments will not show up in Google searches and are not accessible by anyone other than their classmates and myself. Obviously a student could show the course wiki to people outside of the course by logging on in their presence or giving out their login information, but I have yet to have this problem. Wikis are becoming more commonplace in the classroom, although for them to function effectively as teaching aids, instructors must understand what sort of moderation and facilitation is required to encourage wiki use, as well as where and when wiki use is appropriate or useful.[9]

Below I will discuss how I use the wiki for class "discussion" and remote coauthoring; here I explain how the wiki aids in the ritual behavior presentation and the greater goals attached to this presentation. Because the students are required to describe a personal ritual, as well as explaining some of the significance of the ritual, as outlined above, the wiki functions as a platform for pictures, links to videos or web pages that have explanatory value, an outline for the presentation, and plenty of space to organize all of this material. The presenter just pulls up his or her wiki page when s/he presents, and students can follow along. The presenter can add to the wiki on the fly, very easily, which often comes in handy during the question-and-answer period that follows each presentation. Moreover, students are required to ask at least one question or post at least one comment on each classmate's ritual behavior page, and the page's creator must answer and respond to these questions and comments. These presentations are both

---

9. From 2006–2008 I was a member of the Stanford Humanities Lab project, "Co-Creating Cultural Heritage," funded by the Wallenberg Foundation. One primary goal of this project was exploring and assessing the use of digital and collaborative technologies as part of a college-level educational experience, including the use of wikis. One of our major findings was that students do not use wikis as an alternative to classroom discussion and group work unless required to do so, and initial student usage of wikis needs to be moderated and facilitated to "break the ice." When I tied grades to their wiki contributions, designed group activities that required co-authoring via the wiki, and moderated discussions by posting provocative replies to student comments, participation was 100 percent, and the online discussions were as lively and thoughtful as those in the classroom. In other words, as you might guess, technology cannot replace an instructor's teaching and moderation, but it can be a useful supplement, as in the case of the "safe space" I describe above. For research on using wikis as part of coursework, see Brandon and Hollingshead (1999); Lou, Abramin, and d'Apollonia (2001); Godwin-Jones (2003); Lamb (2004); Engstrom and Jewett (2005); Stahl (2005) and (2006); Bold (2006); Richardson (2006); Zumbach, Reimann, and Koch (2006); Han and Hill (2007); Qian (2007); Wheeler, Yeomans, and Wheeler (2008); Lin and Kelsey (2009); Brown (2010); Peters and Slotta (2010); Ducate, Anderson, and Moreno (2011); Naismith, Lee, and Pilkington (2011); Roussinos (2011).

preceded and followed by a more general discussion of the scholarship on ritual behavior, some of which I referenced in the first footnote.

The combination of the presentation, the discussion, and the postings creates an open dialogue about how ritual functions in the students' lives. Students often ask questions that could be considered overly personal, such as, "Do you feel resentment that it is the women who clean up Thanksgiving dinner every year?" or "Why do you think your father and his brother always get into a competition at the dinner table over who took the nicest vacation this year?" Because the presenter, however, has chosen to invite his or her classmates into a discussion of the presenter's Thanksgiving ritual, the other students trust that the presenter is comfortable talking openly about practices, traditions, roles, and norms associated with his or her celebration of that holiday; thus they feel free to ask more intrusive and pointed questions than they otherwise might, both in class and on the wiki. In addition, sharing something personal with the rest of the class helps the students get to know each other better, and that in turn facilitates their really exploring their own, and their classmates,' personal rituals in a more intensely analytical way than they might otherwise be inclined to do. It also opens the door for the course's potentially uncomfortable subjects: death, dying, and death-ritual.

The second pedagogical aid is the use of the wiki to facilitate discussion of the ancient material students encounter in the "death" course. Students are required to post comments on the ancient texts we read and to engage in remotely co-authored assignments, where a group has to articulate an answer to an assigned question. Although the wiki allows them to co-author without having to meet in person, it is not the convenience that I find as useful as offering an alternate venue for discussion. The online discussion is just as lively as the classroom discussion, with the added advantage that students who are reluctant speakers are given a chance to share their "voice" in a virtual and less anxiety-inducing space. While I do require students to initial all their wiki contributions, I still find that on the wiki, they feel freer to express opinions that might be unpopular among their peers, as Walter Penrose notes in his chapter in this volume, and they seem less reticent to disagree with each other.

I think it is very important for them to have the opportunity to articulate their thoughts and engage in dynamic, albeit online, discussion of sensitive issues, the five top controversial issues being suicide, war, "justifiable" homicide, legacy/honor/shame, and the soul/afterlife. The worst thing a teacher can do to shut down a student's capacity for intellectual growth is effectively to silence his or her opinions by not providing a safe space for open discussion. As teachers, we may want to protect the other students from opinions we find offensive, and we may hope to change the mind of the offending student, but honey catches more flies than vinegar, and the change must come from the student's engagement with his or her peers. Likewise, it is good for students to have to articulate why exactly they find a peer's opinion offensive, and having to do that often makes them realize how much more complicated the issue at hand is than they previously had thought. I am able to monitor and moderate the discussion as necessary, but I rarely have to do so. Furthermore, when they return to the classroom after one of these co-authoring or commenting sessions, that openness carries over into the "live" environment, with the added benefit that we can pull up the discussion and start where they left off on the wiki. I have yet to encounter a student who seemed uncomfortable making the transition from the wiki to class discussion; quite the opposite, many seem relieved that they were able to have a launching pad for entering the conversation.

Earlier I discussed an exercise in which the student had to pitch a modern-day adaptation of *Ajax;* remote co-authoring is one way in which the wiki facilitates this exercise. The students also use the wiki for individual presentations on scholarly articles. I assign these articles, which for the most part are archaeological in nature, in the order in which they were written to allow the students to build on each other's articles and presentations, just as the articles I choose build on or respond to each other. They build wiki pages for their presentations, linking to other students' case study presentations and scholarly online resources (like the online *Oxford Classical Dictionary*) as needed to present the important points of each article, any necessary background information (usually historical background or archaeological terminology), and an assessment of how well each scholar makes his or her argument, especially as part of a scholarly dialogue. I find that these personal presentation pages help in making the transition from discussing serious issues, such as why Ajax committed suicide, to looking at large amounts of impersonal burial data. It can be startling for some students; I am used to cataloguing burials, but many of the students are a bit taken aback by the fact that all those little juvenile skeletons stuffed into broken bathtubs or jars are reduced to numbers, graphs, and statistical analyses of social change. Being allowed to juxtapose pictures of individual graves with charts and graphs, to link to other articles that help explain death-ritual phenomena, and to take ownership of one of these case studies, in terms of mastering the material and explaining it to their peers—these things seem to allow students a degree of control over the material that helps them keep in perspective the fact that individual people contribute to all of those graphs, and likewise, those graphs tell us something about society at large.

The students' final essay, which invariably evolves substantially from the proposal to the final copy, is supposed to be an answer to the question "What did it mean to die well in ancient Greece?" I ask them this broad question because, although it requires mastery of the ancient material, it allows them to focus on the aspects of death, legacy, and immortality with which they are most comfortable and which have intrigued them the most. Usually they choose a focus that they find intellectually and emotionally challenging, but they are given the opportunity to sidestep topics that make them uncomfortable. Drafts are required, and I give extensive feedback on these drafts, as well as requiring students to integrate material from the case studies, which are presented after the first draft is due, into their final drafts. My feedback challenges the students intellectually while respecting their preferences not to discuss suicide, or the nature of the soul, or whether a life well lived according to established religious conventions is rewarded in the hereafter. It also allows those students who tire of the absence of women in Classical Studies to write papers about the tight relationship between women and death noted by many scholars, including Maurice Bloch (1982), Sarah Iles Johnston (1999), and Rush Rehm (1996), among many others. I believe that this open-ended approach is extremely valuable in teaching courses about uncomfortable subjects, as it gives the student an "out" if s/he does not wish to take on topics, such as rape, suicide, or pederasty, that come up frequently in Classics courses.

"FINAL" THOUGHTS

I hope that this brief chapter has contributed to the volume by: 1) discussing an example of an uncomfortable issue where some students have to be made uncomfortable in the interests of comprehension, while respecting the discomfort of others; 2) acknowledging the vast differences with which we are dealing when it comes to students', and our own, experiences and familiarity with uncomfortable subjects; and 3) providing some pedagogical suggestions that apply to and are helpful for the teaching of other uncomfortable subjects. Just as the catharsis experienced through watching tragedies performed helped many Greeks learn through suffering—but vicariously—so too do I hope this course helps students better understand the nature and importance of death-ritual in antiquity, as well as what ritual behavior tells us about human society in general, by studying the death and death-rituals of others. Equally important is our own understanding, as teachers, of what experiences and emotional baggage we bring into the classroom when we teach this material. Teaching and writing about dying, death, and death-ritual is one thing when you are going through a relatively smooth patch of life; it is a whole different game when you are seeing the ancient material through the modern filters of war, violence, and suicide attempts, and the terminal illnesses of family and friends—or whatever the uncomfortable subject may be. It is a very fine line between sharing too much and sharing enough to make the students confront, directly and in the classroom, the uncomfortable subjects that, for better or for worse, are part of our humanity.

Teaching about Disability in Today's Classics Classroom

LISA TRENTIN

THE STUDY OF DISABILITY as an academic discipline (formally known as Disability Studies) is a relatively recent development, having grown as a result of increased public activism and scholarly engagement in the mid-1980s. Broadly defined, Disability Studies seeks to augment our understanding of disability in all cultures and historical periods and to promote greater awareness of the experiences of disabled people, so as to use this knowledge to advocate for social change.[1] Today across the United Kingdom, the United States and Canada, numerous institutions of higher education offer an undergraduate degree in Disability Studies or a college diploma in a related field. Despite the growth of the field itself, however, the concept of disability and its use as an identity category (akin to race or gender, for example) in other academic disciplines, such as Classics, has been, by and large, slow to take hold. Recent work on disability in the Greco-Roman worlds has demonstrated the enormous potential of this topic to broaden our understanding of ancient society and culture, yet this research seldom features in the curriculum of today's classroom. While the number of students and faculty with disabilities in higher education continues to increase, a critical engagement with the history of disability is lacking. This chapter calls for the integration of disability in the Classics classroom. What fol-

---

1. As outlined in the Mission Statement of the Society for Disability Studies, the scholarly organization dedicated to the cause of promoting Disability Studies as an academic discipline. See the website: http://disstudies.org/.

lows is a brief examination of the nature of the ancient evidence, its uses and usefulness as a pedagogical tool, combined with the challenging issues it generates, and a reflection on my own experiences teaching ancient disability in the modern university classroom.

MAPPING DISABILITY STUDIES ON THE ANCIENT WORLD AND IN THE CLASSICS CLASSROOM

It was in the early-1990s that the subject of disability in the ancient Greco-Roman worlds began to arouse the attention of the international academic community.[2] Recognizing a vast, but relatively underexplored corpus of ancient evidence, scholars have since sought to integrate the disabled body back into our understanding of ancient society and culture, art and representation.[3] Indeed, the recent spate of collaborative interdisciplinary conferences concerned with the place of disability in ancient society and modern scholarship points to the continued efforts to advance this once marginalized field.[4] Disability constitutes a valuable category of analysis for ancient

---

2. This was, at least in part, a result of the political recognition and support of the disability rights movement with the passing of the "Americans with Disabilities Act" in 1990 and the "UK Disability Discrimination Act" in 1995. No similar federal legislation exists in Canada although the government is currently working towards introducing national disability legislation ("Accessibility for Canadians with Disabilities").

3. The first ever book-length investigation on the topic was Robert Garland's seminal work, *The Eye of the Beholder. Deformity and Disability in the Graeco-Roman World* (first published in 1995, second edition with preface and supplementary bibliography, 2010). Subsequent studies have also been key to the development of this topic in the academy at large: Nicholas Vlahogiannis's book, *Representations of Disability in the Ancient World* (1998a) and his chapters on "Disabling bodies," in the edited volume by D. Montserrat, *Changing Bodies, Changing Meanings: Studies in the Human Body in Antiquity* (1998b) and "Curing disability" in the edited volume by H. King, *Health in Antiquity* (2005) are especially noteworthy. So too are the contributions of Martha Rose. Her book, *The Staff of Oedipus: Transforming Disability in Ancient Greece* (2003), considers the ancient Greek material on physical disability through the lens of disability studies, and her entry in the five-volume *Encyclopedia of Disability* (2006) titled, "History of Disability: Ancient West" is the only one of its kind. Most recently, the edited volume by Christian Laes, Chris Goodey and Martha Rose on *Disabilities in Roman Antiquity* (2013) is the first volume to systematically study the subject of disabilities in the Roman world.

4. New research in the field is significantly supported by the collaborative work of contributors to conferences organized within the last five years, especially in the United Kingdom. The University of Leeds, in collaboration with the University of Kent, hosted a workshop in January 2009 on "Redefining Disability in the Ancient World," which brought together scholars of Classical and Late Antique/Byzantine literature, archaeology and paleopathology to re-assess how the term disability should be used and defined amongst the different fields of scholarship. A related workshop was held at Antwerp in September 2011 examining how people with varying body types and (dis-)abilities were defined and supported in ancient Rome. More recently, the University of Nottingham held a

(socio-cultural) history, one that highlights issues not revealed by traditional categories such as race, gender, class, ethnicity, etc. Approaching the ancient world through the lens of disability studies contributes to a fuller understanding of the lives and experiences of the ancients. It is a logical step then to integrate the study of disability into the Classics classroom.[5] The topic of disability can be implemented in most general art, archaeology, civilization, history, literature, or mythology courses. It also fits well in specialized courses dealing with, for example, ancient medicine.[6] Beyond this, the topic can stand alone as an advanced (under-) graduate seminar dedicated entirely to "Disability in the Ancient World." Although the nature of the evidence itself can generate difficult discussions on issues such as infanticide, in-utero screening, and "sick" humor, if approached with tact and sensitivity, the topic offers great reward.

My work on disability has attempted to plug into existing scholarship by implementing disability studies theory alongside traditional (art-) historical analysis.[7] My research has extended to the classroom by way of my teaching in Roman art and archaeology, civilization and history, first in the Department of Archaeology and Classical Studies at Wilfrid Laurier University, and now in the Department of Historical Studies at the University of Toronto at Mississauga, both in Canada. The integration of this material has proven extremely worthwhile; students regularly tell me that my discussions on disability in the Roman world have opened their eyes to a range of (ancient and modern) socio-cultural issues they had not previously considered.

I must confess too that it is my students who have opened my eyes to issues I had not previously considered: the intense emotional responses and reactions that this material can elicit in classroom discussions which, in turn, informs my approach to teaching the topic. Evidence from ancient Rome generates (sometimes heated) classroom debates, with difficult questions leading to difficult dialogues: What constituted a disability in ancient

---

workshop in December 2011 on "Economies of Disease and Disability from Antiquity to the Middle Ages," which addressed how wealth and economy impacted the lives of impaired people, their careers, and their families in antiquity and medieval Europe.

5. A step that has already begun in the Humanities at large: M. Rose held a two-day seminar with contributions from S. Snyder and D. Mitchell, titled "Teaching Disability in the Ancient World," part of the National Institute of the Humanities series at the University of Illinois at Chicago on "Integrating Disability Studies into the Humanities" during the 2002–2003 Summer Seminars for School Instructors.

6. Baker, King, and Totelin in this volume note that they have included sessions on disability in their courses on Greek and Roman medicine.

7. See Trentin (2009); (2011); (2013b); (forthcoming, 2015).

Rome? How did the ancient Romans understand and explain the causes and consequences of disability (medically, socially and religiously)? How were people with disabilities treated in ancient Rome? How are they treated today? How do modern ideas about disability differ from the past and can we judge an ancient society by our own norms? These questions can be particularly charged for students with disabilities or students with a family member, close relative or friend who is disabled. For some students, personalizing these kinds of questions can be a positive experience, allowing them to engage more fully with the ancient material by applying their own experience and understanding. For others, however, dealing with these questions and the issues thus raised is immensely troublesome and can cause feelings of anxiety, unease and isolation, resulting in reduced participation in class. Herein lies the challenge for instructors: How can one facilitate discussion and dialogue in the classroom in a way that includes *all* students and translates without offense or distress? To think about this, I shall examine some of the evidence for disability in the ancient Roman world, highlighting areas that have proven uncomfortable and particularly difficult to discuss in the classroom based on my own teaching experiences, from which I hope to share techniques for grappling with the sensitive issues of disability, *then* and *now*.

DISABILITY TODAY: STUDENTS WITH DISABILITIES IN THE CLASSICS CLASSROOM

Instructors in today's universities are becoming increasingly aware of the diverse range of students' needs and must respond by providing a variety of instructional, assessment, evaluative and reporting strategies. This is particularly important for students with disabilities who require additional accommodations. The number of disabled students in higher education has increased substantially over the past decade, with 5 percent of university students nation-wide in the United Kingdom, 6 percent in Canada, and 9 percent in the United States being disabled (2006).[8] Despite this, faculty remain largely ill-informed about the needs of students with disabilities and the support required for them to reach their full academic potential.[9] Having spent the last fifteen years in the university system both in the United Kingdom and Canada, I have experienced the reality of this first-hand.

---

8. Konur (2006: 351).

9. On the varying attitudes and perceptions towards students with disabilities (by both faculty and students), see the comprehensive doctoral dissertation by Lombardi (2010: esp. 1–25).

My first direct experience with disability in the Classics classroom came as a graduate student at the University of Nottingham when I volunteered as an academic support tutor for a visually impaired undergraduate student in Beginners Greek. I recall vividly my first meeting with the Disability Support Centre coordinator: she was overjoyed that not only was I a Classics graduate, but my research on deformity and disability surely made me an ideal tutor for this student. I wasn't so sure. On paper, my duties seemed simple: I met the student at the Disability Support Centre twenty minutes before class began, guided her to class, attended class with the student, prepared class notes and offered personal tutoring and mentoring. In actuality, our relationship was more than simply student-tutor; I became a friend and, to some extent, confidant to the student who felt sufficiently comfortable to discuss her classroom concerns with me—most notably, her reluctance to participate in class for fear of drawing attention to herself. Though there had never been any indication of mistreatment by her peers, nor singling her out unnecessarily or unfairly by the instructor, the student nevertheless felt uneasy and this resulted in poor class participation. To me, this seemed quite out of character; on a one-on-one basis, the student was very engaging and animated, but in the classroom, in her first year at university, amongst peers who knew little about her impairment, she became quiet and detached. I cannot, even now, begin to grasp the difficulties of learning the ancient Greek language with a visual impairment. Of course, accommodations were made for the student: the textbook, *Reading Greek,* was available in Braille, all of the class notes I provided were transcribed into Braille, the instructor had ensured everything was read aloud in class and all of the student's exams were conducted orally. Nevertheless there remained obstacles. Although the Disability Support Centre arranged alternative accommodation for the mid-term and final examinations, class tests were more problematic and the instructor confessed to being rather inefficient about arranging alternate facilities for the student; on several occasions the student was tested outside the classroom in the corridor, easily distracted by the commotion of passers-by. After the course had ended, discussion with the instructor revealed that she had had poor communication with the Disability Support Centre and very limited conversations with the student herself about her specific learning needs.

As a result of this experience, and being now myself in the role of instructor, I am keenly aware of, and indeed, a strong advocate for, the benefits of university services for students with disabilities. My familiarity with the system has revealed, however, a serious gap in the transfer of information between student, support service and instructor and that is, without doubt, a pressing problem. At Wilfrid Laurier University the Accessible Learning Centre (hereafter ALC) provides support to both students and faculty individually, but does little to facilitate communication across panels. The decision to disclose information to faculty regarding a disability is one left to the student so as to ensure confidentiality and privacy. A student is encouraged to self-identify with his/her instructor and to discuss his/her need(s) for accommodation. But what happens when a student does not self-identify? What happens when a student's disability is not visible? Not all students with disabilities identify themselves, and not all disabilities are visible. This means that faculty are unable to take the necessary steps to develop and implement appropriate educational strategies with respect to disability-related issues. Moreover, it means running the risk of potentially offending students with unknown disabilities, by using disabling language, whether consciously or not, resulting in embarrassment for the instructor and/or the student's peers. In exceptional circumstances, the ALC will communicate the needs of a disabled student in writing by confidential email to the instructor. Most often, however, the exchange of information between instructor and ALC is relatively minimal—an email at the beginning of the term notifying the instructor that a student with a disability is enrolled in the class and requires, for example, a note-taker, and an email near the end of the term advising the instructor of alternate examination arrangements. In some circumstances, a student will provide documented evidence for accommodation, especially if the accommodation requires the instructor's consent, such as the use of a digital recording device for lectures. Very seldom are instructors given specific details about a student's disability, from the student or ALC. This can put instructors in an awkward position: is it appropriate to ask the student for further details about his/her disability? A student's confidentiality is certainly important, but when does that confidentiality impede the potential for their full integration in the classroom? When, and to what extent, should instructors be made aware of a student's disability? How can instructors help students with disabilities if they are not made fully aware? On the other hand, when a student has self-identified or a student's disability is clearly visible, what resources are available for instructors? How can instructors be coached to deal with the difficulties they might encounter in the classroom, particularly with regard to sensitive course content (e.g., teaching ancient disability in today's Classics classroom)? Sadly, many instructors are left un(der)prepared.

While revising this paper, in the first weeks of a new term, as if on cue with my comments above decrying the gap in communication between student, centre and instructor, I received an email from the ALC supplying me with a list of ten students in my course (of 117) registered with a documented disability. This list included each student's specific accommodations, which were split between examination (the amount of extra time needed to write exams) and classroom (the use of a note-taker) accommodations. The email itself was not unusual. It was the number of students who had self-identified and sought the support of the ALC that struck me. In my first year of teaching, the same first-year course (marginally smaller in size with 96 students), had only four students registered with the ALC, and in the three years thereafter, in all of my other courses combined, only an additional five. More unusual still were the separate emails that followed concerning two students with disabilities necessitating more extensive accommodations, of which I had very limited understanding and no previous experience. I was notified that one student had a memory-related disability (which had been assessed and documented by "a professional in the field") and required the use of approved memory aids (known as "smart sheets") for all examinations. I was given detailed information about the use of memory aids and instruction regarding the procedures for developing these in conjunction with the student and ALC. I was also encouraged to discuss further accommodations both with the student and his/her disability consultant. I did, on both counts. I was also notified (this time with a follow-up telephone call with the disability consultant) about another student in the class who had Asperger's Syndrome. The accommodations for this student were more demanding; in addition to requiring memory aids, the student was also likely to need more contact time with me outside of the classroom. Unfortunately, despite numerous attempts to schedule one-on-one meetings with the student (to discuss class behavioral issues, assignment deadlines, etc.), the student seemed more willing to have the ALC sort this out, rather than speak directly with me, the instructor. The point I draw here is not with the students themselves (more on their cases below) but rather, my amazement at the level of disclosure and the amount of support I was given by the ALC. I still had to research Asperger's Syndrome and think about my own approach to teaching, but my feelings of discomfort (i.e., not being sure how to "handle" the student) were alleviated by the support of the ALC.

As here demonstrated, teaching support is a crucial area that must be addressed if we are to effectively educate all of our students. In recent years there have been efforts to address the difficulties in teaching students with disabilities at the college and university level. Numerous institutions across Canada, the United States and the United Kingdom have begun to offer seminars and workshops for instructors, teaching assistants and tutors to introduce them to the different types of disabilities that they may encounter in their classes, tips for teaching students with different disabilities, facts about the disabled student population at their institution, and an explanation of the disability services offered on campus. Likewise, there is a growing amount of material on teaching students with disabilities, much of which encourages proactive and independent research on the part of the instructor.[10] Ultimately, it is on a case-by-case basis that an instructor forms a pedagogical approach to teaching students with disabilities. This is certainly the case with my own teaching career at Wilfrid Laurier University.

As a relatively small, liberal arts-type college, Wilfrid Laurier University has traditionally been an attractive venue for students with disabilities. According to the ALC there were 830 students registered through the office with some form of disability in 2010. These students account for 6.2 percent of the student population. The University capitalizes on its small campus—which spans a single city block—and the relative proximity of everything on campus as a selling point for students with disabilities. It also offers a number of services for students with disabilities, as well as for faculty and staff. The ALC operates a "Transition 101 Program" for first-year students, which provides a full day workshop for students to orient themselves to the staff, support and services available through the ALC. The Diversity & Equity Office also recently (2010) introduced mandatory AODA (Accessibility for Ontarians with Disabilities Act) training for all employees as well as volunteer staff, an hour-long session outlining our shared responsibility to provide fair educational access to students with disabilities.

In the nearly four years that I taught at Wilfrid Laurier University, I had nineteen students self-identify as disabled, ranging from learning difficulties, physical impairments and autism spectrum disorders. I also had a handful of students who did not formally self-identify; they revealed their circumstances in discussions outside of the classroom. Beyond this, I had countless students speak of a disabled family member or friend and his/her experiences. The presence of these students and their experiences provided the occasion to reflect on my teaching strategies and, whenever possible, implement new teaching techniques and classroom protocol, benefiting, as I have discovered, not only those students with disabilities, but the whole class. Although I make no claim to be an "expert" in the field, nor to have all the "right" answers for difficult classroom situations that might arise, I do hope that sharing my experiences will be helpful to those who have not

---

10. See, for example, Konur (2006), Ben-Moshe, Cory, Feldbaum, and Sagendorf (2005) and Ben-Moshe and Colligan (2010).

taught the topic before, as well as providing a starting point to open up a larger discussion for those who have had similar experiences and can offer additional advice or approaches to teaching.

DISABILITY IN ANTIQUITY: THE EVIDENCE FROM ANCIENT ROME

In the courses I have taught on Roman civilization and Roman art and archaeology, disability features as a key component. I have taught these courses on numerous occasions and have had the opportunity to fine-tune my lectures, to a certain degree. Because the topic generates such rich discussion, both in class and in office hours, I have learned to be less rigid in my approach to teaching, allowing discussion to veer from the syllabus so as to follow the students' interests, without, of course, compromising any of the course content. I was often struck with delight by some of the astute questions posed by my students and their keen interest to know more. On occasion, however, I have been horrified and felt quite disturbed by inappropriate side comments and wholly unacceptable "spastic jokes." I was not alone; other students were similarly offended. In a class where the entire student population is "able-bodied" the topic can cause unease and discomfort because, the ancient Roman world, being quite unlike our own, particularly with regards to its attitude towards, and its treatment of, people with disabilities, often engages controversial and difficult dialogue. Discussion can become doubly uncomfortable when there is a student with a disability in the classroom whose personal experiences might (negatively) impact his/her response to, and engagement with, the ancient evidence and other students.

In a first-year undergraduate course on Roman Civilization, I incorporate a session on "the disabled" under the theme of "Others," which also includes (separate) discussions on women, slaves, and foreigners. My goal is to engage disability studies to interrogate Roman ideas about the 'self' and 'other', abled and dis-abled. As a class we consider a wide variety of sources on disability—archaeological, medical, literary, and visual—and evaluate the reliability of these sources and the context(s) in which they were intended to be read and/or viewed. Students find it particularly unsettling that no testimony of a disabled person exists. The evidence is in fact a patchwork of incidental information about disability, so I warn students that we must be cautious of making sweeping generalizations about the ancient Romans, especially given that our sources derive from the perspective of the able-bodied (elite male). Nevertheless, critical analysis of these sources allows us to ponder questions about the role, status, and treatment of people with disabilities in ancient Rome. This type of analysis in turn opens up possibilities for comparison(s) to the modern world and allows students to recognize the importance of different historical and sociocultural contexts. Highlighting context is especially important when it comes to definitions and terminology, which are difficult areas to negotiate in the classroom. The Romans did not think about nor conceptualize disability as the modern world does and there is no ancient Latin equivalent (or Greek, for that matter) to the overarching term "disabled." The Romans did, however, have an extensive vocabulary to describe an individual who deviated from the "normal" somatotype—*invalidus, infirmus, debilis, deformis,* which can translate as unable, incomplete, weak, ugly, and deformed; but these alone make it impossible to identify specific disabilities. Roman nicknames and cognomina are sometimes helpful here since many are based on definite physical deformities or disabilities, i.e., Strabo (Squinter), Cocles (One-eyed), Caecus (Blind), Balbus (Stammerer), etc.[11] More problematic are the criteria used to determine who is and who is not disabled; the traditional categories of blind, lame, and deaf are not usually questioned, but other, socially ascribed "deformities" like obesity and baldness are often contested, leading students to grapple with different ideas about what comprises a deformity and if that deformity constitutes a disability. An individual may be deformed (e.g., hunchbacked), but other variable physiological and psychological factors will determine whether s/he is also disabled; the significance of these differences is not often considered by students today.

The first year I taught this course, a student with a disability was enrolled in the class. The student approached me in the second week of term with a letter from the ALC to obtain permission for the digital recording of all class lectures. I was not provided any additional information about the student's disability. Although it was only week two, I realized that my class on "the disabled" in week ten could be potentially awkward and I knew that I would have to approach the student in confidence about this, sooner rather than later. The following week I spoke with the student during my office hours and discussed some of the sensitive material to be covered in class. I gave the student the source material and class readings in advance so that she could be prepared for discussion. I also gave the student the option to

---

11. Approximately 40 percent of the names extant from the Roman Republic describe physical abnormalities. On their pejorative use, see Corbeill (2010) esp. 443–44. Others have suggested these were originally playful nicknames that an individual willingly adopted, see Kajanto (1965: 20).

be absent from class if she felt too uncomfortable, with the understanding that a follow-up meeting would be required to address questions or concerns. The student revealed nothing about her disability and was clearly hesitant to discuss her learning concerns with me. In the end, the student did not attend the class, and, to be truthful, at the time, I was relieved. I knew not what to expect from the other students in the class, nor how I would handle difficult discussions. As it turned out, the class was a very engaging and thought-provoking one, as will be discussed below. When all was said and done, I was sorry that the student had not been present to at least listen, if not participate in the discussion that ensued and I stressed this in our one-on-one meeting thereafter. Although the student seemed apologetic for missing the class, it was clear from her body language (crossed arms, fidgeting foot, downward gaze) and the brevity of the meeting (she couldn't get out of my office fast enough!) that she felt uncomfortable discussing the subject with me, even conceptually, since we never spoke in personal terms about her own disability. Perhaps there were underlying issues (bullying, exclusion?) with which the student was still contending. Overall, my meetings with the student were awkward, and I wish now that I had approached them, and the student, more sensitively. I did, however, use the experience to think harder about how instructors can effectively reach out to students in need.

To return to the class which the student missed, discussion centered (as I note now, it so often does) on two areas that commonly generate a variety of emotional responses, from uncomfortable laughter and inappropriate "spastic jokes," to moral outrage and personal offense: the killing of "defective" infants, and the display of the disabled body for entertainment.

THE HORROR! KILLING DEFECTIVE BABIES

Students are often familiar with the (sensationalized) Spartan paradigm of infanticide, but less so with the evidence from ancient Rome. Admittedly, the evidence here is inconclusive and controversial. It consists of highly problematic archaeological remains (the large infant burial at Hambleden in Britain has recently been in the news, Discovery News, May 5, 2011); a single reference to the so-called "law of Romulus" in Dionysios of Halicarnassus (2.15.1–2); a law appearing in Table IV of the Twelve Tables and referenced in a treatise by Cicero (*De Leg.* 3.8.19); also mentioned in a speech by the Elder Seneca (*Contr.* 10.4.16); and a section in the Greek physician Soranus' *Gynaikeia* (2.10) used by Roman parents to judge whether an infant is healthy enough to be raised.[12] In addition to this, evidence from Livy (*Ab urbe condita* 2–4) and Julius Obsequens (*Liber Prodigiorum*) indicates that, in the Roman Republic, the birth of a defective infant could be interpreted as an evil omen and a sign of divine displeasure. In some cases, for example the birth of a dual-sexed infant, we are told of elaborate expiation rites that were performed, followed by the drowning of the infant in the Tiber in order to appease the gods.[13]

First-year students are often shocked and horrified by the practice of infanticide. The "gut" reaction is one of condemnation; this seems a common response to the majority of undergraduate students who have yet to consider the responsibility of caring for and raising a (disabled) child. To be fair, most of the students have little prior knowledge of Roman religion, law, medicine or economics. This can, and has, led to discussion (and arguments) about abortion and euthanasia, themselves difficult topics to address in the classroom.[14] Generally, however, once students recognize the wider context of disability in ancient, especially Republican, Rome, they are not so quick to judge the Romans for being less tolerant than themselves. Discussion then leads to other important questions: What if a disability is not visible at birth? What becomes of parents who choose to raise a deformed or disabled child? What happened to individuals who developed a disability later in life?

Here the comments of one of my mature students, a retired father of three, were particularly helpful. As the oldest member of the class and the only student, to my knowledge, who had children, he discussed his reaction to Roman infanticide based on the only comparison he could make: the birth of his two sons and one daughter and the intense emotional attachment he felt in the birthing room. His children were all "able," but he noted that when each child was born he always ran through the same mental checklist: listen for the cry, wait for movement, check the eyes, ears and nose, count the fingers and toes. The first moments of life were spent ensuring the baby was healthy. Acknowledging that his situation was different from an ancient Roman *paterfamilias,* he highlighted the fact that there was still the latent fear of abnormality. As a Roman Catholic, he would raise his child regardless of physical (dis)ability; his beliefs were not ones of fear of divine displeasure or impending catastrophe and as such he couldn't (shouldn't) pass a moral judgment on the Romans. For him, the practice of

---

12. For infanticide in the Roman world, see esp. Harris (1982); (1994).
13. For birth omens and pollution, see MacBain (1982) and Garland (2010: 67–70).
14. See the chapter on "Teaching Ancient Medicine: the Issues of Abortion" by Baker, King and Totelin in this volume.

infanticide was far removed from the modern world to the ancient world, through time, space and, especially religion. To his comments I directed discussion towards modern prenatal or in-utero screening. It is now fairly routine for obstetricians and/or midwives to perform screening for disease, disability or genetic conditions in unborn infants—a practice which is not so unlike the screening of newborns in the ancient world. Specific disabilities, such as Down syndrome, Spina Bifida and Autism, can (sometimes) be detected, though not with conclusive accuracy. This leaves parents with a difficult decision to make.

On the other hand, however, this mature student did question the treatment of individuals who became disabled later in life. He confessed that he suffered from arthritis in his right knee and walking long distances was becoming increasingly difficult; at some point he would require, at the very minimum, a cane. But he wouldn't (couldn't) consider himself disabled. He was also losing the excellent vision that he had in his youth—did wearing glasses for reading or driving mean he was visually disabled? As he was also already balding, he took to task the stories of various emperors who suffered the "deformity of baldness" (Suet. *Calig.* 50.1; *Jul.* 45.2). What did all of this say about him and the aging process? His reaction was enlightening for the other, younger, students. Plainly put, he noted that as we aged, all of us would inevitably suffer from one "disability" or another.[15] Another student questioned whether it was simply a matter of age, for were we not all already "disabled" in some respect? Other students soon chimed in—those who wore glasses for near-sightedness, a knee brace for a recent football injury, and so on. Using himself as an example proved to be an excellent way of getting the other students to think through the ancient evidence from a modern perspective, while still remaining historically cognizant and morally impartial.

THE HUMOR! DERIDING THE DISABLED

Despite the evidence above, not all defective infants were killed. Indeed, by the Imperial period, it seems that deformed and disabled individuals were raised and fervently traded on the slave market. Plutarch (*Mor.* 520c) states that in Rome the demand for deformed slaves was so great that monster markets (τῶν τεράτων ἀγοράν) emerged where "freaks" of all kinds could

---

15. The Romans themselves thought a great deal about the aging process and the physical ramifications of baldness, deteriorating eyesight, mental instability, etc. For modern discussion, see esp. Harlow and Laurence (2002; 2007).

be purchased. Quintilian (*Inst.* 2.5.11) also claims that deformed slaves were in such demand that some Romans were prepared to pay more for them than for physically perfect ones. Why the fascination with deformed and/or disabled slaves? What fate awaited these individuals? Various sources suggest that deformed and disabled individuals often featured as companions of the elite, and were especially popular at the Roman imperial court, providing a source of amusement and entertainment.[16]

Several ancient authors, including Cicero (*De or.* 2.239) and Quintilian (*Inst.* 6.3.7), state that by the Imperial period, deformed and disabled individuals were ideal subjects for ridicule and derision. Perhaps the most disturbing evidence for this (to a modern audience, at least) lies in the episodes related to the *convivia* of the Roman emperors where deformed and disabled individuals were paraded in often humiliating and debasing contexts for amusement. The emperor Commodus, in one of his "humorous" moments, is said to have served at a banquet two hunchbacks smeared in mustard on a silver platter as a pseudo-meal (SHA, *Comm.*11.1). The infamous emperor Elagabalus is said to have been in the habit of inviting to his banquets eight bald men, eight one-eyed men, eight men with gout, eight deaf men, eight dark men, eight tall men and eight fat men in order to arouse laughter at them all, especially in the case of the last group who could not all fit on one couch (SHA, *Heliogab.* 29.3).

For first year students, episodes like these generate laughter and are considered "funny." Certainly the readers of the SHA also found these stories funny. But how is this humor used to say something about ancient Roman attitudes towards the deformed and disabled? How else might these stories be read? How do they implicate the able-bodied reader/viewer/audience? When does this humor stop being funny? It is only when I pose these types of questions to my students that they begin to consider the implications of their laughter and the significance of this type of representation, and, upon further comparison with the modern world, the implications of similar insults in the world outside our classroom.

The second year I taught this course, class discussion turned to the topic of the humor of disability, spurred on by one male student's desire to share with his peers a few "spastic" jokes. Some students laughed raucously, some giggled uncomfortably, others glared with disdain. The jokes were wholly inappropriate, but rather than reprimand the student, I used this oppor-

---

16. Of course, other employment was certainly available and it is erroneous to make sweeping conclusions. Nevertheless, Imperial sources reveal a picture (whether true to life or not) in which the deformed and disabled were popular household "pets." For further discussion, especially in the imperial court, see Trentin (2011).

tunity to think about "sick humor," and the differences in deriding the disabled in ancient Rome and the modern world. Every society will react differently, and with varying degrees of emotional intensity, to individuals with disabilities, but one seemingly universal phenomenon is the derision of the disabled. The Romans often laughed outright at disabled individuals, they used pejorative language in everyday speech and paraded such individuals in debasing contexts as a source of amusement and entertainment. Today, in many parts of the West, it is politically incorrect to joke about people with disabilities because it perpetuates negative stereotypes and false beliefs about disability. "Spastic" jokes belong within a network of disabling language—language that accepts the assumption that disabilities are bad, unfortunate or denote lack/deficiency; these include still commonly used phrases like lame idea, blind justice, dumb luck, deaf ears, paralyzed with fear, and retarded. Although the student in my class argued that his jokes were "just" funny and he hadn't meant to offend anyone, he clearly didn't understand the implications of this type of disabling humor. One of the female students in the class commented on the fact that her short stature made her a constant target of short jokes and she resented the fact that others found her height a source of derision. As such, she was deeply upset by the male student's jokes and, to return to the ancient evidence, the derision of the disabled in ancient Rome. I wondered how these jokes resonated with the other students in the class registered with the ALC.

I came to understand this somewhat better in a third-year undergraduate course on "The Art and Architecture of Imperial Rome." In this course I included a session on "disabling imagery," again as part of a larger discussion on representing the "Other." My goal is to engage disability studies perspectives to interrogate visual representations of all kinds of *un*Roman, abnormal or physically deviant, bodies. Students were surprised by the very limited repertoire of depictions of physical deformity in mainstream Roman art, given the Roman use of veristic portraiture in the Republic. Large-scale art often disguises or completely eliminates any evidence of physical abnormality (think of the lame god Vulcan on the Albani Puteal or the "weak and feeble" Claudius as Jupiter from Lanuvium), and those representations which explore aspects of abnormality do so with a deliberate desire to shock and amuse (think of the sleeping hermaphrodite now in the Louvre, or the hunchback now in the Villa Albani-Torlonia). On the other hand, in the so-called "minor arts" numerous miniature statuettes survive from the Hellenistic and Roman periods that depict grotesques; popular here are the physically deformed and disabled dwarfs, hunchbacks, obese women, emaciated men, and so on. Though context (public versus private) certainly weighs heavily on function, all of these images articulate a distance and difference between the disabled bodies on display and the non-disabled viewing public. How was this difference understood in the ancient world and how do we make sense of it today?

Displaying deformed and disabled individuals for amusement or entertainment is not a uniquely Roman phenomenon; indeed this tradition extends beyond Rome into modern times. This ancient practice is comparable to that of Victorian American and European fascination with sideshows, dime museums and circuses, where the formally organized exhibition of people with physical, mental or behavioral anomalies was referred to as the "Freak Show." Here, modern "freaks" included: fat ladies, living skeletons, hermaphrodites, spotted boys, giants, Siamese twins and bearded ladies.[17] Showing students images of circus advertisements (Barnes & Bailey) highlights that there is a certain universal fascination with confronting the abnormal, whether that be to point at it or to applaud it. This fascination continues today, albeit in a different disguise: "Buskerfest" (as it is known in Toronto, the largest international street performer festival in North America) replaces born "freaks" with knife-juggling, fire-breathing, body-contorting performers. Moreover, television talk shows and reality programs (e.g., Octo-mom) may now have claimed the cultural position once occupied by the freak show. Indeed, Professor Mary Beard from the University of Cambridge has claimed that the hit "Britain's Got Talent" is a modern day freak show.[18] Here too there is an articulation of distance and difference between the "freak" body on display (the extraordinarily talented or the comically inept) and the "normal" viewing public.

When I taught this course I had a student, unknown to me, with a disability. Her disability was not visible and she had not self-identified. I learned of her circumstances some days later when she approached me in my office hours to talk about how the topic and images shown made her feel—initially uneasy, awkward, and self-conscious, then, after engagement in the class, intrigued and empowered. She had reflected on the fact that her own disability (dyslexia) wasn't obviously visible and that she was thankful for this because it meant less social stigmatization and exclusion. She could understand the reasons for an individual wanting to be represented as "normal," but had trouble with the use of an individual's deformity or disability for "shock factor" or entertainment. She did not find these images

---

17. On the "Freak Show," its history and allure, see esp. Thomson (1996) and Adams (2001).

18. Mary Beard's blog in *The Times Literary Supplement*, "A Don's Life" featured the blog post "A classicist watches Britain's Got Talent" posted May 30, 2009: http://timesonline.typepad.com/dons_life/2009/05/a-classicist-watches-britains-got-talent.html#more

the least bit funny. The student confessed that she found them disturbing, but thought-provoking nonetheless: they made her question different definitions of normality throughout history, and this in turn made her think harder about what exactly made representing deformity and disability so fascinating. The student suggested that "disabling imagery" could be unsettling to even able-bodied individuals since it encouraged all students to question themselves and their conceptualizations of "normal" body types. The student's comments would have provided a unique perspective and a valuable contribution to the classroom discussion, but her feelings of initial discomfort meant that she refrained from offering her input.

I reflected on this meeting much afterwards and thought back to my first-year student in Roman Civilization who avoided the class on "the disabled" altogether and my student whose discomfort translated into inappropriate jokes. There is much value in exposing students to the ancient Roman material on disability, although there are certainly risks in discussing this material if an instructor is not cognizant of the student base and the diverse experiences that each student brings to the classroom. I am still in the process of working out how I can make my classes more "disability-friendly"; how I can ease feelings of discomfort so as to encourage all students, especially those with disabilities, to participate in class. Talking to students with identified disabilities outside of the classroom in advance helps, as do warnings to the whole class that some of the material to be discussed might be potentially disturbing. Remaining sensitive to the presentation of the ancient material and diligent in maintaining a mature and respectful learning environment in the classroom is also important. But more needs to be done. Part of the discomfort in discussing ancient disability lies in the fact that many students have never engaged in serious discussions about disability *today*. Recent attempts to promote diversity in the classroom have resulted in emphasis on issues of race, gender and sexuality, but disability remains largely neglected. Instructors must work towards exposing students to disability perspectives so as to address the wide range of issues that "disable" many people, the implications of which are important for all of us, whatever our ability.

CONCLUSION: INTRODUCING DISABILITY IN THE CLASSICS CLASSROOM

As an undergraduate student the topic of disability featured nowhere in my curriculum. Today the situation is much the same: a poll of the faculty in my former department (which, incidentally, was also the same institution where I received my undergraduate degree, with a number of the same professors who taught me), when asked to what extent they address topics concerning disability in the ancient (Near Eastern, Roman and Greek) worlds, revealed limited to no engagement with this topic.[19] In my current department, the situation is similar. My teaching has sought to change this. My courses in Roman art and archaeology, civilization and history have explored, albeit within a limited context, current research on disability and its usefulness in the Classics classroom. At the University of Toronto at Mississauga in the fall of 2012, I was given the opportunity to extend my scope of impact: I developed and delivered a third year special topics course on "The Body, Physical Difference and Disability in Ancient Greece."[20] In offering this course, my hope was to encourage students to think critically about what it has meant to be physically challenged and impaired throughout history. The course was a success; students commented that they had never considered the ancient world from the perspective of its disabled but enjoyed the new material. This is the greatest merit of implementing disability in the Classics classroom: providing students with new information based on contemporary scholarship and a fresh perspective on issues that are still relevant today, thus giving them a more nuanced understanding of life in the ancient worlds of Greece and Rome. It is thus imperative that we not shy away from the topic of disability, however uncomfortable it might be to discuss, for student and instructor alike.

---

19. A notable exception is the work done by my former colleague Bonnie Glencross, a skeletal biologist with a research interest in paleopathology. Glencross has recently introduced students to the use of skeletal remains and the impact of disability on individuals and communities in a fourth-year course on "Theory in Archaeology."

20. For more detailed information on this course, see Trentin (2013a).

Teaching Ancient Medicine
The Issues of Abortion

PATTY BAKER, HELEN KING, AND
LAURENCE TOTELIN

THE TOPIC of ancient medicine is one that confronts both students and their teachers with a set of difficult issues. All those present in the classroom share the experience of living in a body, whether or not they have reflected on the extent to which their body is their "self," or whether the self inhabits the body; indeed, the subject of ancient medicine itself provides an opportunity to reflect on the philosophical issues related to current perceptions of mind-body dualism. For some, however, due to the nature of the material investigated, the topics covered, and the questions raised in class, ancient medicine will prove to be a particularly disturbing or challenging subject, sometimes at a very personal level. It is the teacher's job to communicate the subject in a mature and professional manner that does not cause the student to cease to engage due to feeling in some way "offended."[1]

As three women who have taught in different universities in the United Kingdom, we have chosen here to present the results of our discussions on how we teach emotive subjects like abortion, euthanasia, birth control, and embryotomy—the process of cutting a fetus into parts so that it can be extracted from the womb—in our Greek and Roman medicine classes. We are interested in how one presents such topics to students without shying away from the realities of past medical practices and the opinions of the

---

1. The issue of "offense" is a pedagogically interesting one; learning may come precisely by having one's core values challenged, but if this is taken too far then the learner may simply refuse to engage.

Greco-Roman medical writers, and we share here our stories about how we have dealt with particular problems concerning student reactions to these. In the course of our discussions, we have realized that our experiences in teaching these topics demonstrate the value of emotional intelligence. Emotional intelligence has become a topic of consideration in educational theory over the past fifteen or twenty years and much has been written about the necessity for good teachers to be aware of both intellectual quality and emotional intelligence in "develop[ing] a holistic learning experience for the student" (Hall 2005: 153). Emotional intelligence is in large part empathy. An empathetic teacher will have an awareness of their surroundings and the ability to sense and understand their students' feelings. When the teacher is attentive to the different emotions and reactions of their students towards certain topics that might be troubling, they can then gauge how to teach the topic in a manner that will encourage a student to engage with the class. An empathetic teacher will also be flexible and able to adapt to unexpected situations that might arise, something all three of us have experienced, and which this chapter will illustrate. Although the majority of the present discussion will be devoted to explaining our practices and our thoughts on teaching these topics, we acknowledge that we have worked in fairly similar situations, and our experiences might not be transferable to those teaching in other societies and types of universities. However, we hope that suggestions of how we deal with particular issues that arise on account of the specific socio-cultural, religious and ethical beliefs of some of our students might assist those teaching in circumstances different to our own.

At the most fundamental level, any group of undergraduate humanities students will have differing amounts of knowledge of their own bodies, as well as differing opinions and beliefs; the example of a history student who told King that her uncle was "having one of his livers removed" should act as a warning against assuming too much prior exposure to physiology. Often it is necessary to explain modern medical views of anatomy or physiology before the students can appreciate the ancient materials, and in evaluations students sometimes comment on how much they have learned from the course not only about their own bodies, but also about ethical issues. Unlike medical students, who can draw on numerous handbooks and monographs developed to help them consult and interact with patients about topics such as abortion, euthanasia, and the ethics of publication (e.g., Ashcroft et al. 2007), humanities students may not have had any prior opportunity to think about medical ethical issues in particular. The other side of this development of the individual through learning about ancient medicine is the "yuk" factor in dealing with ancient medical beliefs and healing practices, which can be precisely what attracted students to select such a course in the first place. We have found that some potential students have preconceived expectations that our classes will provide a source of graphic entertainment, believing the majority of material covered will be stories of horrific surgical procedures and unhygienic medical practices.[2] This preconception can form an obstacle to deep engagement with the sources; strategies need to be developed to give permission to students to find the materials upsetting, while working towards understanding them in their historical context.

The terminology of the body and of bodily processes can be difficult to negotiate in class. The exposure of medical students not just to information about health and disease, but also to ethical debates, often makes them more confident than humanities students in speaking about these issues, for example naming parts of the body without embarrassment. Some students will find the material being studied makes them laugh; often, as for example when comparing medical texts to a play by Aristophanes, this will be entirely appropriate, but at times laughter—and particularly giggling—can be an immature response to discomfort. Students can be very coy when genital organs are being named, and the teacher needs to consider how to negotiate the lines between "technical terms" (penis, vagina, vulva), more vernacular labels (pussy, cock), or euphemisms (down there, private parts). Sexual acts are also difficult to name in class; some students "know it all," others will be genuinely shocked, while in turn some teachers positively want to shock, and others do not. King has vivid memories of saying "cunnilingus" in a lecture to a class of two hundred first-year students in her first year of university teaching. At the end of the class, a group of older students came up to congratulate her for not blushing; this was achieved by avoiding all eye contact and focusing on the back wall of the lecture theater. Totelin felt great embarrassment when she could not recall the technical word "fellatio" while reading a graphic description of that sexual act in class (Archilochus fr. 42). She had to settle on telling the students "we all know what this is referring to, I think." Some students told her at the end of the class that archaic poetry was more fun than they had ever imagined.

A possible way to combat the problem of what language to use in the classroom is to open up discussion early on, by giving students an exercise

---

2. This approach is used by scholarly bloggers such as Lindsey Fitzharris to attract readers; her award-winning blog http://thechirurgeonsapprentice.com/ is subtitled "A website dedicated to the horrors of pre-anaesthetic surgery" (accessed 28 February 2012), later changed to "This website is dedicated to a study of early modern chirurgeons, and all the blood and gore that comes with it" (accessed 8 February 2014).

that permits them to use coarse language about body parts, sexual behavior and venereal disease. Baker had to undertake such an exercise as an undergraduate student in a health class in the United States. The teacher divided the students into three groups. Each group was given a sheet of paper, and the students had to write slang names for parts of the body, sexual intercourse and venereal disease. The papers were passed around every few minutes between the groups and each would add new words to the different topics. These were then read aloud in class. The point of this was to "break the ice" and it seemed to have the desired effect of enabling open, frank and maturely handled discussions between the students and the teacher about AIDS, rape, birth control and abortion. Although Baker found this worked well when she was a student, she has been hesitant to try such an exercise with her own students for fear of offending someone and ultimately being reported; instead, she uses the technical terms. In her experience, she knows that some students would react well to such an exercise, but others are clearly incensed even when technical terms are used, thus making her wonder why they have chosen the topic in the first place. In the United Kingdom there is also an ever-growing audit culture that encourages student comment and criticism. Constructive criticism is useful for teaching development but, since students are now considered "customers," some of their feedback has more to do with their lack of engagement caused by their expectations that they should be given a degree because they are paying the fees. Although Baker's teaching has always been rated excellent in her student evaluations, she is aware of student complaints being taken too far and causing high levels of stress for the teacher. Hence in some instances she has found the audit culture has an adverse effect; it may stifle creative teaching methods because teachers are afraid to cause offense. A discussion of how the different registers worked in antiquity can be a useful alternative means of approach here, for example by assigning a reading from Adams, *The Latin Sexual Vocabulary* or Henderson, *The Maculate Muse*.

While sex is still more of a taboo subject in the classroom than one may perhaps expect, the greatest taboo today remains open discussion of death.[3] King recalls that, in twenty-five years of teaching ancient medicine and sexuality, the greatest reaction of shock she elicited from a class was when she opened the session on death with the words, "You're all going to die, you know. All of you." Horrified, several of the students responded, "You can't say that!" She insisted that it was the one thing she could say, with com-

---

3. See papers by Butler and by Smith and Sulosky Weaver on teaching death, and Sharland on teaching *Lysistrata*, in this volume.

plete certainty. Reflecting on this moment now, she wonders what would have happened if someone in that class had been recently bereaved, or living with a terminal diagnosis. When she taught a module for a Master's course on "Death and Society," she remembers the course convener telling her that he made it clear to the students that nobody who had been bereaved in the previous twelve months should enroll for the degree, as they would not be able to achieve the right level of academic detachment.

As with sexual topics, or death, many medical themes have the potential to be disturbing. Sometimes it is obvious that a particular topic will present problems, but how should the teacher respond? How many "health warnings" should a teacher give to a class, or a potential class member?

Sometimes the issue lies with the members of the group. As Lisa Trentin also discusses in her paper, if the course outline includes a session on "Disability," should the session be taught if any members of the class have an obvious disability themselves? What are the risks of discussing the humor of disability in ancient cultures with a clearly disabled person in the room? While pregnancy is not a disability, in practice it is often treated as such in our society. So what if the teacher for a session on pregnancy is herself clearly pregnant, as Totelin was when, as a junior academic, she took over King's classes during a period of research leave? And not all disabilities are visible. Baker comments that she is at an "advantage" here, being completely deaf in her right ear as she was born without one (microtia).[4] She openly tells students about this in discussions and uses herself as an example for ancient jokes; she explains to them that there is no precise translation of the term "disability" and that ancient sources simply describe those who vary from the cultural norm as incomplete or lame, and she notes that sometimes people had nicknames that give us an idea of what their problems might have been, adding that she herself might be called "one-eared."

We need to think about who we are as teachers, and not just in terms of our own bodies. There exists a large amount of material on teaching techniques, ethics, and theories of learning, much of which encourages self-reflection about our teaching, not only to improve our methods of communication, but also to think about the contexts—socio-political, cultural, and religious—in which the teacher and student are interacting.

The act of discussing our teaching, in the conversations we had while writing this chapter, has forced us to think more about ourselves and our educational backgrounds. King is British, trained in ancient history and

---

4. Microtia is a congenital condition, varying in degree, affecting the development of the inner and outer ear. In some cases the inner and outer ear are underdeveloped; whilst in others one or more parts of the ear are completely undeveloped. In the majority of cases, only one ear is affected.

anthropology, with a doctoral thesis on ancient Greek menstruation that means she finds it easy to talk about body fluids. Totelin is Belgian, trained in Classics, ancient history, and the history of science and medicine in both Belgian and British universities. She finds it important to study ancient medical writings alongside texts that are considered more "literary" (comedy, tragedy, epic, etc.). Baker is an American who studied anthropology and archaeology, history and Classics in both American and British universities and tends to incorporate a large amount of visual, artifactual and written evidence in her teaching. The use of different types of remains raises issues about the presentation of materials; some students, for example, might be comfortable to hear about a graphic procedure or part of the body, but might find representations offensive because they are confronted with an actual image rather than one conjured up from their own imagination. But others might find an image more comfortable to deal with than a discussion. Therefore, the teacher must be prepared for different reactions to the various remains.[5]

Our backgrounds no doubt reflect or influence how we teach, as will be demonstrated below, but also there will be ways in which being women, teaching a class of males and females, must affect our teaching. As women teaching mixed groups, we can choose to play up the male-dominated aspect of the evidence, or speculate about how women could have "played the system": we can teach this material to arouse indignation about how women were treated, or we can try to get past this reaction to understand the material in context. Medical history provides a useful source of information to show that there are multi-variant cultural and temporal differences in the ways that men, women and people in different age groups were defined within their culture. As women, we feel that we are able to say things that, if said by a male teacher, would have been seen as inappropriate or offensive, even if the information we give is identical.[6]

We also need to think about those whom we teach. Our student base can affect the knowledge of our students and the background in medicine they might have. Although all of us teach primarily in departments that offer Classics, ancient history and archaeology, we do encounter different types of student. Baker's are a mix of traditional students who have recently completed their A-levels, and mature students with non-standard entry qualifications. They tend to come from London and the south-east of England; most are studying Classics, archaeology and history.

---

5. At Baker's current institution, students have lodged complaints about pornographic visual images being shown in class; it was the images, not the discussion, that they found offensive.

6. See Liveley in this volume.

Traditional students from the south-east tend to come from middle-class (essentially "white-collar") families with university degrees. There is no medical school at her University (Kent), so she deals solely with students in humanities and social sciences. King taught for eight years in what is now Liverpool Hope University, at a time when 30 percent of the students were mature learners from working-class backgrounds; she then taught for fourteen years at Reading, where the typical student was middle-class and from the south-east of England. She currently teaches ancient medicine only to medical students as a "Special Study Unit," although she is also working in a Classical Studies team preparing a Master's level module on the body, and is thus discussing how ancient medicine plays out in the context of a blend of distance learning and face-to-face teaching. Where one may expect it to be difficult to dissuade medical students from jumping into retrospective diagnoses, in fact they are very sensitive to issues of culture. Totelin, the most junior of the three of us, has taught both ancient history/Classics students and natural science/medical students in various British universities. For the last five years, she has been based in Ancient History at Cardiff (Wales), where the students are mostly from Wales and south-west England, and come from varied social backgrounds. She also takes part in the "Student Selected Component" program organized by the School of Biosciences at Cardiff. Like King, she finds medical students are very aware of the importance of cultural and historical studies, and are therefore keen to take part in class discussions on historical issues.

Almost all our students are white. They come from fairly similar backgrounds and are undertaking university studies in secular institutions where they should ideally be open to different perspectives—as Britain is a multi-cultural society—but, individually, they bring with them diverse experiences related to their sexual health, religious views, ethnic and socioeconomic backgrounds that will influence their views. Thus, we have to find a balance that respects individual students' beliefs, while teaching topics that some will find offensive, others not. Of course, the institution and culture in which one teaches may also determine whether a topic can be taught at all. This point has been raised by Jarvis (2005), who queries when it would be respectful to discuss a topic in a particular cultural context. The subject of abortion, for example, might be more openly received as a topic of study in a secular university as opposed to one that is run by a particular religious group. In 1988, the year in which Section 28 of the Local Government Act—making it an offense to "promote" homosexuality in schools and colleges—was passed, King was teaching in an institution formed from a Church of England college and two Roman Catholic colleges.⁷ In this environment, it was particularly difficult to talk about homosexuality or abortion in class. In theory, if it is made evident to the students that the views expressed in the ancient literature come from a very different society, period and belief system than that within which they now live, it should still be possible to have an open discussion, but "discussion" can be seen by some students as promoting something they deem to be at complete odds with their beliefs.

As for specific individual students, while in most cases there is no way that the teacher can know those medical experiences of the students that are not written on their bodies, it is possible that, in another role (such as personal or pastoral tutor), the teacher is aware of medical or life experiences that may make a particular topic problematic for the student. Such personal issues can also emerge when teaching is one-to-one, such as when supervising a dissertation or a piece of independent study on the topic. In theory, independent study should mean that a student can choose to avoid upsetting topics and focus on something with which he or she is comfortable, but reading around the subject can still produce problems, and avoidance of anything uncomfortable is not a good model of pedagogy. Also, at this level the topic is selected by the student, so the supervisor may find him/herself uncomfortable with it. Working on the topic may even be cathartic for the student, but he or she may still come upon material that is found upsetting, and the discussions of this can be uncomfortable for both parties.

Where a connection between student and topic which may make the student uncomfortable is known to the teacher already, it may be appropriate to talk to the student ahead of the class and discuss with him or her the material to be covered, giving the student the chance to absent him- or herself from a session. But sometimes a more global warning is needed. In particular, even in an age of horror movies, easy access to pornography, and graphic news reporting, any topic involving violence and/or blood needs to be treated with sensitivity. Students with no particular medical problems themselves may find some of the topics inherently upsetting.⁸ They should be given permission to miss classes if, for example, they know they have a bad reaction to the sight of blood, when visual material is being used in class. A good strategy is to warn students a week in advance and give extra reading for those who prefer not to be present for a particular session; even giving them permission to leave quietly during the class if they feel they

---

7. Section 28 was repealed in 2003.
8. See further Liveley in this volume.

are unable to take part can be very helpful. When teaching early modern medicine for the first time using video reconstructions of William Harvey's experiments to demonstrate the circulation of the blood, King found that one student had to leave the room when a live rabbit was the object of a reconstructed experiment. In subsequent presentations of this class she made sure that she shared her own problems with the sight of blood with the students during the preceding session, telling them that the material they would see in the following week had been very difficult for her, too, on first viewing. This made the point that the material was indeed disturbing and allowed students to think about whether or not they wanted to be present; however, it also meant that some students felt they had to be there out of bravado. Baker told one of her stronger students that she was writing the present paper, and asked what she thought about being taught these subjects; the student said she liked them, and had learned a lot about ancient attitudes towards abortion and childbirth, but added that she had also liked seeing the reactions of her classmates, especially many of the males, who were in her words "immature" and "squeamish."

Visual aids are potentially very problematic in a situation in which we are walking a tightrope between the squeamish and those who have chosen to study ancient medicine precisely for the gore. In 1961, a book written about teaching Classics to students in British schools asserted that "visual aids are only aids. They arouse interest and help pupils to imagine how the ancients lived and what they did. They are no substitute for teaching though very pleasant help. Each teacher has to abjure the temptation to lean heavily on them and must decide for *himself* just what part they are to play in *his* teaching. . . . They [visual aids] must be servants, not masters" (from Incorporated Association of Assistant Masters in Secondary Schools, *The Teaching of Classics* 1961: 192; our italics).[9] Baker considers that a reluctance to use such aids is still found in many university classes on Classics; however, having a background in archaeology, she is used to dealing with visual material and feels very comfortable teaching with it. Images can indeed "arouse interest" and help students to concentrate in class, but she notes that such images should play a far more integral role in the lecture. The teacher needs to think carefully about what she intends to illustrate and consider precisely how the illustration can be best used to provoke discussion. In general, in most archaeological classes images are used to show the site and material remains in a manner that makes it possible

---

9. It is not clear to us how to read the "himself" here, since teaching has in modern times been a feminine role.

for the student to visualize the site, but rarely, with the possible exception of issues of cultural heritage, will images of sites, material and even skeletal remains be as disturbing to students as medical images may be.[10]

Depending on the period being studied in medical history classes, modern clinical imagery will most likely not be needed. Students of medicine will be familiar with graphic photographs in their classes, and with the ethical issues that apply to showing modern images of patients; informed consent must be granted by the patient being photographed, and physicians showing these in medical classes will be using the images for clinical purposes (e.g., Creighton et al. 2002). When teaching such students, King uses John Harley Warner's late nineteenth-/early twentieth-century photographs of students posed around the cadaver they are in the process of dissecting (2009). She would be reluctant to use these with humanities students. But ancient images, too, risk disturbing some students. Hence, Baker always warns students before she shows them that certain images might be upsetting. She explains at the beginning of class that images are being shown, although the procedure is also discussed, so that students are given the material even if they feel uncomfortable with seeing the materials associated with a procedure. In general this is done for three procedures: circumcision (figure 4.1), cataract couching, and, in the case of difficult birth, an image of a hook (figure 4.3). Thus, in consideration of the students' feelings she warns them to look away, though she will still describe the procedure; this in practice tends to have the effect of making them look. She is always careful to show scenes that are not very graphic, and safely distanced by being "historical." For example, when discussing male circumcision she will use an image from an Egyptian painting (figure 4.1). She will use the image to talk about the physical position of the physician and the patient, and perhaps the tools used by the physician, as well as discussing whether the image is accurate. However, when she co-taught with a history lecturer on the History of Medicine class, he brought in some very graphic photographs of women giving birth and she realized that some of the female first-year undergraduate students were uncomfortable with this. He gave them no warning about the images, and Baker felt that, for a class on eighteenth-century man-midwifery, it was extraneous and in poor taste to use images of childbirth from a later period. Nor were the images being used to illustrate a particular procedure, or birthing itself, in the period in question. Although Baker uses the imagery of circumcision from Egypt, it is the only image she has found directly related to the subject that is com-

---

10. See Smith and Sulosky Weaver in this volume.

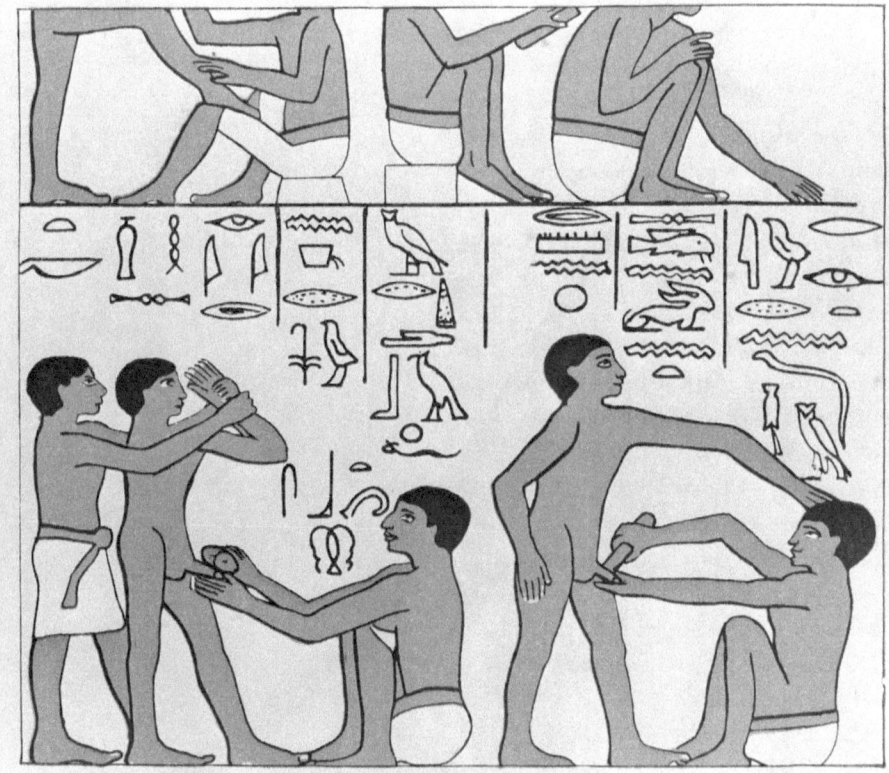

FIGURE 4.1 Egyptian image depicting circumcision

parable, in terms of physician and patient positions, to the very few extant images of surgical procedures found in Greek and Roman remains.

Medical instruments are found disturbing by very many students. King observed real and replica instruments being used to illustrate a lecture for students in the age range 12–18 as part of an enhancement day on 'Roman Medicine', and noted that the only student who fainted during the day did so during a reconstruction of using instruments. Baker brings in real examples to her classes, as well as showing pictures on PowerPoint presentations (figures 4.2 and 4.3). While it is one thing to describe what the texts say, she notes that it is quite another to show the students the actual instruments; this enables them to imagine how a tool might have been held—something

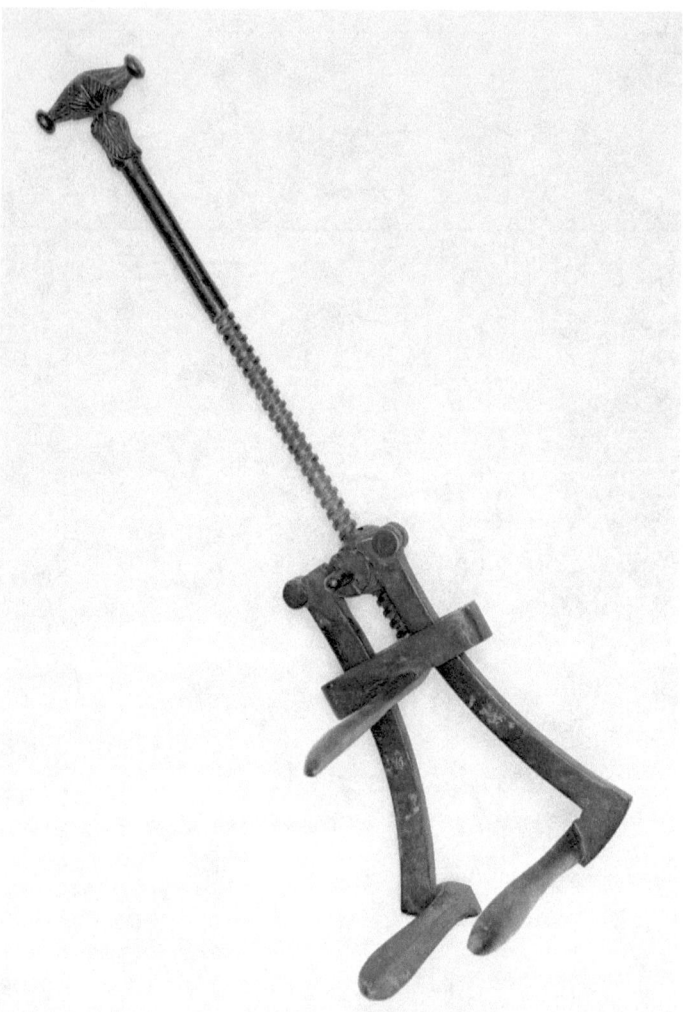

FIGURE 4.2 Roman vaginal specula

we do not in fact know in many cases—to talk about their many functions and to compare them with what is written about them. We actually have very few detailed written descriptions of these tools, so she will ask the students if they are certain that the objects shown are indeed medical tools; this leads to interesting discussions about tools used in treatments even today. King's students were amazed at the similarity between ancient and modern instruments, such as the vaginal speculum (figures 4.2 and 4.4), but King

OBSTETRIC FORCEPS

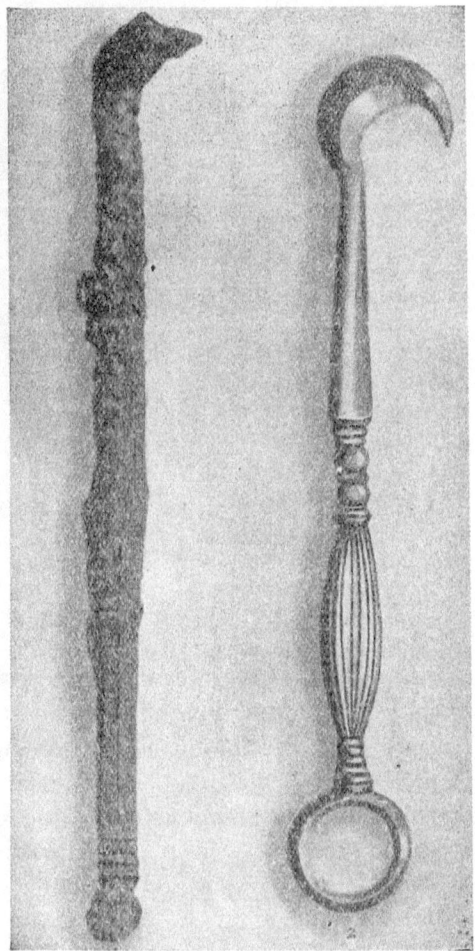

FIGURE 4.3 Roman fetal hook with reconstructed drawing

introduced this instrument as part of a more general discussion of seeing the inside of the body rather than dwelling on the speculum.

For some students, it is precisely their own medical problems and experiences that make them interested in a module on ancient medicine. They come to class as "expert patients," with family members who are health care professionals, or with experience of the illnesses of family or friends. With any condition discussed in class, there is, therefore, a strong possibility that

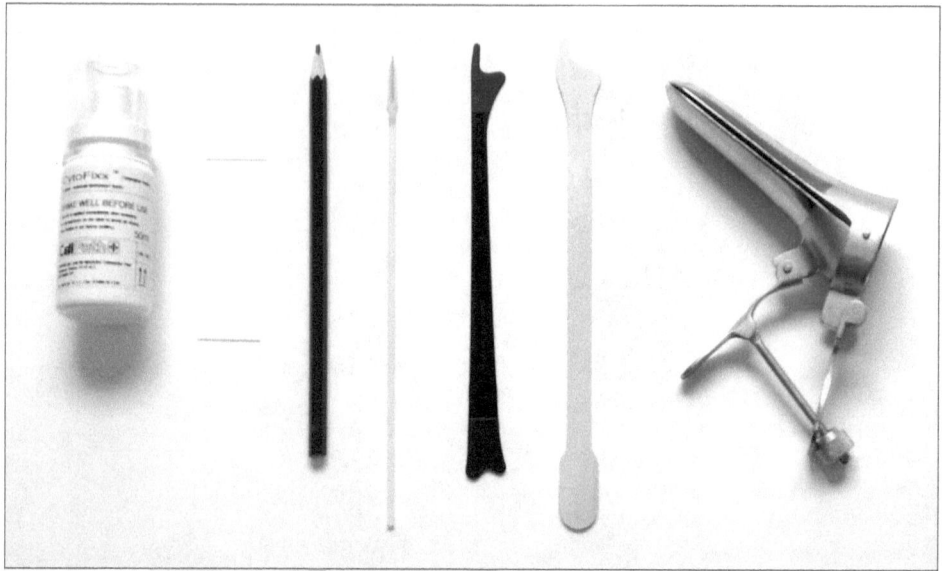

FIGURE 4.4 Equipment used for a gynecological examination. Modern speculum on the right.

someone in the room will have experiences that they may want to share; indeed, preventing students from hijacking the class and making it into a personal confession session can be very difficult. For example, a very talkative student wanted to share with the group her own experience of malaria on holiday in the previous year, but from the front of the room King could see that some students regarded this as irrelevant, while others were keen to hear much more. It was important to allow the student to feel "heard" while also using the role of teacher to feed into the session as a whole the experiences she was describing. When teaching medical students, Totelin found that they wanted to use the Hippocratic Oath as a springboard for discussing their own concerns with modern ethics; while she felt this was appropriate, she was aware that some students wanted to stick to the history.

On occasion, entirely unexpected experiences may be raised by students. For example, when King was teaching on Roman medicine and discussing the use of cabbage as a therapy, she was surprised when a student who was herself a mother intervened to say that cabbage leaves applied to the breasts were indeed a good way of easing pain. This introduced the student's own breasts to the class in a way that could have been embarrassing for her, but in fact the rest of the class focused on the question of the reasons why this remedy could work, and it was possible to move the discussion into a more general one on levels of efficacy. On another occasion, another mature student told the class about her own experience of her baby presenting arm-first; this horrified the younger students, but was valuable in that it made them realize that such things still happen. One of Totelin's mature students, the father of three children, gave a presentation to the class in which he compared ancient birth scenes with today's crowded birthing rooms.

In other cases, students whose own health concerns do not seem to be reflected in the ancient material may be disappointed with this perceived gap; Totelin has found dyslexia/dyspraxia and attention deficit hyperactivity disorder areas relevant here (see also Lisa Trentin's chapter), while King has had students with eating disorders, depressive illness and irritable bowel syndrome looking to find their condition in the past. The mismatch between past and present can be a very valuable way of thinking about not just medicine, but also disease, as culturally determined. Baker mentions to her students the deaf society on Martha's Vineyard, Massachusetts to explain that, in this nineteenth-century community, deafness was the norm, and they had a strong system of communication; so much so, that those who were able to hear were almost excluded (Groce 1988).

Within a course on ancient medicine, it is the topic of abortion that can be the most challenging of all for both the teacher and the students. Bearing in mind the current taboo on discussing death, this topic touches upon both the beginnings of life and its end, and thus has enormous potential to upset and to shock, not least because of the sometimes gruesome nature of the materials. In addition, it can engage very strongly with students' religious and political beliefs. Baker had a female student who told the rest of the class that abortion was a sin; Baker had to insist that other students may have different beliefs about when life begins, and flagged up the importance of respect for other people's opinions. However, there is a value in teaching the topic through a historical perspective because this can allow a student to engage with the issues surrounding abortion as a remote observer. The amount of temporal distance gives students the opportunity to discuss ethical points, and to reflect on their experiences, without feeling that their personal beliefs are directly threatened.

As university teachers, the three of us have taught ancient abortion to audiences of both Classical and medical students. We have found that the apparent disagreement between sources, and scholarly attempts to explain this away, allow students to engage with the debates; these issues are not specific to the topic, but the topic offers an accessible way of dealing with them. We have taught it in different ways: as a two-hour seminar taking its starting-point from the Hippocratic Oath, within a lecture on women and ancient medicine, as part of a lecture on ethics, or at the level of one-to-one supervisions for an extended essay. In this chapter, we will not be presenting a "right" way to proceed, but we hope that our different experiences will help those who have not taught the topic before, or who have found it in some way difficult. While Baker and King do not devote a whole session to "abortion," preferring to move to the topic organically from a related topic, Totelin has taught a full session devoted to the "abortion clause" in the Hippocratic Oath.

We have all found that the Hippocratic Oath is a good way to start a discussion on abortion in ancient societies. Baker always begins by bringing in two different modern translations of the Hippocratic Oath along with copy of the original Greek.[11] One translation reads, "I will not give an abortion" (Lloyd 1978: 67); the other, closer to the Greek, states, "I will not give a pessary for an abortion" (Jones 1957: 298–99). Baker then translates the Greek for the students, which demonstrates to them very clearly how helpful it is to know the original language, and allows them to think about what the Greek might actually mean. She goes on from the Oath to address the question of when, for ancient writers, "life" begins. The seminar also considers works of Aristotle, the Hippocratic writer of *On the Nature of the Child* and Soranus' *Gynecology*. While it is inevitable that students do begin discussing these issues from their own perceptions, the use of other medical texts with different views introduces a range of positions with which students can identify.

While discussing the issue of when life was thought to begin, it is worth noting that an encounter with the ancient texts is potentially a liberating experience for those who have had an abortion, as it allows them to consider different answers to the question of whether they have destroyed a "life." As it was believed in antiquity that female fetuses took longer to develop and become active than male fetuses, this provides a way of thinking about "life" in connection with gender. The question of when a "late period" becomes an "early abortion" is one that students find engaging; they are often unaware of how common early miscarriage is, even today.

Like Baker, King teaches abortion within a session on the Hippocratic Oath as the foundational—and contested—document of the western medical tradition. Rather than moving on to the issue of when life begins, she works to challenge modernizing readings not only of the "abortion clause"

---

11. Various translations of the Oath can be found on "Medical Oaths," http://www.med.umn.edu/phrh/oaths/home.html (accessed 8 February 2014).

but also of the "euthanasia clause"; this defuses the issue of abortion by placing the discussion within the context of translating between cultures more generally. Her aim is to show that both clauses share a concern with the control of dangerous drugs and the risks of these being in the hands of lay people who may use them in ways that the physician does not think are appropriate. She then returns to abortion in a later class on ancient pharmacology, where she raises the question of whether the recipes of the Hippocratic corpus represent "men's knowledge" or "women's knowledge." Both Totelin and King discuss the effect these remedies would have had on women's bodies (causing bleeding and/or causing the uterus to contract), and note that ancient remedies purporting to increase fertility often contain the same ingredients as abortive compositions. Students are always surprised at the contents of the Oath—King has sometimes started her class with a brainstorming session asking the students to come up with what they expect to find in this document, in order later to underline that the parts we hear about in modern life are not those dealing with caring for one's teacher! After teaching within an introductory module on the History of Medicine for the History Department, Baker now has copies of modern versions of medical Oaths available for perusal if they are needed; King did not use these in her "Greek and Roman Medicine" module, but included them when teaching reception in a different module on "Hippocratic Medicine," where students were asked to think about changes in medical Oaths over time.

Totelin has taught the topic of abortion to two very different audiences. For ancient historians, she covered it in a lecture focused on the topic of women and ancient medicine, where she stressed how problematic it is to assume that ancient gynecological texts reflect women's knowledge. As part of a module for medical students on the Hippocratic Oath, she devoted an entire session to abortion, doing exercises very similar to those used by Baker and King, in terms of comparing it with other medical Oaths. She discussed the reception of the abortion clause in antiquity, looking in particular at the places it is mentioned in Scribonius Largus (a first-century pharmacological writer, who considers the prohibition of abortion to be a sign of humanity) and Soranus (a medical writer active around 100 CE, who provides evidence for an ancient debate between those who opposed abortion and those who prescribed it with discrimination).[12] She also looked at some—rare—ancient anti-abortion laws, where men's rights to an unborn heir come to the fore. This provided a useful contrast

---

12. Scribonius Largus, *Compositiones*, prologue; Soranus, *Gynecology* 2.19.

to modern abortion laws which center on women's rights. This led on to a discussion of the use of history as part of the *Roe v. Wade* case in 1973, where Ludwig Edelstein's interpretation of the Oath (whereby the Oath represents the view of a marginal Pythagorean group) was used to discredit its moral hold on American medical ethics (Edelstein 1943).[13]

Alice Knight, one of Totelin's medical students, decided to produce a piece of creative writing for her final assessment. She reflected on what she would feel as a GP faced with a case where a young mother of three children came to ask to abort her twenty-week fetus:

> " . . . How do I know whether I've made the right decision? Of course it was a tough decision to make, and surely I have to respect my patient's decision. But is it fair? There were no deformities, or congenital conditions detected so far. As far as I was concerned she was carrying a perfectly healthy fetus. . . . I was the second medical practitioner to sign the form to allow her a termination of pregnancy. What would Hippocrates the "Father of Medicine" have to say about that? The original Hippocratic Oath emphasizes "do no harm" and yet I have just put pen to paper and signed to allow the abortion of a healthy twenty-week old fetus. Do no harm to whom? To the unborn child? To the mother who's already struggling to manage? Or to her other children? . . . And yes, maybe I have gone against Hippocrates. I have authorized an abortion (although that being said, not by a pessary), but what we have to understand is that things change with time. Yes, in this instance I feel this was the right decision to make."[14]

Interestingly, in addition to mentioning the abortion clause of the Hippocratic Oath, Alice focuses on the "do no harm" clause; this is not in fact from the Oath but from *Epidemics* 1.11, "As to diseases, make a habit of two things—to help, or at least to do no harm," although the Oath echoes this in stating "from [what is] to their harm or injustice I will keep [them]."[15] She knows, as do all her peers, that fetuses can now survive after twenty-four weeks of gestation.

The composition of the student group also affects the reactions to some key stories in the ancient history of abortion. Medical students will laugh at

---

13. US Supreme Court. "Roe v. Wade – 410 U.S. 113" (1973). Justia. http://supreme.justia.com/us/410/113/case.html (accessed February 4, 2014)

14. Laurence Totelin wishes to thank Alice Knight, as well as the School of Biosciences, Cardiff University, for allowing her to reproduce parts of this essay.

15. From Heinrich von Staden's translation of the Oath (1996), which is available here: von Staden, H. "The Asclepion"; "Hippocratic Oath." www.indiana.edu/~ancmed/oath.htm. (accessed February 4, 2014)

the story in *On Generation/Nature of the Child* of the flute-girl who aborted a six-day-old "seed."[16] The girl was told to jump up and down to cause an abortion. When she does this, an egg-like mass falls from her body which, after six days, shows the formation of the umbilicus. Most ancient history students, with very little knowledge of the processes of conception and implantation, will not see the joke. Ancient historians will probably be more shocked by the medical descriptions of abortion and childbirth, as most do not know that today anything that relates to birth is still rather "messy," and involves blood, sweat and tears. Both ancient history and medical students tend to be disgusted by the "barbaric" methods used for abortion in the ancient world. Yet, when one of Totelin's dissertation students looked on the web for evidence relating to ancient gynecological remedies, he was surprised to find sites recommending the same "natural" remedies as those listed in the Hippocratic texts.

King also uses the Oath when teaching medical students, in her case as a Year Four Special Study Unit where her theme is the history of dissection. She begins the module with a discussion of the Oath; students comment that, while the Oath is always mentioned in passing within their medical training, they much appreciate the opportunity to analyze it in detail, clause by clause. King's purpose here is to emphasize to the students the differences, rather than the similarities, between the ancient and modern worlds; these students rarely have much historical background, and are otherwise likely to elide the two in inappropriate ways. She does not invite ethical reflection on the rights and wrongs of abortion, but uses it as a way of thinking about respect for the body, relevant to the question of human dissection, its value and possible objections to it.

Embryotomy—which in some cases can be seen as a very late abortion—is a particularly sensitive example of a potentially upsetting topic. Baker and King have both included this in their syllabi, King as part of a session on surgical interventions, showing that the Oath's prohibition on cutting does not extend to the rest of the Hippocratic corpus. King highlighted the verb *temnein,* to cut, and so also discussed in this session anal fistula and hemorrhoids, meaning that the material was not entirely gendered as female. Baker warns the students that they might like to leave the room; this invitation is needed for male students as well as females. It was upsetting for a student whose girlfriend had recently had a miscarriage. Totelin has never taught the topic, and feels incapable of doing so; she finds the graphic descriptions in texts so upsetting that she fears she would respond to them in class by tears or inappropriate laughter. But her students have

---

16. *On the Nature of the Child* 13 (Lonie 1981: 7, 159).

still found this material when reading for independent study; her (male) students were shocked when they came across descriptions of embryotomy whilst reading for dissertations on the topics of midwifery or surgery.

Abortion raises the wider question of how far the teacher can expect students who have personal experience of what is being discussed to speak out. This depends not just on the size and the atmosphere of the class, and the personality of the teacher, but also on the personality of the students. Even if it is probable that some students in the class might have had an abortion, they rarely speak out, as there is still a sense of shame attached to this decision. Pregnant students, however, may be vocal; they too have had to make difficult decisions. One of Totelin's students argued that the United Kingdom law (two medical practitioners to sign the request) was not really respected, and that she had been asked by her physician at twenty weeks of pregnancy whether she wanted to abort her baby. This had angered her—it also shocked Totelin. One has to find ways to re-center the discussion after this type of intervention. Totelin wishes she had acted in the following way (she did not): she could have spoken about the reasons for having an abortion in the ancient world and whether they differ from those in the modern world. She could also have discussed the different expectations put on different "types" of women in the ancient world. Thus, while the young flute-girl in the Hippocratic story had to abort to keep her value, ancient "respectable" women were expected to carry children.

Finally, how do we assess work in a course on ancient medicine? We have found that the topic lends itself to innovative teaching and assessment methods which can themselves be inclusive, in that they allow students whose strengths lie outside the traditional essay format to shine. Baker's student presentations have included a group acting out a Game Show with Galen, as the host, making himself more knowledgeable than the contestants. When King first taught "Greek and Roman Medicine," she asked all students to prepare group presentations to be performed at the start of each weekly two-hour session. Some were highly original; for example, the "Roman medicine" presentation which was organized as a consulting room with "patients" coming in to explain their symptoms to the "physician" who invariably ended each appointment with a recommendation to use cabbage. Others raised interesting questions that could be discussed in class afterwards, such as the one on "Did Alexandrian medicine use human dissection?" which included animal organs acquired from the local butcher being produced, apparently from within the student playing the part of the person being dissected. In addition to helping students think about the extent to which animal bodies were seen as adequate guides to the human body, the presence of an assistant dressed anachronistically in a modern nurse's uniform initiated a discussion on assistants in ancient medicine. Another group acted out a birthing scene on the table at the front of the lecture theatre; King was slightly concerned in case an administrator chose that moment to come in, as this was the week in which the university checked that classes were taking place in the right size of room. However, on those occasions where the students were not well prepared or had drawn on unreliable sources found online, the amount of time spent after the presentation in tactfully correcting errors eventually made King abandon this method of engaging the students. She did this with reluctance, as these presentations clearly engaged the students and led to useful discussions. Totelin has set her medical students the task of producing their own version of the Hippocratic Oath; several included an "abortion clause" on the lines of "I will respect the woman's right to choose and maintain the integrity of her own body," and one particularly original response was to produce a musical version in which the student expressed the joy, anguish and huge sense of responsibility involved in being a physician. One of Totelin's ancient history students wrote a medically-themed play in the style of Plautus for an independent study; it involved a dishonest Greek doctor tricking a Roman *paterfamilias* out of his money with complex but useless therapies.

As teachers of ancient medicine, we hope that our experiences will be helpful not only to those who offer modules on this topic, but to others teaching potentially difficult subjects. We would recommend ancient medicine as a means of engaging students, challenging their assumptions, and showing them that many of the same concerns we deal with today were present in the past. Within such a course, abortion—and related areas concerning birth and the female body—is often the most difficult subject to teach but, as we have shown here, the issues it raises are frequently more extreme versions of teaching challenges we find throughout such a course. Emotional intelligence should enable the teacher to create a safe space within which individual students, bringing to their studies a range of past experiences, can allow material from the past to help them think about their own lives.

The "Whole-University Approach" to the Pedagogy of Domestic Violence

SUSAN DEACY AND
FIONA MCHARDY

THIS CHAPTER addresses issues relating to teaching domestic violence in ancient Greece in the HE classroom. Our decision to develop and teach material on this subject related primarily to the direction of our own research in 2009 when we created our MA module "Gender and Crime in Ancient Greece" which includes sessions on violence against women. This choice of teaching and research material was particularly timely, coinciding as it did with research undertaken in schools on partner exploitation and violence in teenage intimate relationships by Christine Barter et al. for the National Society for the Protection of Children (2009), and the drafting of a call to end violence against women and girls[1] by the U.K. government (2010). At the same time, there has been an increasing interest in this area of pedagogy, not only among classicists, but also among colleagues from other disciplines, including at our own institution.[2] This chapter draws on our own experiences of teaching domestic violence in ancient Greece, current political initiatives, nationwide research into the everyday experiences of young people and pedagogical advances to make a case for

---

1. Defined as "any act of gender-based violence that results in or is likely to result in, physical, sexual or psychological harm or suffering to women, including threats of such acts, coercion, or arbitrary deprivations of liberty, whether occurring in public or private life" following the United Nations Declaration on the elimination of violence against women (1993).

2. See James (2008); Koster (2011) and the introduction to this volume.

a "whole-university approach" to domestic violence. This approach which is currently being advocated within U.K. schools involves commitment by all members of the community (staff and students, male and female, etc.) to ending all forms of violence and abuse.³

The research discussed in this chapter is part of a project titled "Teaching Sensitive Subjects in the Classics Classroom" for which we received funding from the Higher Education Academy in 2011.⁴ The idea to undertake a pedagogical project on this subject came about following the roundtable discussion on teaching rape organized by ourselves together with Nancy Sorkin Rabinowitz in April 2009 at the Classical Association conference in Glasgow.⁵ Our focus in the "Teaching Sensitive Subjects" project was not on controversial subjects (i.e., ones which make students debate passionately), but on troubling subjects such as domestic violence, abortion and sexual abuse (i.e., ones which might affect individuals in the class to such an extent that they might struggle to join in discussions, experience distress, or feel the need to miss the session in question). The main aim of our project was to gain expertise on teaching sensitive topics both from fellow classicists and from colleagues in other disciplines.⁶ We also built up resources that cite relevant literature, and websites offering support on various issues including rape, and domestic abuse for our University's VLE site. While the focus was primarily on ways in which staff can handle teaching this material and deal with possible problems experienced by students, the project also looked at the impact of teaching the topic on academic staff, and at options for staff training. As Shirley Koster (2011) has demonstrated, staff who teach about gender tend to become involved in the "emotional labor" of dealing with student responses to the teaching material, especially coping with what she terms "traumatic disclosures" such as experiencing domestic violence (2011: 64). Therefore, we also reflect on ways in which staff as well as students can cope with the challenges of studying domestic violence in ancient Greece.

---

3. Ava Project and Home Office (2010: 8).
4. The project was funded by the HEA Subject Centre for History, Classics and Archaeology under the Teaching Development Grant Scheme. The scope of the project was larger than the scope of this paper. We would like to thank all the anonymous participants in the project who have made this paper possible.
5. See introduction for the similarly-themed events which preceded the Glasgow roundtable in the United States following the publication of Sharon James's 2008 paper.
6. Since Jan 2012, we have been interviewing selected U.K. academics. Data derived from these interviews are used in this paper.

TEACHING DOMESTIC VIOLENCE IN ANCIENT GREECE

The decision to teach domestic violence in ancient Greece came about through our plans to write a book dealing with issues of gendered violence.[7] By working together we could more fully develop our existing areas of expertise[8] and the study of domestic violence offered much potential. Few scholars had dedicated studies to the topic and much of the material available was for late antiquity.[9] David Schaps had published an article arguing for the prevalence of domestic violence in antiquity based on his reading of Zeus in the *Iliad* in 2006; Sarah Pomeroy had approached the issue from a feminist perspective in her book *The Murder of Regilla* in 2007; and Lloyd Llewellyn-Jones had presented a version of his now-published paper discussing the extent of wife beating at Athens at a conference in Cardiff in May 2009.[10] Our aim was to take their work further by considering the applicability of various modern theoretical approaches—including feminist theory, criminological studies, psychology and evolutionary psychology—to case studies taken from Greek myth and literature.

Our term-long module, Gender and Crime in Ancient Greece, devised jointly by ourselves in 2009, and designed with similar goals in mind to our research project, was first taught in autumn 2009 by Susan Deacy, and subsequently in autumn 2011 by us both. As part of an MA in Historical Research, the module forms a compulsory element for students on the Classical History Pathway, and an optional element for students on the General History Pathway. The 2009 contingent was composed of both "classical" and "general" students, and of both men and women. There was again a mixture of male and female students in the 2011 class, but it was this time composed exclusively of classicists. Both classes included students from diverse cultural, social and ethnic backgrounds as is typical at Roehampton. The syllabus includes examination of uxorcide, domestic violence, infanticide, "honor" killings, and rape through consideration of ancient sources and modern theoretical materials. To help students grasp some of these new theoretical approaches, we arranged for input from colleagues in other disciplines. In 2009, a session was led by a specialist in Victorian gender and crime who discussed how she adopts a multi-methodological approach to the study of infanticide. Another guest lecturer was a criminologist who discussed so-called "honor" crime in the United Kingdom. After each of these sessions,

---

7. Deacy and McHardy (forthcoming).
8. Deacy (1997); (2013); McHardy (2005); (2008a); (2008b).
9. See, e.g., Clark (1998); Parca (2002); Dossey (2008).
10. Schaps (2006); Pomeroy (2007); Llewellyn-Jones (2011).

the students discussed the applicability of these approaches to their studies of the ancient Greek evidence. Encouraging the students to reflect upon new theoretical methods of treating ancient evidence is a significant part of their development as Master's students and central to the Historical Research MA as it is designed. However, at the same time, this mode of study opens up the contemporary connections between ancient Greece and current issues in a way which can be both inspiring and challenging.[11] These differing responses are made clear in statements made in student end-of-tem evaluations from 2009. The responses indicated that students had valued the comparative approach. Comments included: "I have really enjoyed this module, particularly its focus both on modern debates and ancient Greek history"; "I loved the two external speakers and the way their topics interlinked with the module"; "Looking at the contemporary theories on crime and also the research seminar on nineteenth-century England has given me a different perspective on ancient Greece and has led me to consider the applicability of universalist approaches." At the same time, it was clear that students had been inspired by the teaching method to take a comparative approach in their essays.[12] For example, one student applied psychological research into mother–son violence to Greek mythology, specially focusing upon the Clytemnestra–Orestes relationship. Another student compared gender violence in ancient Greece with evidence from modern Nigerian culture. On the other hand, the challenge faced by some students in studying this material was spelled out in one evaluation. One student said that their "least favorite topic" was honor crime: "it was very interesting, but very upsetting." The method employed appeared to have brought the students on this module closer to the subject matter, and they had become more deeply affected by the material under discussion than we had anticipated. The creation of a document containing advice, contact details of support staff on campus and links to supportive organizations which are now posted on the module's VLE site was a first step in dealing with the issues raised.

Colleagues interviewed as part of our Teaching Sensitive Subjects project have spoken of similar experiences. One colleague has used comparative modern material to break down the distances between the students and the ancient material with great effect. In a session where students would not be expecting a discussion of rape, the lecturer showed the Eurymedon

---

11. See James (in this volume) who suggests a "more global context for rape in antiquity by turning to modern comparative materials."

12. The module is assessed by an essay of 4,000 words. Students choose their own essay topics following discussion with the tutors.

vase. At first the students laughed. But then the laughter died away when the lecturer showed an image of American soldiers laughing over the naked bodies of Iraqi prisoners. Then the lecturer used the images to explore rape as a metaphor for military domination. This technique is designed to shock and to make the students think through what the ancient material means. The pedagogical tactic employed is very different to the ones discussed by James, Thakur and others in this volume where a warning is given that difficult content is about to be shown. In this example the tactic helps students grasp the ancient material in an abrupt but memorable way. But what might the impact of this tactic be on a student who had suffered rape? The worry is that students might be ill prepared—they do not have the option of absenting themselves from the class or of looking away as is suggested by some of the contributors to this volume when dealing with potentially difficult material. As suggested above, the provision of suitable supportive materials can help tutors to challenge their classes academically, while supporting affected students. But tutors must also be properly prepared to tackle problems which arise from the employment of shock tactics in teaching this material. One classicist commented, "when I first started teaching on these subjects (rape, sexual violence, abortion, etc.) I approached these subjects as 'edgy' topics good for galvanizing seminar discussion/debate. My focus was 'academic'/'intellectual'/'political' and my teaching would usually involve some element focusing upon these subjects through the lenses of feminist theory and criticism." But, with deeper experience as a personal tutor this lecturer came to realize that "individual students . . . had first-/second-hand experience of these issues and—while some found talking/reading about these issues liberating / releasing—some found them incredibly difficult (and I found myself talking about these issues more and more outside of the classroom)." We will discuss the issue of how staff should prepare for and be trained for dealing with such students in detail below.[13]

We are also not alone in finding that our students have been particularly affected by material relating to domestic abuse. One interviewee noted that students have been particularly affected when they learn about domestic violence in antiquity: "The most feedback I've received about sensitive subjects has not been about sex at all, but about domestic violence. . . . I warned the class beforehand that some of this can be difficult. I talked through anthropological evidence and I showed some slides (with an added warning beforehand) of Pakistani girls disfigured by beatings or by cutting

---

13. See also Koster (2011: 62).

off noses and ears. Horrid stuff but valuable instructive material; we talk about 'honour' violence and 'honour' killings. Some of the girls in the class later told me that the images had haunted them for weeks after." Another notes, "the ancient world was not necessarily a nice place to be; it could be cruel, bloody, coarse, debased, vulgar, and depraved. Amid the beauty of ancient art, literature, and philosophy, there is also a harsher reality." As the interviewee commented, this "reality" can be disguised by the sugar-coated translations which some classicists have given for ancient terms for sexual abuse: these are "woefully inappropriate . . . and I'm happy to get my students thinking why this might be." These scholars agree that facing the challenges the ancient world presents in class is educationally beneficial, but that care needs to be taken about the mode in which the subjects are addressed.

A further potential issue which became apparent during our teaching of the session dedicated to domestic violence was a lack of awareness among students concerning the nature of domestic violence in either modern or ancient societies. In both renditions of our module, the domestic violence session focused on discussion of pertinent classical sources[14] along with two scholarly papers, one non-classical (Wilson and Daly 1998) and the other classical (Llewellyn-Jones 2011).[15] The article by Wilson and Daly argues that spousal violence can emerge when men seek to assert control over their wives, notably over their reproduction or sexuality. The suggestion is that such violence is universal and ubiquitous, especially in cases where there are questions relating to paternity. Based on evidence of ancient Greek concerns with paternity and control over women, acceptance of the hypotheses of Wilson and Daly suggests that domestic violence would have been prevalent in ancient Greece. The article by Llewellyn-Jones (2011) gives examples of spousal violence in ancient Greek sources and posits that such violence was frequent even though there are not abundant ancient examples. Students were asked to consider each time four possible explanations regarding the lack of evidence for spousal violence in ancient Greece as posited by Llewellyn-Jones: first, that domestic violence did not happen; second, that it happened only infrequently and was regarded as abnormal; third, that it happened but was deemed a private matter; fourth, that domestic violence

---

14. Zeus and Hera in the *Iliad* (1.562–70, 15.16–21); Synodinou (1987); Schaps (2006); Alcibiades' treatment of his wife (Plut. *Alc.* 8.4) and passages where men kill their pregnant partners (e.g., Hdt. 3.31–3, Diogenes Laertius 1.7; Suetonius *Nero* 35; Philost. *VS* 555; Hyg. *Fab.* 202 Coronis; Apollodorus *Bib.* 1.20; Pomeroy (2007).

15. Llewellyn-Jones's paper existed only in conference paper form in 2009.

was so routine that it did not warrant mention in the sources.[16] In each rendition of the class students first felt that domestic violence probably occurred only infrequently because there was a lack of evidence (point 2 on the list), but when they had studied and considered the modern materials and statistics on domestic violence their opinions changed and they decided that violence was probably frequent (point 3 or point 4 on the list).

In the discussion of these points it is necessary to think deeply about what constitutes an act of domestic violence and define what is or is not appropriate. It was apparent from the discussions in class that students held different views on this subject and moreover that they were inclined to deny the frequency of violence in Greece based upon their assumptions. These assumptions are of concern because students appear to lack awareness of the prevalence of violence in intimate partner relationships. That is to say that the students in our classes did not deny that domestic violence occurred in ancient Greece because they see Greece as a distinct and idyllic society, but that they lacked awareness of the prevalence of such violence in any society, including our own. It is possible that the students have all led sheltered lives, but it is important to note that any assumption that they will not have encountered domestic violence either first or second hand because they are university students is inappropriate since domestic violence occurs in all sectors of our society across age, social class, race and religion.[17] Indeed, as discussed below, research in U.K. schools indicates that the prevalence of abusive behavior including sexual and physical violence among young people in intimate partner relationships in the United Kingdom is shockingly high. The research also shows that most of them do not report their experiences as they feel them to be a normal part of life. The implication of these findings is that students may be underestimating the occurrence of acts of violence in society because they do not recognize that controlling behavior is abusive, but they deem it to be a normal part of an intimate partner relationship. The possibility that some students have experienced domestic violence, but have not fully recognized their experiences, means that defining and debating what constitutes domestic violence in one of our classes could bring about a recognition that a student has been affected by abuse, but has normalized it. Such a student might not be aware that the material studied would be difficult for them personally until

---

16. Llewellyn-Jones (2011: 254–55).

17. See Straus (2004) for university data which is in line with data for other sectors of society. Like Koster (2011: 64–66) we have learnt about students' experiences of domestic violence in personal tutorials and through their mitigating circumstances documentation and have also received confidential revelations from staff aware of our research topic.

they were in the class discussing it. As a consequence it might be difficult for a student to decide to miss that class. At the same time it is possible that perpetrators might reach a fuller understanding of the implications of their acts through such in-class discussions.[18] We shall set out below the evidence which supports these views and put forward arguments about how best to deal with the issues raised here.

DOMESTIC VIOLENCE IN THE UNITED KINGDOM: PREVALENCE AND POLICY

While it has long been acknowledged that domestic violence is prevalent throughout the United Kingdom and elsewhere, the actual extent of the abuse is unclear because of underreporting.[19] Disputes over definition also create difficulties. For example, many feminists argue for a broad range of activities, some deemed criminal (battering and murder) and some not (insults, jibes), to be included in a "continuum" of violence,[20] while statistical reports tend to include only criminal violence which has been recorded within the justice system. Statistics based only on officially reported incidents do not give the full picture and fear, embarrassment and denial can prevent reporting even in surveys.[21] Moreover, men may be particularly ashamed to be perceived as victims of violence.[22] Because of this issue, the British Crime Survey carries out a self-completion mode to assess prevalence of domestic violence.[23] The data gathered in this survey suggest that in the United Kingdom, more than one in four women will experience domestic abuse in their lifetime, often alongside years of psychological abuse.[24] In a survey conducted in eight schools in England, Scotland and Wales in 2009 among boys and girls aged between thirteen and seventeen, results indicated that levels of sexual and physical abuse were startlingly high, but that the majority of the young people surveyed had not told anyone about what had happened to them.[25] Many had even thought their

---

18. See Koster (2011: 64) on the guilt felt by some of her male students.
19. See e.g. Wilson and Daly (1998: 199–200).
20. See e.g. Mooney (2000: 94); Edwards (2006: 56).
21. Mooney (2000: 3–4); cf. McWilliams (1998: 132–5); Edwards (2006: 44). See also HM Government (2010: 6–7).
22. Edwards (2006: 45, 50), Barter et al (2009: 47–48).
23. Reported rates of domestic violence in the self-completion mode are five times higher than in face-to-face interviews (Flatley et al. 2010: 58).
24. See HM Government (2010: 5).
25. See also Flatley et al. (2010: 57) which notes the low reporting rate for sexual assaults.

experiences to be a normal part of being in a relationship. In the survey a quarter of girls and 18 percent of boys reported some form of physical partner violence, while one in three girls and 16 percent of boys reported some form of sexual partner violence, although girls were much more likely to report sustained violence.[26] Having a partner who was more than two years older was a significant risk factor for girls, with 75 percent experiencing physical violence and 75 percent sexual violence.[27] This research indicates that it is insufficient to examine police records to gain an accurate picture of the extent of domestic abuse. It also highlights the prevalence of violent behavior in the relationships of young people at an age just before they enter institutions of higher education. Indeed earlier research by Straus indicated that the rates of physical and sexual violence in universities at that time matched the rates reported in U.K. schools in 2009.[28]

Of particular note in the conclusions of the U.K. school survey was the way in which many young people expressed the notion that violence within an intimate partner relationship was normal or acceptable. The problem of normalization is not restricted to adolescents. It is also typical for women in abusive relationships to normalize the violent behavior by saying "nothing really happened."[29] In research conducted among women in London many expressed the view that violence in their relationship was caused by their own "transgressions" and blamed themselves for what had happened.[30] As Merry notes, "whether a person describes herself as abused depends on how she interprets a slap, a blow or an insult."[31] At the same time, the lack of depictions of domestic violence as a criminal activity on TV shows, combined with an emphasis on other forms of crime in the media, might lead someone watching crime on TV to become unable to identify themselves as a criminal.[32] Among teenagers the problem is exacerbated. As researchers working on teenage domestic violence and abuse for the AVA (Against Violence and Abuse) Project suggest, "because of a lack of experience in constructing respectful relationships and because of their peer group norms it can be difficult for teenagers to judge their partner's behavior as being abusive."[33] In some cases, such as the constant monitoring of a partner by

---

26. Barter et al. (2009).
27. Notably this trend is supported by Daly and Wilson's theories regarding the increased risk for the young "wives" of older men (1998: 216).
28. Straus (2004).
29. Kelly and Radford. (1998: 74).
30. Mooney (2000: 187–88).
31. Merry (2009: 22).
32. Mooney (2000: 127).
33. Ava Project and Home Office (2010: 3).

using mobile phones or social networking sites, respondents were unclear on whether this monitoring constituted a control on their lives and curb on their freedom, or the loving concern of their partner.[34] One respondent in the survey suggested that control in a relationship was seen as normal: "Everybody does it [control one's partner], I thought he was weird and then I talked to my friends and all their boyfriends are the same."[35] The young people also tended to view coercion to have sex as a normal feature of teenage life.[36] Although this research focused on school children aged thirteen to seventeen, there is no reason to believe that teenagers moving from school to university would suddenly change their attitudes because they are now eighteen. Indeed the research among adult women cited above indicates that normalization of violence is not isolated to young people. Moreover, the environment at university where many young people are away from home for the first time and can be experiencing relationship problems without familial support makes it all the more pressing that universities take these points into consideration. The evidence of relationship violence including rape on U.S. campuses suggests that the problem could be equally prevalent in the United Kingdom.[37]

Following on from this research, the U.K. government launched a major advertising campaign aimed at young people in which they sought to question and change attitudes towards partner violence.[38] The shift in government policy from focusing on judicial responses after violence has happened to prevention of violence and changing attitudes in society is understandable given the attitudes displayed by the young people who took part in this survey and their inability to recognize and deal with their experiences.[39] The campaign shows typical scenes of teenage interaction such as a young man pressuring his girlfriend into having sex through an escalation from emotional control to violence. It asks the participants to consider "If

---

34. Barter et al. (2009: 114).

35. Ibid. 150.

36. Ibid 185. See also Burman and Cartmen (2005) based on research done among young people in Scotland which has similar findings.

37. See James (2008: 12). The experiences on U.S. campuses and what we can learn from them will be discussed in greater detail below.

38. The teenage relationship abuse campaign originally ran in February and March 2010 and re-ran from September to November 2011. Adverts can be seen and debated on the "This is Abuse" website (http://thisisabuse.direct.gov.uk/).

39. As articulated by Home Secretary Theresa May (HM Government 2010: 3). The "Real Man" campaign run by Women's Aid has similar aims, but targets especially the adult male population. http://www.realmancampaign.com/. Cf. also the "Tackling Violence" campaign from New South Wales which has released an educational DVD called "Change your ways: Australian Men Talk about Domestic Violence" aimed at young players of rugby league (NSW Office of Communities 2012).

you could see yourself, would you stop yourself?" The aim of this ambitious campaign is to alter impressions of what kinds of behavior are acceptable by drawing in both victims and offenders, and also other members of society, to ask whether they would tolerate this form of behavior. On the website, young people have written extensive comments about the commercials, sharing details about their own relationships and condemning the violent behavior demonstrated in the advertisements. The comments indicate the prevalence of the type of scenarios depicted in the advertisements among the young people who have contributed to the forum as well as the negative impact these experiences have had on their self-confidence in the long term. The comments also indicate that many of those involved find it hard to recognize inappropriate behavior or to leave the relationship even when they do. Some writers identify themselves as sixth-form students about to go to university.

As part of the same campaign, teaching materials aimed at children in Key Stages 3, 4 and 5 (age 13–18) were published with the aim of helping young people to recognize and avoid abuse.[40] The focus is on educating both potential victims and potential abusers in an attempt to eradicate abuse by demonstrating that it is unacceptable in all circumstances. This "whole-society approach" permeates the policy document, action plan, advertising and teaching materials with which the government has been involved and is made explicit in the teacher's guide published by the AVA project and the Home Office (2010). The guide suggests that all members of the school community should work together to ensure support is available, to bring about the prevention of violence and to promote equality. Steps regarding support include ensuring that all staff are well informed about the school's child protection procedures and how they relate to teenage relationship abuse, that information about support services be posted in the school and that students have access to counselors there.[41] Steps intended to prevent violence proactively include age and ability appropriate lessons on teenage relationship abuse for all students and training for all school staff promoting awareness of teenage relationship abuse and gender equality. Measures aimed at creating an equal environment include a working group of staff and students to develop, deliver and monitor a strategic approach to promoting respectful relationships and gender equality in the school. The role of this group is to ensure that there is clear leadership and commitment to develop a "whole-school approach" to stop teenage relationship

---

40. Women's Aid and HM Government (2010).
41. Ava Project and Home Office (2010: 7).

abuse. The guide also recognizes that "There may be staff in the school that have experienced or are experiencing relationship abuse themselves. Discussing relationship abuse may therefore raise issues amongst staff so it is vital to provide appropriate support."[42] The steps suggested here include some points which are not pertinent to adult students at university level such as child protection legal issues, but two of the key points regarding provision of support for students and provision of training for staff map well onto our Teaching Sensitive Subjects project goals. The idea of setting up an educational program suitable for university students also has merit.

DOMESTIC VIOLENCE AND THE "WHOLE UNIVERSITY"

As classicists working on an interdisciplinary pedagogical project we discovered that we were facing not just a problem connected with teaching ancient evidence for domestic violence, but a university-wide problem which demands a "whole-university approach." This includes educating and supporting both students and staff. The University provides Student Welfare Officers as well as student counselors. Nevertheless students will often turn first to a personal tutor or to someone who has taught them.[43] Some staff do not consider it their job to spend time on supporting students who make disclosures to them concerning issues in their personal life. However even these colleagues need adequate training in how to refer students in difficulties to a counselor or student welfare officer. We consider that the overlap between personal and academic subject matter demonstrates the need for staff to be trained in providing more "hands on" and sensitive help.[44] As Shirley Koster notes, she chose to get training in counseling.[45] Another colleague of ours undertook training outside the university on dealing with crisis situations following a situation in which a student revealed over a protracted discussion that she could not cope with sitting an exam and was struggling with her studies because she was an alcoholic. A recent in-house training session for lecturing staff in our department was designed to work with a small group of colleagues (maximum 8). Each tutor wrote down a particular situation that they have had to deal with. The topics were drawn out at random for discussion by the group with input from the University Counselor. The Counselor also provided notes for tutors including "dealing

---

42. Ibid. 6.
43. Koster (2011: 62, 64–5)
44. See James (2008: 12).
45. Koster (2011: 75).

with a crisis." Important things for staff to learn that arose from the session included things *not* to say to students (e.g., "my door is always open . . . "), how to set boundaries (e.g., concerning the minimum and maximum time to be spent on pastoral care),[46] and when to refer the student to someone else. In addition staff are not obliged to keep things confidential unless they have stated explicitly that they will. It is therefore important that staff should not promise to keep things secret, not least as this may affect their ability to share the burden of any problematic revelation. It is preferable that this kind of in-house training is made a standard part of staff continuing professional development programs rather than being made available only to those who demand it.

Our institution currently has no educational program for students to offer instruction in either physical or sexual abuse. Instead these issues are dealt with on an individual basis by the student welfare team. In many U.S. colleges programs offering education on rape and domestic violence are available. Foubert's peer education program which has been in existence since 1993 has as its goal ending rape on campuses. This program, initially aimed at men, appealed to men as potential helpers of a friend rather than as potential rapists, and to bystanders, who were encouraged to intervene to stop the attack. The program makes use of a video in which a police officer is attacked and raped, goes through a hospital examination and is subsequently ribbed by his colleagues. This scenario was chosen to try to encourage men to develop deeper empathy by thinking themselves into the situation. There is a focus on how they can help (e.g., by referring for counseling, and avoiding saying negative things) and intervene.[47] The subsequently-developed women's program likewise focuses on how to help a friend. In addition, it looks at how to identify threat, believing that a focus on the warning signs (e.g., excessive alcohol consumption and controlling behavior) are vital. The program also stresses that women need to avoid blaming themselves for rape. They are therefore encouraged not to blame the victim.[48] The dual approach focusing on men and women separately is significant in this program as it sees the need to educate both (potential) victim and (potential) perpetrator. There are also peer education programs on interpersonal violence such as the "One Act" program at the University of North Carolina at Chapel Hill. This training teaches students to recognize the early warning signs of interpersonal violence and take

---

46. Cf. the case made in Koster (2011: 74) for establishing boundaries for our professional practice.
47. Foubert (2011: 3–4).
48. Ibid. 4–6.

preventive action.⁴⁹ At the same university, the student organization Project Dinah runs a week long awareness campaign to increase knowledge about interpersonal violence.⁵⁰ This model, combining a student-led awareness campaign with an educational program, is one which we hope to emulate at our own institution. At the same time we hope to address both victims and perpetrators. Teaming student education on violence with adequate support for those affected and training for staff such as suggested in the "whole-school approach" above would be valuable in creating a joined-up approach to tackling this issue.

Our experiences of the difficulties in teaching this material also lead us to suggest that support and counseling be available to staff as well as to students. At the training session for departmental staff at our institution we discussed what happens when staff are affected by subjects raised by students. The University Counselor made the suggestion that one solution could be a tutor "buddy system" where tutees can be referred to another tutor if the problem affects a particular staff member too closely such as when a member of staff has suffered a bereavement. Our University's counseling system is also available for individual members of staff. Sharing our experiences with colleagues is also valuable. We have so far done so at a national symposium in Bristol (May 2012) and two national conferences in Reading (April 2013) and London (September 2013). The interest generated among colleagues about these events indicates a need for these topics to be discussed more extensively. The creation of regular sessions where staff can share experiences in an informal way is a positive and useful way of talking through issues connected to teaching sensitive subjects.

CONCLUSIONS

While it is good practice for classicists to be prepared and to be trained to support students on an individual basis, universities as whole units should grapple with the issues surrounding domestic violence through student and staff training in the "whole-university approach." The kind of material now available to schools needs to be extended to HE to raise awareness among students and staff alike as to the prevalence of domestic violence and partner abuse, and to support vulnerable students once they have made the transition from school to university. Support needs to be provided for "mature"

---

49. http://campushealth.unc.edu/oneact
50. http://projectdinah.webs.com/

students and for lecturers who may, themselves, have experienced domestic violence. Strategies also need to be put in place to support those students who have been, or continue to be, perpetrators. As "front-line" professionals, lecturers need support to be able to support students effectively, concerning strategies for teaching aspects of the subject in class, in how to deal with disclosures from troubled students, and in how to deal with the challenges of emotional labor.

Teaching Uncomfortable Subjects
When Religious Beliefs Get in the Way

Polyxeni Strolonga

Teaching Classics entails exploring subjects that may generate distress among students.[1] This volume focuses on a range of such subjects that have been identified as sensitive for discussion, from rape and race to homosexuality and death, since ancient norms and attitudes on issues of sexuality, religion and tolerance differ markedly from our own. Evidently, what troubles students is not only the nature of the topics, but also the personal, sometimes biased perspectives that students bring into the discussion. How receptive the students are to new and controversial ideas depends to a great extent on their personal experiences and the education they are receiving, both formal and informal. Regardless of their background, it is my belief that education should challenge students in a productive way and invite them to engage with ideas that may be provocative and foreign to their own values and beliefs. My experience teaching at a private university that is owned by a specific denomination has given me some insight into how to teach students to think critically about social issues that may be controversial, while at the same time maintaining the necessary respect for their moral principles and religious beliefs. In this chapter I discuss how students

---

[1]. I would like to thank Ariana Traill, Shawn O'Bryhim, Zach Biles, Athanassios Vergados, Angeliki Tzanetou and Judith Chien for their thoughtful feedback. Also, I am thankful to the anonymous reviewers and the editors of this volume for their constructive criticism. Finally, I am grateful to my students, whose thought-provoking responses to our readings challenged some of my own ideas and beliefs about the ancient world and my students' lives.

in faith-based education may respond to aspects of the Classical world that are uncomfortable to them because of their religious background, and how the instructor—especially one who does not share their faith—can help them reflect on their uneasiness when they encounter such topics.

For three years I taught at a university whose student body was rather homogeneous, being primarily white and predominantly affiliated with the same church. Most of my male students older than nineteen years of age had served a two-year mission either in the United States or in foreign countries.[2] Thus many of them were exposed to foreign cultures and ideas and had examined religious or cultural differences. This experience made them more open-minded than their younger classmates or than a conservative religious student is expected to be. Especially students who were studying Classics were very receptive to provocative topics, acknowledging that the field they chose involves the exploration of ideas that may be counter to their beliefs. For them the obscenity or the "impropriety" of the texts they read did not interfere with their faith. In a class on archaic lyric poetry for example I met no opposition or uneasiness from the students when we read the Cologne epode (196A West) attributed to Archilochus and discussed Henderson's article on the interpretations of the love-making scene.[3] The students displayed a great degree of maturity and could separate their religious beliefs from the study of antiquity. Since most students discovered Classics later in their studies, they had perhaps learned through their educational experiences how to face any challenges that Greek or Roman culture would pose.

However, in the case of Classical Civilization classes, students who were for the first time exposed to the Classical world were more sensitive about uncomfortable subjects and sometimes reluctant to engage in a discussion of such topics. My focus in this chapter is confined to students who were enrolled in three Classical Civilization courses: Greek and Roman Mythology, Introduction to Greek and Roman Literature and the Golden Age of Greece. In the first two classes the student body was primarily freshmen while more advanced students attended the third. As I will show, it is not only age, declared major, and exposure to foreign cultures but also the personal level of conservatism that may affect how students of faith respond to sensitive subjects.

The first issue to address is what makes subjects difficult to talk about in the case of religious students, especially for those with no previous back-

---

2. While for males the mission was obligatory, for women it was optional at the time.
3. Henderson (1976).

ground in Classics. The students' discomfort stems primarily from focalizing Greek and Latin literature—to use a framework familiar from narratological theory—*and* from their expectations from faith-based education. When we ask our students to engage with sensitive narratives, we assign them the role of both the narrator, i.e., "the agent who narrates a story," and the focalizer, i.e., "the agent who perceives the story."[4] Through focalization[5] a student presents a narrative from a personal angle and attaches to it his/her emotional reaction.[6] According to Irene de Jong's scheme the student plays the role of a "primary narrator-focalizer" who embeds the focalization and narration of "a secondary narrator-focalizer," the latter being in our case the ancient author or his characters.[7] Religious students cannot always be detached from the narrative nor can they dissociate themselves from the ancient narrators. For example, my students often characterized Greek or pagan (in their words) gods as evil, merciless and unkind, differentiating them from their own perception of a benevolent and forgiving God. Some students could not grasp the reasons for believing in anthropomorphic, capricious and immoral gods and pitied the Greek worshippers who had to venerate them. Although religion is perhaps not an uncomfortable subject *per se*, it is a charged topic for students of religious background, who often compare their beliefs to ancient ones.

If we think in terms of focalization, it is perhaps easier to comprehend why students can be critical of primary sources, since they read texts through a modern (in this case a religious) lens. My goal was first to teach them how to engage in an objective discussion of the narratives and in narratological terms to show them how to leave aside emotional focalization that blurs the distinction between the ancient narrator and the modern focalizer. When students for example were using the term "marry" as a euphemism to describe a sexual relationship (e.g., "Apollo wished to marry Daphne" or "Zeus wished to marry Io") since the two concepts are interdependent in a Christian culture, I had to ask them to focus on the language chosen by the author and be faithful to the story.

---

4. On the definition of these terms see Nünlist (2003: 61).

5. I use this term loosely to point out the conflicted outlook we may encounter as a student tries to keep up with the narrative but also to voice his/her views. For example as Irene de Jong (1987: 33) explains, the narrator and the focalizer can be characters of the story, i.e., they are internal, or they do not coincide with them, i.e., they are external (e.g., the poet). I however assign the role of the focalizer and narrator to the reader, the student, who re-presents orally an ancient narrator's story. As de Jong (1987: 33) notices every narrator is a focalizer.

6. On emotive focalization and focalization in general see Rimmon-Kenan (1983: 71), Gennette (1980); Bal (1985); de Jong (1987: 31–5).

7. de Jong (1987: 34).

At the same time, when we encourage students to voice their personal views, we gain an invaluable insight into their perspective on antiquity, and we may aid them in developing their own self-awareness. Within this framework, teaching Greek religion to religious focalizers can be highly effective as long as foreign concepts are familiarized. I often stressed for example the notion that although the ancient Greeks perceived and defined their relationships with the divine in a different way (e.g., anthropomorphism), certain convictions, like the belief that proper worship and devotion to the divine should be rewarded, are still valid nowadays. To this end, ancient sources that expressed similar questions and emphasized the unfairness of the gods who did not reciprocate after receiving offerings proved to be of great value. For example Eurycleia's (H. *Od.* 19.363–69) complaint about Zeus' ungratefulness instigated a good discussion of modern views on divine benevolence.[8] It was also helpful to point out that the notion of a merciful God has been always questioned by non-believers, since suffering abounds in our world. Asking students to view their beliefs from a different perspective, ancient or modern, could lead to the realization that monotheistic religions must confront some of the same questions as ancient polytheism.

The manifestations of reciprocal relationships between gods and worshippers were another issue that attracted the attention of my students. For example, when I mentioned that there was no notion of paradise in Homer's *Nekyia,* they were uncomfortable with the idea and expressed their puzzlement by asking why Greeks did the "right thing" if they knew that there would be no reward in paradise. The discussion of narratives in the underworld, then, turned into an exploration of issues of morality. By bringing in some of my research on reciprocity in archaic poetry and Greek religion and the notion of the free gift (i.e., giving without the expectation of reciprocation)[9]—which is not, but should be compatible with the institution of religion—I explained that altruism and morality (however defined) should be unconditionally practiced without the expectation of a reward. When I taught the same topic to my students in another class, I instigated the discussion by asking about the implications of the absence of paradise in a Christian sense from *Odyssey* 11 and the punishment only of those who challenged Zeus (i.e., Tantalus, Sisyphus, Ixion and Tityus).[10] It was thus

---

8. For mortals' complaints in Greek literature about gods showing ingratitude see Parker (1983: 114–18).

9. On the notion that free (i.e., without strings attached) gift does not exist, see Marcel Mauss (1990); Laidlaw (2000).

10. Tsagarakis (2000: 111) makes a plausible argument that if the "Homeric Man" believed that

useful to invite students to interpret a phenomenon through their views, thereby showing how deficient such an approach can be.

Not only religious but also cultural biases may affect students' focalization of narratives. One student asked me, for example, whether Greeks practiced polygamy, since Agamemnon brought Cassandra as a second wife, confusing to a certain extent concubinage and slavery with polygamy. While it is necessary to encourage our students to focalize the readings and voice their personal view, we also need to train them to analyze ancient cultures based on objective criteria and the social or religious conventions of the period they study.

Students in faith-based colleges also anticipate that their learning experience will lead to growth and serve as a guide for virtuous living.[11] One of my students complained that Plato's *Symposium* did not edify, uplift or educate him in a way that would benefit him. The focus and aims of faith-based education were also reflected on the evaluation forms that included questions asking whether the Gospel was incorporated in the class and whether the course had strengthened the students' faith. Both questions showcase the direction of faith-based education and imply a particular outlook on teaching. Although these two questions were not applicable to a Classics course, in the case of Greek and Roman mythology a student noted with disappointment that during the whole semester the name of Jesus Christ was never mentioned. Since I could not shape my classes to address such expectations, it was useful to explain to my students the teaching outcomes I planned for my classes. I pointed out that even though Classical texts do not directly pertain to current religious beliefs and dogmas, they provide us with certain tools that can analyze and explain human nature. It was important therefore to show that the study of Classics can be beneficial for students of all faiths, genders and beliefs, and that the lessons of antiquity can be applied to their own lives and be appreciated even within a strict religious context. For example, while Hippolytus' decision to retain his virginity was very appealing to my students, whose religion promotes chastity, my discussion of this matter in terms of extreme devotion helped them reevaluate the contemporary conflict between religious and social norms. Most students—not just the conservative ones—are prompt to make clear-cut distinctions between "good" and "evil," "moral" and "immoral,"

---

the gods punished "perjury, the maltreatment of suppliants and similar offences," he also believed that since the soul ended in Hades, the wrongdoers were punished after death. However, this belief is not implied in the *Nekyia*.

11. On ancient views about moral education and virtuous character in Plato's *Republic* and Aristotle's *Nicomachean Ethics* see Verbeke (1990); Smith (1999); Curren (2000); Barrow (2007).

"right" and "wrong." While Medea's murder of her children, for example, was easily frowned upon just as was Jason's adultery, it was harder for students to see at first the multifaceted motivations of her actions. In cases like this, it has always been useful to ask students to argue about a controversial topic from both sides.

As I have shown, religious or other presumptions may distort students' view of the Classical world and increase their uneasiness in the case of sensitive subjects. In order to address the students' distress it is important to employ strategies to allow them to express their feelings towards their readings. For example, I explored my students' first response to Plato's *Symposium* by asking them to answer anonymously three questions:

1. Plato's *Symposium* can be treated as praise of homosexual love. Did you feel uncomfortable as you were reading it? If so, in what way? Were there any particular parts that made you more uncomfortable? If you did not feel uncomfortable, why not?
2. In what way do you think modern beliefs and attitudes towards homosexuality affect a modern audience's perception of the *Symposium*?
3. Is the *Symposium* a valuable reading? Yes, no, and why?

To my surprise the responses varied significantly. While I anticipated that my students would view the text through the lens of their religion, I was pleasantly surprised by the maturity and open-mindedness of the majority. Some expressed their interest in the text without being offended by the content. One student wrote: "I did not feel uncomfortable. I am accepting of all beliefs, attitudes and cultural opinions. I had no problem with it because it makes sense given the time period." Others accepted the fact that they had to read something they did not agree with while not becoming disturbed. One student noticed that the arguments in the *Symposium* about beauty and love could be transferred to any relationship. All students who mentioned that they felt a bit awkward nevertheless regarded the *Symposium* as a valuable reading, because they accepted diversity and because it offers an excellent insight into Greek culture. One student explained the problem: "Most people, especially in our culture at our university, look down on homosexuality as morally wrong and unnatural. It can be difficult to accept that the *Symposium* was written in a time when such attitudes did not exist." Few students saw no value in reading the *Symposium* or stated that, even though they did not feel uncomfortable reading it, they did not think it should be studied. The very few students who acknowledged that they felt uncomfortable reading the *Symposium* expressed a certain degree of anger that they were forced to read about (in their own words) sins, inappropriate topics and acts against human nature. One student stated emphatically that s/he did not feel uncomfortable but s/he was "grossed out," adding that "stating that Greeks were homosexuals would be enough." At the same time the defenders of the *Symposium* also expressed their views strongly. One student noted for example that the reading does not have to be uncomfortable just because you may not agree with it or because it is culturally awkward, adding that: "we are in college to expand our minds and to become exposed to life, not to hide from it." Overall, the majority of the students appeared to have no problem reading the *Symposium*. As one student put it, "I would not choose ignorance over awkwardness."

A few students refused to take the poll, making apparent that we cannot reach all students who are uncomfortable engaging in a discussion about their feelings, at least with this technique. In my case, it could perhaps be more difficult to make my students express how they felt and to convince them that I was interested in their responses, since I did not share their faith and I am a foreigner (thus, clearly a different focalizer). Although my students were very accepting of me and even appreciated the fact that they had a "real" Greek as their professor, nevertheless it could be easily assumed that I endorse or promote Greek culture, or that I cannot understand their reaction since what was bizarre for them was presumably ordinary for me and I would naturally be more receptive of my ancestors' beliefs. My students may have thought I could not question Greek customs and therefore I would be prompt to disregard their criticism. A culture barrier could also (but not necessarily) be responsible for their reluctance to share their thoughts with me, since I did not fit the typical profile of a professor at that university, being young, unmarried and a foreigner: the *Other* that they sometimes struggled to comprehend in their readings. In addition, since students in faith-based colleges usually tend to respect authority and refrain from challenging it, they may not have wanted to share any views that could conflict with those of the professor. All of these speculations were never really confirmed by my students directly or indirectly; in fact my colleagues who shared their students' faith noticed as well that students rarely complained to them openly about readings. Nevertheless, raising these issues may assist our understanding of the professor's personal impact on the discussion of sensitive topics.

Within this context, the anonymous questionnaire has proven to be of great use to me. I could see a wide spectrum of responses to uncomfortable readings and, moreover, I had access to the justification of the students' feelings. The anonymity allowed them to freely criticize the readings themselves or even my choice of the readings. The questionnaire became a forum of free speech and expression. Moreover, the explanation the students provided for their reactions helped me understand their mentality and prepared me to address these issues.

I employed the questionnaire as a teaching tool when we discussed the *Symposium*, since fewer students were eager to express their views in front of their classmates. In the class after I had read my students' replies, I was able to address their concerns and show that it is insufficient to criticize Greek customs based on contemporary beliefs. I also explained the value of the *Symposium* beyond the context of homosexuality in terms of the idealized *eros* that overrides carnal desire and also in philosophical terms with the Theory of Forms. Considering that some of my students would marry before they finished college and that all valued the institution of marriage, which according to their religion was eternal, the notion of an elevated love that goes beyond physical attraction was very appealing to them. The questionnaire approach therefore showed that, first, students can talk more openly about these topics anonymously and, second, considering the variety of responses, that the level of uneasiness differs from student to student, even in the case of a very homogenous, religious and, in theory, conservative group of students.

The multiple responses to the *Symposium* also reflect the difficulties that are faced by an instructor who tries to accommodate students with different perspectives. This was apparent in the case of one student who objected to reading Aristophanes' *Clouds* because of his aversion to the characters, whom he identified as crooked and immoral. The relationship between father and son did not fit into the ideas of social propriety and congenial familial relationships that were promoted and encouraged by the student's religion and culture. Although a quiz was assigned on the particular play, he refused to read it and suggested that he could be tested on a different topic.[12] After the student, who was a freshman and had not yet served a mission, expressed his concerns to me, I felt the need to cancel the quiz and make the reading optional, considering that there might be other students who felt the same but were not brave enough to express their feelings.[13] In class the following day, I had to explain my decision and even felt the need to apologize for not anticipating their distress. However, as I mentioned to

---

12. Sharland in this volume mentions a similar problem when a student refused to translate a section from *Lysistrata*.

13. Sharland discusses walkouts by students. Although she attributes students' reactions to their families' conservatism among other reasons, I never had the impression that students were influenced particularly by their familial environment.

them, I would not apologize for Aristophanes, who uses characterization to provoke laughter by creating characters that exaggerate and go against social norms. I explained, too, that while comic devices have various effects on diverse audiences of different periods, characters worse than the audience can generate laughter even in contemporary societies. I thus tried to contextualize what was perceived as immorality within the genre and the scope of the play.

To my surprise, another student, a junior and a former missioner, opposed the cancellation of the quiz and claimed in class that he was against censorship. He had read and enjoyed the play, and he found the other student's sensitivity extreme, immature and inappropriate. I realized that it was difficult for me not only to predict which readings would be troubling, but also to deal with students who would not respond in the anticipated way to uncomfortable readings. I felt that Aristophanes divided my classroom and that I had to reconcile students who were rigidly conservative with those who were more open-minded. Therefore, I had to teach tolerance not only of Greek ideas, but also of opposite views, a valuable lesson for students who are exposed at an early age to absolute religious thinking.[14]

My solution was to teach the *Clouds* and discuss the play in a way that even students who had not read it could follow my lecture. I also spoke to the protester student and the conservative one separately. I encouraged the one to respect his classmate's sensitivity and the other to feel free to express his discomfort, while being more willing to read even "inappropriate" texts. In retrospect, it was perhaps not effective to make the reading optional, especially since neither the department nor academic divisions[15] placed any restrictions on what should be taught, and encouraged intellectual challenges that could make students step beyond the confines of their comfort zone. In fact, some colleagues disagreed with my decision to cancel the readings, while others acknowledged that they refrained from using Aristophanes' comedies in order to avoid such complaints. Occasionally students in other classes in the field of humanities would complain to administration about explicit or immoral readings, but to my knowledge the professors were always supported and students' concerns were toned down. Nevertheless, prompted by my student's reaction I felt at that point that excusing my students from reading the *Clouds* was the solution for avoiding more griev-

---

14. Cf. Lauriola's (2011) assignment on modern misuses of the word rape and how she taught her students to show respect through the way they use their language.

15. The institution, however, imposed "limited academic freedom" as far as the Honors Code and discussions about the Church were concerned. On academic freedom at religious universities see McConnell (1990) and Andreescu (2008).

ances. The mixed responses from the students, though, led me to realize that as educators we often enter our classroom having our own biases, anticipating certain reactions from students of a certain faith, race and gender, but that our projections cannot always be accurate.

An instructor's biases fall into two categories: on the one hand we cannot predict the negative response by the students to a text, because we are blinded by our own open-mindedness and the long exposure to our discipline. On the other hand we anticipate some distress based on our assumptions about certain types of students and perhaps adjust our teaching accordingly. Teaching at a faith-based institution, for example, seems more challenging, since greater sensitivity to uncomfortable subjects is expected. However, I have faced similar sensitivity among students outside faith-based schools, and as Sharland in this volume and I have shown, it is very uncommon that students overreact to uncomfortable topics; even in the case of the anonymous questionnaire it was only a small minority that expressed their distress over reading the *Symposium*. Instructors often bring their own agenda into the classroom when they feel uncomfortable with certain students' mindsets. Students can be too conservative for our taste, but our job is to instruct them how to be more open-minded and tolerant, not to judge their worldview.

We as educators have the duty to be receptive and respectful of our students' beliefs, while widening their horizons and challenging them to examine topics from many angles. To this end, making the uncomfortable topics relevant to the students' own experiences may appease their distress from engaging with ideas that are counter to their morals. When, for example, I taught Greek homosexuality in my class on the Golden Age of Greece with upper-level students, I talked about it in terms of taboos, which change from time to time. I gave the example of polygamy, which was acceptable in the past but banned later on. I also avoided modern terms such as pedophilia that do not really apply to ancient homosexuality and perhaps make students more uncomfortable. At the same time I refrained from mentioning sensitive current topics such as Proposition Eight, an issue that had caused a great division in my students' communities, where protests took place often even outside their churches.

In a similar framework, when I talked about the Eleusinian Mysteries I referred to some negative depictions of my students' religion by other Christians, who regard it as a mystery cult. My students could comprehend the secrecy of the Eleusinian Mysteries, since at their temples they also performed rituals which should not be revealed or discussed. To adjust our teaching to our students' background can thus be very fruitful.[16] Even though I had not studied my students' religion extensively, I was aware of certain viewpoints and rituals; I used this knowledge several times in class, not only to help them find connections between the past and the present, but also to show them that I was a part of their community and aware of their belief system.

Another technique to relieve the students' uneasiness was to prepare them for what they would encounter in the readings. When I taught Aristophanes' *Frogs* in another class, the students expressed no concerns. I had warned them in advance about the context and language of Greek comedy and gave them a short introduction to comic devices. I followed the same practice before I assigned readings on Herodotus, another author whose explicit scenes have created some level of uneasiness. Such a technique allows the students to approach Greek culture based more on ancient beliefs and less on their own perspectives, without excluding the expression of their own sentiments. Another useful technique that allows students in a conservative environment to voice their views lies in the type of exercises that they are assigned. Paper topics that make students contemplate their own experiences may motivate them to express themselves. For a paper that asked the students to compare and contrast female characters in the writings of Herodotus, Aeschylus, Sophocles, and Euripides and discuss gender biases, a student felt the need to mention a relative's divorce, which is strongly discouraged by the student's religion, and to emphasize the negative way in which the female divorcée was treated by the community.[17] Such a paper topic allowed my student to find a venue for her frustration at double standards for women in her culture.

To conclude, my teaching experience in faith-based education taught me some valuable lessons. First, students cannot always express their level of uneasiness, unless they have opportunities to do so anonymously or privately. Second, not all students react to uncomfortable readings the way we expect, and thus, we cannot always predict which readings may generate discomfort. Third, it is important to show the value of sensitive subjects for the students' education and to employ their experiences to teach them how to approach these topics with a different mindset. I will end my paper with an answer that a student gave on the questionnaire for Plato's *Symposium*,

---

16. See for example how Widdows (2011: 31–32) adjusted her teaching of rape for a male audience.

17. On how a class can affect our students on a personal level, see James (2008) and other chapters in this volume.

which I think encapsulates all the points I am trying to address: "We of course carry our biases into the story with us, which is, I think, something that is unavoidable, and if our biases are at least acknowledged, they can actually facilitate learning."

7

Too Sexy for South Africa?

Teaching Aristophanes' *Lysistrata* in the Land of the Rainbow Nation

SUZANNE SHARLAND

WHAT, WOULD YOU IMAGINE, is the most uncomfortable subject to teach in the South African Classics classroom?

Race? Given South Africa's long colonial history of racism and oppression, including the notorious *apartheid* regime which between 1948 and 1994 deprived the majority of the country's population of a vote and of all the other rights and freedoms which accompany true democracy, this is not a bad guess. As a white South African female lecturer teaching a student body which over a period of twenty years has transformed from majority white to majority black, I am constantly aware that I am addressing learners whose racial identity and cultural background may be different from my own. So when Ovid claims that the Ethiopians got their color when Phaethon flew his father the Sun's chariot too close to the earth,[1] or the Penguin translation has Juvenal's speaker warn the cuckold that his adulterous

---

1. This plays on the putative etymology of *Aethiops* as "someone with a (sun-)burnt face," reflecting the fact that Mediterranean-type coloring was the norm for the Greeks and Romans, and anything outside of this norm would have to be explained. See Ovid *Metamorphoses* 2.235–36: *Sanguine tum credunt in corpora summa vocato / Aethiopum populos nigrum traxisse colorem*—"It was then, they believe, that the peoples of Ethiopia became black-skinned, because the blood was drawn to the surface of their bodies." It doesn't help much that Libya is said to become a desert at the same time, and the disheveled-haired nymphs are bewailing their dried-up pools and other water sources (237–39). I've explained to my students that I consider this silly and naïve rather than actively racist, and strangely, I haven't as yet had any complaints.

wife may yet make him the nominal father of a "picaninny,"[2] or the film *300* (Zack Snyder 2007) portrays every black person who appears on the screen as a villain, alarm bells start going off in my mind. However, South Africans are rather used to discussing race, and I have found that the best policy is to ask the students directly whether they think something is racist or not, and if so, why (that, or use a different translation, preferably one's own).

If race is not the most volatile subject in the South African Classics classroom, then what is? Disease, perhaps? South Africa at present has one of the highest rates of HIV infection in the world, especially among young people (and the province of KwaZulu-Natal, in which I currently teach, has the highest infection rate in South Africa),[3] so it follows that, in this HIV/AIDS global capital, many of my students may be HIV-positive. When looking at how ancient pre-rational medicine attributed illness to the gods' agency, as with the plague sent by Apollo in the first book of the *Iliad*,[4] I find it useful to point out the parallel with those who claim that AIDS is a punishment from God, to show that this is essentially the same irrational idea, attributing disease to divine agency rather than to germs and viruses. Unfortunately, however, South Africans on the whole are very reticent on the subject of HIV/AIDS. Perhaps it is a result of the confusion sown by the denials of former president Thabo Mbeki and his government,[5] but even now, with anti-retroviral medicine and other treatments being made freely available by the current government, comparatively few South Africans are open about their HIV-status and even fewer

---

2. This offensive term is Green's translation of *Aethiops* at Juvenal *Sat.* 6.600 (1974: 149). The cuckolded Roman husband is imagined becoming the father of an Ethiopian (*esses / Aethiopis fortasse pater,* 599–600), and is compelled to hide his *decolor heres,* his heir with an "off-black" face (Green 1974: 150). All of this is a potential minefield for the Classics lecturer. At the *African Athena* conference at Warwick in 2008 African American classicist Shelly Haley discussed the offense caused by some of Green's translations.

3. UNAIDS (2009); Setswe (2009). According to Setswe, 25.8% of adults between the ages of 15 and 49 in KwaZulu-Natal are HIV positive.

4. *Iliad* 1.43–67.

5. Thabo Mbeki made a number of controversial statements about AIDS during his premiership (1999–2008), even going so far as to question whether HIV causes AIDS and to ban the use of antiretroviral drugs in public state hospitals. His government was therefore accused of refusing appropriate medical treatment of HIV-AIDS to its citizens in need of this. The current president of South Africa, Jacob Zuma, has not fared much better. During his rape trial in 2006 (of which he was acquitted), Zuma revealed to the Johannesburg High Court that, in order to prevent catching the Human Immunodeficiency virus, he had taken a shower after having unprotected sex with an HIV-positive woman. Although he subsequently apologized for this statement under pressure from AIDS education groups, Zuma has been satirized repeatedly in the South African media for this lapse of judgment, especially by the cartoonist Zapiro (aka Jonathan Shapiro), who has famously caricatured Zuma as a figure with a showerhead growing out of his head. This image has been exploited extensively by Zuma's political enemies, most recently by Julius Malema.

could be described as AIDS-activists. So, for all the wrong reasons, disease is not a major issue in the South African classroom.

In fact, the most controversial issue in the South African classroom seems to be sex; at least, this has been my own experience of teaching Classics in South Africa. On two separate occasions at different South African universities, in two very different cultural settings, students have exhibited such extreme reactions to my attempts to teach Aristophanes' *Lysistrata* that they have refused to engage with the play at all. In both cases, the students came from what one could describe as broadly Christian fundamentalist backgrounds and cited religious reasons as the motive for their flight from this text. The first incident took place when I was teaching at a conservative[6] Afrikaans-speaking university in a semi-rural setting in 1999; the second occurred at an English-speaking university in an urban area in 2009. In both incidents, the students were in their late teens or early twenties. In either case, all of the students concerned were white (I shall return later to why I think this could be significant). In one case, the class was a Classical Civilisations-type class of about forty students who were looking at a portion of *Lysistrata* in translation; in the other case, the class was a group of four students doing third-year Greek, and the idea was to read as much of the play as possible in the original, given the number of periods allocated to the class. In the first case, those rejecting Aristophanes were a triad of young male Theology students; in the second, the complainant was a female student majoring in Ancient Greek. In both instances, the strong reactions were those of a minority, as the rest of the students in either class seemed to respond favorably to the text. In both cases, I suspected that the particular students' reluctance to engage with *Lysistrata* had more to do with embarrassment about sex than with religious concerns.

An intense reaction of this nature to issues of sex and sexuality could potentially occur not only when a lecturer or teacher of Classics is treating *Lysistrata* or another of Aristophanes' comedies, but in relation to a host of other topics, such as homosexuality in ancient Greece or erotic imagery from Pompeii. One could anticipate a similar reaction in students from many other conservative religious communities worldwide, but my point in this chapter is that in South Africa, this type of response has the weight of a particular history behind it: ironically, in reacting in this fashion, my students were behaving in a manner which was in line with the official attitudes to sexuality, religion and education promoted by the former *apartheid* regime. The system of *apartheid* was based not only on racial segrega-

---

6. See below my discussion of the meaning of "conservative" in the South African context.

tion (*apartheid* is an Afrikaans word that means "separateness," "apartness," or "segregation"), but also on a very strictly interpreted form of Calvinist Christianity, on patriarchal dominance and sexual conservatism. The South African Nationalist Party, the government behind this system, incorporated all these elements into their education policy which they called "National Christian Education." This illegitimate government ruled South Africa for almost half a century, so it is not surprising that it left its mark on the collective psyche of the nation and on the learners who passed through its education system, perpetuating the culture of a generally very conservative minority—the Afrikaner.

"CONSERVATIVE" IN THE SOUTH AFRICAN CONTEXT: ISSUES OF LANGUAGE, CULTURE, AND RELIGION

The racist policies of the *apartheid* government in South Africa towards black people, the history of the struggle to end this form of oppression, the imprisonment of Nelson Mandela for several decades until his release in 1990, and finally, the emergence of the "New South Africa" after the first democratic elections in 1994, are well known.[7] Less well known to the international community is the extent of the "divide and rule" policy of the *apartheid* regime, which not only insisted on the separation of white and black, but also encouraged the development of distinct group identities within these broader racial groupings. Not fully realized by outsiders, perhaps, is the degree of bipolarity (for want of a better term) within the South African white community itself, which comprises roughly two distinct groups divided on linguistic and cultural grounds, the "English" and "Afrikaner."[8] Culturally and politically, the term "conservative" has particular nuances in the South African context, since it tends to be most often applied to white Afrikaans-speaking South Africans (i.e., Afrikaners). In comparison to English-speaking South Africans, during the *apartheid* era

---

7. Much of the background can be absorbed by reading Nelson Mandela's autobiography *Long Walk to Freedom* (1994), which is also a history of the struggle to end *apartheid*.

8. This differs from the United States, where people from many different nations have contributed to the resulting community. The fact that South Africa comprises a much smaller area than the United States and never attracted such intensive European settlement as North America, Australia or New Zealand, may go some way to explaining the binary system of settler group identities that resulted. The "English" and the "Afrikaners" do not comprise ethnic groups in the strict sense, but are rather linguistic and cultural communities. Max du Preez notes (2003: 50) that in his home town of Kroonstad most of the English-speakers were not English at all, but Jewish and Lebanese.

Afrikaners in general were (and in many cases, remain) more likely than English-speakers to have roots in rural areas, to be religious rather than secularly minded, to follow the Christian ideal of sanctioning sex only within marriage (officially, at least), to be politically conservative (tending to right-wing as opposed to left-wing politics), to openly express racism towards black people as well as towards other groups, and to organize their households in a patriarchal manner.[9]

The divisions in South African communities of European origin can be related directly to distinct phases in the history of colonial rule in this region. Between 1652, when the first European settlement at the southern tip of Africa began, and the early nineteenth century, when the British assumed control of the Cape of Good Hope and surrounding areas,[10] voluntary immigrants to the region were predominantly of Dutch and German origin, although other groups, most notably the French Huguenots, joined the mix. In addition, there were a number of involuntary immigrants: because the indigenous Khoisan population was disinclined (understandably) to work for the colonists, slaves were brought to the Cape from Dutch colonies in the East, from India, the East Indies, Madagascar, Mozambique and other regions in Africa,[11] to work not only as agricultural laborers, but also as skilled artisans and servants. In the days of early Cape settlement, white women were particularly scarce, so it is not surprising that miscegenation took place from the beginning of the colonial period: in addition to the inevitable relationships between mostly male colonists and their female slaves, research has shown that over a thousand interracial marriages took place during the period of Dutch rule at the Cape.[12] Many of the offspring

---

9. Even nowadays, many Afrikaners assert, citing the Christian apostle St. Paul (Ephesians 5:22), that they recognize the husband as the head of the household, and defer to his judgment in all important matters, rather than accommodating a more egalitarian arrangement; in practice, this results in a proliferation of strict patriarchs terrorizing their wives and children in a near modern facsimile of *patria potestas*. I should add, however, that there have been tremendous changes among white Afrikaans-speaking South Africans within the past fifteen years or so, with younger people increasingly adopting more liberal attitudes with regard to religion, sexuality and family life.

10. Britain first seized the Cape in 1795 in a bid to prevent the sea-route to India from falling into French hands, but gave it back to the Dutch Batavian Republic in 1803 (Muller 1981: 100–109). In 1806 Britain took over the Cape again, this time on a more permanent basis (Muller 1981: 115). British sovereignty over the region was internationally recognized by the Congress of Vienna in 1815.

11. Du Preez (2003: 25).

12. Du Preez (2003: 29). Along with this went an interesting linguistic development: gradually, in relative isolation, the seventeenth-century Dutch spoken at the Cape began to change and evolve, to absorb the flavors of the slaves' speech and even some French from the Huguenots who intermarried with the Dutch, until an independent *patois* emerged, initially dismissed as "Kitchen Dutch," but later known as *Afrikaans* (literally, the "African" dialect or version of Dutch).

of these unions were accepted in colonial society, and, ironically, are among the ancestors of the Afrikaner.[13]

Soon after taking over the Cape at the start of the nineteenth century, Britain began a policy of forcing the Cape Dutch to learn English, and of actively encouraging British settlement in southern Africa. After 1834, the new regime further infuriated Dutch farmers by putting into practice the Abolition of Slavery Act without adequately compensating the slave-owners for their loss (at least in the opinion of the former slave-owners). Dissatisfaction with the new rule resulted in many farmers of Dutch descent leaving the British-controlled areas of southern Africa from 1838 onwards, and pushing increasingly into the interior in wagons pulled by teams of oxen (a phenomenon endlessly celebrated by school history textbooks of the *apartheid* era as "The Great Trek"). On their journey into the interior, with the Christian Bible their only literature, the Afrikaners developed an image of themselves as "God's chosen people," like the Israelites of the Old Testament. South African history text books from my generation would cite many examples of the proof of God's beneficence toward the Afrikaner,[14] the villains of the piece being the dastardly English-speaking representatives of the London Missionary Society, who inexplicably championed the end of slavery and later supported the rights of black farm workers against their Afrikaner masters.

In the interior, the Afrikaners or Boers ("Farmers"), as they came to be known, established a number of independent republics, the chief of which were the Orange Free State (*Oranje-Vrijstaat*) in the region between the Vaal and the Orange rivers, and the South African Republic (*Zuid-Afrikaansche Republiek* or *ZAR*) in the area north of the Vaal river and south of the Limpopo. The Afrikaner pioneers saw these states as places where they could at last, in peace and without outside interference, practice their own culture, speak their evolving Dutch dialect rather than English, where they could worship their Old Testament-inspired God in their own manner, and where

---

13. Research has suggested that Afrikaners have approximately 7.2% "non-white" ancestry (Du Preez 2003: 29). This may be, in a roundabout way, the underlying reason for the peculiar anxiety exhibited by this group concerning issues of race; the Afrikaners' claims of so-called "racial purity," which pervaded the *apartheid* era, may be seen as a backlash in a population which was already to some degree racially mixed but which chose to ignore or suppress this fact.

14. The most significant of these was the Battle of Blood River (16 December 1838), on the eve of which Sarel Cilliers led the group of pioneers in a prayer, according to which they made a "covenant" with God, promising to build a church and commemorate the day if they were granted victory over the Zulus, their opponents. When the victory did fall to the pioneers, this was taken as an indication that God was indeed "on their side." In a show of solidarity, British settlers and their Black followers apparently provided reinforcements for the Afrikaners under the command of Andries Pretorius (Muller 1981: 166).

they could treat the black servants that they had brought with them as they saw fit. Britain did not express much interest in these republics until it was, quite by accident, discovered that they contained great mineral wealth, and that the South African Republic, in particular, lay atop some of the richest mass deposits of gold in the world. Fortune-seekers from all over the world flocked to these previously unknown republics in an unprecedented Gold Rush. To cut a long story short, Britain's interest in gold superseded any prior political treaties that she may have made with the republics, and in 1899 war ensued.[15]

The South African War (1899–1902)[16] was the world's first modern war. Not only did the Boer forces outwit the British with guerrilla tactics, but, chillingly, this war likewise foreshadowed subsequent twentieth century conflicts in its high proportion of civilian deaths. Largely because the Boer commandoes depended for their survival in the field on a widespread network of sympathetic farm-dwellers, the final phase of this war saw the British adopting a scorched-earth policy: farmhouses and crops, anything that could sustain the commandoes, were summarily torched, Boer women and children were systematically rounded up and herded into the world's first war-time concentration camps, so called because their aim was literally to concentrate the civilian population in a limited area rather than having

---

15. In 1852 Britain, apparently hard-pressed by too many financial commitments in southern Africa, signed the Sand River Convention, a treaty which recognised the independence of the South African Republic (Muller 1981: 178). In 1870, diamonds were discovered in an area then known as Griqualand West, which was claimed by both Boer republics and the Griqua tribe. When in 1871 the Griqua chief Waterboer appealed to the British government for help in this dispute, Britain responded by annexing Griqualand West, including the diamond fields (Muller 1981: 304). The discovery of gold in an area of the South African Republic known as the Witwatersrand in 1886 boosted Britain's imperialist ambitions even more. Negotiations between Paul Kruger, President of the South African Republic, and the Portuguese at Delagoa Bay (now Maputo) resulted in a railway being built between the landlocked republic and the coast. The completion of this railway in 1894 raised the specter of a potentially wealthy power in the region entirely independent of Britain but open to negotiating with other European powers (Muller 1981: 317–18). This consideration was one of the factors that encouraged British imperialist Cecil John Rhodes to attempt to provoke the ZAR into war with the failed Jameson raid of 1895 (Muller 1981: 322–24).

16. This conflict is known to English-speaking South Africans as the Boer War or the Anglo-Boer War, and to Afrikaner patriots as *Die Tweede Vryheidsoorlog* or the "Second War of Independence," referencing a prior conflict in 1881 known as *Die Eerste Vryheidsoorlog* or the "First War of Independence," in which the republics were, incredibly, able to stave off attack by Britain. The chief battle in the "First War of Independence" was the Battle of Majuba Hill on 27 February 1881, at which Boer fighters, using guerrilla tactics for the first time, decisively defeated British forces. This victory is paralleled only by that of the First Anglo-Zulu War two years previously, in which an army of Zulu warriors crushed a British force of invaders at the Battle of Isandlwana on 22 January 1879 (on this battle and the concept of an "African Thermopylae," see Murray 2009: 51–68). In either case, however, Britain eventually regrouped and retaliated, to the detriment of both the Zulus and the Boers.

them spread over the entire war-zone, where they were optimally positioned to assist the enemy. Whether intentional or not, unsanitary conditions and overcrowding in the thirty-one concentration camps positioned at various locations around the region resulted in the deaths of over 26,000 women and children, and an untold number of their black servants.[17] This preventable loss of civilian life (some would call it genocide) is something that the Afrikaners have never forgotten; it is this, and not the Great Trek, that proved to be the defining crucible of Afrikaner national identity.[18]

The concentration camps and other casualties of the Anglo-Boer War are central to the development of the Afrikaner world view, and may help to explain their passionate hatred of the British government, and corresponding animosity towards English-speaking South Africans.[19] Unwillingly incorporated in the Union of South Africa in 1910, Afrikaans-speaking white South Africans looked to mythologies and reconstructions of their past in order to establish a new collective identity. The early decades of the twentieth century saw the rise of Afrikaner nationalism, culminating in the centenary celebrations of the Great Trek in 1938, when there was a symbolic attempt by Afrikaner nationalists to duplicate the historical migration

---

17. The total number of deaths in the concentration camps, including the deaths of adult male inmates, was 27,927, of whom 4,177 were adult women and 22,074 were children below the age of 16 (Muller 1981: 356).

18. The most poignant description of what many contemporary Boer families must have endured comes from the short story writer Herman Charles Bosman, speaking as his story-teller *par excellence* Oom Schalk Lourens: "I was in the *veld* [field or grassland] until they made peace. Then we laid down our rifles and went home. What I knew my farm by was the hole under the *koppie* [cliff or outcrop] where I quarried slate-stones for the threshing-floor. That was about all that remained as I left it. Everything else was gone. My home was burnt down. My lands were laid waste. My cattle and sheep were slaughtered. Even the stones I had piled for the *kraals* [enclosures for animals] were pulled down. My wife came out of the concentration camp, and we went together to look at our old farm. My wife had gone into the concentration camp with our two children, but she had come out alone. And when I saw her again and noticed the way she had changed, I knew that I, who had been through all the fighting, had not seen the Boer War" (MacKenzie 2006: 26; translations of Afrikaans words are given in square brackets).

19. Afrikaners derisively term the British *Rooinekke* ("Rednecks"), because of the tendency of the typical Anglo-Saxon complexion to burn under the fierce South African sun. They deride English-speaking South Africans as *Soutpiele* or *Souties* ("Saltpricks" or "Salties") due to their historical attachment to Britain, the idea being that the English have one foot in England, and one foot in South Africa, so that their genitals fall into the salty Atlantic ocean in between. Throughout the early to mid-twentieth century, Afrikaans-speaking and English-speaking schoolchildren would often come to blows, or insult each other with name-calling. One of the favorite rhymes used by Afrikaner children to insult their English-speaking peers, was: *Rooinek, val jou vrek/Anderkant die Koeliekerk*, which is virtually untranslatable, but essentially expresses a wish that the English-speaking *Rooinek* child should fall to his or her death behind a non-Christian (and non-white) place of worship. English-speaking children would retaliate with the rather simpler taunt: "Afrikaner, *vrot* banana!" (*vrot* is itself an Afrikaans word which refers to over-ripe or rotten fruit or vegetables, and which, like many terms, is also commonly used in colloquial South African English).

into the interior in celebration of this feat. Some ten years on, Afrikaner nationalism had grown to such an extent that the Nationalist Party, led by one Daniel François Malan, who openly espoused views of national self-determination and segregation on racial grounds (subsequently labelled *apartheid*), won the national elections and thereafter formed the first exclusively Afrikaner government of South Africa in 1948.[20]

As noted, the system of *apartheid*, which went hand-in-hand with Afrikaner nationalism, was based not only on racial segregation, but also on Christian religious fundamentalism (as interpreted by the Afrikaners' Calvinist churches),[21] patriarchal dominance and sexual conservatism.[22] During the *apartheid* era, when the government consisted almost entirely of Afrikaners, the viewpoint of this minority group was imposed on everyone in South African society. In terms of "National Christian Education," everyone was forced to learn the Afrikaans language and to study the history of South Africa as seen from the perspective of the Afrikaner.[23] In the 1970s and

---

20. Needless to say, only white South Africans were allowed to vote in this election.

21. One of the peculiar features of the *apartheid* system was "its heavily ideological nature and its quasi-religious status" (Richardson 1986: 4). Proponents of the system of *apartheid* claimed to have found Biblical verses which apparently supported their theories of racial superiority and inferiority, and which were used to justify *apartheid* or "separate development," as it was sometimes called. By contrast, in 1982 the World Alliance of Reformed Churches (WARC) declared *apartheid* a heresy and suspended the membership of two of its South African Churches. The Dutch Reformed Church was permitted to re-join the WARC only in 1998, when it had thoroughly renounced *apartheid* and agreed to end its system of racially separate congregations. Of the Afrikaner establishment's ministers of religion, Beyers Naude (1915–2004) had been one of the few clerics brave enough to condemn *apartheid*. By contrast, the mainly English-speaking Anglican (Episcopalian) and Methodist churches, among others, vigorously opposed *apartheid* from its inception, and were a major thorn in the side of the South African Nationalist Party regime over the years. Two of the Anglican Church's most significant anti-*apartheid* campaigners were Father Trevor Huddleston and Former Archbishop Desmond Tutu, the latter of whom subsequently played a central role in the Truth and Reconciliation Commission, coined the term "Rainbow Nation" (used in the title of this chapter), and who remains, in a sense, the voice of South Africa's collective conscience.

22. Not only was the *apartheid* regime essentially racist, but, as a "nanny" state, it also attempted to impose Christian (more strictly, Calvinist) moral values on its citizens. All forms of pornography were banned, and a notoriously rigid Board of Censors was tasked with previewing all books, films and other media made available to the South African public, in order to ensure that Christian sensibilities were upheld, and that no encouragement of non-racism or "Communism" enlightened the populace.

23. Proposed instruction through the medium of Afrikaans in township schools was the catalyst that sparked the 1976 Soweto Uprising. Nelson Mandela, imprisoned on Robben Island at the time, heard about this mass uprising of schoolchildren from the young prisoners who started arriving on Robben Island in August 1976: "On 16 June 1976 fifteen thousand schoolchildren gathered in Soweto to protest the government's ruling that half of all classes in secondary schools must be taught in Afrikaans. Students did not want to learn and teachers did not want to teach in the language of the oppressor" (Mandela 1994: 575). The shooting and killing of a number of schoolchildren by police caused the protest to spread throughout South Africa.

1980s,[24] when *apartheid* was at its height, all state schools in South Africa were required to start the day with a Christian religious service, including the singing of hymns and the reciting of prayers,[25] and study of the Christian Bible was also a compulsory part of the school curriculum.

Growing up in *apartheid* South Africa, I resented the Afrikaner-dominated Nationalist Party government's influence on my education. Like many English-speaking South African schoolchildren, I hated having to learn the Afrikaans language, which at the time I saw as a useless exercise. I felt impatient with what I perceived, even then, as the mythology and propaganda of the Afrikaner masquerading as history lessons: even the sections on international history in our curriculum seemed designed solely to place the Afrikaner's quest for self-determination in historical perspective. More broadly, I resented the crude nature of the system of *apartheid* which was at that stage threatening to bring my country into international disrepute (even though, as a white person, I benefited from this system in many ways). I now realize that I built up a great deal of prejudice and resentment, not necessarily towards individual Afrikaners, but towards the collective. In short, I was racist towards them. I now see that I took a great deal of childhood trauma with me from my schooldays,[26] when, in the late 1990s, I went to teach Classics in a conservative Afrikaans environment. Buoyed by the romance of the New South Africa, I anticipated and indeed expected that even conservative South Africans would let go of their past and embrace the country's new constitution. However, the university at which I was teaching was one at which the *apartheid*-era concept of "National Christian Education" was still endorsed and practiced, five years after South Africa's first democratic elections.[27]

---

24. Born in November 1966 in Cape Town, I spent most of the 1970s in primary school, and was in high school from 1980 to 1984. My education is largely thanks to the *apartheid* government, which spent roughly ten times the amount of money on every white child's education compared to what it spent on that of a black child (see Richardson 1986: 18 n. 4). The observations about South African schools in the 1970s and early 1980s are courtesy of my own experiences.

25. This describes the protocol at Christian government schools during the *apartheid* regime. I'm afraid I have no idea what took place in schools where the majority of the pupils were Jewish, Hindu, or Muslim (many of which would have been private schools at that stage), but given the *apartheid* principle of "separate but equal" (which never actually worked in practice), it is likely that religious services appropriate to the school's cultural context were conducted.

26. Jonathan Jansen has recently cautioned (2011: 5) that South Africans may be more traumatized by *apartheid* than they realize. He also notes that insufficient time has been allotted to mourn past injustices (2011: 6).

27. I should note that this university was not a privately-owned or independently funded institution, but was a public university funded substantially by the state coffers. Despite this, the university continued with its narrow Calvinist agenda as if no changes had taken place on the broader South African stage. Only Christians could be appointed to positions at this university, and all new

CASE ONE (1999): *LYSISTRATA* IN THE LAAGER[28]

In 1999, as noted, I was teaching a newly-introduced Classical Civilization-type course called Ancient Culture (*Antieke Kultuur*) in the above-mentioned conservative Afrikaans-speaking university. As is the case with most Classical Civilization courses world-wide, Ancient Culture was taught entirely in modern translation and required no prior acquaintance with any ancient language (one of our selling points). Part of my motivation for using *Lysistrata* in this context was that there was a published Afrikaans translation of this comedy readily available,[29] which is not always the case with every play. My modus operandi was for the class to read a portion of the play out aloud, with different students assuming different roles. We would then discuss the portion just read, and I would explain any points of interest or obscure Classical allusions that appeared in the portion of text. Everything was going smoothly (or so it seemed), when suddenly three first-year male students seated in front got up in unison and left. I do not recall if they said anything upon leaving so abruptly, but it soon emerged that they had left because they felt *Lysistrata* offended their religious beliefs. I was amazed and rather devastated: I had been trying to make the course interesting for the students, and I had not anticipated such an extremely closed and negative reaction.

Upon scrutinizing the portion of text we had been reading for clues, I came to the conclusion that Aristophanes' reference to Athenian women's genital depilation could well have been the deciding factor: *met die donker driehoek skoongeskeer* ("with the dark triangle completely shaven"),[30] as the

---

appointees were compelled to complete a course instructing them in the Calvinist philosophy of teaching adhered to by this university. However, the South African Constitution, which came into effect on 4 February 1997, enshrined the right to freedom from discrimination on the grounds of religion and belief, among other things (Section 9 of the Bill of Rights). The university in question has since joined with another university in a reconfiguration process and appears to have abandoned, at least formally, its strict and exclusive stance on religion.

28. A *laager* was a defensive circle of ox-wagons used during military operations or skirmishes during the period of the Great Trek (for example, at the Battle of Blood River in 1838). The expression "*laager* mentality" has also often been used metaphorically to describe the isolationist, inward-looking tendencies of white South Africans in general, and conservative Afrikaners in particular during the *apartheid* era. I use it here to characterize what I perceive as the students' frustrating lack of openness towards other cultures or foreign ideas in the incident I describe.

29. I felt that the lively translation of Van Rensburg (1970), which has also been used by several dramatic productions of the play in Afrikaans, would serve my purposes in making the comedy accessible and intelligible to my students. As noted, I had used this translation for two years prior to this without any problems emerging.

30. Van Rensburg (1970: 14). While the idea of shaving appeals to modern practices, the Greek παρατετιλμέναι (Ar. *Lys.* 151) here suggests plucking rather than shaving. As for the question of

Afrikaans translation of J. P. J. van Rensburg rendered it, may just have been too much for them to take. Looking back, I now realize that I may have been a little too optimistic in trying to read this play in such a conservative religious context, but I had taught the play for two years prior to this with no unfavorable reactions. The university timetable had, in fact, been changed that year, for the first time allowing first year Theological students to fit the Ancient Culture course into their schedule, which may explain why the problems emerged only in 1999, and not before, when a bunch of secularly-minded Law and Arts students had been the chief recipients of the course.

One of the students who walked out of my class came to see me a short time later, to apologize and explain where he was coming from, as it were. He came from an extremely conservative Christian background, it transpired, with a domineering, rather obsessive father. (This father, an independent source revealed, was so extreme in his religious fundamentalism that he refused to allow novels, even ones with a broadly religious theme, under his roof. Instead, everyone had to read only the Bible.) The student explained that he did not want to react to things in the way that his father did, yet he found himself doing so all the same. I explained to the student that the whole cultural approach of the ancient Greeks towards issues of sexuality was entirely different to the modern one, and that I would be misrepresenting Aristophanes if I did not allow him to speak for himself (even if only in modern translation). He said that he understood that, but felt that it would be better if I went and studied the ancient texts myself, and then just reported on them in summary (and obviously, sanitized) form. I felt that this was not being honest about the ancient Greeks, and was tantamount to lying about them. Although I was grateful for the student's courage in coming to speak to me, ultimately we had to agree to differ. I perceived with amazement the extent to which I was in the middle of a major cultural clash, one that was centuries in the making. This was a clash of the pagan, Classical world, on the one hand, and the fundamentalist Christian one, on the other; it was also a clash, to my mind, between secularly-minded liberal English-speaking South Africans, and conservative,

---

how much hair the Athenian women removed, Martin Kilmer has suggested that, based both on the evidence of Old Comedy and of vase painting, it appears that Athenian women did not completely depilate their genitals, but may only have trimmed or shaped their pubic hair: "... the two methods of depilation commonly used for the genital region, plucking and singeing by lamp, were used not to strip the genitals bald, but to reduce and probably to shape the pubic hair. The result of this must have been to make the vulva more visible; and the literary evidence makes it clear that the point was to increase sexual attractiveness" (1982: 111).

religious Afrikaners;[31] it was a true clash of cultures—the Classical and the Christian—and one which I would see again, in a context where it was somewhat more unexpected.

CASE TWO (2009): LEAVING OUT *LYSISTRATA*

The second time I had trouble with my choice of Aristophanes' *Lysistrata* as a text for study came about a decade after this. In 2009, I was teaching in an urban historically English-speaking South African university situated in one of the country's major urban regions. I was due to teach Aristophanes as an author for a Greek third-year class to read. In the previous year, I had taught Aristophanes' *Peace,* and was considering the *Frogs* as a possibility. However, the fact that at least two of the four students in the class were pursuing or had recently pursued postgraduate research in Classics which focused on women and gender studies, encouraged my selection of *Lysistrata;* in fact, one of the students actually suggested this text due to her research interests, and later, when the possibility of change was raised due to one student's unhappiness about the play, the three other students were against altering their choice.

I began this section of the module with an introductory lecture on Old Comedy and Aristophanes, outlining the characteristics of the genre, looking briefly at what is known about Aristophanes' life and mentioning some of his other plays, and then explaining the plot of *Lysistrata.* After this introduction, I set the students a number of lines to prepare for our next meeting. Shortly before this next class, one of the students came to see me in my office and explained that she did not feel that she should study the play, making it clear that it offended her religious beliefs. She was a student who was quite openly a born-again Christian and also a very competent student in Greek, so we discussed the possibility of her doing a self-study in some other author. For some reason I felt empathetic towards the student and understood where she was coming from, and I also understood, without her having to spell it out, that she would not back down from the stance she was taking. But there was also, understandably for me, a feeling of *déjà vu*— here, again, was a fundamentalist Christian taking offense at Aristophanes'

---

31. On the other hand, I should note that there is also a very down-to-earth undercurrent within Afrikaner culture that I find appealing and which is rather Aristophanic. After I had related the incident of the students' walk-out to various university colleagues individually, every one of them independently suggested that what the students had really been doing after walking out was masturbating in the toilets!

Lysistrata. Not again! At the same time, I felt renewed admiration for Aristophanes. Why was it that this particular play, well over two thousand years old, still had the ability to shock in the twenty-first century? It was nothing short of incredible.

I'm afraid that I did not engage with this student much after she declined to read the play. Some people may have admired her stance, and her willingness to stand up for her beliefs. It must have taken courage, I shall grudgingly admit. This student was alone in her rejection of Aristophanes, and not part of a threesome acting in unison as in the first case. I now regret that I did not interview her more thoroughly, but I think I felt somewhat resentful, based on my previous experiences with this play: it is really hard not to take such rejection of one's teaching personally, and at that stage I did not much feel like talking to her. One of her acquaintances told me that he thought that this student, who came from a conservative religious background, was not herself as conservative as her parents were, but that she may have been reluctant for her parents to know what she was reading. Living at home in a close-knit family, she would not have been able to hide what she was translating from her family, nor presumably would she have wanted to do so.

A colleague of mine who is originally from Germany, was shocked at this student's refusal to read what was being prescribed, and suggested that giving in to her demands may set a dangerous precedent: what would happen if, in future, for example, a Muslim student decided that they did not want to read a text for religious reasons? I could see that this was a potential problem, but I thought that, in practice, this was unlikely to happen. Personally, I have never had any complaints from Muslim students, who comprise a substantial minority both in the South African population and in our student body. Under *apartheid*, although tolerated, Islam was severely marginalized by the powers-that-be, despite being a presence in South African history from the early days of foreign settlement, when it was a religion identified chiefly with the slave population at the Cape.[32] It was also a religion mostly practiced by those who, while not identified as indigenous Africans, were certainly not classified as "white" either. This historical background may go some way to explaining why Muslim students, at least in my experience, seem cautious about speaking out about things that they may find offensive or shocking. By contrast, Christian students, especially fundamentalists, can be vociferous in their condemnation of any-

---

32. Slave-owners at the Cape even encouraged their slaves to convert to Islam, since if they converted to Christianity, their masters would, according to law, have been compelled to set them free.

thing that they perceive as contradicting or "being against" their religion. Since Christianity was until recently South Africa's state religion, and was championed everywhere, particularly in education, it is not surprising that some Christian students should have a sense of entitlement that goes way beyond the simple question of human rights or freedom of religion. People from modern European societies, like Germany, where the education system and public life have for some time been mostly secular in nature, and where a substantial portion of the population would describe themselves as atheists or agnostics, simply do not grasp the extent to which issues of religion still consume many South Africans.

Another suggestion was that we should try to read the bits of *Lysistrata* that are "not about sex." As everyone knows, this is impossible: infused with *double entendres*, witty references to obscure Athenian mating habits, and some not-so-subtle jokes, Aristophanes' *Lysistrata* is, to borrow a phrase from Roald Dahl, a play simply "soaked in sex."[33] It was eventually decided that this student would study a prose author with another colleague of mine, while the rest of the class continued to read Aristophanes' *Lysistrata*. This was admittedly a compromise, but sometimes, as we in South Africa are well aware, a compromise is necessary to keep the peace. And *Lysistrata* is, after all, a play about peace.

LYSISTRATA:
GENDER, CULTURE, AND THE SOUTH AFRICAN CONTEXT

The intense reactions to Aristophanes' *Lysistrata* which I experienced on two separate occasions in the Classics classroom were, I should stress, the responses of an extreme conservative minority within the student body, and are not in any way representative of South African students in general nor indeed of its broader society.[34] As noted, many topics in Classics could elicit this type of reaction. Yet in my experience at least, nothing else has elicited such an intensely negative reaction as this charming comedy about

---

33. In Dahl's novel *My Uncle Oswald,* the heroine Yasmin Howcomely is described as "absolutely soaked in sex" (1979: 96).

34. On the contrary, Betine van Zyl Smit has pointed out that *Lysistrata* is the comedy of Aristophanes most often produced in South Africa (2005: 254). Several Classical scholars in South Africa have worked on Aristophanes, including Betine herself, and earlier, Geoffrey Chapman at the (then) University of Natal. Chapman's inaugural lecture delivered in 1984 (published in 1985) was entitled *Women in Early Greek Comedy: Fact, Fantasy and Feminism* (see discussion in Lambert 2011: 80–81). More recently, Martine de Marre of the University of South Africa has also published on Aristophanes and women (2001: 37–65).

a female sex strike to stop a seemingly endless war. Could the problem lie in the fact that *Lysistrata* so unabashedly portrays adult female sexuality, even if largely within the confines of marriage, a context supposedly sanctioned by Christianity, and of a distinctly fictional variety? Is there such an underlying misogyny in the Christian tradition that its proponents somehow cannot stomach the sexual and political empowerment of women and the foregrounding of female values that the plot of *Lysistrata* endorses? Why is the prospect of women using sex to end a war so problematic? Or is it all simply a result of inexperience and immaturity on the part of the particular students?

I shall analyze and briefly explain what I think was going on in the two cases I have cited taken one by one, given the different cultural contexts and the decade that separates these two occurrences. In the first example, the students were all white male Afrikaners who were studying theology at what was then, even by Afrikaans standards, a very conservative institution. These students would have been at high school during South Africa's first democratic elections, and thus much of their schooling prior to this would have been in the atmosphere of the "Old South Africa." Parental attitudes have been cited as an influential factor in both cases, and in the first case, as we have seen, these are likely to have been extremely conservative. While not all students who reacted negatively would necessarily have been supporters of *apartheid*, it is striking that a "National Christian" approach to education was, in recent memory, the official approach to education sanctioned by the *apartheid* government, and one which continued to be endorsed by the university at which this incident took place.

My point here is that in 1999, because of South Africa's history and also ironically because of the very changes that had been taking place since 1994, those students coming from a Christian background, particularly if white and male, would have had a sense of entitlement that those coming from a different cultural perspective would not have had: as Afrikaner Christian white males, they would have felt entitled to complain and to have their complaints taken seriously. At the same time the seemingly rapid changes that were taking place in the larger South African society may have caused a sense of outrage and a perception that traditional values and customs were breaking down—Lysistrata and her neatly plucked pubic hair were probably just the last straw. The students who walked out of my *Lysistrata* class in the first case were in addition representatives of a peculiarly reactionary group within Afrikanerdom, a minority within a minority: one of the students (not the one who came to speak to me), I was told, was a member of a religious sect called the *Verbondsvolk* ("People of the

Covenant"), a religious group that was extremely right-wing in its views. This group would in all likelihood have opted to return to pre-1994 South Africa or to a facsimile thereof if this were at all possible. My "nationality" (as an English-speaking South African) and female gender may have also been perceived as a problem in this conservative environment. The three students who walked out of my class may well have come from backgrounds in which animosity towards Britain and towards English-speaking South Africans was stressed. Some of these students may have thought that as a woman I should not have been lecturing theological students in the first place, given St. Paul's notorious views on women as instructors. It is quite clear to me that I may have had better luck teaching *Lysistrata* to the Amish.[35]

The second case of Aristophanic resistance, which occurred in 2009, involved, as noted, a particularly religious female student in a secular context. In this case, the student would have been too young to have experienced *apartheid*-style "National Christian" education, having started school around the time of the first democratic elections. Ten years on, most South African schools were by now thoroughly racially mixed, and Christianity, although still the dominant religion, had been tempered by the introduction of comparative religious studies in schools. Although the negative reaction to Aristophanes' *Lysistrata* took a little longer this time (about 24 hours as opposed to being instantaneous), it was also pretty immediate. Like the Afrikaner male students in the first example, the female Christian student did not reject Aristophanes' *Lysistrata* after an in-depth investigation of gender politics in the play,[36] nor after witnessing the hilarious scene between Myrrhine and Kinesias (both slang names for genitals),[37] nor after pondering the possibilities of the "lioness on the cheese-grater" position for intercourse.[38] Rather, simply after attending my introductory lecture and

---

35. See 1 Timothy 2:12: "I do not permit a woman to teach or have authority over a man; she must be silent." This verse is often used to justify the exclusion of women from the priesthood, notably in the particular church which ran the Theological School attached to the university where this incident took place. The three students who boycotted my class were all studying towards degrees in Theology under the auspices of this church, which comprises an extremely conservative minority even within the ranks of the Afrikaner. Since historically, this church even went so far as to warn its members against the dangers of dancing, among other things, they are sometimes jokingly dubbed "South Africa's Amish," with reference to the group called the Amish in the United States. My throwaway line here suggests that the real Amish may not even be so conservative.

36. On this see, e.g., the discussion of Taaffe (1993: 48–73).

37. See the discussion of Stroup (2004: 59).

38. It is uncertain whether the "lioness on the cheese-grater" mentioned at Ar. *Lys.* 231–2 is just an elaborate joke, invented by Aristophanes, or is an actual Athenian fifth-century slang term, used particularly among women, for a sexual position (or is a term Aristophanes and other Athenian men

maybe starting on the translation that was prescribed for homework, the student concluded that the play was not for her.

In this case, the student's perspective may not have been one of entitlement so much as embattlement; she may have perceived herself as the lonely voice of Christian morality crying in the wilderness. Although the student's extreme Christian approach is unusual in contemporary South Africa, for me it is the more worrying of the two examples. I am not entirely satisfied with the resigned manner in which I handled her complaint, although I realize, in retrospect, that my own Christian background and previous experience with similar objections from students resulted in a paralysis brought on by guilt: for all my Classical training and disbelief at the student's degree of conservatism, at the same time some small part of me felt guilty about exposing this pure, saint-like student to the pagan profanities of Aristophanes! But guilt is not a useful emotion. A more important question for me is: what should I do if something like this happens again?

DIALOGUE AND *DIALLAGE:* RECONCILIATION IN THE SOUTH AFRICAN CLASSICS CLASSROOM?

The theories of the twentieth-century Russian thinker Mikhail Mikhailovich Bakhtin on dialogue, Carnival and the lower bodily stratum have often been applied to Aristophanes in recent years—although Bakhtin himself was not unfortunately as forthcoming about Aristophanes as many scholars would have liked.[39] Nevertheless, given the manner in which Bakhtin defined the serio-comical genres of antiquity which he identified as the precursors of dialogic novelistic discourse,[40] it is clear that Aristophanes belongs with them and influenced many of them. Bakhtin comments: "In the ancient period, early Attic comedy and the entire realm of the serio-comical was subjected to a particularly powerful carnivalization."[41] Aristo-

---

would like to imagine sex-mad housewives would use among themselves). Although many scholars have supposed that the "lioness on the cheese-grater" refers to the dorsal-ventral position ("doggy style"), Stroup (2004: 54 n. 32, cf. 55 Figure 5) suggests that it "might refer more generally to an identifiably feline raised-rump posture associated with hunting, claw-sharpening, and sexual availability." Prince, however (2009: 161–70), noting the ferocity, nobility and potentially transgressive domination of the "lioness" image, suggests a variation of the "woman-on-top" position. If a real sexual position is indeed meant, it may have been some variation of what is nowadays called "Reverse Cowgirl," which has the advantage of being both a rear-entry and a "woman-on-top" position.

39. For the application of Bakhtinian theory to Aristophanes, see e.g. Platter (2007: 1–25).
40. See Bakhtin (1984: 106–27).
41. Bakhtin (1984: 129).

phanes' *Lysistrata* lends itself well to interpretation as a "carnivalized" text: first performed on the occasion of the festival of the Lenaia in 411 BCE, this fantasy play celebrates the temporary overturning of male and female social roles in order to bring about an end to the on-going Peloponnesian War. The provocative sex-striking women led by the exemplary Lysistrata engage in the ancient equivalent of "tactical frivolity" as they occupy the Acropolis and the treasury. In her anti-hierarchical *agon* with the magistrate, Lysistrata instructs the *Proboulos* on the lessons that the *oikos* can teach the *polis*.[42]

The men, by contrast, have the tables turned on them: they are stuck at home and are at their wits' end, increasingly desperate househusbands, as their tumescent groins indicate, until they finally agree to stop the war. With its focus on sex as a way to end a war, the play puns throughout on the lower bodily stratum, with clever *double entendres* and constant allusions to sexual practices. In the end, the peace treaty is mapped out on the body of the naked and nubile Reconciliation (*Diallage*). Although I would hesitate to call it a feminist or even proto-feminist piece (apart from Lysistrata, the tippling sex-mad women, almost entirely without any self-control, are all portrayed according to standard ancient Greek stereotypes), in Bakhtinian terms, *Lysistrata* is a thoroughly joyous and life-affirming exercise in hope and renewal. If the original purpose of Aristophanes' obscenities was apotropaic, in other words, to repel evil spirits, envy and the like, what does this say about those whom the rambunctious vivacity of his comedies still chases away nowadays? The answer is far from flattering.

In attempting to apply Bakhtin's ideas to the pedagogical context, it seems that the most applicable one is the concept of dialogue, which informs virtually all of his concepts. It would seem that the most important thing is to keep the students talking about their reactions, even if they admit to finding something shocking. In her chapter in the present volume, Polyxeni Strolonga suggests that lecturers cannot always predict how learners will react to a particular text or topic: she makes the point that while even students from very conservative backgrounds may sometimes surprise us with their openness to new ideas, not every student shocked by an issue under discussion will necessarily feel empowered to voice their reservations in class. Strolonga suggests conducting anonymous questionnaires on students' responses to potentially shocking material in order to give even the shy students a chance to speak out about things that may be bothering

---

42. Ar. *Lys.* 571–86. The wool-treating imagery taken from the women's experience in household tasks is brilliantly applied to the organization of the state. On the question of women and the *oikos-polis* divide, see the reconsideration by Foley (1982: 1–21) of the arguments put forward by Shaw (1975: 255–66).

them. Overall, the expression of shock itself may be a useful didactic exercise: it is healthy for us to acknowledge that not every culture is the same as ours, and that even something written many centuries ago may offend us. Shock may be a useful reaction in that it also shows how a(live) with potential a text like Aristophanes' *Lysistrata* still is. In Bakhtinian terms, Aristophanes' *Lysistrata* is truly "unfinalizable"—always open to new interpretations, and new responses, never a closed book.[43]

---

[43]. I would like to thank Steve Collings of the University of KwaZulu-Natal for looking at my paper from an ethical perspective and for giving it clearance. I would also like to thank the editors and the anonymous readers for their helpful comments.

Pedagogy and Pornography in the Classics Classroom

GENEVIEVE LIVELEY

> Behind the complexities of the arguments about pornography often lies a philosophical discourse about representation and education, seeing and knowing. . . . As a consequence, pornography strikes very deep into the sociocultural formation of education, knowledge and cultural awareness.
> (Wicke 2004: 63)

INTRODUCTION

Questions of whether, when, where and how to introduce sexually explicit, erotic, or pornographic material (in both visual and written form) into the university classroom have been considered on both sides of the Atlantic for several years now, with academics teaching pornography in departments of literature, history of art, law, gender, cultural, and media studies all sharing ideas and answers across different subject disciplines, countries, universities and departments.[1] In the social sciences, arts and humanities, the academic analysis of porn has become a broad and broadly respectable field of scholarship, in which a range of sexually explicit material is subjected to scrutiny. Identified by its academic readers as a distinctively interdisciplinary field (a status it shares with Classics), pornography certainly "jumps many disciplinary boundaries and critical barriers" as it enters the

---

1. See in particular Curry (1996); Kirkham and Skeggs (1996); Kleinhans (1996); Williams (1999) and (2004); Driver (2004); Amy-Chinn (2006); Lehman (2006); Reading (2006); Attwood and Hunter (2009); McNair (2009).

university classroom.² It also forces its teachers and students to re-examine their existing preconceptions and to redraw the lines that distinguish between (for example) high and low—or no—art, public and private, reality and representation.

In this chapter, I want to explore the potential for adopting a cross-disciplinary approach to "professing porn"—or "porno-pedagogy" as Gideon Nisbet describes it—in Classics and ancient history in order to see what we can learn from other subjects and to see what lessons about pornography in the classroom we, in turn, might share.³ It's my contention that the transgressive character of pornography—both ancient and modern—makes it "good to think with" and therefore "good to teach with." As Brian McNair suggests:

> If one task of the academic is to engage and enthuse students, to teach them to think and analyse in a mature and confident manner, then the zone of the sexual is potentially fertile territory. . . . Talking about pornography—its meanings, attractions, functions—brings the private sphere of the bedroom into the public realm of the classroom, and permits engagement with topics that are still difficult to raise in other contexts.⁴

This is not to suggest that pornography in the classroom is an uncomplicated "good thing." Nor do I intend to rehearse here second and third wave feminist arguments against and for pornography—either inside or outside the classroom.⁵ Certainly, the introduction of sexually explicit material (whether or not it involves the representation or humiliation of women) into feminist classrooms can be seen as anti-feminist to the extent that it potentially undermines the "'safe space,' the ethical and democratic environment" with which, as teachers, we aim to provide our students.⁶ However, the preponderance of successful pornography classes taught by feminists in Women's Studies courses across Europe and North America suggests that pornography can be taught safely, ethically, and respectfully—especially in the feminist classroom.⁷

---

2. Wicke (1993: 67).
3. Nisbet (2009: 152 n.4). As part of such "porno-pedagogy," Nisbet suggests (153) that "Pornography is read as a social document . . . or as a gender-and-identity toolkit."
4. McNair (2009: 559).
5. For a "classic" debate on this subject see Richlin (1992b: xii–xxii).
6. Miller-Young (2010).
7. On teaching pornography in the feminist classroom (and for nuanced definitions of the same) see Sedgwick (2003), and Miller-Young (2010). Mireille Miller-Young (2010) defends her teaching of sexually explicit material in the feminist classroom thus (with particular resonance for those of us who teach classes on gender and sexuality in the Classics and ancient history "feminist"

In the Classics classroom it can be difficult to *avoid* teaching pornography. As Catherine Johns has observed in her work on "erotic images" in ancient Greece and Rome, "it is impossible to study either classical antiquities or classical literature without encountering material which is of a forthrightly sexual nature."[8] Indeed, while the line(s) distinguishing the erotic from the pornographic may be drawn differently in different classrooms, Isabel Tang's *Pornography: The Secret History of Civilisation* locates the classical world as the birthplace of modern pornography and identifies the rediscovery of Pompeii (and the creation of the Secret Museum to house its "pornographic" artefacts) as a key moment in the history and pedagogy of pornography.[9]

Inherently interdisciplinary in its subject range, classical pornography embraces sexually explicit material as diverse as the Pompeian and Herculaneum wall-paintings and artefacts once collected in the Naples "secret museum," graphic depictions of sex acts on Attic pottery and Arrentine ware (and related Roman silver ware such as the notorious "Warren Cup"), ancient erotic handbooks, Horace's obscene epodes and Ovid's literary rapes.[10] Add to this, miscellaneous works of reception both inside and outside of the traditionally acknowledged Classical tradition such as the "erotic" classical paintings of the Victorian Pre-Raphaelites, Charles Mee's drama *Orestes 2.0,* HBO's sexually explicit *Rome* series (2005–2007), Starz's graphic series *Spartacus: Blood and Sand* (2010), Adamo's pornographic *Private Gladiator* trilogy (2002), and Guccione's *Caligula* (1979). In showing, reading, and teaching such material, issues of sexual exploitation and the abuse of women, men, children, and animals challenge us at every turn, raising difficult ethical and educational questions too. Drawing upon my own experiences of teaching pornography in British undergraduate and postgraduate classrooms (not as an example of best practice but as a springboard for ideas and a suggestion of possibilities), I will consider not only the pedagogical, personal and professional risks but also the opportunities that may be opened up by the difficult subject of "professing porn."

---

classroom): "I provide techniques for the analysis of pornography as a variant and historically contextualized visual culture, film genre, and sector of the sex industry. Prompting students to consider the technological, socioeconomic, and cultural context of particular images as they are produced, circulated, and consumed also means positing how sex functions as a site of desire, power, and knowledge through the specific textual forms."

8. Johns (1989: 15).
9. Tang (1999).
10. See Grant (1975); Boardman (1978); Johns (1989); Richlin (1992b); Kampen (1996); Blanshard (2010).

PROFESSING PORN

I don't teach any courses dedicated solely to pornography or erotica per se, but I do teach a range of courses in which I make extensive use of sexually explicit material—including some modern pornography. In a course on "Configurations of Gender and Sexuality," for example, I include a range of ancient sources that illustrate various classifications of broadly defined "pornography": straightforward representations of sex acts and images of male and female genitalia (predominantly images and artefacts from Pompeii); representations of the same that *appear* to be designed, at least in part, for the purpose of sexual titillation or arousal (Greek symposium ware and Roman wall paintings, predominantly from Pompeii's *lupanaria* and domestic *tabellae*); representations, not necessarily making direct reference to sex acts or genitalia, involving the sexual humiliation and degradation of men and women (including Catullus' hendecasyllables, Horace's *Epodes*, and Ovid's rapes); and, in a closely related sub-category, representations of prostitutes (drawing upon the etymology of *pornographos* as "whore-writing").[11] Students deal with all of this material intelligently and sensitively, noticing *topoi* and patterns in erotic scenes, exploring issues of gender and power, context and consumption. The material that shocks them most (or makes them least comfortable) is inevitably that which most challenges their preconceptions about sexual behavior (ancient and modern), as based upon their own prior experiences and observations. For them sex is "private," and the presence of attendant *cubicularii* in the background of many pornographic scenes is more disquieting to them than the sex acts shown in the foreground. In a similar vein, the act of bestiality graphically depicted in a Pompeian garden statue group of Pan penetrating a goat shocks them less than the shared eye contact and apparent *tendresse* that the two figures seem to exhibit. And the presence of erotic *tabellae* in the House of L. Caecilius Iucundus (the friendly paterfamilias featured in the Latin textbooks of the Cambridge School Classics Project whom many students first encounter in the school classroom) is regularly the feature that students report as the most personally disconcerting aspect of the course.[12]

In the "Configurations of Gender and Sexuality" course the pornographic material presented to students is exclusively ancient, but in a

---

11. Amy Richlin's Introduction to *Pornography and Representation in Greece and Rome* (1992b) provides one of the best critical orientations for Classicists attempting to map the multifarious and nuanced classifications of pornography.

12. Students report that learning pornographic images were discovered in the House of Caecilius is something akin to discovering porn in the bedrooms of their parents.

course on Ovid's *Ars Amatoria,* as part of a wider analysis of the text's ancient and modern reception as an "obscene" work, I ask students to evaluate a range of modern pornographic and quasi-pornographic responses to it. Alongside various English translations exploiting the pornographic potential of the poem with "erotic" illustrations and titillating blurbs,[13] we look at Walerian Borowczyk's 1983 film *Ars Amandi* or *Art of Love,* and the 1989 special "Sexual Arts Issue" of *Forum* magazine featuring an illustrated translation of the first two books of the *Ars Amatoria* by Peter Jones.[14] Jones presumably deemed the third book more appropriate to the women readers of *Cosmopolitan* and omitted its precepts from his contribution to the *Forum* magazine's special "196 pages (not to be missed!) on oral sex, masturbation, sm, massage, sexual surprises and more. . . . " Indeed, Jones assumes an exclusively heterosexual male audience for his text and shapes his translation and his precepts accordingly—encouraging students to consider the objectification and "othering" of women in books 1 and 2 of the *Ars* from a fresh perspective.

Unlike Jones, Borowczyk incorporates elements of all three books of the *Ars Amatoria* in his classic "porno" *Ars Amandi,* together with features from the *Remedia Amoris* and *Amores.* The elegant cinematography of this work is characteristic of Borowczyk: framing the most explicitly sexual scenes and providing a narrative structure for the film, Borowczyk presents a toga-clad "Ovid" lecturing first to a group of young men and subsequently to a group of young women—roughly mirroring the divisions of the *Ars Amatoria* and suggesting both male and female "students" as Borowczyk's own intended audience. However, the central protagonist of the film is a young woman who, contrary to the conventions of pornographic cinema, remains (for the most part) fully clothed throughout the movie. Indeed, despite the film's publicity blurb claiming that it "tells several stories that teach men how to love and be loved by women," the "Jezebel" label under which the video of the film is produced and distributed also suggests the possibility of a projected audience primarily of *women* as the viewers of this "soft-porn" *Ars*—leading to thoughtful classroom discussions about the gender and

---

13. See Gibson (1996: 4). A particular favorite with students is *The Lover's Manual of Ovid* translated into English by E. Phillips Barker with drawings by A. R. Thomson, published by Basil Blackwell of Oxford in 1931. This translation seeks to supply the *Ars Amatoria* "with an English dress" but rather more successfully supplies it with English undress. Notable are the sexually suggestive line drawings accompanying the text: "Deeper" illustrating a bare-breasted *puella,* and "The New Milky Way," which depicts a naked female sun-bather relaxing while a friend appears to tickle her back with a stick.

14. This special edition of the "Forum Collection" magazine (June, 1989) featured a specially commissioned translation by U.K. Classicist and journalist Peter Jones.

sexuality of Ovid's own target audience (his textual disclaimers notwithstanding) for each of the three books of the *Ars*, as well as a finer appreciation among students as to how this two-thousand-year-old poem might once have offended Augustan *decorum* and laws.[15]

Significantly, students have responded very differently when shown short extracts of this film to when I have asked them to view it in its entirety. The viewing of excerpts has tended to provoke laughter and a superficial commentary, with little attempt made to draw connections between Borowczyk's film and Ovid's poem, whereas extended viewing has elicited far more thoughtful—and often genuinely insightful—discussion about generic codes and conventions; the gaze; different cultural configurations of sex, sexuality and gender; Ovid's own "cinematic" style; the function of humor; and, naturally, the tensions between reality and representation thrown up by both *Ars*. Indeed, my experience of viewing modern pornography in a classroom context echoes that of Mark Jones and Gerry Carlin (Lecturers in English literature at the University of Wolverhampton, who sparked a media storm in the United Kingdom in 2004 for including pornographic films in a course on "Unpopular Texts"). They suggest that:

> Two minutes of pornography is titillating. Ten minutes is boring. Extend the viewing in this environment and critical analysis is the only option left. Watching pornography in a classroom becomes a Brechtian experience, causing discomfort and alienation. Porn then reveals not just flesh, but also its formal conventions, its repetitive narratives, its tableaux of power, its cold ideologies, its descent into bathos.[16]

I would hesitate to characterize my own classroom screenings of Borowczyk's *Ars Amandi* as offering students a wholly "Brechtian" experience: reflective detachment from the material upon the screen is very often compromised by exclamations of humor and revulsion from the students, even after ten minutes viewing or more. However, I too find watch-

---

15. The differently gendered emphases in the publicity material for the film's cinema and video releases are probably the result of a considered marketing strategy and relate to differently gendered audiences: male consumers would be more likely than women to pay to see the film screened in a 1980's porn cinema, whereas women (or heterosexual couples) would be more likely to purchase the film in its video format. On the mass marketing of porn, see Nisbet (2009). My students are often shocked to learn that films such as the *Ars Amandi* would have been viewed in "public" spaces such as "adult cinemas" (while noticing the parallels with their own viewing of the film in the "public" space of the classroom). In the internet age, porn is a "private" business. See Reading (2009) on the internet and teaching porn.

16. Jones and Carlin (2004).

ing extended extracts of modern pornography in the classroom context a useful pedagogical tool: recognizing and analyzing the conventions, narratives, and configurations of sex, gender, and power played out in a modern pornographic context teaches students to recognize and analyze the same features in an ancient text, artefact or image. It may be significant (or at least noteworthy), however, that the "modern" pornography I utilize in this way appears to most of my students as decidedly "old-fashioned." Produced before most of the undergraduates in my classes were born, the sex scenes and naked bodies (male and female) represented in Borowczyk's film of 1983 and the 1989 special "Sexual Arts Issue" of *Forum* magazine graphically illustrate the fact that sex, no less than pornography, is a cultural construct, shaped by the socio-historical conditions, ideologies and aesthetics of its time—just as our responses to it are configured, in turn, by our own twenty-first century cultural horizons.[17] Viewing and discussing pornographic material that is temporally and culturally distant from our own horizon is often easier precisely because of the stance of critical "distance" that it permits us to adopt toward it. And it is perhaps for this reason that I do not include more recent pornography in my teaching: there is a line, it seems, (drawn somewhere towards the end of 1989) that I am unwilling to cross; I am comfortable teaching Guccione's *Caligula* (1979) but not Adamo's *Private Gladiator* (2002). The critical distance I create by staying on one side of this arbitrarily drawn temporal line demarcates a "safe space" both for my students and for myself: a personally no less than intellectually secure space in which I feel *safe enough for now* to take risks as a (female) teacher, as a feminist, and as a Classicist.

This relates, in part, back to my disinclination to describe the pedagogy of pornography as a wholly or straightforwardly "Brechtian" experience. Pornography—whether ancient, modern (or 1980s)—is essentially a "body genre."[18] Different definitions of pornography place different emphases upon the body, so that the label "pornography" might apply to *any sexually explicit material;* to sexually explicit material *primarily or wholly intended to arouse* its viewers/readers; or to sexually explicit material that is *offensive, obscene or disgusting.*[19] In each classification, however, bodies are central to

---

17. Students inevitably comment upon the "hairiness" of the bodies—male and female—and an apparent penchant for orgies in this material, attributing these features to the perverse tastes and aesthetic sensibilities either of the 1980s or (somewhat bizarrely) of "Europeans."

18. See Kleinhans (1996).

19. Definitions of pornography are notoriously problematic. Attempts by scholars of modern pornography to define a history and a genre for their subject by looking back to the ancient world (and especially to ancient etymologies) are both common and commonly confused. See Tang (1999). Reading (2006: 124), for example, suggests saliently that "the boundaries of what constitutes

the definition of pornography: the representation of bodies involved in sex acts and/or the representation of sexual body-parts feature in the broadest definitions; sexual and physical arousal in the bodies of an audience feature in more nuanced definitions; and equivalent bodily reactions involving disgust, trauma, and damage feature in others. Teaching pornography, then, necessarily involves a potentially uncomfortable focus upon bodies—not only those on the screen or in the text, but those in the classroom, too. And while it may be relatively easy to establish and maintain a critical distance from those other bodies on the screen, in the text, or on the page, our own bodies (and those of our students) present more of a challenge. As Nguyen Tan Hoang has pointed out:

> Teaching porn is different from other modes of pedagogy, because it activates and disavows bodily reactions from teachers and students, thus highlighting the fact that both are sexual subjects, [and that] teaching and learning are both embodied practices.[20]

Teaching porn certainly presents a unique set of challenges to both teachers and students in this respect. When I teach ancient comedy, I want students to have an appropriate—that is a physical, bodily—response to the primary material under consideration, as well as to my teaching of it: I want them to laugh. What sort of reaction is appropriate, what sort of response do I want, what response can I expect, from students when I show them sexually explicit, erotic, or pornographic material?

Nguyen's observation that teaching, learning, *and* pornography are each concerned fundamentally (albeit in very different ways) with the body helpfully reminds us that "embodied" responses are always already part of the pedagogic process. As part of this process, I am prepared to risk making both my students and myself potentially "uncomfortable" by dealing with challenging material but I want to manage that potential discomfort as sensitively, sensibly and as ethically as possible.[21] Whenever I bring sexu-

---

pornography are . . . so porous and differentiated over time and between people and places that [only] showing students a specific text can serve to clarify exactly what it is one is critiquing." Her appreciation of the cultural, geographical and historical differences attending pornography in the modern world, however, does not extend to the ancient world and she confidently asserts (also on page 124) that the ancient Greek etymology of pornography reminds us that it means straightforwardly and simply "writing about sexual slavery."

20. Nguyen (2010), cited in Miller-Young (2010).

21. In this respect, teaching pornography shares fundamental similarities with teaching other subjects in the Classics classroom, such as gender and sexuality, or race, power, class and identity, where there is a similar focus upon bodies and 'embodiment.' On the similarities between these

ally explicit material into the classroom, then, I explicitly acknowledge the challenges that it presents to all of us in that room. I encourage students to comment aloud upon what they are viewing or reading while they are viewing or reading it, and I actively participate in this class commentary myself. I encourage students to laugh and giggle at the material they find ridiculous. I provide handouts with (mock-serious) directions that these are to be used as "screens" to hide behind if students see anything that they can't bear to look at. I confess to my own sense of discomfort in teaching this material and (as an inveterate blusher) prepare them to be sympathetic and sensitive to signs of embarrassment in themselves and others. I use pornographic teaching materials only in my teaching of optional, final year, small seminar classes. I introduce the most explicit materials only in the final weeks of each course when students have had time to develop a sympathetic rapport both with their group and with me, and when the classroom environment is a safe and relaxed learning space. I follow the suggestions of other professors of porn and encourage students to "see themselves as lay-experts bringing their own knowledges and opinions to the classroom."[22] I talk to my students, I listen to them, and I adapt my teaching style to suit the requirements of each new group. I remain mindful that I am teaching material of which some colleagues (and some students) disapprove, and which others find merely frivolous. I try to learn from other professors of porn.

PORNO-PEDAGOGY

Two key "lessons" for professors of porn emerge from the extensive body of research written and published on this difficult subject, each of which could be usefully carried across into Classics and ancient history classrooms. The first concerns the importance of content warnings and repeated opportunities for students to "opt out" of viewing, reading, talking, and writing about porn. While it might reasonably be argued that any undergraduate or postgraduate degree in Classics or ancient history *should* include as part of its mandatory syllabus some teaching and learning on issues of gender and sexuality, race, power, class and identity, the case is hard to make for pornography (either "soft" or "hard core") as a "core" topic of study

---

subjects see Miller-Young (2010). See also Endres in this volume on teaching Plato's *Symposium* in the context of a Gay and Lesbian Literature class.
    22. Smith (2009: 574).

in the Classics classroom—despite its obvious intellectual and pedagogical affinities with these other subjects. In Classics and ancient history, courses containing extensive or exclusive reference to pornographic material are unlikely to be core or compulsory for undergraduates, so students likely to be shocked or offended by such material can simply elect not to take the classes in which it features. Even where a course makes no use of modern pornographic images, students can find themselves viewing explicit images of same-sex sex for the first time, discussing masturbation and dildos with their peers, contemplating stories and scenes concerning bestiality, rape, and pederasty—uncomfortable subjects for many undergraduates, upsetting and offensive for a few. It follows then, that proper content warning is essential in enabling students to make informed choices in these circumstances and course descriptions should themselves be explicit about the nature and form of any sexually explicit content. Clearly, the professor of porn must proceed with sensitivity and ensure that her teaching of pornographic material is delivered with the informed consent of her students.

Yet, here, I find myself compromised by the idea that, as university and college teachers, we *should* be challenging our students, forcing them to question their preconceptions, prejudices and beliefs—including (and perhaps especially) those concerning sex and sexuality. Like Peter Lehman, "I tell all my students that if they can get through college without encountering disturbing, upsetting ideas that challenge the belief system they bring into college, they should ask for their tuition money back."[23] As a professor teaching porn in American universities and mindful of the potential for exposure to sexual harassment charges that his subject brings, Lehman acknowledges, however, that "Content warnings or signed student consent forms are . . . a serious pedagogical issue."[24] However much we might want to challenge student preconceptions and prejudices by teaching (with) pornography, we can only do so with their consent.

The use of formal student consent forms may seem slightly excessive in the context of the Classics classroom (particularly in U.K. universities) where the viewing of "hardcore" material (and, hopefully, the risk of lawsuits) is less likely. But one advantage of this approach is that it prompts students at the outset to take the course and its sexually explicit material seriously, to think seriously about their own personal and intellectual engagement with "challenging" material. An appropriately worded content warning can successfully achieve similar results, however—without carrying

---

23. Lehman (2006: 16).
24. Ibid.

quite the same risk of *preparing* students to be shocked and offended as the consent form potentially bears. Again, Lehman offers a useful formulation that might be adapted for use in Classics and ancient history:

> This class includes sexually explicit materials and anyone offended or disturbed by viewing, reading, or discussing such materials should not enroll in the class. If any material should prove unexpectedly disturbing, students should simply leave the screening or lecture and meet with the instructor. . . . Similarly, if any students are uncomfortable with a discussion topic with classmates outside class, during office hours, or at any other time, they should simply indicate that they are uncomfortable and do not wish to discuss the topic further. This course presumes that students have a mature interest in exploring and discussing issues of sexuality and representation in an open and un-pressured environment.[25]

In my own teaching, I tend towards the use of short and relatively low-key content warnings on the unit descriptions that students use when making their option choices, which are then reiterated on the unit program/outline to highlight individual classes where I plan to introduce particularly explicit material—typically: "This unit/class contains sexually explicit material." I then follow this up with a verbal caveat at the start of the first class and again at the start of any subsequent class dealing with the analysis of potentially problematic material. My colleague, Kurt Lampe, who teaches Slavoj Žižek's film, *The Pervert's Guide To Cinema,* and reads Charles Mee's play *Orestes 2.0* (which includes in its dialogue an excerpt from the memoirs of a porn star) as part of a course on Greek tragedy, uses this simple but effective formula: "Warning: this class/drama contains graphic language and content."[26] Indeed, once enrolled in a class that they have been forewarned will contain sexually explicit material, students should, good practice suggests, be given further opportunities to opt out of discussions that make them uncomfortable. Lehman's consent form offers a salient reminder that this right to "opt out" should be extended—and explicitly so—to discussions outside of the classroom, both with other students and with teachers. It is also worth considering the importance of the "opt out" when setting students assignments and assessments, designing essay options and exam papers so that students can again exercise some degree of choice in the material that they are asked to analyze.

---

25. Ibid. 17.
26. *Orestes 2.0* by Charles Mee: http://www.charlesmee.org/orestes.shtml

The second (and related) lesson that Classicists and ancient historians can draw from teachers of porn in other disciplines is the need for candor and openness in every aspect of the teaching process. Some teachers design "ice-breaker" exercises to help establish a community of shared experience based on "confessions" that everyone in the class has already watched, looked at or read some kind of pornography outside of the classroom; others require their students to keep an online journal, wiki or blog recording their expectations of and responses to the class and the material studied within it; almost all stress the value of personal honesty and frankness on the part of the teacher.[27] An open dialogue between teacher and students appears to be the hallmark of ethical porno-pedagogy and various strategies to manage this are readily open to Classicists and ancient historians: we can ensure that we only teach porn in sufficiently small seminar groups so that we are able to monitor discreetly each and every student's participation and engagement; we can reserve the teaching of porn to students in their final year when they should have already developed sufficient confidence and experience in sharing their ideas openly in the classroom; we can talk openly and honestly with our students about our own sexual subjectivities, and our own attitudes and responses to pornography; and we can listen carefully and respectfully when students talk.

Indeed, Alan McKee's inspiring article on professing porn—"Social Scientists Don't Say 'Titwank'"—makes a strong case for encouraging students to develop and use an appropriate critical vocabulary in their studies of sexually explicit material, suggesting that the formal language used by teachers and academics can have a distancing effect in discussions and analyses of pornography which is not always desirable in the classroom.[28] It is essential to have an open discussion with students at an early stage as to the critical idiom and language that is to be used in the classroom and in written assignments (which may not be the same). But, in my experience, different students and different classes feel comfortable using different modes of expression: some students and some groups prefer the critical distance engendered by more formal language (discussing "breasts" instead of "tits," for example), whereas others feel most comfortable bringing the same language they use outside of the classroom into class and into discussions. I often receive emails from students asking whether it's acceptable for them to use colloquial phrases (such as "fucking") in their essays and dissertations (sometimes it is) and now include McKee's essay in relevant

---

27. See McNair (2009) and Miller-Young (2010).
28. McKee (2009).

reading lists to help assuage fears that "Classicists don't say 'fuck'" (sometimes we do).

CONCLUSIONS

As Classicists, we may be cautious about how we engage with pornography in the classroom—particularly in its modern configurations. And we are right to be cautious. As Henry Jenkins advises in his essay "So You Want to Teach Pornography?"

> Go in with your mind open. Make responsible and ethical decisions. Be ready to promote an intellectual rationale for your decisions. And watch your back.[29]

There is a lot at stake in porno-pedagogy. Get it wrong and we risk, at best, a giggling group of students assuming that their own "lay-expertise" qualifies them to assess and/or dismiss any sexually explicit material uncritically; at worst, alienated, offended and upset students, and hostile colleagues. But the rewards of teaching pornography—or, perhaps a better formulation for Classicists and ancient historians might be teaching *with* pornography—is well worth these risks. In courses on sexuality and gender, on Greek and Roman art, on the Roman elegists, and on the Classical tradition, some degree of engagement with pornographic material is almost impossible to avoid. And, as Gideon Nisbet points out,

> ... we *should* engage with it, if we are at all serious about our declared interest in reception of the ancient world in contemporary popular culture, because pornography is *the* definitive popular-cultural form: a global economy and language whose representations of the ancient world are in some ways the best index we have of what [the ancient world] means. . . .[30]

So, pornography—both ancient and modern—is both a necessary and a desirable feature of the contemporary Classics classroom, it seems. Our challenge is to teach it ethically and responsibly.

---

29. Jenkins (2004: 7).
30. Nisbet (2009: 154). Thanks to Kurt Lampe, Alex Wardrop, Vanda Zajko, and all the students in my Configs of Gender and Ovid classes.

Challenges in Teaching Sexual Violence and Rape
A Male Perspective

SANJAYA THAKUR

INTRODUCTION

Subjects such as rape and violence against women are encountered in a myriad of different texts in various genres and in nearly every course offered by Classics departments. Yet, discussion of them is often avoided. And it is an obvious reality—but it is worth pointing out here—lots of men teach Classics courses. Yet, while attending the 2008 Feminism and Classics conference, and then the subsequent APA/AIA roundtable and panel in 2009, I was struck by how few men were in attendance. At the 2008 Feminism and Classics conference, only about 15 percent of the attendees were male. At the roundtable in 2009, for most of the session I was the only male in attendance, though two others eventually joined the group that had at least twenty participants. So, while much fruitful discussion has transpired on the topic of teaching sensitive issues and the texts in which they occur, few men have become involved.

I believe the standard practice for many men is to steer clear of discussions (or even acknowledgment) of sensitive and possibly controversial topics in the classroom. In informal conversations with a number of colleagues at other institutions such impressions have been reinforced. The majority of individuals I have spoken to are aware that these issues are prevalent in the texts we cover and on the minds of our students, and yet they say that they avoid teaching subjects such as rape for a variety of reasons:

(1) their desire not to offend, (2) they are afraid to somehow treat them "inappropriately," and they perceive they do not possess adequate knowledge or training to discuss such topics, (3) their own comfort level with the material and subject, (4) their uncertainty of how even to begin a discussion about them, (5) they find them (or believe their colleagues and superiors might find them) unsuitable for discussion in an academic setting, (6) they hope other faculty or departments will cover them. Consequently, most often they avoid any mention of, let alone engagement with, these issues. Yet these are issues that should and must be discussed.

Many male junior faculty members with whom I have spoken are also concerned that one misstep (in which they come across as insensitive or do not handle issues "properly") might ruin their careers.[1] Some colleagues have reported to me fears (whether rightly or wrongly based) that students might take issue with such discussions on their evaluations, and that their evaluations will be lower as a result. Since such evaluations are critical in tenure reviews for many, the answer is to "play it safe" and avoid topics which might cause conflicts, ill-will, or elicit contentious feelings or discussions. Some feel apprehensive that they are traversing into subjects where female faculty "own" the exclusive purview and authority. A second challenge is far more subtle—that men lack (or feel that they lack) a support community or network. The truth is the scholarship on rape and sexual violence against women is dominated by female scholars.[2] Even if one were to glance at the contributors of this volume, few men would be found. Many men still, I think, hear the word/term "feminist" and equate it with some sort of innate hatred of men, or dismissal, rejection and illegitimacy of male perspectives, and thus feel they have no authority to offer their own scholarship on these subjects.[3] I remember reading the first line of Amy Richlin's (1992a) article "Reading Ovid's Rapes": "A woman reading Ovid faces difficulties." and I immediately thought, "Wait, I do too! And so should (and do) men."[4] The stereotype still exists that men will be looked down upon

---

1. Female instructors face their own set of challenges, some of which are discussed in James's chapter.

2. Male scholarship on sexuality has primarily been focused on homoerotic relationships between males.

3. For some historical perspective see Hallett (1993) and Richlin (1993).

4. I am using Richlin's line here as a bit of a strawman—it will become clear that I have great admiration for the article and Richlin's work. However, my thoughts on the line are that it creates a barrier and sense of exclusivity, rather than acknowledging that every reader should be uncomfortable with Ovid's depictions of sexual violence and abuse. I do not think her omission is intended as a slight, by any means, but I believe it is reflective of a perception that men cannot appreciate these texts or relate to them in the same way women can, perpetuating a gender segregation in scholarship and study, and the stereotype that one can only teach sexuality as it directly relates to your own

or not accepted as legitimate scholars if they teach or write about these subjects. These are challenges for men who want to discuss such topics, and many must also combat stereotypes from other men who still believe that these issues should be written about and discussed by women (one anecdote I share below will hopefully dispel this myth). Some men have reported to me that they feel they risk alienation at both ends of the spectrum, from feminists who believe they lack training, expertise and understanding, and from males who define their teaching and scholarship as anomalous or inappropriate. But these perceptions are not true, I can attest to a group of scholars who have welcomed male participants and would give advice to any scholar, no matter their gender. The degree to which these concerns are valid varies, but I will advise that by carefully planning and situating such discussions, negative outcomes might be lessened when compared to the positive feedback students might provide. Some of these are issues related to perceptions of authority. I have found it important to make an upfront statement that any non-victim cannot truly understand what a victim has gone through, but I think as a scholar and teacher that a discussion of sensitive issues, like rape and sexual violence, has a place in the classroom.

I would argue that avoiding a discussion of rape and sexual violence is irresponsible. Students are made aware of issues such as rape and sexual violence from their very arrival on most college campuses, through events at orientation and various programs throughout their college career.[5] Furthermore, arguments that these topics are or should be handled by others are simply an excuse to avoid engagement. So how does one responsibly teach and become comfortable leading discussions concerning this material? I hope to offer some suggestions and advice, drawn from my own experience.[6]

I want to share one recent event which has fomented my resolve that men must be involved in these discussions in the Classics classroom. In preparation for this piece I reached out to my colleagues and took the

---

gender. But I believe in the past twenty years since that article was written discussion of "troubling" subjects has moved beyond being merely acceptable, to being expected that all professors will discuss these issues in literary texts. Also see Lauriola (2011) and Widdows (2011). Widdows's article is an excellent companion piece to this chapter; there she details some of the challenges facing a woman teaching rape texts at an all-male college.

5. At my institution such issues are discussed during (at least) four separate events students are required to attend during freshman orientation. I am confident in asserting that such issues receive similar prominence during orientations around the country. Also various awareness campaigns are almost ubiquitous on college campuses throughout the year.

6. It is quite possible many will disagree with my approach or have other suggestions. I believe a good place for such continued dialogue is the Cloelia website, found at http://wccaucus.org/.

opportunity to visit classes where subjects such as rape and sexual violence were being discussed. It was in one particular course that I realized the power and significance a male voice discussing these issues can have. The subject being discussed was rape, and a student forwarded his opinion that rape really did not have a clear definition, and seemed unable to define (in his mind) consent.[7] I decided (politely, but firmly) to involve myself and challenge the student's definitions, preconceptions and general ignorance in the course of the class discussion. I may not have changed his opinion, but it was the impact on the other students which was significant. I was struck by the amount of feedback I received after the class. Numerous students emailed me; in particular it was female students who stated things like, "thank you for demonstrating that not all men have such ignorant opinions" and "you challenged him in a way I never could have." The most significant thing for me was that students, and even the female instructor, stated that they were uncomfortable directly engaging the student in the way that I did. The instructor elaborated, stating that the fact the response came from a male gave it a different level of validity in the eyes of some of the students. Perceptions are important, and I realized afterwards that although an absence of male voices addressing these issues might not in any way be a validation of them, some students might interpret silence in such a way. For this reason I am adamant that these topics are not exclusively female issues, but issues which ought to be discussed whenever they appear in texts in our classes.

Though I now realize how important it is to address these issues in the classroom, I once avoided teaching and discussing them, although I would not say it was a conscious decision. It was upon hearing Sharon James's paper at Feminism and Classics V and doing research for my own gender and sexuality course that I began to recall all the times I had heard, for example, the story of the rape of the Sabine women, and how the fact that it was a rape was glossed over.[8] Much like later artistic depictions of the event (such as Rubens's famous painting), or even Livy's own summary of the aftermath of the rape, the violence and details of the actual event were not mentioned. I then realized that I too had avoided in directly engaging with such topics, there and elsewhere in teaching ancient literature and culture.

I do not need to state that sexual violence is prominent in our society, especially on college campuses. But I do think some statistics are worth citing, especially when one considers the audience present in a classroom.

---

7. To be honest, I have not encountered this attitude in one of my own classes; what I hope to emphasize here is the impact a discussion of such issues in a Classics classroom might have.

8. Now published as James (2008).

There is a possibility, nay, probability, that some students in your classroom have been, or will be, the victims of sexual assault.[9] I also think it is important to describe where I teach and what courses I teach to illustrate how and in which contexts I address these issues. I teach at Colorado College, a small liberal arts college of about two thousand students. Our students take only one class at a time, for a month, each class session about three hours in length. The result is that classes often have the feel of a graduate seminar, in that in depth discussions are commonplace. I taught a course on "Gender and Sexuality" for the first time in 2008–9, and regularly since. In preparation for that course I spent a great deal of time selecting texts and translations, and reflecting on what I wanted my students to learn in the course. My strategy has been to try and select a broad range of texts from Greek and Roman culture and pair each with select scholarly articles that emphasize a different theoretical approach or focus on a different aspect of gender/sexuality. I am primarily concerned with the role of women in society and literature, but the course has included extended discussions of pederasty, homoerotic relationships between men, between women, sexual violence, and rape. In each other course I teach I now include a unit on the role of women and address "troubling subjects" where they occur in literature. For

---

9. Sharon James's chapter in this volume addresses the issue of having a perpetrator of sexual violence in your classroom. Government statistics (Fisher et al. 2000: 10) show about 5% of female students will or have been victims of sexual assault, but even the authors of the study acknowledge the numbers are probably much higher. Colleges and universities are required by the Clery Act to report the number of incidents that occur on campus (Officially the *Jeanne Clery Disclosure of Campus Security Policy and Campus Crime Statistics Act, and the Higher Education Opportunity Act*. My thanks to Dr. Heather Horton, the former Sexual Assault Response Coordinator at Colorado College, who provided me with these statistics and bibliography, and discussed the variability in reporting procedures around the country). If one is interested in examining the statistics at a specific college or university, or gathering aggregated data from groups of institutions, the following website contains such information: http://ope.ed.gov/security/. A few notes of caution when looking at Clery Act statistics: first of all they only reflect officially reported incidents. Second, they include only events that occur on campus, on public property adjacent to campus (i.e., sidewalks) and non-campus property—some institutions define fraternity houses, under this category, but others do not, creating a great deal of variability about how different campuses compile their data. Events that occur, for instance, in off-campus student housing are not included in the Clery reporting (although some institutions, my own being one of them, include them in their annual reports). Third, counselors (for example) who receive information in confidence are not required to report, so many campuses do not have data that might be reported to those individuals. Counselors could report such acts without naming particular individuals to maintain confidentiality, but are not required to do so. Such decisions are at the discretion of the college or university. Some campuses work with the counseling staff to collect aggregate data which is included in the Clery reporting. Some institutions report very low numbers of sexual assaults for a year (sometimes zero); perhaps they are accurate, but one must wonder about the means in which they collect data and the consequences of "disguising" the actual number of assaults associated with their institution to increase their statistics/reputation at the expense of those who have been, and could be, victimized.

example, I teach Livy 1, a text I am going to focus upon below, in three different courses—a freshmen introductory Classics seminar, Roman History, and in my course on Gender and Sexuality. Obviously all three courses have a different focus, and different constituencies, but my goals in each are primarily those I stated above—to consider how the scenes of rape and sexual violence are presented in the context of the works in which they occur, how a particular author characterizes the details therein, and how the choice to present sexual violence and rape affects the broader narrative. As an Ovidian scholar I know these subjects are central to the proper presentation of such texts as the *Metamorphoses* and the *Ars Amatoria*, and likewise for nearly all ancient texts.[10] Even though my experiences have been shaped, in part, by the institution at which I teach, I have tried in what follows to offer some suggestions which could be applied no matter the type of institution and size of course being offered.

CLASSROOM ADVICE[11]

I have divided this section of my paper into three parts: (1) activities to undertake before entering the classroom, (2) suggestions for time in the classroom itself, and (3) activities related to time outside of the classroom.

(1) Prior to Entering the Classroom

Before entering the classroom and introducing "troubling subjects" in class, proper preparation is paramount. And by this I mean preparation on a number of fronts. First, I advise reading scholarship on the particular texts you will be examining. This seems like a no-brainer, but it may take time to find scholarship which aligns with your own approach. I like to select one article which I share with students, sometimes to be read by all as an assignment, in other cases as supplemental reading for those who might be interested in pursuing issues further. I will provide two examples when I discuss Livy and Ovid below. Furthermore, if you are not sure how to begin

---

[10]. I actually end my Gender and Sexuality course with Ovid. I think he is by far the most challenging and complex author to teach. His treatment of rape and violence are so nuanced, and in the case of the *Metamorphoses*, so varied, it makes instruction (and reading) quite challenging. Richlin's article (1992a) that I mentioned above (and will return to below) is a must read. See also Curran (1984) and Johnson (1996).

[11]. For other useful advice see James's chapter in this volume.

a discussion, or are unfamiliar with literature that might be applicable to the texts you are studying, most colleges and universities have Women's Studies departments or programs (or similar), and I know that faculty/staff in these areas would be thrilled to see that, rather than avoiding these issues, instructors are willing to engage with such topics. I even think an email to colleagues can be appropriate, not only asking how others approach these topics, but if they include such discussions in their courses.

I think one of the most critical steps that instructors can take is to create a well-balanced syllabus which gives students the opportunity to engage with these issues across a range of texts. I often create assignments where a student might discuss at greater length the issues and scenes we read about, after some personal reflection and thought about what transpired in the classroom. It is also worth noting that there is always a level of apprehension—you never know how each class, or student, will react to the material, but if well-prepared one can alleviate many of the pressures related to teaching these topics.

Subjects such as rape elicit deep emotional responses; I always include a friendly reminder in introducing the discussion that students should focus upon specific topics, words, themes or moments in the text, rather than offering general opinions or statements. Being prepared for a range of responses, including silence and temerity, is crucial. For example, some students tend to think their experience is universal, to think exclusively within their own cultural experiences, and have difficulty understanding other cultures and societies, let alone ancient ones. Others view history progressively and deal in absolutes—"ancients were savages, now we are civilized." When confronted with texts and scholarship that fly in the face of their views, they often adhere all the more strongly to them. Others absolve or dismiss these issues in the text as characteristic of ancient societies and beliefs and not applicable to modern cultures. When they start to deal with the ramifications of what they are reading about, discussing, and learning, the experience can be transformative—that, in certain instances, ancient literature deals with these issues far more directly than can be found in many canonical modern texts.[12] Though you cannot predict how every student may respond to a text, you can consider various scenarios and plan accordingly, especially with regard to your initial approach to the topic.

---

12. For example, Ovid's *Amores* 1.7 (see Greene 1999), 2.13 and 14.

(2) In the Classroom

A classroom discussion or lecture on rape in texts is not something to spring on students. I always begin the course, or portion thereof, with an introduction. I do not have a formal statement I read, because I think it would make a difficult subject feel all the more rigid and uncomfortable. I always begin with an introduction to the material and what issues I want the class to focus upon. I include in that introduction a discussion of student attitudes, and my expectation for participation. I state that I expect students to participate in the discussion, but if they feel uncomfortable for some reason with a certain aspect or direction of the discussion they can remain silent.[13] After class I make sure to sit down privately with those students and discuss why they chose not to participate, allowing them to discuss the topics with me in a more comfortable space, or steering them towards counseling if warranted. If I do send a student to a counselor, I make sure to follow up and check on their wellness. I think it is important to remember that just because you, the instructor, feel comfortable discussing these topics not all students will, for a variety of reasons. Though I want them to become aware of these issues, to think about these topics, and hear them discussed openly, I personally do not want students to do so until they feel ready. I try to keep students involved, and say that if a student does not feel comfortable they should talk to me before class. I also advise making available a list of resources for students who might need to deal with, or would like to discuss, events or issues within their own lives. I want to create a venue for students to discuss these issues/experiences where they might be more comfortable and, where they can, in certain cases, receive the help that they need. Such a list might be comprised of a campus Dean of Students, sexual response coordinator, counselor, chaplain, etc. You might also provide a list of local resources/organizations outside your college or university, as some students believe that information, even though confidential, will be spread on campus, and "people" will find out. In addition, some have counselors whom they have seen in the past or find the idea of leaving campus more comfortable. My goal is to find them the help they might need, wherever that may be.

I want to prepare the classroom for a respectful discussion of such topics and facilitate dialogue, and to create an environment that fosters discus-

---

13. For example, when discussing Livy 1, if a student remains silent in our discussion on the rape of the Sabine women, I try to involve them in discussions of other episodes in the book where they might feel more comfortable.

sions, reflective thought, and maintains respect for every person's viewpoint, even if they initially might be extreme.[14] I try to stress the following: I begin with the simple caveat that these are indeed sensitive issues that are going to be discussed. I directly address what we are discussing (rape, pederasty, sexual assault). I am clear with my goals for the class session, typically how an author presents the issue in a certain text and how such choices affect our reading and interpretation.[15] If I am concerned about how a group may respond, I offer a series of questions for students to consider and have them take a few minutes to write a response—this diminishes the chances of a someone thoughtlessly shouting something out (though it still happens in their writing, but at least there is time for some reflection). I direct students to consider how such issues function within the text and how an author presents a story. I then use my knowledge of literature, ancient culture and history to develop their understanding of both the text itself and the historical circumstances which led to its production. And I share such information with my students. Though it might not be completely possible, my goal is that everyone should feel that the classroom is a safe space, and to assist in this effort I tell students to think before they speak, and to avoid personal anecdotes in discussion, as these are often tangential and highly emotionally charged—keep the focus on texts.[16] In general, my experience is that participation is almost universal, what is a greater challenge is focusing the discussion on the texts in question and how the "troubling" subjects actually function within them.

One must be aware of the pressures certain students feel, in particular those who might have experienced sexual violence in some form.[17] I lecture

---

14. In such (rare) cases where I have found students who initially might espouse extreme viewpoints (like in certain circumstances that acts of sexual violence can be condoned), I try to dispel the belief by engaging with the student, or moderating a discussion closely. I see my role as an educator; I want to force students to explicate their positions and demonstrate that they need to be founded on more than impressions. One cannot convince all, rather, as I stated in my earlier anecdote, being a vocal advocate and ally is a role I see as important.

15. If one is lecturing, or even in class discussions, I think it is advisable (at least at the beginning stages of teaching these subjects) to concentrate on the role such acts serve in a purely literary context. I have found students like to speculate about society and offer general thoughts on a topic, but are less inclined (as with many topics) to investigate in depth how an author presents a certain issue within a text.

16. Students might include such personal details (if they deem them applicable) in written assignments, but they are directed to focus on the texts in question. I encourage them to speak with a qualified counselor if they wish to discuss personal experiences. I hate to be blunt, but I am not a psychologist or counselor, and am unqualified to handle such issues properly—I encourage students to address such issues with qualified staff by providing a list of people whom they can talk to on campus.

17. Some statistics are cited in fn. 9 above.

on respect, especially in cases where students might disagree with an opinion put forth in a scholarly article, by another student in the classroom or the professor. One should also be cognizant that there is also pressure on male students in these classes. In many Greek and Roman texts males, generally speaking, do not come off looking that enlightened. Males might feel under attack, and thus overreact—again I have found it is important to keep the focus on the text at hand. Be prepared to act as mediator as much as instructor and make sure to remind students to leave the day's discussion in the classroom, if discussions become heated. More often I have found students express a general frustration with ancient (and modern) attitudes towards issues of sexual violence. You can close your discussion with a reminder that resources are available for those who want to discuss personal issues in response to reading/discussing the selected text(s) and post online, or have available in your office, a list of individuals students might contact.

(3) Post-Class

It is critical to create a space for students to synthesize what this all means—I think reflection in a writing assignment is best. By the end of my gender course I ask students a question about rape in select episodes from Ovid's *Metamorphoses* (though they have the option of writing about issues of rape and sexual violence at earlier moments in the course). As I said at the outset, I discuss "troubling" issues in a range of different texts at numerous moments in each course; often I make the assignment question dealing with "troubling" topics reflective across a course or unit, so students have time to digest what they have read and discussed.

I think many men (and women) are terrified at the thought of a student entering a faculty member's office and revealing that they have been raped or have been the victim of some form of sexual violence, and I can tell you it does, and might happen. Realize the trust the student is placing in you. Be sympathetic and offer your support, but know to whom you should refer the student, and take the appropriate steps to ensure their personal safety and welfare. Every college or university has a different power structure, but I think asking the Dean of Students' office and finding contact information for your sexual response coordinator (or similar) is crucial.[18] However, this

---

18. Each college or university should have policies if you do discover something has happened to a student while enrolled at your institution. If, as often happens, something has occurred prior to the student's enrollment at your institution, you should have contact information for counseling

is clearly a situation which we as professors are not professionally trained to deal with. Know the policies of your college or university. Concentrate on dealing with issues that arise in the classroom or assignments. Be prepared to discuss questions students have about an assignment, but recognize that these might lead to revelation of a personal issue. Direct the student to seek help, separate from the course, then work with the student on the assignment.

Let me repeat, awkwardness and nervousness are normal feelings in treating these subjects. The greatest challenge is that you never really know how an individual student, or class, will react to the material and even how you might react to their statements. Frankly discussing these topics with other faculty, staff and colleagues before you teach can help one prepare, especially in making oneself more comfortable talking about such topics. These issues can be personal and elicit highly-charged, emotional responses. I have found the best way to approach them is to place them in a scholarly context. For the remainder of this chapter I want to take a close look at a pair of episodes from Livy's first book, the rape of the Sabine women and the rape of Lucretia, and offer a few observations, primarily to get the ball rolling to reveal some different avenues one can pursue when examining text and the issues of rape and sexual violence that occur therein.

LIVY 1: A CASE-STUDY

Livy 1 is a good example of a text that is frequently taught in a range of introductory Roman civilization and Roman history courses. The episodes of rape and sexual violence therein should be discussed and acknowledged because these episodes are critical to any reading of the book and Livy's work in general. First consider how the issues of sexual violence relate to your lesson plan, i.e., what do you want the students to get out of the text. My goal is for students to recognize how both the female characters and acts of violence committed against them (and occasionally by them) function within the context of the book and Livy's work as a whole. I also want to look beyond the acts of violence in and of themselves to consider why an author chose to center episodes around acts of violence against women.

---

services at your institution available. In my case students have not revealed that they have been victims of rape during my "gender and sexuality" course, but during other courses. It is no secret that I teach a course on gender and am involved with our Feminist and Gender Studies program. One cannot generalize about why individual students feel comfortable coming to particular faculty members, but they do.

I focus on Livy's language and imagery, how he presents these scenes both in and of themselves, in relation to each other, and to other episodes within the book. My comments here will be brief, but I hope illustrative of the multitude of directions one can take in reading and discussing these episodes.[19] I also couple ancient texts with scholarly articles. Students see how Classicists and academics have researched, thought about, and discussed these issues at length. Good articles can offer greater historical depth and background than one can in the best of lectures or discussions. Furthermore, they can offer different perspectives than your own.

Rape of the Sabine Women

The rape of the Sabine women is an abduction story, but non-consensual sexual intercourse between the Roman men and their Sabine captives is one of the outcomes. In fact repeated sexual acts must occur until the women become pregnant and are able to help populate the growing city. Livy begins the episode by explaining (1.9ff.) why the Romans needed wives, and how neighboring tribes were unwilling to intermarry because of the dubious origins of Romulus' citizenry. Livy details how Romulus carefully plans and executes the seizure of the women. Romulus sends envoys to announce the festival, and decorates Rome. Upon their arrival, the guests take tours of the town, the spectacle then begins, and a signal is given. The men race (*discurrit*, as a single collective) to snatch young women (*virgines*) and the beautiful ones (*excellentes forma*) are given to senators; at this point I pause for a discussion on the relationship between beauty and sexual violence in ancient literature and myth.[20]

Livy then moves to the girls' parents; conspicuously absent are the girls' reactions beyond a single line.[21] Livy follows with the awkward scene of Romulus trying to comfort the young women as if they had all somehow

---

19. I include selections from Livy 1 in the courses I mentioned above. The book receives greater focus (and is read in its entirety) in my course on "gender and sexuality." The bibliography on these episodes is immense, but I have found the found the following studies particularly valuable: Arieti (1997), Bryson (1986), Claassen (1998), Joplin (1990), Stevenson (2011); focusing on the Sabine women: Hemker (1985), Miles (1995: 180–219), Wiseman (1983); focusing on Lucretia: Calhoon (1997), Donaldson (1982), Feldherr (1998: 194–203), Matthes (2000: 23–50).

20. The relationship between beauty and rape is discussed in my "gender and sexuality" course, in which texts such as Ovid's *Ars Amatoria* are also read. The issue/myth of behavior, beauty and dress as somehow provoking and condoning acts of sexual violence is one my students are eager to discuss and dispel.

21. *Nec raptis aut spes de se melior aut indignatio est minor:* "The stolen maidens had no more hope for themselves, nor were less indignant."

been gathered together, and telling them to soften their anger (*mollirent iras*), and that "often gratitude arises from injury" (*saepe ex iniuria postmodum gratiam ortam*). The class discusses why Livy presents Romulus and the episode this way. The first sentence in section 10 illustrates the further glossing over of the girls' emotions: *iam admodum mitigati animi raptis erant; at raptarum parentes tum maxime sordida ueste lacrimisque et querellis civitates concitabant.*[22] It is the parents who look like the victims of rape, and it is they who must resist Romans. The class considers Livy's conclusion that women, by nature, are won over by sweet words,[23] the stereotypes of women and men perpetuated by this episode, and how such a "happy" ending sets the stage for the women to intercede later between their Sabine families and Roman husbands.

I couple my reading of Livy 1 in my "gender and sexuality" course with Sandra Joshel's article on Lucretia and Verginia (1992). I have found the article an apt companion to discussions because, in addition to being well-written, it reviews a range of episodes, not all of which one can discuss in detail in class. Joshel (1992: 117) illustrates how, for Livy, "innocent women were raped or killed for the sake of preserving the virtue of the body female or body politic." I agree with her characterization of women as "catalysts" for male action (1992: 121), except in that it reduces the violence committed against these women to a literary motif. Joshel asserts that, "women function as obstacles or embody spaces, often between and separating men" (1992: 121) and that "the space that is Woman is equated with a chastity that should render the space of the home or between men impenetrable" (1992: 122). Thus rape, or attempted rape, appears as a penetration of space. For Joshel, Livy's women and the actions committed against them are viewed almost exclusively within the literary context of Livy's work. In some sense this further distances the reader from the graphic violence committed. One of her arguments is that such extreme actions in the text are necessary for the episodes to achieve their desired effect (1992: 123). And she goes on to explain the role the sexual violence plays in Livy, providing historical background for the period in which Livy is writing and his literary goals for the work.

---

22. "Now already the spirits of those seized had been mitigated; but then at that moment the parents of those seized, with befouled clothes, were attempting to arouse their states to some action with both tears and complaints."

23. *Accedebant blanditiae virorum, factum purgantium cupiditate atque amore, quae maxime ad muliebre ingenium efficaces preces sunt.* "These arguments were reinforced by the endearments of the men, who excused their actions by their desire and love, which represent effective entreaties beyond all others in appealing to a woman's nature." On the use of *blanditae* see Miles (1995: 205–8).

Joshel's point that (1992: 125) "for history to be a source of models for emulation, it must demonstrate an unequivocal pattern" helps to explain why sexual violence against women becomes a theme in Livy; for it to serve this function it must be repeated and occur to such an abnormal degree that the events become memorable. In light of these arguments my classes discuss how women are objectified and silent at moments which they might be most vocal.

For all its excellent points, the article does not try to comprehend sexual violence and the act of rape itself on a human level, rather focusing on its representation in literature. To examine the depiction of sexual violence and its presence in this episode, I introduce Ovid's *Ars Amatoria* 1.101–34.[24] For those who argue that the rape of the Sabines should solely be read as an abduction story, or that such activity was somehow more socially acceptable then, I turn to Ovid. The story of the rape of the Sabine women forms a long digression in Ovid's discussion of where to find women in Rome. He attests that the circus has a long history of being such a place, and introduces the episode in this way. Ovid's focus is solely on the abduction scene itself and does not address the unwelcome sexual advances that soon followed, nor is his conclusion to the episode satisfactory for most modern readers. But I would argue his text does introduce the rapes themselves into a reader's mind, forcing one to consider the fate that followed the capture of these young women. I often give the passage to students in class and use it to initiate discussion or as a companion piece following an initial discussion of Livy 1.

I am also interested in how one text informs reading of the other. Students do then have to consider the episode in the context of the *Ars Amatoria* 1 (a text which is assigned in my "gender and sexuality" course). In Ovid's version the focus falls on different aspects of the myth, and he emphasizes female perspective at points in his storytelling. In Livy the men are *Romana iuventa*, in Ovid *viri*, and so at the outset of Ovid's version, the tone of the abduction changes, as Ovid includes an age disparity between abductor and abducted (cf. *viros*, 102, *puellam*, 109, *virginibus*, 116). The women are first the objects of the male gaze (109). The women are objectified and considered booty (*praeda*, 114), soon to be grasped by the men's *cupidas manus* (116).

Ovid follows with a pair of similes which compares the girls to doves and young lambs, and the men to eagles and wolves. These similes empha-

---

24. Ovid also provides a version in the *Fasti* 3.187–234. The story is also found in Cic. *Rep.* 2.12–14, Dion. Hal. 2.30–47, Plut. *Rom.* 14–19.

size that the girls are absolutely terrified (*timidissima*, 116, full of fear again in 119, *timuere*, and pale, 120), but the simile also masks the actual physical abduction of the young women. I always pause discussion at this point to reflect on Ovid's choice to present the scene in this way and how such imagery creates certain impressions and feelings for the reader. Ovid continues to drive home the girls' fear (*timor,* 121, 126).[25] He then immerses the reader in the chaos of the scene, moving the reader from person to person, and adding depth to our imagined vision, as well as focusing on individuals here and there to populate the scene (*pars . . . pars,* 122; *altera . . . altera,* 123; *haec . . . haec, haec . . . illa,* 125).[26] The men, in contrast, operate as a collective; they lack individual identity and struggle to capture the women, again objectified as booty (*praeda,* 125), prizes of battle for the warrior Romans.

Ovid closes the episode with a direct quotation from one of the Roman men: "Why do you ruin your tender eyes with tears? What your father is to your mother, I will be this to you."[27] The contrast in tone and image between this line and those which precede it is striking. It also makes a wonderful talking point, as is Ovid's desire to "be a soldier of Romulus."[28] It is also important to emphasize what is not in this scene. Ovid does not include any description of sexual acts, despite the greater female perspective. The scene also assimilates rape to marriage, especially as the Roman men state this line to the Sabine girls while they literally have them slung over their shoulders (*sublatam . . . vir tulit,* 128). Rather than simplifying our reading of the event, Ovid's presentation complicates it in many ways, and in so doing offers a means to tackle further issues related to rape, sexual violence and the ways in which they are presented (or avoided) in literature.

Rape of Lucretia

Livy's first book concludes with the rape of Lucretia and the fall of the Roman monarchy. He begins the story in section 57; after a debate about

---

25. 121: *nam timor unus est, facies non una timoris.* "For their fear was one, but not one was the face of their fear."

26. 122–25: *pars laniat crines, pars sine mente sedet / altera maesta silet, frustra vocat altera matrem / haec querita, stupet haec; haec manet, illa fugit.* "Some tear their hair, others sit mindless. One is sad and silent, another calls the name of her mother in vain. This one complains, this one is dumbstruck, this one stays fixed in place, that one flees." If one just quoted these three lines, I think they alone could be used for comment beside Livy.

27. 129–130: *atque ita "quid teneros lacrimis corrumpis ocellos? / quod matri pater est, hoc tibi" dixit,* "ero."

28. 131–32: *Romule, militibus scisti dare commoda solus / haec mihi si dederis commoda, miles ero.* "Romulus, you alone knew to give pleasing things to soldiers. If you would give these pleasing things to me, I would be your soldier."

the character of their wives, Tarquin, Collatinus and some of the other young Romans leave Ardea. After seeing other wives feasting and at leisure, they find Lucretia weaving away with her maids. Here Livy is clear that Tarquin intends to rape her.[29] Later, in section 58, Tarquin returns to Collatinus' house and is led to the guest bedroom for the night, but he proceeds to Lucretia's room where he rapes her. He gives a short speech identifying himself, threatening to kill her if she speaks.[30] We discuss why Tarquin identifies himself and how rape can be viewed as a statement of power and control, rather than purely sexual gratification. Tarquin then attempts to persuade Lucretia to submit willingly, as if such a thing were possible.[31] Finally he threatens to kill a slave and place him beside her body if she does not submit. Military vocabulary is prominent throughout the episode as it often remains in characterizations of acts of sexual violence today; Tarquin conquers her (*vicisset*) and returns to Ardea a victor (*victrix*). Lucretia is merely saddened (*maesta tanto malo*) after the act, and Livy provides no details on actual rape, or aftermath. The entire encounter is completed in a few sentences. Nonetheless the rape is quite different from the rape of the Sabines; here conquest is achieved through a sexual act, by someone known to the victim; there is no long term relationship between the parties, as in the Sabine story.

Ovid tells this story as well, in the *Fasti* (2.685ff), part of the entry commemorating the Regifugium. Ovid's version serves as a useful comparative text. Much of his narrative has the feel of a dramatic production. As in Livy, after the debate, the husbands return to Rome, see the other women drinking (739–40) and Lucretia weaving (741–42). She speaks to her faithfulness for her husband (745–54), but even here her tears have an appeal (*lacrimae decuere pudicam*, 757). Collatinus tells her to set aside her fear (*pone metum*, 759), a theme seen in all of these rape scenes. Meanwhile Tarquin is seized by lust (*raptus caeco amore*) and burns (*furit* 762, cf. *cupit* 766). Ovid then describes how every part of her physical body

---

29. I.57: *ibi Sex. Tarquinium mala libido Lucretiae per vim stuprandae capit.* "At that time an evil desire to rape Lucretia by force seized Sextus Tarquin." This is an apt moment to mention the inadequacy of modern translations, which often come up with creative terms that obscure what is transpiring, especially for students who would never use these terms. Sélincourt's (2002: 101) Penguin translation (a widely used text) is "debauch"—archaic indeed.

30. "*tace, Lucretia*" *inquit;* "*Sex. Tarquinius sum; ferrum in manu est; moriere, si emiseris vocem.*" "Silence Lucretia," he said, "I am Sextus Tarquin; a sword is in my hand; you will die, if you let out a sound."

31. *tum Tarquinius fateri amorem, orare, miscere precibus minas, versare in omnes partes muliebrem animum. ubi obstinatam videbat et ne mortis quidem metu inclinari, addit ad metum dedecus.* "Then Tarquin confessed his love, begged her, mixed threats with prayers, turned the woman's spirit in all directions. When he saw she remained obstinate and could not even be persuaded by fear of death, he added disgrace to her fear."

appeals to Tarquin, but so does her virtue (763–64). Once Tarquin returns to Ardea, he recalls all of her attributes again (770–74). He burns with lust (*ardet,* 779, cf. 762), and as an enemy (787) this unfriendly guest returns to Collatinus' house. In line 790 Lucretia is merely *infelix*—the description does not do justice to all that she will suffer. Tarquin's speech (795–96) is reminiscent of the Roman male's speech which occurs in the *Ars Amatoria* passage discussed above, but then Ovid switches to Lucretia's perspective (797ff.). He focuses upon her silence and fear, punctuated by questions she asks herself during her rape. We discuss the emphasis on fear, considering fear as inward-looking, providing insight into a character's feelings, but also as something the rapist desires. The initial words 801, 2, 3 all describe questions she addresses to herself.[32] Such brevity speeds up the action, and gives the reader a sympathetic look at the chaos and panic she faces. Such a style follows that seen in Ovid's description of the Sabine girls at the moment of their capture. Our minds race like Lucretia's; Tarquin's actions then slow the scene down. Tarquin entreats Lucretia by prayers (*precibus*), bribes (*pretio*) and threats (*minis*).[33] The ordeal is lengthy and culminated by a second speech which Tarquin delivers (807–9). Livy says Lucretia is defeated by fear (or rumor), and her rape is reduced to one word, submission (*succubuit*), and comes after twenty lines building up to it. Ovid then inserts the narrator, which is worth pause in any discussion of this passage. Tarquin's exit is never described; he is never quoted again, nor is his perspective on the aftermath of the rape described. Lucretia calls upon Collatinus, Brutus and her father and when they see her they are affixed by fear (*metu,* 822) as she was during the rape itself. When she describes what happened, Ovid does not provide any detail, but merely says she stated as much of her story as she could.[34]

In teaching these and other Ovidian texts, I assign Amy Richlin's aforementioned "Reading Ovid's Rapes" (1992a).[35] The article concludes with a

---

32. 801–3: *quid faciat? pugnet? vincetur femina pugnans. / clamet? at in dextra, qui vetet, ensis erat. / effugiat? positis urgentur pectora palmis.* "What could she do? Should she fight? A woman who fights will be conquered. Should she scream? But there was, in his right hand, a sword which forbid it. Should she flee? His hands pressed down hard on her breast."

33. 804–5: *tum primum externa pectora tacta manu /instat amans hostis precibus pretioque minisque.* "Then for the first time her chest was touched by another's hand. The enemy lover pressed her with prayers and bribes and threats."

34. 827: *quaeque potest, narrat; restabant ultima, flevit.* "And what she was able, she told; the end she held back, and wept."

35. She also discusses the rape of the Sabine women (1992a: 166–8). In my "gender and sexuality" course we also read selections from the *Amores, Heroides* and *Metamorphoses*. I advise including one additional episode, in particular. Ovid's account of the rape of Callisto in the *Metamorphoses* (2.401–507) illustrates that both sexes can be implicated in the suffering of a victim (see Johnson

variety of approaches in reading and interpretation, but privileges none, while clearly pointing out that none in and of themselves are satisfactory. The article also deals with the harsh realities many scholars avoid, that "the nature of Ovid's rapes surely bears on the lives of the women who heard his poems and live[d] in the sign system that produced the canon." Richlin includes the reminder that "content is never arbitrary or trivial; content is not an accident of a text but an essential" (1992a: 159). It is simple to say that women, in these stories, are objectified, that they arouse male sexual desire and have the power to cause men to deviate from acceptable social customs and behavior, but Richlin forces one not only to consider why these forms of violence are selected, but the implications of these actions. Ovid's version allows one to examine the episode from the perspective of the perpetrator *and* the victim, and elicits many comments on Ovid's, at times, "realistic" portrayal of the victim. I think it is safe to go further and ask whether there is something about societies which define themselves through acts of violence against others that prefigures violence against women, especially in mythological accounts. This is in no way to excuse or justify these acts committed against women, but to offer a possible avenue for a further expansion of discussion beyond the immediate text, if one wants to discuss sexual violence in a broader context. My goal here has not been to depict Ovid as a savior, by any means. Ovid's versions are still literary and highly stylized, and each serves particular functions in its specific work. But to some students these texts offer a level of "relief," that someone else so long ago continued to think about these episodes and addressed some of the issues that they themselves are concerned with.

SOME FINAL THOUGHTS

I have tried to relate a number of issues surrounding the teaching of "troubling" subjects and some avenues for preparation and discussion. I firmly believe that their discussion in the classroom is a must, and that they should be viewed as a legitimate part of our field, and subjects everyone within Classics should be prepared to engage with and discuss. I think so many of these topics are central to understanding Classical literature and culture that an avoidance of them is simply not teaching the material, texts

---

1996). After her rape, Callisto is dismissed by Artemis and her companions from their company; they treat her with disgust and disdain, all from a group one might initially believe would be sympathetic since they do not like men to begin with. Callisto is transformed as punishment by Juno. Made voiceless she wanders with nowhere to turn, until her eventual, second, transformation.

and subject matter we possess and avow to study. I hope that discussions on pedagogy can continue amongst Classicists and that colloquia on these topics become less segregated and involve a more diverse constituency. I also believe we must begin by stating explicitly that it is not only acceptable for men to talk about these subjects, but that it should be standard practice for any teacher. One place to begin is to organize a panel or discussion for faculty who teach gender, sexuality and other "sensitive" topics at your institution. Hosting an event amongst your colleagues within a department, or across programs, might also garner interest. I believe there exists a degree of trepidation among even those who teach these topics that they are not handling them as well as they could, and open discussions could help uncover best practices.

I cannot relate the degree of response I have had when telling people I am writing on this topic, often along the lines of "you're crazy, but thank you. I am eagerly waiting to read it." "Crazy," I think, because they are inexperienced and feel intimidated in dealing with these topics in the classroom and "eager" because they actually do want to deal with topics they know they have been avoiding. Male apprehension might be a result of perceptions rather than realities; I believe most of what I have stated in this chapter will be applicable to any reader, perhaps defined by some as more acceptable as it comes from a male. If so, so be it. I hope that any Classicist, no matter their gender, or how they self-identify, will step forward and become part of this ongoing discussion. I have tried to be as honest as possible in this piece, because perceptions and stereotypes do exist; my goal is not to offend or cause controversy, but to include advice, suggestions, and opinions shared with me, and I hope to have enlightened at least a few through a sincere appraisal of the attitudes that exist and challenges we all face as teachers and colleagues of those who teach these subjects.

Talking Rape in the Classics Classroom
Further Thoughts

SHARON L. JAMES

THIS ESSAY follows up on two previous publications of mine: James (2008), originally a paper presented at the Feminism/Classics V conference, in a panel on feminist pedagogy, and James (2012), on teaching rape in Roman love elegy. In those articles, I focused on my own experiences teaching Latin texts that present rape—often repeatedly, and in ways that modern students find very disturbing. My purpose here is not to rehash my prior work but to enlarge my overall discussion, with the aim of presenting what I hope will be a useful set of principles, probabilities, and preparatory tactics, as well as readings, that can help other instructors.

I begin with the standard feminist gesture of self-placement: I'm a middle-aged tenured female Classicist, with teaching experience in both large public universities and small liberal arts colleges. Like most Classics professors, I'm Caucasian and have therefore lived a life of white privilege. It has been a life intensely aware of limitations upon and hostility toward women in multiple forms: lowered expectations, veiled sexism, open misogyny, sexual discrimination, violence, and rape. I have personally experienced all of these behaviors except for rape. For reasons I cannot figure out, let alone try to explain, I have been, over the past thirty-five years, the repository of an astonishing number of rape disclosures. These have come from close friends, acquaintances, students, and even sometimes from people I barely know; they come in conversation, in office hours, in consultation—almost always unexpectedly. Whether something in me elicits these disclosures, I can't say, but I estimate that I've heard the sentence, "I was raped" (or an equivalent), probably 150 times. More than once have I gained the impression that the discloser had not yet told someone as close as a husband about a rape that took place before she met him. For some reason, people seem to trust me with this information, to consider me a safe person and even a safe place. I rarely hear any detail, and I hasten to note that I never, ever seek any; often, the mere disclosure has seemed to be enough for the person making it.[1]

As I kept hearing this sentence, over the years—no doubt often because I was teaching rape texts, such as Ovid's *Metamorphoses,* and because I was writing about depictions of rape in ancient literature (as in James 1997 and 1998)—I became increasingly conscious of the problems of talking about rape, or teaching it; I have further become aware that rape is an epidemic on college campuses. The turning point was my discovery, mentioned below and in James (2008), that I had unwittingly seated a student next to the male student who had raped her in a previous year—a discovery completely unrelated to our readings in that particular class. At that point, I began to think more systematically about rape in colleges and universities, and how it affects students, both those who have experienced it and those who fear that they will.

In this essay, I draw on nearly three decades of teaching experience, ranging from small Latin and Greek courses to mid-sized translation classes to large lecture courses. This chapter discusses the way students think about rape, their tremendous sensitivity to the subject, and how teachers can prepare for this difficult classroom conversation. It thus expands briefly on my previous articles to include other issues, aiming to include the especially sensitive situation of male professors and teaching assistants (on which see especially Thakur in this volume), and the difficulties of integrating the topic of rape in something like a course on Roman history. A further topic is a consideration of pedagogical and consultational (i.e., in office hours rather than in class) risks and limits. Lastly, I seek to begin providing a more global context for rape in antiquity, by turning to modern comparative materials that can be invaluable both in shaping the intellectual content of their class presentations and in preparing for almost inevitable, and almost inevitably difficult, conversations in the office as well as the classroom.

---

1. I note that my age seems to make no difference in the number of rape disclosures I hear from students. I think some students are more comfortable telling a younger professor and others are more comfortable with an older professor. I suspect, with no way to support my suspicion, that female students will be readier to tell a younger male professor than an older one. In my own case, the disclosures from my students probably keep coming because I do teach rape texts, but as I discuss below, they may come in any class, from basic Latin to a large lecture course.

A final preliminary note: it might be thought that certain types of classes or instructors are unlikely to wind up discussing rape with students. But even those teaching, say, elementary language or philosophy may well find themselves facing just this problem. It remains true that students are more likely to tell a female teacher than a male teacher that they have been raped, but the rule is not absolute. I know more than one male graduate teaching assistant who has been informed by a female student that she was raped over the preceding weekend and would need to miss class sessions periodically because of the legal process or that she had been raped during the previous year and that the case was finally coming to trial.

This situation can arise in *any* class, not only in those that deal with rape. The diminishing stigma of having been raped means that some young women feel ready to speak of it to a professor or TA, in a fairly matter-of-fact way. Disclosure of rape to college instructors is thus increasingly likely. In addition, as I noted in James (2008), rape is a pandemic on college campuses. More than once have I had to say to colleagues, "no, it isn't merely *possible* that a student of yours might be raped in college some day—you have *already* taught students who were raped in college, and many of them were raped by other students. What's more, almost every female student personally knows a rape victim."

Thus, even those who are not teaching a sensitive subject may end up needing advice and resources, when a student comes in to the office (or sends an email) to say, "I was raped, and I'm going to have to miss some class."[2] Even responding to such a disclosure requires preparation; see section V below for discussion of my own (numerous, by now) such experiences and some suggestions on how to handle these announcements. But it's important to keep in mind that many students who have suffered rape won't mention their assault: they may not want to think about it; they may not want it to be a potential problem for their performance in class; they may even think they must "tough it out" and learn to be non-reactive to the subject of rape. Just because nobody in a given class tells you that she was raped does not mean that nobody in that class has been raped. It's wise, particularly in designing and teaching a large class, to presume that at least a couple of your students have suffered rape, and that the majority of them know someone who has been raped. I proceed here below with the presumption that those students are female, chiefly because the majority of rape victims are women but also because the likelihood of learning from a

---

2. See, to give only a single citation on the subject of rape among college students, Minow and Einolf (2009), with their bibliography.

male student that he has been raped is virtually nil. It has happened to me a few times, but the number of this particular revelation is absolutely dwarfed by the number of women from whom I have heard about sexual assault. The stigma on male rape victims is so great that they often suffer their trauma in silence, even for decades afterwards, but I cannot even hazard a guess about how frequently male students have been raped. My use of female pronouns here represents my experience, but I remain aware that men too suffer rape.

I. TALKING RAPE IN THE CLASSICS CLASSROOM

The teaching of rape texts is not limited to the Classics classroom, as the subject comes up in courses from art history to world literature to film. But it may be fair to say that of necessity Classicists face the subject more frequently than do teachers in other fields, for one simple reason: Greek myth overflows with accounts of rape, and we cannot avoid Greek myth, even in courses on Latin poetry. Early Roman history is replete with rapes—from Rhea Silvia to the Sabine women to Lucretia—so even a class with no apparent relation to sexual violence, such as "Roman Civ," must address the subject somehow or risk upsetting and alienating students. These accounts have usually been downplayed, even dismissed, even by the ancients themselves. Using terms such as "seduction" or "dalliance" is a way of evading the discomfiting fact of rape. Teachers have good reason to be nervous about the topic, and perhaps even to avoid teaching it altogether. I have male friends who have stopped teaching, say, Ovid's *Metamorphoses* in translation classes, precisely because of the unavoidable problem of discussing rape. I have even been brought in to teach class sessions on rape texts simply because a male colleague was so uncomfortable talking about the subject.[3]

Such solutions as euphemistic language, avoidance of brute physical realities that are evident in the ancient materials, abandoning works like the *Metamorphoses,* are unsatisfactory pedagogically and intellectually, as well as personally. When we make such choices, we present a sanitized version of antiquity to our students; and if we treat rape lightly, with euphemism or

---

3. I suspect that many male professors would like to be able to teach ancient rape materials in a way that allows them to acknowledge the actual nature of rape, and in a way that does not leave them somehow implicated in the conspiracy of silence that continues to make rape a source of shame for its victims. I recommend beginning with Thakur in this volume and then moving ahead: students are very responsive when they see their professors acknowledging rape as brutal rather than trivial or unimportant.

hasty dismissal, our students will know that they are being cheated. They may never say so to our faces, particularly not in a large lecture course, but they will feel it. They may send impassioned, even enraged, emails, which cannot be ignored; sometimes they complain in their written course evaluations. In the past it may have been possible to sidestep and soft-talk rape, but no longer: students, especially female students, are highly politicized (as they should be) on the subject of rape, and they can become deeply offended by its depiction in ancient materials and its elision in the instruction of those materials.[4]

The questions, then, are these: how should we take such feelings into consideration, in preparing our classes? how should we talk about the subject? how do we prepare to deal with students who come in to the office, often very upset, to talk or complain about rape? what limits do we put on discussions, both in class and in the office? in the office, how do we negotiate delicate conversations?

The first step—well before teaching a class that discusses rape materials—is to investigate campus and local resources: there is a rape crisis center in every college town, and every campus health center has counselors and therapists. The office of the Dean of Students has further resources. Staff in those offices are eager to help teachers who will be dealing with the subject of rape. They're glad to give out brochures, cards, or flyers. In contacting these offices, I keep things simple: I say that I'll be teaching, of necessity, texts that depict rape in disturbing ways; that I want to be able to offer resources to students who are upset; that I'll be glad of any advice, or suggestions; and that I'd like any informational materials they have available.

I keep these materials in my office, as students upset about rape rarely want to be so identified in front of other students. They'll come to a professor's office to seek guidance but will rarely state in public that they (or, for example, a close relative or friend) have suffered rape.[5] Angry outbursts do occur in class, and should be expected, especially with particular materials (such as the Archilochus' Cologne *Epode* or Ovid's poetry), but they tend to be based on political, rather than personal, grounds.

Find out if your institution has a policy for dealing with rape. My university requires instructors to notify the office of the Dean of Students if we believe that a student is a danger to himself, herself, or to others. In one situation, I did so, as I had evidence that a student was continuing to

---

4. In fact, male students frequently have the same reaction, for several reasons—one of which is that they have seen the effects of rape on a close friend or relative.

5. For accounts of an exception to this general, rule, see Kahn (2004; 2005), discussed below; in my view, such disclosures are most likely to be made in an all-female classroom.

put herself into a dangerous situation with a violent man. As I was completing this chapter, revelations about the appalling sexual abuse of young boys in the Penn State football program were coming out. The persistent institutional protection of a serial pedophile rapist at Penn State serves as an unpleasant warning that campus policies do not always exist to protect on-campus victims of crime. So it is important to know what your institution requires of you, if you should learn from a student that she (or he) has been raped.

The next step is to read scholarship on rape in antiquity. Students will ask questions about attitudes toward rape, about law on rape, about resolutions for rape. It's important to be prepared for these questions. Section VI, below, lists some starting points. Equally important is modern comparative material from both so-called Western nations (by which is usually meant Western Europe, North America, Australia and New Zealand) and non-Western countries. Sexual values, attitudes toward rape, and treatment of women in many places on the planet today are hardly different from those of the ancient world, and there is excellent, accessible scholarship on the subject, to which I return below. These materials have helped me to provide what my students have told me is an invaluable opportunity both to reflect on motives for and realities of rape and to gain broad perspectives about the history and contemporary practice of rape as a constant global presence, a recurrent human event. The international scholarship is particularly valuable in providing cross-cultural and culturally sensitive perspectives on rape. Faculty at ethnically diverse campuses will find these materials especially helpful, but they have much to teach Classicists in particular, as I discuss below.

An excellent starting point is Madeline Kahn's 2004 article, "'Why Are We Reading a Handbook on Rape?' Young Women Transform a Classic," and its follow-up in her 2005 book. Kahn provides a gripping example—and one that reads like my own early teaching autobiography—of the way students may respond to Ovid's *Metamorphoses* in a myth course. The rage of her women students is more widespread than many instructors may know, and her account of their reactions is electrifying. Anybody preparing to teach a mythology class should read at least the 2004 article. Further recommendations for readings follow, in Section VI.

It's helpful to prepare a handout with some information on the materials and on how students might approach them. I've developed such a handout for teaching Ovid in translation classes. It states plainly that Ovid repeatedly depicts sexual violence, with focus on male motives for rape and awareness of female fear of rape. I list some questions that students might ask as they're reading: how should they react when the *praeceptor amoris* presumes that his male pupils will *want* to commit rape? do they think they are supposed to identify with Ovid's male pupils in general, or is it possible that these males are being depicted in a way they might question? whose perspective on the fleeing Daphne of *Met.* 1 is being invoked-theirs or Apollo's? Apollo is depicted as shallow; how does that depiction affect their interpretation of the way he "reads" Daphne as she tries to escape him? For Terence's *Hecyra* and *Eunuchus*, I ask students to focus on how he invokes the way women actually experience rape (a subject I discuss in James 1998), and how the rapes in his plays are showcased rather than treated lightly or passed over.

Finally, it's crucial to design assignments so that students are not *forced* to write about rape. My exams offer students a choice of questions and topics, so they can always avoid writing about rape. I do not make up paper topics for students, but I've found that many students—the ones who have not been raped but fear that they might be raped—actually want to write about rape. When talking to a student who is casting about for a paper topic, I never suggest rape. I don't have to: the subject pulls them in. The process of analyzing patterns of rape in, say, Ovid, Greek myth, New Comedy, seems to offer them a chance to think about cultural values, social practices, and the persistence of rape throughout history. I've heard often from students that these materials made them more aware of their own vulnerability to rape, and caused them to take more precautions. But I never propose the subject, let alone require it. For all the times I've been told by a student that she was raped, I know that the majority of such students are not telling me, so I never presume that I'm talking to someone who has not been raped.

II. PREPARING TO TEACH RAPE MATERIALS

The first point is this: expect to go rather slowly when teaching a text that involves rape. It is not possible to buzz through, say, two or more books of the *Metamorphoses* or a play of Terence in a speedy fashion. Even if students don't speak up and out, or don't voice objections and alarm, the instructor must raise the subject. When putting together a schedule of readings and assignments, plan for the disturbing episodes of rape to take at least an extra half-class session. It's only fair to let students know in the beginning of the term that they will be reading and studying materials that are disturbing, that involve rape. At the end of the first day of any such class, I make that announcement, and I say that rape was common in the ancient world, as it is now, though it was defined very differently—a subject to be discussed as it arises; I further add that judging from my past experience more than a few students in the class know someone who has suffered sexual assault, and that they will find the materials upsetting. I let them know that they can come to my office, that I'll never ask anybody any personal questions, and that I'm not a counselor or therapist but can direct them to on-campus resources if they're interested. The wording I use is neutral:

> At this point, I have to let you know that some of the materials we will be studying depict rape, and in what many people find to be a very disturbing fashion. I don't know that there is any way to depict rape that *isn't* disturbing—I hope not—but in my experience students find these depictions particularly upsetting. Ovid has been accused of being pro-rape. In my opinion, his depictions of rape are deliberately discomfiting, though not everybody takes my particular view. You can expect to be disturbed by what we're reading, but we can't avoid the subject. Rape is a very sensitive subject, and we will discuss carefully, with respect for each other, the ways in which our materials depict it. I've found in the past that these texts are especially upsetting to students who have known someone who was raped. If you are upset by the readings or discussions, please come see me in my office. I'm not a counselor or therapist, and will never ask any personal questions, but I can point to very helpful resources on campus. In class, I expect everybody to treat these materials with great care and to be sensitive to each other. Nobody will *ever* be forced to talk about rape, either in class or outside of class. If I could avoid the subject, I probably would, but it's part of our class materials, it was part of life in the ancient world, and it's a significant, repeated event in Greek and Roman mythology. So we *must* deal with it in this class, but we'll do so with respect and sensitivity.

The precise contents of this announcement are adjusted to the specific material. Students tend to respond somberly: they seem to appreciate the advance warning and, particularly, the promise that class discussions will be conducted with sensitivity. The follow-up notice should come in the form of a reminder, shortly before any day in which rape will be featured in the readings: "on Monday, we'll be discussing one of those disturbing episodes of rape that I mentioned on the first day of class; you'll probably find your readings to be unsettling, and we'll talk about how and why they are unsettling. But remember that nobody will be required to talk about rape in class." If I have a study guide, I distribute it before students do the reading.

III. TALKING RAPE IN THE CLASSROOM

In class discussions, my tactics vary depending on the class I'm teaching: small language class, reading in the original; seminar-sized translation class; large lecture class. I begin by saying that the ancients were disturbed by rape, but that they defined it legally as occurring only to citizens and they allowed it to be legally and socially resolved by marriage, although we don't know how often such a resolution took place. This information, which I've usually mentioned at least once before, is absolutely shocking to modern students, and I structure in time for their shock, chiefly by making it part of the discussion. Fairly early on, I say that the same remains more or less true on much of the planet today, and I offer citations to that effect. I point out that even though rape was considered a crime only when it was perpetrated upon citizens, the legal restriction did not keep non-citizen women from feeling any less personally violated, and that male perpetrators would have observed resistance among their own household slaves, even if they neither respected that resistance nor considered their physical force to be rape.[6] I can link this aspect of the lives of the enslaved in antiquity to the lives of enslaved persons anywhere, as one of the many evils of slavery (see DuBois in this volume). Students tend to understand that in any system of slavery, the enslaved do not own or control their own bodies, so they can assign this form of rape in antiquity to slavery in general. But they have a harder time understanding that rape of a free non-citizen was not considered rape, and I encourage them to find that fact problematic and troubling.[7] This is one of the vantage points at which students can use two sets of eyeglasses, the ancient and the modern: this issue permits them to understand the perspectives of ancient citizen society, on its own terms, and then to critique that perspective as one of exploitive privilege of anyone not fortunate enough to be a citizen.

---

6. At Lysias 1.12, Euphiletus' wife accuses her husband of wanting access, behind her back, to the maid, whom he had "dragged about" (εἷλκες) on a previous occasion. The application of violence indicates resistance by the slave. Xenophon's Ischomachus tells his young wife that she is more appealing to him than a slave who must be forced into sex (*Oec.* 10.12); as Pomeroy (1994: 308) notes, "Xenophon is the first Greek author to recognize that an ordinary slave may be reluctant to have sexual intercourse with a master." Xenophon may have been the first extant Greek author to put this reluctance into prose, but it was already acknowledged in texts dealing with the enslaved Trojan women (and is later found in Plautus' plays, as well as in Ovid's love poetry, as I argued in James 1997). In any case, every slave-owner would have observed the phenomenon. On the Trojan women, see particularly Scodel (1998).

7. On this point, it may be helpful to quote this remark: "Just because a woman doesn't call it rape doesn't mean she doesn't feel violated. She may not have the language, or she may never have been asked" (Heise, Moore, and Toubia 1995: 21–22).

The horror of students at the prospect of a woman's being forced to marry the man who had raped her is universal, and it offers a means of helping them to understand marriage in antiquity, and in much of the world today, as a social institution rather than a personal relationship and a personal choice. But the process of walking them through the equation, so to speak, is slow and delicate. On this point, drawing on modern analogues is very helpful, although it's also painful for students, who are horrified to find out that ancient sexual values continue to flourish on the planet.[8] My researches into the subject indicate that in some parts of the world, murder by their own families is a common fate for girls and women who suffer rape, and that in many countries and cultures, physical abuse followed by rejection and ostracism is standard. Greek myth records this behavior, but otherwise our ancient sources do not tell us if rape victims in the ancient world met with similar treatment from their families.

A lesson from the contemporary world helps students to develop a more complex, sensitive, and nuanced understanding of the problems of rape in antiquity: when contemporary evidence tells them that they can't simply dismiss the ancients as, well, ancient and therefore not relevant to themselves, or as anomalous, they must take the subject seriously and think about it systematically. In addition, students who might be tempted to say something like "well, it wasn't really the same back then" (a sentiment I've heard) do not manifest the same reaction to learning that, say, a ten-year-old girl raped by her neighbor, right-now-this-minute-as-they-are-reading-or-sitting-in-class, might be brutally beaten by her family members when they discover the rape; if she's lucky, she'll be allowed to live and become engaged to the rapist, rather than being killed (for just such a narrative, see Shalhoub-Kevorkian 1999: 162).[9]

Using such contemporary materials requires care and sensitivity, as one can neither simply dismiss other cultures as barbaric (and therefore hardly worth thinking about) nor downplay horrific abuse of women on the basis of cultural relativism. For one thing, victims who are willing to go public have already recognized rape as a crime and a personal violation, so they

---

8. These analogues are easy to find in current news media; for a scholarly report, see Shalhoub-Kevorkian (1999), who reports on young Palestinian girls forced to marry the men who raped them. Her discussion of their distress, as they seek counseling in secret, is both very moving and very enlightening for considering the same phenomenon in the ancient world.

9. Another example: on learning that his 14-year-old daughter had been raped by her father-in-law, a man in India publicly demanded that she kill herself: "'You whore! You will listen to me!' . . . Nathula lunged toward his daughter. 'Get back into that room!' he screamed. 'Do as I tell you to do! If you don't kill yourself in five minutes, I will do it for you!'" (Weaver 2000: 52).

certainly do not downplay it.[10] There are activists and organizations everywhere protesting violence against women, lobbying against laws and practices that further abuse rape victims (such as having to marry the rapist, or being raped, in a police station, by policemen who consider a woman attempting to report a rape to be fair game for themselves).[11] Finally, there are thoughtful, supportive, innovative programs around the world for helping rape victims in ways that are culturally sensitive and effective.[12]

Information on contemporary international attitudes toward, sociocultural treatments of, and law governing rape is so widely available as to be almost overwhelming. The materials tend to divide into two chief categories: rape as war-crime and marital rape (i.e., does a given culture understand the concept of marital rape?). Your students will be more interested in the issue of rape as they personally experience it, fear they will experience it, or as experienced by someone close to them. There is plenty of material on this subject, much of it in such periodicals as the *Journal of Interpersonal Violence* and *Violence Against Women*—but a great deal of information is on the internet. Used with care, these materials can both help students to understand and discuss, with sensitivity, rape in antiquity and to become more aware of the world they inhabit.

In holding class discussions of such materials as Ovid's *Metamorphoses*, the rape plots of New Comedy, visual depictions of mythic rapes, Archilochus' Cologne *Epode*, it's crucial to let students know that you share their distress. But teachers should also be prepared to experience the anger of students against themselves, for merely having assigned such unpleasant

---

10. The sources that transmit testimony of such rape victims are too numerous to list here; eloquent and heartbreaking examples may be found in the articles of Nadera Shalhoub-Kevorkian (see especially 2001; 2003).

11. See, e.g., Maboe (1994); Heise, Moore, and Toubia (1995); Johnson (2009); see also the website of the organization Women for Women's Human Rights, an NGO established in Turkey in 1993 (http://www.wwhr.org/index.php); the organization RAINN (Rape, Abuse, and Incest National Network) has a webpage called International Sexual Assault Resources, where are listed the websites of organizations in eighteen countries that work to help victims of sexual assault: http://www.rainn.org/get-help/sexual-assault-and-rape-international-resources. Victims' Assistance Online has numerous further resources, including international efforts to combat sexual assault (http://www.vaonline.org/sa.html) and links to such organizations as Men Can Stop Rape (mencanstoprape.org) and UN Action Against Sexual Violence in Conflict (http://www.stoprapenow.org/). There are many other resources on-line. I note the following: "Rape crisis centers outside of the United States are not affiliated with RAINN, and RAINN has not certified the services they offer. Links are provided solely as a courtesy to international visitors." Even if (or when) these websites and organizations close down or merge, other resources will easily be found with a few minutes' time on internet search engines.

12. For a few examples, see Agger (1994); Maboe (1994); Shalhoub-Kevorkian (2000 and 2001); Weaver (2000).

materials. (Hence the necessity of a first-day warning.) It's also crucial to make sure that students aren't insensitive to each other. Male students are often extremely uncomfortable, as though they are being assimilated to the exploitive and abusive attitudes of the rapists in the ancient works, so it's important to say early on that not all men are rapists, that you don't consider your male students to be like Tarquin or Tereus. If you find out, as I did once (and as a former graduate student of mine did as well), that you do have a rapist in the class, one who raped another member of the class, consult with your institution's legal advisors. They will almost certainly say that you cannot mention the situation in class. If you know who the victim is, you may assure her in office hours that you will not advert to the situation in class, you will not identify her to anybody ever as having been raped, and that you'll understand if she wants to avoid certain class discussions—if, say, the rape of Lucretia is on the syllabus, you'll review it with her in office hours so that she won't have to come to class.[13] Teaching in such a situation is fraught and can be very disturbing, but it can happen to any teacher, male or female, in any class. Thus every teacher should really be prepared for handling a rape disclosure.

IV. OFFICE CONVERSATIONS

In office hours, I've been asked by students who have made a rape disclosure to me if they can be excused from a day focused on rape. I tell them yes, they can come to my office and we'll talk only about the readings, so that they'll know any materials that might turn up on an exam. In these conversations, I ask only once if the student is seeing a therapist; if the answer is no, I urge her to do so. In these conversations, I proceed slowly and take my cues from the student: if she makes eye contact and is very calm, I look directly at her. If she's anxious, I talk even more slowly and make it clear that I understand her concerns and will accommodate them as best I can. Sometimes a student will use circumlocutions, such as "some of the things we've been reading/talking about in class are very upsetting because of something that happened to me" are not uncommon. In such cases, I then do not use the word rape in conversation or email with the student; I substitute a phrase like "this disturbing subject." Thus, for example, when I've promised to tell such a student in advance that a given class session

---

13. For me, it was a large lecture course, for my former graduate student, it was a fairly small course. In both cases, other students in the class knew about the situation, but it never came up in class meetings.

must deal with rape, I write to her and say, "this is just to let you know that the readings for Wednesday's class do contain disturbing subjects, and you may prefer to miss class; if so, let's set a date to go over the necessary materials." A student in a lecture class might say that she would like to sit in the back of the room and be prepared to leave when the unnamed disturbing subject comes up; I always agree. To their own surprise, such students often find the readings therapeutic—a word I've heard regularly—but this result is not guaranteed; as Kahn (2004; 2005) demonstrates, they also may find the readings to cause a vivid and terribly distressing revival of sexual assault.

V. RESPONDING TO A DISCLOSURE OF RAPE

Students may identify themselves as rape victims in a number of ways, and as I've noted, they don't necessarily limit that identification to female instructors. They will very rarely do so in a public setting: they tend to come to the office; sometimes they'll use email. It is very common for them to miss class for a week or two before they come to explain their absence; I've found that they often tell themselves that they should "solve" their problem independently, or that they thought it might go away if they waited. It is crucial to note the obvious here: a student who makes a rape disclosure to you has made a decision to trust you. You must continue to earn that trust by not showing agitation in the office and—most importantly—by making sure that your in-class behavior toward the student does not change.

If a student reveals to you in the office that she has been raped, keep a relaxed body posture and a low-key but sympathetic voice. Never ask questions. I say something like, "I'm so terribly sorry to hear it. I can't tell you how many women I know who have suffered the same thing."[14] I then proceed to ask, gently, if they are getting counseling and I add that I can point them to on-campus and near-campus resources. They almost always are, in fact, receiving counseling of some sort, and I say I'm glad to hear it. At this point, the student usually takes over, but if she sits and looks frozen, I ask, again using a gentle tone, if she is finding our materials disturbing. She'll usually nod; sometimes she can't make eye contact. I then say, "these

---

14. Anybody who does not want to say "I can't count the number . . . " may say something like, "I'm so terribly sorry to hear it. It's extremely common, and that fact is tragic." Calm sympathy is what students are usually seeking. They will almost never want to provide details or to seek therapy from their professors, so an expression of genuine sympathy that does not raise the emotional temperature in the classroom is both welcome and also a way to keep the conversation focused on the class and their own work in it.

materials really *are* disturbing, and I can see that they would be especially distressing for you. That's why I gave advance warning in the beginning of the term." If I'm teaching Ovid or Terence, I usually say that I think those two poets know how disturbing their works are, what a violation rape is, and that they're exposing the disingenuities and cultural inequities that excuse and even encourage rape. I then reassure her that I will not ask her any personal questions, because I'm not a counselor, and that I'll do what I can to make the class less difficult for her. In my experience, these students really want to finish the class and do well in it, and I always tell them that they won't have to write about rape on an exam or in a paper.

In response to an email disclosure of rape, I write back something very similar: "I'm so sorry to know it; I can't tell you how many women I know have been through the same thing, and I understand that you might be very uncomfortable with the materials." I immediately add, "I'm not permitted to discuss this sort of subject electronically, as email is not a private or secure medium of communication. Please come see me in my office so that we can make arrangements for you to finish the homework/course/assignment in the way that is least distressing for you." I then notify an administrator—my department chair or the Dean of Students—that I have received such a communication, though I don't give the student's name or any details.

If the student making the disclosure is male, you will probably be hearing something like, "I was sexually abused as a child." My procedure is pretty much the same as for women students, although I may add at some point that I'm aware how much harder it is for men to make such a statement; I will also say, very shortly after the initial disclosure, that I'm horrified to keep learning, year after year, how extremely common sexual abuse of children both male and female is, but I'm very glad that there is increasing awareness of the problem and that resources to help are increasing rapidly. It's appropriate to ask, at some point, if the readings are proving to be difficult, and then to proceed as above.

Overall, the most important points are that we must keep students aware that we're not therapists, without making them feel pushed away, and that we must maintain a student's privacy. Never reveal to anybody, even a campus official, anything told to you in confidence by a student—unless you believe that the student is a source of danger to anybody, including himself or herself. In that case, consult immediately with the Dean of Students and follow any required institutional procedures. I can't say that teaching rape gets easier over the years, but I can say that preparation makes all the difference in the world, and that experience will be your own best teacher.

VI. RECOMMENDED READINGS

Begin with Kahn (2004; 2005): there is no better preparation for understanding the rage that young women may feel when reading what appear to be casual, even enticing, depictions of rape. Kahn's sensitivity to her students is a model for all instructors. Thakur (in this volume) is essential reading, especially for male instructors; his attentive treatment of specific works and Latin phrases is invaluable. See also Liveley (2012), for a superb discussion of teaching rape; her list of suggested readings offers very helpful background. Lauriola (2011) and Widdows (2011) discuss different experiences teaching rape in the Classics classroom; see Jeppesen-Wigelsworth (2011) for statistics about rape of college students. Studies of individual rape texts and episodes, or authors whose works feature rape, are too numerous to list here, but are all widely available; the edited volumes of Porter and Tomaselli (1986) and Higgins and Silver (1991) are good resources for beginning to gather a larger historical context. Richlin (1992a), whose reading of Ovid is quite different from mine, and Scafuro (1990) are essential; see also Johnson (1996). For studying rape in antiquity either generally, Doblhofer (1994) is a starting-point for an overview; the essays in Deacy and Pierce (1997) are also helpful. Historical inquiries into ancient attitudes toward rape include Harris (1990; 1997; 2004; 2006), who argues that we should not use the term rape to denote sexual assault in antiquity because the ancients didn't think of it the way moderns do. I differ strongly with his argument, as not a single ancient source records a woman's own words, and analogous modern comparative evidence, as I've discussed above, demonstrates that women in cultures with sexual values very close to those of the ancients identify their rape experiences as personal violation rather than property damage. But Harris's review of ancient Greek materials is virtually comprehensive and thus useful for preparing to teach rape materials.

Among the most helpful and illuminating sources on modern comparative evidence is, as already noted, the work of Nadera Shalhoub-Kevorkian (1999; 2000; 2001; 2003). Gil and Anderson (1999) provide a stunning narrative of a rape case in contemporary China and the way the victim dealt with her experience; it is highly recommended reading, as it demonstrates concisely that ancient sexual values are alive and well on the planet today—but that women can and do work out ways of dealing with their trauma. Parrot and Cummings (2006: 95, with citations) offer a short list of cultures that retain patriarchal sexual attitudes. Heise, Moore, and Toubia (1995) is essential and enlightening. Agger (1994) provides an exemplary model of sensitivity in counseling rape victims; see also Kalu

(2004) and Maboe (1994). Johnson (2009) gives a riveting account of how women in Russia have been organizing to combat both rape and socio-legal attitudes toward rape. Ramos Lira, Koss, and Russo (1999) show how international and ancient sexual values are still to be found in the United States Minow and Einolf (2009) provide recent citations for studies on the high incidence of rape among college students; they demonstrate the high rate of rape among sorority members in U.S. colleges—a subject many will prefer to avoid in class, but should not avoid in preparing for classes. I strongly recommend Rozée (1993), for an eye-opening set of perspectives. The readings listed here are only the tip of the iceberg: thoughtful, searching, sensitive studies of rape abound, and they are invaluable in preparing to teach, and in dealing with, the subject of rape in the Classics classroom.[15]

---

15. My acknowledgments here are brief, but my debts are many. I'd like to thank the editors and referees of this volume, as well as Alison Keith, Genevieve Liveley, and Barbara Gold. My greatest thanks are numerous but necessarily nameless: they go to my students over the last three decades, who have taught me so much about how to deal with the subject of rape in the Classics classroom. They have been extraordinary teachers.

Teaching the Uncomfortable Subject of Slavery

PAGE DUBOIS

THE PROGRAM for our panel at the American Philological Association in 2011 described the topic as teaching "uncomfortable" subjects in the Classics classroom, although the theme has since morphed somewhat, from "troubling" to "sensitive" and beyond (see introduction). I seem to have gotten stuck on "uncomfortable." And I should begin by saying first I believe that part of our responsibility as teachers is sometimes to make comfortable students uncomfortable, and in addition, that I'm not sure that the topic of slavery in ancient Greece and Rome *is* an uncomfortable subject for today's students. When I teach students the language of the ancient Greeks, in courses where the reading focuses on the Greek texts, they accept without question the fact of ancient slavery. Recently teaching Andocides' legal oration *On the Mysteries,* his defense against the death penalty first performed in 399 BCE, I found that the students were interested in the details about everyday life that appear in the text, including the presence of slaves. For example, the revelations concerning the sacrilegious performance of the Eleusinian mysteries in Athens itself, in 415 BCE, were made by slaves. Andocides recalls that the citizen Pythonicus stood up in the assembly and said:

> "Alcibiades the general, as I shall prove to you, has been performing the Mysteries with others in a private house; and if you vote to give immunity

to whom I tell you to, a servant of one of the men present here, though he is uninitiated, will tell you the Mysteries." (11)[1]

The word translated here as "servant" is *therapon*, but as is revealed later, this man is a slave. We discussed the ubiquity of slaves in private houses, and their exposure in legal situations in which they were always vulnerable to torture. Later in our reading of this oration, we came upon another circumstance in which slavery figured, and which afforded the occasion for further discussion of the precarious lives of slaves, and their exploitation by their masters. The informant Diocleides tried to implicate not only Andocides, his family and friends, but also many others in the episode of the mutilation of the herms, which took place on the eve of the Athenian navy's expedition to Sicily in 415 BCE. Diocleides claimed that he had seen conspirators gathering, some three hundred of them, by the light of the moon, because he had a slave at Laurium and was going to "collect a payment" [38]. That is, he had leased out one of his slaves to work in the deadly silver mines at Laurium in southeast Attica, and was on his way to take the money owed to him for the leasing of this man's labor. The incidental appearance of these individual slaves, their presence or absence taken for granted by the actors in this drama, allows for an extended discussion of the ubiquity and invisibility of slaves in the world of ancient Athens. Later on, we learn that Andocides himself, a man eager to demonstrate his filial piety and devotion to family, friends, and city, was not guilty of the crime of mutilating the herms because he had broken his collar-bone while riding. He recalls: "To show that this was true, I handed over my slave for torture to prove that I'd been ill and hadn't even been getting up from my bed" [64]. There are several such moments in this oration, and here too the students, reading the text in Greek, seemed not in the least uncomfortable with the fact that slave testimony in the Athenian law courts was acceptable only if derived through torture.[2] Such reactions have made me worry about students' capacity for historical empathy.

I no longer have to contend with the traditional idealization of ancient Greek and Roman culture, especially among Classical studies majors. Once upon a time, when high-school and freshman university courses on Western civilization were the norm in the United States, the glories of ancient Greece and Rome were standard fare. The Greeks invented democracy, philosophy, and drama, and we were their worthy heirs. In my experi-

---

[1]. Gagarin and MacDowell (1998: 104). All citations of Andocides refer to this translation.
[2]. See duBois (1991).

ence, students no longer arrive with these illusions; if they remember anything about the humanities, it is possibly some elements of global culture or multi-culturalism, or a smattering of American history, but their ideas about ancient Greece and Rome seem derived from books like Rick Riordan's series *Percy Jackson and the Olympians,* or from "games" in which ancient heroes are resuscitated with little attention to their former lives in ancient mythology. Reminding them of the painful facts of ancient slavery merely to demystify the glories of ancient architecture or philosophy or literature, or the Athenian invention of the jury system, seems pointless. Classicists themselves tend to cast a critical eye on those glories anyway, these days.[3]

But teaching as I do at a large public university, I have other sorts of courses beside those in ancient Greek, graduate seminars on comparative slavery studies, undergraduate courses on comparative slavery, or on texts read in translation that concern slaves and slavery. I teach a course on ancient Greece and Rome in cinema and television, and a freshman lecture course with two hundred students, a survey of ancient civilizations including the ancient Near East, ancient Greece, ancient India, and ancient China. Especially in these general education courses, there is little prior knowledge of antiquity. It is in these courses, courses using texts in translation and films, that I have most difficulty concerning a degree of discomfort about slavery. If Classics majors themselves accept slavery and the torture of slaves in Classical Greek and Roman antiquity without turning a hair, the general education students go beyond such acceptance, to *identification* with ancient slaves. But this is a particular brand of slavery based on their prior viewing of movies and television. If students have seen movies about antiquity, going back to the beginning of the history of film, they have experienced ancient Greece and Rome from within the monotheistic perspective of Judaism and Christianity.[4] And in most cases, among my students, they have uncritically idealized the slaves of ancient Greece and Rome, as martyrs, as underdogs, as Christians before or after the fact.

In *Ben Hur,* for example, one of the first narratives to be filmed, in 1907, published as a novel in 1880 with the subtitle: *A Tale of the Christ,* Judah Ben Hur, a nationalist hero of ancient Israel, spends time as a slave rowing in Roman galleys. In a later version, the film starring Charlton Heston made in 1959, Heston-Ben Hur is a charismatic leader who calls on

---

3. See duBois (2001); (2003); (2010a); (2010b).
4. On these films, see Wyke (1997); Joshel, Malamud, and McGuire (2005).

the Zionist impulses of viewers of that film, made soon after the foundation of modern Israel, even as he encounters Jesus in the course of his life. Jesus, whose face is never shown, gives the thirsty Ben Hur water after he has been made a slave for resisting Roman domination of Israel; Ben Hur returns the favor as Jesus carries his cross to Calvary, and at the end of the film, as Ben Hur's mother and sister are cured of leprosy by the radiant light that signals Jesus' death, he seems to join his beloved Esther and his family in conversion to Christianity. The galley slave, adopted by a Roman senator, is freed and becomes a leader of his people, only to become a follower of Jesus. His sufferings as a slave, whipped by various cruel overseers, are overshadowed by his stature, physical and moral; the movie, in a sort of family romance, suggests that the nobility of Ben Hur's character can easily overcome the momentary obstacle of enslavement. And the identification of the audience is solicited for Ben Hur himself, a magnificent specimen of manhood, Jew and Christian at once.

In the 1960 film *Spartacus,* starring Kirk Douglas, once again the heroic slave stands at the center of the narrative. This is but one in a long line of dramatic presentations of the story of the Thracian slave, including theatrical drama and even ballet. Although the life of Spartacus predated the birth of Jesus, there are here too moments in the film which point to the imminent arrival of Christianity, as well as allusions to the Nazi Holocaust of the Jews in the Second World War. As Spartacus is dying on the cross, crucified along with his followers by the Romans, we see Jean Simmons carrying his infant son, riding off into the future; the scene condenses the representations of the baby Jesus and his mother, dressed in blue, with the visual presentations of the death of Jesus. And again, the hero is a magnificent slave.

A whole series of films concerning antiquity solicit this explicit or implicit identification of the contemporary audience with ancient Israelites enslaved in Egypt, or with Christian or proto-Christian slaves, supporting audience projection into their situation of humiliation and degradation, but with a constant irony. The film-going audience knows that the humble and oppressed slaves embody the future, that the Israelite slaves will conquer Canaan and establish the kingdom based in Jerusalem, and that Christianity will eventually seize hold of the Roman Empire, and defeat "paganism." So the slaves' sufferings are ennobled and justified, seen as a necessary and transitory martyrdom before the inevitable victory of the meek.

Other films in this category include *The Robe* (1953), based on a best-selling novel by the Congregationalist minister Lloyd C. Douglas, who also wrote *Magnificent Obsession* (1929). Marcellus, the decadent Roman character, is rescued from depravity by his slave Demetrius, played by Victor Mature, who is purchased by Marcellus in a slave auction in Rome. Demetrius is the moral force in the narrative, becoming a Christian after he and Marcellus participate in the crucifixion of Jesus and receive his robe; Demetrius is linked to a utopian community of Christians who are filmed with light radiating from their beatific faces, and who argue against economic exploitation. Demetrius, now freed, is tortured by the Romans, but healed by the Christian Peter, and here again, the slave emerges as the moral center of the drama. In the sequel to this film, *Demetrius and the Gladiators* (1954), Marcellus has gone to heaven, and his former slave undergoes several career changes, including Praetorian guard, Roman tribune, and gladiator. Although at one point he abandons Christianity, in the end he returns to the faith and carries the robe to Peter, along with the message that the new emperor Claudius will not persecute the Christians as Caligula had. *The Silver Chalice,* made in the same year as *Demetrius and the Gladiators,* is also based on a successful novel. A Greek slave, Basil, sold by his own uncle into slavery, is played by Paul Newman, who crafts a cup to contain the holy grail from the last supper; the slave becomes a Christian after he wins his freedom. Again, the slave is good, is Christian, is artistic and sensitive, and chooses art and virtue over pagan decadence. In my course on films about antiquity, these films, many of them already well known by the students, seem to at least temporarily reinforce their identification with ancient slaves. Although there was a similar idealization of the ancient slave Spartacus in the Soviet Union, and a famous ballet based on his life, the audience was encouraged not only to see Christianity in the slave, but also proletarian class consciousness.

In more recent years, students have seen Ridley Scott's *Gladiator* (2000), and the cable television series *Spartacus: Blood and Sand* (2010) as well as a "prequel," *Spartacus: Gods of the Arena* (2011), with more to come. In *Gladiator,* the central character, the general Maximus, played by Russell Crowe, although not a Christian, is an elite Roman enslaved and made a gladiator. Like other slaves in movies based on the ancient world, he proves his inner nobility and defeats all enemies in the arena, including the emperor Commodus, and is the brilliant and admirable protagonist in a fantasmatic representation of the restoration of the Roman Republic. The film was a huge international success, and again centered audience identification on a heroic slave character. In the STARZ television series retelling the often-told story of the Thracian slave Spartacus, the emphasis has rested not only on the semipornographic erotic life of the Romans, including the former Xena, Lucy Lawless, playing a Roman matron, but also on the heroic brutality, gory battles, and bloodthirst of the slave gladiators. These slaves are models of heroic masculinity for some viewers. For many students, raised on violent video games, identification with these characters seems effortless.

The late Gilles Deleuze, in his influential work on cinema, described the ways in which Hollywood has used antiquity allegorically: "the American cinema constantly shoots and reshoots a single fundamental film, which is the birth of a nation-civilization, whose first version was provided by Griffith" (Deleuze 1992: 148). Deleuze here refers to *Birth of a Nation*, released in 1915, which recounts the history of the Civil War in the United States, the impact on North and South, and the foundation of the Ku Klux Klan, the murderously racist group organized after the abolition of slavery to maintain white supremacy in the southern United States. He goes on to draw the parallel with the cinematic traditions of the Soviet Union: "It has in common with the Soviet cinema the belief in a finality of universal history; here the blossoming of the American nation, there the advent of the proletariat" (148).

Deleuze points to the narcissism of cinema in America: "it and it alone is the whole of history, the germinating stock from which each nation-civilisation detaches itself as an organism, each prefiguring America" (149). He points out that as in the 1923 version of *The Ten Commandments*, which featured a parallelism between the ancient world and the United States, the "decadent nations are sick organisms" (149). America is the cure.

If the Bible is fundamental to them, it is because the Hebrews, then the Christians, gave birth to healthy nation-civilizations which already displayed the two characteristics of the American dream: that of a melting pot in which minorities are dissolved and that of a ferment which creates leaders capable of reacting to all situations (149).

American film treats all genres to some degree as "historical." Biblical and toga epics, Westerns and gangster movies, all look to a past that is fictionalized and treated as a myth of origin for the United States. And of course, with Griffith at the origin of these traditions, the issue of slavery in the antebellum period, the rise of the racist clan after the American Civil War, and the abjection of African Americans from the "melting pot" is part of the continuing development of the cinematic trajectory in America. Slavery, which might seem to have been the tragic situation of the Israelites in the *Ten Commandments* (1956), was the "natural" condition of African Americans, and this double history of slavery affects the teaching of antiquity in my classrooms, where many students, as noted above, identify with the enslaved Israelites, with the colonized slaves of the Romans, but not with the slaves who inhabited their own nation from the sixteenth to the nineteenth century, and beyond. Ancient slaves, usually represented as white, are noble characters resisting tyranny; the African American slaves of D. W. Griffith are base, and prone to rape white women.

DELEUZE, following Nietzsche's analysis of three aspects of history, makes the point that, of the "antiquarian," the "critical" or "ethical," and the "monumental," this last aspect:

> favours the analogies or parallels between one civilization and another: the great moments of humanity, however distant they are, are supposed to communicate via the peaks, and form a 'collection of effects in themselves' which can be more easily compared and act all the more strongly on the mind of the modern spectator. (149)

Monumental histories, such as those of ancient Babylon, or Israel, communicate with the film-makers' present. Hollywood filmmakers assume that the white ancestors of their audiences share their hatred of white slavery, and possess an innate desire for freedom and an identification with the heroic slaves of the Israelite and Roman past, an identification that takes for granted the white privilege of most filmmakers and spectators. The situation in these ancient settings is allegorized to encompass what the American directors assume is a natural hunger for freedom and escape from bondage, a naturalization that echoes American ideas about the foundation of the nation, even though the nation was in fact built on the genocide of indigenous people and the enslavement of Africans. The myth of escape from oppression, the "huddled masses yearning to be free," from Emma Lazarus's poem, inscribed on the Statue of Liberty, informs profoundly these accounts of antiquity on film. Ancient—almost always white—slaves are heroized, the underdogs belatedly breaking off from a site of decadent beginnings, and forming a new noble nation, distinct from the Roman tyrants, the aristocratic oppressors, in films from *Ben Hur* to *The Robe* (1953), to *Demetrius and the Gladiators* (1954), to *Spartacus* and then to *Gladiator*, which features the displaced Western hero, noble of character and although enslaved, demonstrating his true nobility in the face of the depraved emperor in the arena. Deleuze observes that the Hollywood film not only considers ancient and modern civilizations to be parallel, but, citing the Soviet film pioneer Sergei Eisenstein, he also points out that:

the principal phenomena of a single civilization, for example, the rich *and* the poor, are treated as 'two parallel independent phenomena,' as pure effects that are observed, if necessary with regret, but nevertheless without having any cause assigned to them. Hence, it is inevitable that causes are rejected from another perspective, and only appear in the form of individual duels which sometimes oppose a representative of the poor and a representative of the rich, sometimes a decadent and a man of the future, sometimes a just man and a traitor, etc. (149–50)

This description anticipates the situation in Ridley Scott's *Gladiator*, where the central character is a slave, but where the issue of slavery is never addressed; the condition of the leading man is nothing like that of the ordinary slaves in the drama, and his natural superiority emerges in the course of the drama. In the "duel," the "man of the future," the "just man," in the person of the slave gladiator Maximus, confronts the decadent, rich, traitorous emperor Commodus, and defeats him not in the name of the anonymous slaves of the Roman empire, but for the sake of the restoration of the aristocratic Roman Republic. All this an allegory for a return to the simple values of the American republic. Like John Wayne and other Western heroes, this lonely, courageous, tragic hero looks back to a paradise lost. The new television *Spartacus*, continuing the themes of blood and sand and voyeurism, focuses not on slave rebellion but on the gory combat and homosocial bonding of "world extreme cagefighting," an American mixed martial art. The causes of slavery or poverty are never addressed; the heroic slave gladiators accidentally, unjustly fall into the hands of evil Roman soldiers or slave-traders.

And for American students, these ancient slaves are the good guys, the world-historical subjects of a new world, soon to be free, and it is difficult to make them see otherwise, even with Hecuba, or Andromache, or an Aristophanic Xanthias. These ancient Greek characters, from Athenian tragedy and comedy, stand in some sense for the real slaves in the Athens of their first audience, and suffered humiliation and defeat in their possession by free persons, whether their fates are treated tragically or comically. They are not the bearers of a New World of freedom. In the film *Spartacus*, Tony Curtis, in a once-censored scene, escapes from the decadent Roman aristocrat Crassus, played by Laurence Olivier, who tries to seduce him with talk of oysters and snails. Homophobia links up with identification with the collective slaves surrounding Spartacus, who die on the cross with their hero as he gazes down at his family moving toward the dawn of Christianity, presaged in the voice-over that begins the film. If there are titillating aspects of ancient slavery, a whiff of sado-masochism in such TV presentations as *Rome* and *Spartacus,* with lascivious Roman matrons like Lucy Lawless, the former Xena, dominating slaves sexually, this adds to the unconscious pleasures of identification.

As Deleuze argues, referring to the orgy of decadent nations represented in historical, monumental films:

> [I]t is a matter of Good and Evil, with all the temptations or the horrors of Evil (the barbarians, the unbelievers, the intolerant, the orgy, etc.). The ancient or recent past must submit to trial, go to court, in order to disclose what it is that produces decadence and what it is that produces new life; what the ferments of decadence and the germs of new life are, the orgy and the sign of the cross, the omnipotence of the rich and the misery of the poor. (151)

These are familiar and comforting narratives for Americans, histories that parallel the myths and ideologies that sustain their sense of living in the greatest nation in the history of human kind. Slavery in ancient contexts especially does not make them uncomfortable; they see it as the prelude to the establishment of a new and better world.

What *does* make my students uncomfortable, and, as noted above, I have to say too that I believe that part of our responsibility as teachers is to make them uncomfortable, is to think critically about the history of slavery, *including* slavery in the history of the United States. It may seem perverse to argue for making students uncomfortable, in the context of this volume in which other essays take up the difficult and painful questions of rape, violence in the family, homophobia, sexism or racism. Of course if students have been the victims of such oppressive treatment, they need to be protected from further trauma as class discussion touches on these questions in Classical texts. But I do think that we can be too protective of students who want to remain comfortable, not to hear about matters they have not been exposed to, and which are often suppressed in the ideology of the United States in particular, which has an intense investment in seeing itself as the "greatest nation on earth," refuge for the refugee, home of family values and patriotic fervor. The history of the United States might indeed make them uncomfortable, if they read it from the point of view of indigenous people, decimated at best, exterminated at worst, or from the perspective of the descendants of the "middle passage," the forced kidnapping, purchase, enslavement, transportation of Africans from Africa to the Americas. Many died; those that survived were sold into terrible conditions.[5]

---

5. See Hartman (2008); Rediker (2007).

Although this information may make some African American students "uncomfortable," it has seemed to me that most appreciate attention to a neglected part of American history, and that making the oblivious uncomfortable is teaching them. Just as, in a course I teach on evolution, prehistory and ancient civilizations, when I remind the students that we are all Africans, descendants of the earliest Homo sapiens from Africa, the black students in the class seem to enjoy this reminder, while some white students, especially those from evangelical Christian anti-evolution backgrounds, scowl at me.

If some contemporary students have no trouble identifying with Charlton Heston as Judah Ben-Hur, or Kirk Douglas playing the Thracian slave Spartacus, or Russell Crowe as the enslaved gladiator Maximus, or the late Andy Whitfield playing the new Spartacus, many of them are, like the secession-celebrating citizens of South Carolina, in deep denial about the history of racialized slavery in the United States, its defining presence in the nation's foundation, in the constitution, and its persistence after the civil war, in what Douglas Blackmon (2008) calls "slavery by another name," the virtual re-enslavement of black men in the South in the prison system in which they furnished free labor for many of the mines, railroads, urban construction, and factories. In the course of a blistering indictment of racial abuse in the Southern states, he documents the dependence of such companies as U.S. Steel on the forced labor of African Americans returned to slavery by the criminal justice system:

> Only by acknowledging the full extent of slavery's grip on US society—its intimate connections to present-day wealth and power, the depth of its injury to millions of black Americans, the shocking nearness in time of its true end—can we reconcile the paradoxes of current American life. (402)

Blackmon cites the end of World War II, and the return of African American soldiers from the front, as the moment at which calls for racial justice triumphed over the centuries-old survival of slavery in the United States.

But the criminologist and historian Loic Wacqant has described different racist regimes that have succeeded one another:

> Not one but several "peculiar institutions" have successively operated to define, confine and control African-Americans in the history of the United States. The first is *chattel slavery* as the pivot of the plantation economy and inceptive matrix of racial division from the colonial era to the Civil

> War. The second is the *Jim Crow* system of legally enforced discrimination and segregation from cradle to grave.... America's third special device for containing the descendants of slaves in the Northern industrial metropolis is the *ghetto*. ... (Wacquant 2002: 41)

The final institution, still in force, is "the carceral apparatus," which he describes as joined to the ghetto to produce the hugely disproportionate numbers of African American men in America's prisons. Wacquant establishes a genealogical link between mass imprisonment and slavery. The present-day criminal justice system in fact continues to exploit the labor of inmates, many African American, who are virtual slaves. All of this makes many students, especially non-African American students, very uncomfortable.

In addition to this legacy, and continuation of African American slavery in American society, reflected in popular culture, in music and television and films, and in the everyday exploitation and incarceration of black Americans, there is also the persistent fact of slavery around the world and in the United States in the present. For example, there are collections of accounts, in slaves' own voices, of their experiences of enslavement in the present. Here is one such account, a first-person narrative from modern Greece, the story of "Valdete," a young woman from Albania:

> We were living on my mother's pension payment, since my father was unemployed. When I was sixteen I had to go to Athens and work there for my living. There I was introduced to a guy from Fier [in southwest Albania], who first promised to marry me, but very soon cheated me and made me a prostitute.
>
> I was unlucky, living with a cruel person who treated me as a slave. I stayed with him for more than two years. During that time I was working ten to twelve hours a day, and he got all my profits. The first thing I experienced in the morning was beating and torture by him. (Bales and Trodd 2008: 56)

To read this first-person account juxtaposed with the texts describing the prostitutes of Classical Athens decreases the distance between the present and the past. And lest we imagine that such things happen only in other places, far away from the United States, I ask my students in courses on slavery, both graduate and undergraduate, which always include this comparative aspect, to read the narratives collected from slaves in America, like this one from "Joyce," collected in 2002:

"Was doing migrant work since I was nine or ten. Went to school with Mormons. Only black in the school. . . . Worked many years on the camp. And they be beating on you and pistol-whuppin' you. . . . Never got paid a cent. . . . . Sometimes till 9 PM with the truck lights on picking sweet potatoes in North Carolina. Locked up each night in a compound with barbed wire, guarded by dogs. They'd make a count of everyone before bedtime, and they'd be walking with a rifle outside the hall when people slept." (Bales and Trodd 2008: 220)

Children, boys and girls, are enslaved in sex trafficking, in domestic labor, in agriculture. There's the story of Miguel, from Mexico, an undocumented farm-worker, who "felt like a slave" from the moment he arrived in the United States (Bales and Trodd 2008: 143–44); Maria, also from Mexico, who worked as a domestic slave: "The third day in the house he told me that he had bought me, that I was his slave, that he paid $200 for me, that I was there to do whatever he wanted to do to me. . . . He beat me, raped me; every day he abused me mentally, physically, emotionally, spiritually. . . . After I reached eighteen, he sent me to work in the factory and I brought my check back" (166–67). Compare this to the scene of Diocleides in Athens in 415 BCE, going to Laurium to collect the wages for his slave.

I try to undo white students' imaginary sense that their skin color protects them from slavery, convince students that in antiquity slaves were often Greeks, not the heroic founders of a new nation, but rather the tortured, beaten, short-lived victims of their masters, and I find it useful, even though many elements of the situation have changed dramatically, even though slavery in capitalism is different from ancient slavery, to have them read not just texts from antiquity, and American ante-bellum slave narratives, but also these first-person accounts collected from some of the thirty million present-day slaves, some of them in the United States. This does, and should, make everyone uncomfortable.

Teaching Ancient Comedy
Joking About Race, Ethnicity, and Slavery

BARBARA GOLD

IN A CLASS on "Ancient Comedy: Then and Now," which was, by design, slanted heavily towards works concerning women and rape, e.g., Aristophanes *Lysistrata, Thesmophoriazusae, Assemblywomen;* Menander *Epitrepontes;* Plautus *Casina, Truculentus, Bacchides* and *Cistellaria;* and Terence *Hecyra* and *Eunuchus,* I taught many plays that deal with issues that often cause discomfort among the students in a variety of different ways: slavery and torture of slaves, rape, gender-crossing, cross-dressing, forced prostitution, and baby-swapping, to name but a few (see James 2012; this volume). I was ever mindful of the fact that this was billed as a class on *comedy* and that the students were expecting it to be funny. To counter this expectation, we took as a guiding principle Woody Allen's pronouncement about comedy: "Primarily I want the audience to laugh. If they laugh and don't think, then I'm successful; if they laugh and think, then I'm very successful. If they think and don't laugh, then I've had it."[1] So I tried to give the students plenty to laugh about. But also to think about.

I told the class that we would look at comedy as a social document: at what comedy tells us about, *inter alia,* the changing lives of women, the treatment of slaves in ancient societies, and the differential social strata that the various types of characters inhabit. Further we would investigate how humor works: what is funny, to whom is it funny, why is it funny,

---

1. As quoted in the *Independent,* London, 13 May 1995 (cited in Balme 2001: xxix).

and at whose expense is the joke made (comedy almost always has a butt). The students were chagrined on hearing my intended plan, since they were expecting a class on jokes and humor, not on potentially uncomfortable and difficult issues. The course was designed to be performative and interactive in nature: in each class, groups of students read aloud and performed for the class scenes from the play we had read for that day, and, at the end of the course, the students put on, for the entire campus, two plays that they wrote and produced, based on ideas, themes, and tropes from the ancient comedies we read that they transposed into a contemporary setting. The plays that they wrote included certain themes and devices from the ancient plays, such as cross-dressing, use of a chorus, reversal of fortune or social status, divine figures, and attempts to topple social institutions. One play, for example, centered on the President of our college (a woman), who, in order to infiltrate a fraternity and investigate its drinking habits, cross-dresses as a man, gets drunk herself, and ends up in bed with a "prospie" (a prospective student). The real identity of the President is uncovered by the fraternity boys, and the President (the socially and culturally dominant figure) is compelled, through a series of clever machinations on the part of the fraternity members, to support and abet the outrageous behavior of those below her (the students in the fraternity).

The students were thus frequently encouraged, through dramatic readings, performances, active discussion, and writing their own scripts, to live, to feel and to enact the different characters and situations in the plays. They had to interact with each other, in sometimes uncomfortable scenes, on two levels: in their own voices, and as the characters in the plays whose views and behavior they assumed. Some students were more willing than others to take on a character's voice, mannerisms, gender and point of view; others retained their own personalities and behaviors, simply reading the scene without taking on the character. But even those who did not allow themselves to identify with their character of the moment stepped out of their own shoes when they interacted with students reading opposing roles in the scene. It was the *interaction,* carried on in front of an audience, that caused them to think more deeply about what their character might have felt, how some characters would have been open to abuse, and how those characters might have reacted.

Another significant factor in the reactions of the students to the material in this course is that I teach at a private liberal arts college, which has a 200-year history of being largely wealthy, white, male, and privileged. Here politeness is generally the prevailing mode of behavior (at least superficially). Many students are reluctant to raise and grapple with delicate and difficult issues, or do not even recognize that such issues exist. Furthermore, I suspect that many of the students take Classics courses precisely to avoid having to grapple with difficult issues; students (and, sad to say, many professors) often view Classics as a "safe" space away from disturbing issues, a place where they can read old books that will not force them to contend with what they think of as contemporary problems.[2] Thus, in order to get students to do this kind of engaging, one often has to force the issue. If we choose to teach a course on the ancient world in such a way as to bring up issues that are present in the text or even foregrounded by it but which can safely be ignored if we decide not to highlight them, we run certain risks. (This risk-taking is perhaps why most of my own professors managed to curtail or even avoid altogether discussions of matters like gender, not to mention rape and sexuality.) We risk making some or all of the students uncomfortable, and indeed making ourselves uncomfortable too. We risk having to alter our pedagogies in order to accommodate these less traditional and more incendiary topics. But we take these risks in order to do what any good teacher must do: unsettle presumptions, defamiliarize the familiar, and make the students engage with the messiness of life, "reveal what's going on beneath and behind appearances."[3]

This chapter will fall into two parts. Before I discuss the ways in which I attempted to teach plays that deal with issues around slavery, race and ethnicity, I will give some historical background on the plays themselves—in particular on their audiences—and on how jokes work.[4] There has long been discussion about the physical setting and audiences of Roman New Comedy. Where were the plays performed? Who comprised the audience? How and to whom were jokes about issues like slavery and rape pitched? How did the marginalized groups who are so prominent in these plays (slaves, prostitutes, courtesans) react to the jokes about the groups to which they belonged? And when we refer to "slaves" in Rome, what exactly do we mean?

Many scholars who make the argument that these plays were written for the mainstream ruling class assume that the plays were always pre-

---

2. Compare here Pearcy's remark about a similar view of Classical works and themes in neoclassical drama in nineteenth-century America: "Neo-classical dramas could raise political issues, but it is striking how often in America a classical setting seems to mute political receptions or remove them to a safely remote time or space" (Pearcy 2013).
3. Lisa Miller, "Harvard's Crisis of Faith," *Newsweek* 2/22/10, 43.
4. Much of this work has been done in a forthcoming article by Amy Richlin entitled "Talking to Slaves in the Plautine Audience." I thank her for sharing this work with me in advance of its publication, and I am grateful for her well-supported insights into the genesis and settings of Plautine plays and for asking important questions concerning how joking about slavery works.

sented at the various *ludi* or institutionalized festivals sponsored by this same ruling class, and they ask why these men would sponsor publicly-funded plays that undercut their authority and position.[5] But there is no reason to think that the plays were performed only at state-sponsored *ludi*; they may well have been presented more casually at local, rural fairs and markets, and outside of Rome. This sort of monolithic thinking undercuts the complexity of both the historical and physical backdrops of these plays, and the language and reception of the texts. Who was "the audience"? Not only upper-class citizen males. Women, lower classes, slaves and soldiers were also present. Because of the differences in their status, they would not have responded in the same way as those who were free men or of a higher social class. Indeed the plays would have appealed to each of these constituencies in a different way, and each member of the audience would have heard, seen, and noticed different words, gestures, things said and unsaid, differently.

Slaves in Roman comedy are a puzzle because they inhabit a double register: since they are slaves, they are always vulnerable and constantly under threat of being beaten or otherwise punished, yet they often have starring roles in these plays (e.g., Pseudolus in Plautus' play of that name or Chalinus in Plautus *Casina*), and they famously outwit their masters at every turn. Most scholars have assumed that the notional audience (or the audience at which the playwright was actually aiming his words and which he expected to sympathize with his point of view) was in fact comprised of slave-holding Roman male citizens, and that such an audience would have enjoyed and laughed at the jokes on themselves (when the slave characters bested them) for several reasons. First, the plots were not a serious reflection of reality nor a reflection of what went on in their houses. *Their* slaves were well-behaved and kept in line; *their* wives were modest and discreet and knew their place. Second, this was a fantasy, a play on stage, and the fantasy (of slaves outwitting masters, of wives ending wars by going on sex strikes) would end when the play ended. There was no danger of it threatening them in real life. They could keep the plots at arm's length. Third, the constant threat of punishment to the wayward slaves was perhaps enough to make the slave-holding citizens confident that such slaves would always receive the appropriate payback for their anti-social behavior.

When we use the term "slave" in the context of ancient Rome, what exactly are we referring to? Certainly not what was meant by slaves in

---

5. See McCarthy (2000: 18): "I am emphasizing the logic for thinking of Plautine comedy as part of the public transcript because it gives a firm basis for arguing that it is the desires of the dominant in Roman society, rather than those of subordinates, that exert the primary force shaping these plays."

eighteenth–nineteenth-century America, when slave was a racially-loaded word. We might mean (and often do mean) men captured in wars (and such slaves would often have been well educated), or female slaves (often born to other Roman slaves or captured in wars), or about-to-be freed slaves, or slaves born to homebred slaves living in Roman households and reasonably well-treated, or slaves sent to work in the mills or mines who had short, execrable lives. But—and this needs to be made quite clear to the students—we do not mean people of color. Most Roman slaves would not have been racially differentiable from free Romans. Slaves who were prisoners of war would perhaps have been ethnically distinct, but students should be dissuaded from thinking of Roman slaves as being and looking like American slaves (for student attitudes toward slaves in the ancient world, often defined by contemporary movies, see duBois's essay in this volume). To be a slave was to hold a certain class and status, but the origins and circumstances of these slaves varied widely.

Amy Richlin, in a forthcoming work on Plautus, makes the following statement about the reception of comedy by different members of the audience: "the plays themselves deliver something for everyone: a plotline for the elite (to some degree), scenes for the underclasses, language on all levels. . . ."[6] So each member of the audience would have viewed each scene or heard each line a bit differently. As is also true of satire, joking language can be used to deliver double or triple meanings, and to hide whatever unitary truth might be lurking behind the comic screen. Slaves speak in double-talk, intending to send one message to the master and another to a fellow slave or another less dominant character. So, for example, Tyndarus' aside about Philocrates in Plautus' *Captivi* notes:

ut facete orationem ad servitutem contulit (276)

how he has cleverly adapted his language to slave jargon!

Here, Tyndarus' statement could mean one of two things: that Philocrates (who is masquerading as a slave) is very good at sounding like he is a slave; or that Philocrates is cleverly speaking in code, hiding one meaning beneath another, as slaves must do.

Or consider the sexual innuendo present in Plautus' *Casina,* when Chalinus, a slave, speaks to Lysidamus, his master, about Olympio, another slave who is listening in:

---

6. Richlin (forthcoming).

CH. adsunt quae imperavisti omnia: (358)
uxor, sortes, situla atque egomet. OL. te uno adest plus
    quam ego volo.
CH. tibi quidem edepol ita videtur; stimulus ego nunc (360)
    sum tibi,
fodico corculum; adsudascis iam ex metu, mastigia.
LY. tace, Chaline. CH. comprime istunc. OL. immo (362)
    istunc qui didicit dare.
LY. adpone hic sitellam, sortis cedo mihi.

CHALINUS: Everything you ordered is here: wife, lots, water, and I myself.
OLYMPIO: (breaks in) With *you* here there's one thing more than I want.
CHALINUS: It may well seem that way to you. I'll sting you now, I'll
    pierce your little heart. You're already
    scared and sweaty, you whipping post
LYSIDAMUS: Be quiet, Chalinus.
CHALINUS: Take this fellow in hand!
OLYMPIO: No, you take *him* in hand! He's *used* to being taken in hand!
LYSIDAMUS (bringing things back under control): Bring the urn here.
Give me the lots. (II.6; translation by James Tatum, adapted)

The English translation nicely highlights the complexity and sexual innuendo of the word *comprime* in line 362, which can mean both "to get control over someone" and "to rape someone." Likewise the phrase *didicit dare* (362) can mean that he is used to getting punished or he is used to being on the receiving end of a homosexual rape.[7] Lysidamus, the master, and Olympio, the other slave, are hearing quite different things from Chalinus' remark, and the two meanings of the word can apply equally well to Lysidamus, who has both the authority and position to punish the slaves and also elsewhere in the play engages in homosexual encounters with both men (and they with each other: II.8; III.6, IV.4, V.2).

James Scott, in his book *Domination and the Arts of Resistance* (written about Malay peasants), talks about the "hidden transcript" of a subaltern's speech (as opposed to the "public transcript" that displays institutionally-supported values and events). The sentiments expressed by a slave in such a hidden transcript would allow him or her to express feelings of anger and retribution "in the teeth of power" (Scott 1990: xiii) while at the same time

---

7. See further for the sexual enslavement of characters in the *Captivi*, Leigh (2004: 90–91).

also offering a refuge of denial or disguise. Scott's theory is nicely encapsulated in an Ethiopian proverb quoted as an epigraph by Scott: "When the great lord passes the wise peasant bows deeply and silently farts." As Scott points out, since these "hidden transcripts" are meant to be hidden, they are somewhat difficult to locate or bring to light, but, he claims: "The recovery of the nonhegemonic voices and practices of subject peoples requires, I believe, a fundamentally different form of analysis than the analysis of elites, owing to the constraints under which they are produced."[8]

Then there is the matter of how jokes work and how discourse is framed and understood: the reception of and response to comedy also depends on whether the playwright has a willing listener and on finding an appropriate butt for the jokes. If we are to believe Freud's and Bergson's theories of laughter and joking, every joke needs an audience that shares the jokester's prejudices and presuppositions. This audience or target group provides reassurance and reinforcement and allows the jokester to say things that he otherwise would not dare to say. There also needs to be a third party, the butt of the joke (who may or may not be present). Thus A tells a joke to C (the listener/audience/confidant) about B, a third party who is the victim or butt.[9] This model works to some degree in comic/slave humor: the slave needs an audience and also needs a butt for his jokes. But since the full meaning of these jokes is usually double and must be hidden, the audience is split between the listener who hears and understands and another listener who hears but does not understand. The butt of the joke or action is also shifting: the teller himself (the slave) is the butt of the action of the play, or at least would appear to be, but he is in fact in charge of the jokes, for which the true butt is the master.

With so many ambiguities interlaced throughout a comedy and so many different layers of speaker and audience, it is clear that there can be no one dominant or totalizing way to read or approach comedy. It offers no easy or obvious answers; it both reinscribes normative values and also "provides a site of resistance to them."[10] The ontological and epistemological uncertainty that was generated by theatrical performance and that allowed the viewers to engage in role-switching throughout the play was present in both the bodies on stage and in the spectating bodies. The spectators—slave-owners and slaves alike—left the theater full of the ambiguities presented

---

8. Scott (1990: 19).
9. See on this Gold (1994).
10. See Rabinowitz (1998: 3). She is talking here about tragedy but this holds equally well for comedy.

in the plays. The ancient comic writers do the double business of reaffirming the ideals and norms of society while also leaving ample room for uncomfortable reflection on issues like slavery and rape. Some characters exemplify social norms; others, from marginalized groups, voice views critical of the social mores. Comedy thrives on confusion and the temporary disturbance of social order.[11] Each member of the audience will find different things to laugh at depending on how he or she is socially and personally situated.[12]

With this background in mind, I would like now to focus on the recent course I taught on Ancient Comedy and on one student in particular whose presence in the class caused me to rethink how I should be teaching it. In this class, I had, out of 23 students, about an equal number of men and women but only one student of color (African American). In a college such as mine, which still has only a very small number of non-white students, the demographic of the class was not surprising; even less so in a Classics course, which traditionally does not draw many students of color. Since the class would read many plays focused on issues of gender, unequal social status, and slavery (which might include discussion of both race and social rank), I had to think carefully about the demographic of the class and how these issues would affect different members of the class in different ways.

The most interesting student in the class was my African American student. I'll call him Jack. Jack was a first-year student, but not at all shy. I observed that most of the students in the class were made very uncomfortable by reading aloud and performing gender-bending scenes such as Aristophanes' *Thesmophoriazusae* or Plautus' *Casina* (the discomfort was made evident by the giggling, the reluctance to read certain parts, the exaggerated macho behaviors); in fact, they were aghast when I suggested that I was quite happy to have men playing women's roles and vice versa. But Jack was delighted to play, for example, the role of Pardalisca, the maid in *Casina*, modulating his voice to appear feminine, or to take roles in which a male

---

11. See Gold (1998: especially 27).

12. For a discussion of the reception and translation of Classical comedy and the importance of the receiver's historical and personal context, see Cook and Tatum (2010: 311–30). This chapter concerns the African-American poet and novelist Rita Dove and her poem "Arrow," which confronts a reading that Dove attended of Aristophanes' *Thesmophoriazusae* in a translation by the well-known Classical translator William Arrowsmith. Arrowsmith tries to replicate the effect of some of the Greek dialogue by using black urban English. Dove (and others) found his ethnic stereotyping racist and offensive, and Dove wrote her poem "Arrow" in response. Arrowsmith defended his translations as a way to "celebrate our differences" (Cook and Tatum 2010: 319, 412 n. 6, citing Scharffenberger 2002: 459) and as not meant to harm or offend (Scharffenberger 2002: 459). Cook and Tatum propose that Dove's poem could be referring to institutional racism (316), and they point out that "the appropriation of those [black speech, whether rustic or urban] languages could never be a neutral act" (315).

is acting the part of a female (such as The Kinsman in Aristophanes *Thesmophoriazusae*); perhaps Jack had had more experience in life than some other students at playing both public and hidden roles and at expressing himself by donning other masks? When Jack performed such parts (with gusto and hilarity), the rest of the class was amused but also taken aback at his willingness to engage so freely with the Other.

When it came time to talk about slavery and the mistreatment of slaves, which one can hardly avoid in Roman Comedy, I thought carefully about introducing the subject to the class.. When in Plautus' *Truculentus*, Callicles arrives with his slaves, driving two maids ahead of him with goads and whips, and says to Syra, Phronesium's maid: "rogitavi ego vos verberatas ambas pendentis simul" ("I questioned you both when you were strung up by your thumbs on the whipping post," 777), or when Truculentus says to Astaphium: "neque istuc insegesti tergo coget examen mali" ("This back is one field that will never know a whip's furrows," 314),[13] or when Phaedria in Terence's *Eunuchus* (165–69) goes looking for gifts to give to Thais, an Ethiopian slave-girl and a eunuch (presented as examples of two exoticized and half-human beings), I felt that I needed to contextualize the issues that these scenes raised and to carefully encourage discussion of their reactions. I was aware that the issue of slavery would or might resonate differently for the one African American student in the class (even though it was not racially-based slavery, as I took pains to explain repeatedly). I wondered how to include him fully in the conversation without seeming to put a spotlight on him. Or how to find out what his thoughts were without opening him up to embarrassment in front of the other students. I kept waiting for the moment when it would be clear that Jack was uncomfortable and I might need to steer the conversation in a safer direction (and is this, as duBois asks in her essay in this volume, always the best thing to do?). And for the moment when I would have to try to explain why these jokes are now or ever were "funny."[14] But Jack seemed unperturbed by these frequent references to torture of slaves, and the other students, inexplicably to me, who were otherwise full of wise-cracking comments on other uncomfortable issues like rape, had nothing to say at all.[15]

---

13. Fitzgerald comments, "Plautine comedy is riddled with references to beating, though, as Erich Segal pointed out in a classic study (1987), the presiding Saturnalian spirit ensures that beating, constantly threatened, is always postponed" (Fitzgerald 2000: 33). But this is not true: there are many passages in comedy (including Plautus *Truculentus* 777 cited above) that refer to whippings and beatings that *have* taken place or backs that *are* furrowed.

14. See Parker (1989).

15. My experience with trying to bring up, in a sensitive way, the difficult issue of slavery and the mistreatment of slaves, differs from that of Sharon James, who discusses teaching texts on rape in this volume. She reports that many of her students are eager to talk about both the rape texts and,

Jack came to see me in my office one day, and there he shed some light on his reactions or lack thereof. He said that because we were talking about slavery in an ancient Roman context and not slavery in the United States of the eighteenth–nineteenth centuries, the subject did not have a personal impact on him or make him uncomfortable (once again I was reminded that Classics courses provide a safe space to discuss potentially explosive issues because they feel so far removed from our students in time and space). Our context was a different time and a different place, and most of these slaves were not people of color (some, of course, like Phaedria's present of an Ethiopian slave-girl to Thais in Terence's *Eunuchus*, were). He mentioned in contrast a course he was taking simultaneously with mine on the Old South. In that course, he felt uncomfortable in the way that slavery was presented and discussed, and the topic seemed much more real to him for obvious reasons. As a requirement for that course, he had to go to a three-day conference held at an off-campus venue. He mentioned that there, out of approximately one hundred people at this conference, he was the only black person present except for one janitorial worker (the racial imbalance at this facility underlined the continuing importance of race in the United States). This class, he said, had made him uncomfortable in a way he never felt in my Comedy class (he never articulated why exactly, but I inferred that his discomfort came from the way the professor handled discussion of a slavery that was very much based on race).

Another rather surprising reaction to these plays and their portrayals of racial and ethnic issues and slavery was contained in Jack's final essay on Terence's *Hecyra*. In discussing the notional audience of this play (and others), Jack said the following:

> Although the notional audience probably was adult free men, I believe [that] this play has commentaries about a multitude of social relationships. I doubt that any ancient citizen would fail to gain from seeing such

---

sometimes, their own personal experiences (the latter in one-on-one conversations in her office). James and I both think it is extremely important to contextualize such difficult issues (rape, slavery) by discussing them in both ancient and modern contexts. Clearly her students discuss rape in her classes (or in some of her classes) more openly than mine were willing to discuss slavery. I suspect that the students' willingness to open up depends on a number of factors: whether the course has been offered before and whether the instructor is known to bring up such issues (my comedy course with its focus on women was offered for the first time); what kind of course it is and how large (a Latin class; a small seminar; a large lecture class); how clearly and consistently the subject is raised; what sort of texts are read (I think that comedy seems farther removed from the students' real experience than, for example, elegy does). James concludes a list of steps an instructor might want to take when preparing to teach rape by saying: "Don't be surprised if they don't want to talk about rape" (James 2012: 555).

a telling portrayal of their society. Women, men, slaves and prostitutes all have a place in this play. . . . Terence masterfully creates an abbreviated social structure that speaks to the rights, ambitions, and hardships of everyone within it.

Although I would have a hard time agreeing with the idea that women, slaves, and prostitutes felt fulfilled, justified or gratified by seeing the portrayals of themselves in these plays, I can see how Jack was able to find a way of reading these plays that would allow the marginalized and oppressed members of the society and the audience—and himself—to somehow see themselves reflected in the plots and actions.[16] Others have found ways to read slavery and rape that mitigate the horrors beneath them: the threats were rarely carried out and the plays only show a world turned upside down for the moment, a place that never really existed; or in the plays the slaves were nearly always more clever than their masters; or the slaves are usually sympathetic characters.[17] But these seem to me to be rather specious justifications for barbaric practices. Jack's method of trying to understand was more honest. Jack finally remarked that he did not find *Hecyra* funny at all, but he did find it his favorite play to "think about" (or, as we'd say now, to "think with").

What are the lessons learned from teaching this course in this way and from having Jack as my student? What would I do differently in the future? I would say first that it is easier in many ways to teach difficult and uncomfortable issues such as rape, slavery and the torture of slaves in courses on the ancient world, where students feel somehow protected from having to deal with these issues because the plays are so far separated in time and space from themselves. I know that students who discuss such issues in Women's Studies or Africana Studies classes have a much more visceral and personal reaction and that it is much harder for the professor to negotiate these discussions.[18] But in some ways, the feeling of separation that Classics

---

16. The situation is similar for violence directed against women in Roman comedy. Rape scenes are often mistranslated so as to imply that the sex is consensual; see Packman 1993 for good examples of such translations. But, as James points out (1998: 45–46): "The absence of any ameliorating or mitigating circumstance or element in the characters of these two young rapists [in Terence's *Hecyra* and *Eunuchus*] might well leave what Smith (1994: 30) calls 'a more reflective portion of the audience' . . . reflecting uncomfortably on love, sex, rape, and marriage in Rome."

17. See on this Parker (1989: 233–46). For example, Duckworth (1952: 288) says that "the cunning slaves are in a minority and the instances of ill-treatment are extremely few."

18. I think that an entirely different type of student takes courses in Africana Studies or Women's Studies, and that they expect there will be wide-ranging and open discussions of difficult issues (which does not mean that it is easy to teach them in those disciplines either). Many students take courses in Classics precisely because they think they will not have to engage with these difficult and

students often have makes it more difficult to teach these issues, precisely because they do not seem "real" to the students, and the students refuse to engage with them in a thoughtful way. When we were discussing one of many of the rape scenes (which are often translated in such a way that they do not appear to be rape but rather consensual sex or "boys will be boys" scenes),[19] one of my students (a male), who was looking increasingly frustrated and angry, argued that I was making too much of these rape scenes, that rape was not the same in antiquity as it is now, and that we should not overplay its importance. The students might have felt the same way about discussing slavery but did not want to articulate it in class.

Thus, in Classics, we have a divide to cross that sometimes gives a false sense of protection to the students and makes these all too real issues seem unreal to them.

Another lesson learned is that students who are not in the demographic group under discussion can easily remove themselves from the discussion, thinking "this is not about me" (for example the male student who minimized the importance of the rape scenes in these plays). Not one woman in the class felt that I had overemphasized the importance of the rape scenes. I imagine too that the white students in the class were farther removed from our discussions about slavery. Jack disconnected himself in some ways, but he also found a way of reading that allowed him to become a part of the notional audience that he constructed.

What would I do differently in the future? I would give the students more historical background on who slaves were in ancient Rome and compare Roman slavery to American slavery. I would explain more about the system of concealment and doubletalk that slaves had to inhabit, and have them act out, in a mindful way, scenes of beatings or threatened beatings. I would have the students examine plays in which the ethical nature of slavery seems to be at issue, and ask questions about what makes someone a "natural slave" versus one who has been wrongfully or temporarily enslaved.[20] And I would examine with them different translations, some of which gloss over the brutality of actions in the plays and others of which are more clear about what is happening.

It is clear that pushing students to read aloud and perform makes them see sides of these issues that they do not see from simply reading to themselves or class discussion. When students take on the mask of a character

---

personal topics, and their expectations differ. There is also a more mixed demographic in Women's Studies and Africana Studies classes than we usually tend to get in Classics courses.

19. See for good examples, Packman (1993) and Smith (1994).
20. See the discussion of Plautus *Captivi* in Leigh (2004: 86–95).

unlike themselves, it both forces them to consider how such a character might have thought about being a slave or a woman, and also allows them to behave differently than they would if they were not in a performative environment. The double strategies of performance and historical contextualization when used together punch home the significance of uncomfortable topics and make it possible for us to suggest ways in which the students can confront them profitably and honestly in their reading and in their own lives.

13

Difficult Dialogues about a Difficult Dialogue
Plato's *Symposium* and Its Gay Tradition

NIKOLAI ENDRES

> When we recognize the *Phaedrus* and the *Symposium* as interpreting our experiences, we can be sure that we are having those experiences in their fullness, and that we have the minimum of education. (Bloom 1987: 133)

I TEACH in the English Department at Western Kentucky University, which currently enrolls about 20,000 students, many of whom are first-generation. My two specialties are the Classical tradition and queer studies, which I combine in my Gay and Lesbian Literature class.[1] This popular course (judging from enrollment) begins with Plato's *Symposium* and uses Platonic love as a thematic thread throughout the semester.[2] While strictly speaking this is a comparative rather than Classics classroom, the *Symposium* (and the *Phaedrus*) remains an iconic text in all of later gay literature. However, the issue of pederasty (*erastes* and *eromenos*), or more broadly the relationship between an older man and a younger man, always raises problems. To American students, the *Symposium* (and partly the *Phaedrus*) presents erotic choices that they find strange, off-putting, or just void of love—in short, controversial.

---

1. I hereby would like to acknowledge the many (controversial) contributions my students in Gay and Lesbian Literature have made throughout the years to this essay, to the course, and to my intellectual development. I would also like to thank the WKU Office of Research for its generous support.

2. For a more detailed description of this course, see Endres (2009). I assign the following texts from Classical antiquity: Plato's *Symposium, Phaedrus*, and *Laws;* Petronius' *Satyricon;* Juvenal's Satires 2 and 9; excerpts from Suetonius' *Lives of the Caesars;* Sappho; and all the extant Greek and Roman sources dealing with lesbian activity.

Moreover, this relationship reoccurs in seminal texts of same-sex world literature: Encolpius and the Pergamene boy in Petronius' *Satyricon*, William Shakespeare and young Mr. W. H. in the Sonnets, Lord Henry and Dorian Gray in Oscar Wilde's *The Picture of Dorian Gray*, Gustav von Aschenbach and Tadzio in Thomas Mann's *Death in Venice*, Michel and his Arab boys in André Gide's *The Immoralist*, Jim Willard and Ronald Shaw in Gore Vidal's *The City and the Pillar*, Hadrian and Antinous in Marguerite Yourcenar's *Memoirs of Hadrian*, Alexander the Great and Bagoas in Mary Renault's *The Persian Boy*, Shunsuké Hinoki and Yuichi Minami in Yukio Mishima's *Forbidden Colors*, Harlan Brown and Billy Sive in Patricia Nell Warren's *The Front Runner*, and many more.

This prevalence seems to aggravate the problem, but it also hints at a solution. While Plato's speakers present erotic attachments that come across as abstract and difficult to American students ("difficult" as in the theme of this volume), looking at their later manifestations humanizes them. All the homoerotic relationships mentioned above maintain the age discrepancy, but the younger man/*eromenos* is in many cases no longer a minor (of course, Classical antiquity did not conceptualize teenagers the same way modern law does). Moreover, many of the issues that Plato's speakers gloss over (for example, why does a young man feel attracted to someone much older? will their love last? what is the role of monogamy? how exactly can the physical be transcended? why is the *eromenos* supposed to feel *philia* rather than *eros*? and what is the difference? how do women fit into the picture?) feature prominently in those later texts.

What I have found helpful in the classroom is a preliminary examination of Platonic love, which may very well leave students uncomfortable, but eventually they come to a better understanding of Plato's complex erotic relationships and a realization of why the *Symposium* has offered a validating model to "gay" men throughout the centuries. In what follows, I present five later texts, from different cultures and histories, showing how they can be used to address the difficulty students have in understanding Platonic love. I first discuss those texts' controversies and then explain my pedagogical strategies.

THE CONTROVERSY

(Classical) pederasty remains controversial, well beyond the classroom. A special issue of the *Journal of Homosexuality*, devoted to same-sex desire in Greco-Roman antiquity and in the Western tradition (2005), originally included an essay by psychologist Bruce Rind on pederasty. As the editors Beert Verstraete and Vernon Provencal point out in their introduction, nowadays pederasty is often conflated with pedophilia and sexual assault: "Unfortunately, one statement in the abstract of his paper was misconstrued by certain sectors as advocating pedophilia, which made it the subject of media controversy" (Verstraete and Provencal 2005: xxviii). While the essay was subsequently deferred, the issue remains in the spotlight with revelations about child abuse in the Catholic church; the football scandal at Pennsylvania State University; accusations against the former Prime Minister of Italy, Silvio Berlusconi, that he paid for sex with a 17-year old Moroccan prostitute; the arrest of a Mormon polygamist a few years ago for allegedly arranging marriages between underage girls and older men; controversy over the age of consent, which differs widely by state and country; or the statutory rape charges against Roman Polanski. Teachers can thus assume that students are aware of the issue but probably quite hesitant to talk about it.[3]

THE CHALLENGE

While I also teach the *Symposium* in Mythology, in Humanities: Greece and Rome, and in World Literature, where I sometimes hear a few homophobic grumblings, the students in Gay and Lesbian Literature know to expect an open forum on male and female homosexuality and are overwhelmingly gay friendly. What, then, is the challenge? First, being around eighteen years old, students are close in age to many teenage victims of sexual abuse and may thus feel particularly vulnerable. (However, I have never had a student who told me that he or she was abused as a child, unlike Sharon James, who has taught students who have been raped; see James 2008.) Second, many students are interested in discussing sex, but not all of them are comfortable doing so in class. Third, students are quick to dismiss someone like Gustav von Aschenbach, who wants to have a sex life past forty, as a dirty old man. Fourth, students almost impulsively see the minor in an intergenerational relationship as a victim. Fifth, I can confirm Sharon

---

3. For Classics teachers, one could add here the controversy over James Davidson's *The Greeks and Greek Love: A Radical Reappraisal of Homosexuality in Ancient Greece*: some of its biggest provocations concern the exact—sexual or not—nature of the *erastes/eromenos* bond (Davidson desexualizes it), the age of the *pais* in *paiderastia* (Davidson thinks it ranges from the late teens to the early twenties), the onset of puberty for Greek males (Davidson locates it much later than modernity does), sanctions for sexual assault of boys under eighteen (Davidson suggests the death penalty), sexuality as constructed (Davidson adheres to a more essentialist camp), or Davidson's demolition of "the fable of paedophile Greeks" (2007: 70).

James's observation that more and more students come to literature, Classical and modern, with an interested or subjective approach. One example: students really relate to E. M. Forster's *Maurice,* because, as they see it, it is a coming-out story in college, even though it dates back an entire century; yet notably, Forster's Clive turns to Plato in order to seduce Maurice: rather than ask the unspeakable "Are you gay?" he wants to know whether Maurice has read the *Symposium.*

A DIALOGUE ABOUT LOVE?

In the *Symposium,* seven speakers present seven different versions of *eros.* Students find most of them troubling. Phaedrus comes across as old, stuck in the past, and focused on the dead (although his mention of same-sex couples and the military usefully triggers discussion of another controversy). Pausanias, of course, gets to the crux of the issue:

> When an older lover and a young man come together and each obeys the principle appropriate to him—when the lover realizes that he is justified in doing anything for a loved one who grants him favors, and when the young man understands that he is justified in performing any service [*hupourgein*] for a lover who can make him wise and virtuous—and when the lover *is* able to help the young man become wiser and better, and the young man *is* eager to be taught and improved by his lover—then, and only then, when these two principles coincide absolutely, is it ever honorable for a young man to accept [*charisasthai*] a lover. (*Symp.* 184d–e)

In addition to the older/younger gap, students have a hard time with Pausanias' idea (widely held in past centuries) that love between men is heavenly and superior to the bond a man and a woman forge in marriage. At the same time, Pausanias' vision of a long-term relationship, "I am convinced that a man who falls in love with a young man of his age is generally prepared to share everything with the one he loves—he is eager, in fact, to spend the rest of his own life with him. He certainly does not aim to deceive him—to take advantage of him while he is still young and inexperienced and then, after exposing him to ridicule, to move quickly on to someone else" (181d–e), immediately appeals to my students. Unfortunately, I explain, Pausanias is describing an anomaly, for common belief held that an *eromenos* ceased to be desirable to an older man with the growth of his beard and the subsequent loss of his (androgynous) beauty.

To love bearded men is more meaningful for Pausanias, because only with age and maturity does a beloved develop a sense of fidelity—the very basis of a lasting relationship. Pausanias knows what he is talking about: his attachment with Agathon celebrates its tenth anniversary at the moment of the *Symposium* (see *Protagoras* 315d–e).

About Doctor Eryximachus there is something too clinical—literally: he elaborates on "the science of the effects of Love on repletion and depletion of the body" (*Symp.* 186c). Students are initially baffled by Aristophanes, but when I interpret his speech as the beginning of "romantic" love—the search for a soulmate, the desire for one's other half, the pursuit of the whole—students soon facetiously rechristen Valentine's Day as Aristophanes' Day. (Many students are also familiar with the movie *Hedwig and the Angry Inch,* which features Aristophanes' ideas about the origin of love.) The question is whether such love works. Martha Nussbaum, for example, objects to such a fusion: "For what [the split creatures] thought they most wanted out of their passionate movement turns out to be a wholeness that would put an end to all movement and all passion. A sphere would not have intercourse with anyone. It would not eat, or doubt, or drink . . . it would be complete" (1986: 176). A fruitful discussion of the validity and feasibility of romantic love in our time ensues. It seems that students approach Aristophanes' speech most comfortably, which may very well be due to the absence of the two halves' age difference. Here we have two similar (actually, identical) beings desperately in love with each other.

Three speakers remain. Agathon, who rhapsodizes that "Everyone knows that Love has extraordinary good looks, and between ugliness and Love there is unceasing war" (*Symp.* 196a), is too full of himself, too campy, "too queeny" (in the words of an openly gay student I taught a few years ago). Socrates, the ugliest man in Athens who likes to surround himself with male beauty, pontificates in terms too abstract, too hard, too ideal. Alcibiades usually evokes a lot of sympathy for being deeply but unhappily in love: "the moment he [Socrates] starts to speak, I [Alcibiades] am beside myself: my heart starts leaping in my chest, the tears come streaming down my face . . . " (215e). As David Halperin explains: "the Socratic community is a theater of frustration and torment. Indeed, Socrates . . . is a lover himself, yet he contrives to be surrounded by other lovers to whom he represents, in turn, an object of love, even as they are objects of love for him" (1986: 68). Platonic love is difficult.

The course now moves on to how these philosophical relationships are put into literary practice and how later writers deal with some of the greatest difficulties in Plato.

A BOY WHO LIKES SEX

While the *Satyricon* is unique in the syllabus presenting a non-hierarchical attachment between Encolpius and Ascyltus, it features a traditional account of Greek pederasty, "usus formosorum" (85.2), in the story of the Pergamene boy (sections 85–87). Eumolpus, now a rather lecherous old man, tells a tale about his younger days. Visiting a family with a beautiful but sheltered son, Eumolpus reveals an insidious scheme: "Whenever at the dinner table the subject of pederasty came up, I lit up with such anger, I begged them with such savage severity not to rape my ears with this obscene talk, that the parents (the mother especially) came to view me as one of those philosophical saints." Now students' alarm bells start ringing. Eumolpus takes the boy to the *gymnasium*, instructs him, makes gifts—first a pair of doves, then two fighting cocks—and has his way. When Eumolpus fails to deliver on the promise of a Macedonian stallion (a gift so big that it smacked of prostitution), the *ephebus*, who had boasted to his friends about his lover's wealth, threatens to turn him in: "I'll tell my father." Will Eumolpus be punished? Eumolpus never tires in his seductions and once again gets what he wants: "for the truly conscience-free, no challenge is too great." Then Petronius completely twists the story, with victimizer and victim switching roles:

> With bad feeling vanished, I was reconciled to the boy, and having enjoyed his favor I fell asleep. But the boy was at the end of puberty, an age eager for passive pleasure; he wasn't happy with a single encore. He roused me from my doze and said, "Don't you want to?" Really, it wasn't a troublesome duty. He got what he wanted, though he must have been rather oppressed by my panting and sweating, and I fell asleep again, exhausted by ecstasy. Less than an hour later he poked me and said, "Why don't we do it again?" This was too much. I flared up with annoyance and turned his own words back on him: "Go to sleep, or I'll tell your father."

What are the pedagogical opportunities of this exchange? I bring in the issue of sexual harassment here, which all students are very sensitive to. We discuss how quick we are in believing the victim, especially when the accuser is young and the accused old (or, when a woman is the accuser and the accused is a man; teachers may want to bring in the case of Dominique Strauss-Kahn here). Also, we easily overlook the complexities of the case, namely the fact that Eumolpus was much younger back then and therefore not that much older than the boy. Equally uncomfortably, we ignore that the boy took the initiative here and that he enjoys sex with an older man. Can this be real? At this stage, students have gotten pretty emotional and probably appreciate some academic research. I therefore send them to the library/internet to investigate sexual harassment—with several uncomfortable findings: sexual harassment does not need to be motivated by sexual desire (such as straight men harassing a gay man); ninety-five percent of women have received some kind of sexual material (phone calls, letters, emails) at work; statistically, virtually any manager or supervisor will be accused of sexual harassment during his or her career (see Howard 2007: 69, 13, 134); a large number of sexual harassment claims is fraudulent (see Henagen 1998). Sexual harassment has more than one side.

SEX IN THE CLASSROOM

The Picture of Dorian Gray (1890–91) focuses on another aspect of the controversy: the educational corruption of an impressionable youth by an older man. At the beginning of the novel, Dorian is depicted as a *tabula rasa:* twenty years old, innocent, orphaned. The fact that Dorian has no father is relevant, for it is a situation akin to Pausanias' erotic model, the older man acting as a surrogate father for the boy. (Instructors may want to turn to biography here and note the similarities between Wilde and his young lover Lord Alfred Douglas.) Lord Henry, Dorian's older mentor, is the seducer of the novel: "Nothing can cure the soul but the senses, just as nothing can cure the senses but the soul" (30). Henry believes that "if one man were to live out his life fully and completely, were to give form to every feeling, expression to every thought, reality to every dream—I believe that the world would gain such a fresh insight of joy that we would forget all the maladies of mediaevalism, and return to the Hellenic ideal" (28). However, he is only a spectator of life, a detached *voyeur* who is taking an inexpressible delight in Dorian's corruption: "he had been an evil influence to others, and had experienced a terrible joy in being so" (156). For Henry, Dorian is a means of peeping through a hole into a show, free of any danger and charge, and watching how someone is practicing the theories he is afraid to experience himself. Students certainly speculate about Henry's (and Dorian's) homosexuality, and while Henry's kind of second-hand experience by means of his mastery of Dorian can certainly be read as sublimated homosexuality, I stress a different aspect in class. On what clues, I ask my students, could Dorian have picked up that Henry is a fraud?

One of Wilde's most memorable statements is "Education is an admirable thing. But it is well to remember from time to time that nothing that is worth knowing can be taught" (1242). Henry's teachings have a pedagogical value on the surface only. Jeff Nunokawa observes:

> When Lord Henry imagines the scene for seducing a young man as a classroom rather than a bedroom, he joins a faculty imagined by a well-known tradition of anxiety hard at work in the climate of scandal and controversy that beclouded Oxford and Cambridge during the second half of the nineteenth century, a tradition of anxiety which predates the Victorian period by about two thousand years, and which shows no signs, even now, of waning. (1992: 316)

Since Greek homoeroticism often conflated the sexual and the educational, students cannot always disentangle the two. While modern education is non-erotic, it is still a relationship of unequal power, usually between an older teacher and a younger student. Here I remind the class that Socrates, in whom the erotic and the educational coincided according to Alcibiades, got into trouble exactly for corrupting the youth of Athens, although those charges were of course hardly sexual. But the classroom is not the only contested site in the Classics and comparative literature classroom.

SEX IN THE LOCKER ROOM

Coaching may be even more fraught than teaching, for not only is it an educational relationship but also, by definition, physical. In *The Front Runner* (1974), forty-year-old Harlan Brown is a closeted coach who trains three openly gay runners. One of them, 21-year old Billy Sive, falls in love with him, but Harlan resists Billy's advances. Before coming to his current college, Harlan was at Pennsylvania State University, where he was fired for homosexuality.[4] A 19-year old runner had fallen in love with him and, when feeling rejected after Harlan failed to respond to his advances, made false allegations of sexual harassment; Harlan, for fear of exposure, refused to contest them legally. Although Harlan has feelings for Billy, he does everything to discourage him from a relationship. He even cruelly hits him in

---

4. In light of the Jerry Sandusky scandal at Penn State, Warren may be commended for an uncanny prescience, but it should be noted that Harlan suffers from a *wrongful* accusation. Still, next time I teach the class, I plan to draw detailed parallels between Warren's imaginative rendering in 1974 and the almost daily revelations about college coaches abusing young athletes.

front of the class. At that point, Billy's friend Vince straightforwardly tells Harlan that Billy is in love with Harlan and utterly miserable. Harlan then lets go his emotional iron fist, and they become a couple. Of course, only at a fictional liberal school, where the faculty is composed of recovering alcoholics, ex-convicts, handicapped Vietnam veterans, a gay couple, and other unconventional professors, is such a relationship possible.

This is our next uncomfortable dialogue: consensual relationships between a student and a teacher/coach. In Plato, such a bond is highly valued. Socrates is always roaming around the wrestling schools and watching beautiful boys, and once they had exerted themselves, he would gladly engage them in dialogue. Socrates never gets carried away, although when he sees gorgeous Charmides, he feels the flames of desire. We also know that all (male only) athletes at the Olympic Games exercised in the nude, that the athlete in his very nakedness resembled the nude statues of gods, that the perfect body represented the democratic body politic, that paintings frequently depict Eros chasing young athletes with hot desire. The gymnasium and the palaestra provided sites for rigorous exercise and philosophical inquiry. Not so in the twenty-first century, when most schools have explicit policies outlawing amorous relationships between students and teachers/coaches.[5]

Students are uncomfortable with three aspects here: homosexuality and sports in general (which remains one of the last taboos), a relationship of unequal power, and a young athlete actively pursuing his coach (who is usually seen as the predator). This is why *The Front Runner* is such a valuable text, for Warren is at pains to show how Billy and Harlan negotiate a successful relationship that transcends their asymmetry, a romanticized notion of gay marriage: "We saw it simply as a formal public declaration of

---

5. My university, for example, states the following policy in the Faculty Handbook: "Sexual relations between students and faculty members are fraught with the potential for exploitation. The respect and trust accorded a professor, as well as the power exercised by the professor in an academic or evaluative role, make voluntary consent by the student suspect. Even when both parties initially have consented, the development of a sexual relationship renders both the faculty member and the institution vulnerable to possible later allegations of sexual harassment in light of the significant power differential between faculty members and students. If a consensual relationship has existed or develops between a faculty member and a student, the instructor should not thereafter have undirected responsibility for the advising, supervision, evaluation, or grading of the consensual relationship partner's performance. The faculty member must disclose the consensual relationship to his or her immediate superior, normally the department head or college dean, and make arrangements to end advising, supervisory, evaluative, or grading responsibilities for the consensual partner" (2011: 16). This policy also applies to a consensual relationship between a coach and a student under his or her supervision.

our love for each other, of our belief in the beauty and worth of this love, of our intention to live together openly, of our rejections of heterosexuality. Neither of us was a blushing bride led to the altar. Neither of us was bound to obey, or to be the property of the other. We were two men, male in every sense of the word, and free" (193).

Harlan coaches Billy to win an Olympic gold medal; in fact, it is *because* Billy is in love that he is athletically successful, which echoes Phaedrus' speech in the *Symposium*. Since a lover would never desert his beloved in extreme jeopardy ("He'd rather die a thousand deaths!"), an army of lovers might conquer the whole world; Phaedrus closes his panegyric on love with the most famous homoerotic couple of antiquity: Achilles and Patroclus (ironically, this very relationship troubled even ancient readers because of an unclear distribution of sexual roles). I add that Warren views Achilles' funeral games for slain Patroclus as the origin of the Greek Olympics and uses their love as a plea for queering the canon: "Yes, the real *Iliad* belongs to us gay people, as totally as the stories of out gay baseball players and out lesbian tennis divas also belong to us. Mark Bingham, rugby player who died a hero's death on 9/11, has the roots of his courage in ancient soil" (*The Lavender Locker Room* 13). Unease thus often gives way to admiration when we finish *The Front Runner:* Warren brings out how love can harmonize people of different ages, how the gay athlete can run faster than his straight competitors, and how the younger man/*eromenos* manages to convince his coach to accept his love.

A 53-YEAR-OLD MAN AND A 14-YEAR-OLD BOY

Death in Venice (1912) causes the most trouble to students. Because of all the Platonic borrowings, Mann clearly invites a comparison to the *Symposium* and the *Phaedrus*. Aschenbach is described as an older man who fits many of the Platonic requirements, not least his nobility of spirit: Aschenbach's works have become textbooks, "whose style children were encouraged to emulate" (60). Aschenbach feels "paternal kindness" (28) toward pre-pubescent Tadzio (his armpits are hairless), whose father is absent and whose mother fails to apply educational rigor to her son. How does Aschenbach court Tadzio? Several vase- and wall-paintings in Kenneth Dover's *Greek Homosexuality* (1989: 93–94) show that an *erastes* puts his hand on the shoulder of an *eromenos* (with varying results) in order to court him while his other hand usually reaches for the boy's genitals. Critic

George Bridges wonders why Aschenbach did not lay his hand on Tadzio's head or shoulder, since "such a gesture would not at all be improper, given the fact that their paths cross every day" (1986: 41). The answer is simple. Because Aschenbach has been vigorously transporting himself back to the fourth century BCE (even directly addressing Platonic characters), his gesture would have been an erotic attempt at courtship. It is also an excuse students are wary of: just because *paiderastia* worked for the great Greeks does not mean it can be imposed on our society (no one would think of doing the same with Greek slavery). In any case, even though Aschenbach and Tadzio never make more than eye contact, Aschenbach has a uniquely Platonic reaction when watching Tadzio. His mind literally gives birth: the verb Mann uses is "kreißen," which denotes a woman's giving birth to a child (nowadays this verb survives only in the noun "Kreißsaal," delivery-room). However, this spiritual begetting comes with a warning:

> It is surely for the best that the world knows only the lovely work and not also its origins, not the conditions under which it came into being; for knowledge of the origins from which flowed the artist's inspiration would surely often confuse the world, repel it, and thus vitiate the effects of excellence. Strange hours! Strangely enervating effort! Strangely fertile intercourse between a mind and a body. (39)

Strange! Mann could not have described better how students react to Aschenbach's interaction with Tadzio.

What is a teacher supposed to do here? A canonical work—widely known as novella, opera, and film; heavily anthologized; read by countless 14-year-olds in the German classroom; published by a Nobel Prize laureate—that features the attraction of a 53-year-old to a 14-year-old. What I have found helpful is moving away from Aschenbach ("old lecher," "dirty old man," "pedophile," are predictable student dismissals) to Tadzio. Recalling the Platonic background, I ask them how Tadzio was supposed to have reacted to Aschenbach. Michel Foucault describes a precarious balance for the lover and the beloved:

> [The *erastes*] was in a position of initiative—he was the suitor—and this gave him rights and obligations; he was expected to show his ardor, and to restrain it; he had gifts to make, services to render; he had functions to exercise with regard to the *eromenos;* and all this entitled him to expect a just reward. The other partner, the one who was loved and courted, had to

be careful not to yield too easily; he also had to keep from accepting too many tokens of love, and from granting his favors heedlessly and out of self-interest, without testing the worth of his partner; he must also show gratitude for what the lover had done for him. (1990: 196)

Why does Tadzio not respond to Aschenbach's advances? Evidently enough, he does not particularly like the old man, and he certainly does not *love* him, which is anyway a desire (*eros*) he is not supposed to feel, only *philia* or "friendship." If Tadzio had responded to Aschenbach's erotic advances, had encouraged him in his wooing, had submitted to him without reasonable resistance, a Greek audience would have dismissed Tadzio as "easy" because, as Pausanias warns, it "is shameful to yield too quickly" (*Symp.* 184a).

But the strangest thing here is that Aschenbach, never at a loss for Platonic quotes, fails to refer to a passage in the *Phaedrus* where Plato seems to condone sexual desire, even on the part of the *eromenos,* where *eros* is reciprocated, where a life-long relationship depends on *anteros,* "counter-love," where the age difference becomes virtually irrelevant. In Socrates' allegory of the charioteer, when the lover's soul sees the boy, "it opens the sluice-gates of desire and sets free the parts that were blocked up before. And now that the pain and the goading have stopped, it can catch its breath and once more suck in, for the moment, this sweetest of all pleasures" (*Phdr.* 251e). Now, to give in to sexual desire is of course far from ideal for Plato, but it need not be too bad. If the lovers respect each other and sex is not their main goal, they will grow wings, too: "If . . . they adopt a lower way of living, with ambition in place of philosophy, then pretty soon when they are careless because they have been drinking or for some other reason, the pair's undisciplined horse will catch their souls and together bring them to commit that act which ordinary people would take to be the happiest choice of all" (256b–c). Socrates strikingly contends that these lovers will attain blessedness as well, that sex can be a happy choice (for the rest of one's life!), that there is more than philosophy to the good life, that love need not equal a zero-sum game.

E. L. Marson offers one explanation for Aschenbach's omission: "the excuses for homosexual sensuality in Plato and Plutarch are forgotten by [Aschenbach] because to recall them would be too much of a temptation" (1979: 122). This is very suggestive, and I add that by the standards of the *Phaedrus, both* Aschenbach and Tadzio would feel *eros,* sexual desire, which only re-emphasizes why Aschenbach and Tadzio's relationship is so troubling to us. According to our sexual belief system, *neither* a man in his fifties *nor* an early teenager is supposed to have an active sex life. There certainly is much food for thought here.

SEX AND THE SAMURAI

In order to show that the problematic age difference is not limited to Western culture, I assign Mishima's *Forbidden Colors,* which is peppered with Platonic references. First a brief synopsis. Old Shunsuké Hinoki is a tremendously successful writer but failure in his private life; three marriages to a thief, a madwoman, and an adulteress who kills herself with her lover have turned him into a cynical misogynist; all he wants now is exact revenge on women, for which he enlists the help of an irresistible gay youth, Yuichi Minami. According to Shunsuké's plan, Yuichi will play Don Juan to women but never touch them.

Some cultural background may be helpful here: during the Tokugawa period (1603–1868), as Gary Leupp documents, homosexual behavior flourished in Buddhist monasteries, male brothels or teahouses linked to kabuki theater, and samurai mansions. As in ancient Greece, the relationship usually involved a mature man (such as a monk) and a boy (his acolyte), often called "older brother" and "younger brother." Unlike the usual Greek model, however, the pair sometimes swore life-long loyalty and certified their bond with a written oath (1995: 43–44). Similarly, the samurai of Japanese feudalism often established intimacy with young boys. Many of these boys were educated in monasteries, where they had experienced the "brotherhood" just described. Adult warriors would then do martial training with youths to prepare them for the battlefield; in return, they would receive sexual gratification (1995: 47–57). Gregory Pflugfelder points out the difference between Japanese homosexuality and heterosexuality, *nanshoku* and *joshoku* respectively:

> The pleasures of this realm [*nanshoku*] sprang neither from purely physiological processes, as the medico-scientific model of 'sexuality' suggests, nor from a lofty spiritual source, as the term 'love' often implies; instead, more akin to the Greek 'eros,' they partook equally of physical and emotional elements, both of which were understood to pose a similar degree of threat to the unenlightened soul. (1999: 25)

In the realm of male eroticism, we find *shudō,* which meant "not so much the 'way of youths' as the 'way of *loving* youths,' an erotic path that younger males traveled only in their capacity as sexual objects, and females could not tread at all" (27). We are very close now to Greek *paiderastia* and to Plato's androcentric world, and we even have equivalent concepts to *erastes* and *eromenos: nenja* and *wakashu* (or, earlier, *nyake*), "the two asymmetric halves of the *shudō* couple, each role complementing and predicated upon the existence of the other" (40).

What, then, is the trouble with *Forbidden Colors?* Shunsuké, whose relationship with Yuichi recalls a father and son model (141), closely adheres to instructional principles—only to pervert them utterly:

> Yuichi's face never left Shunsuké's heart day or night. In his torture, he reviled him; by all the mean names he knew he cursed this false youth in his heart. Only then was he at ease in the knowledge that he clearly detested this young scoundrel. With the same mouth he had used to sing praises of Yuichi's complete absence of intellect, he now ridiculed him for his lack of intellect. Yuichi's inexperience; his annoying lady-killer pose; his self-centeredness; his intolerable self-love; his outbursts of sincerity; his capricious naïveté; those tears; all the rubbish of his character. (177)

All the rubbish of his character. What if the youth—popularly seen as child-like, pure, innocent—is bad? In Plato we never find out what the *eromenos* feels or, to be precise, we only know what the beloved is *not* supposed to feel. And even if an *eromenos* like Alcibiades pours out his heart, he only meets with laughter. Here we have a youth with a destructive sex life who becomes more corrupt than his corruptor. Furthermore, Mishima brings out something that has been troubling students all semester long. Women always seem to play second fiddle in these relationships, and even when the older man is/was married (Lord Henry, Aschenbach, Alexander the Great), wives are kind of meaningless. Mishima excavates the full brunt of misogyny. The question is whether he is still true to Plato. In the *Symposium,* the male guests prefer to drink among men only; in order to enjoy a homoerotic atmosphere, they quickly dismiss the flute-girl in fairly derogatory terms: "let her play for herself or, if she prefers, for the women in the house" (176e). But at the same time, the highest authority on love is also accorded to a woman. Students eagerly discuss the various gender troubles here: closeted older men who have affairs with young males, bisexual men, gay men who put down women, clueless wives, and much more. Because misogyny is so profoundly offensive, students are particularly eager to engage with it in all its facets.

NO CONCLUSION TO CONTROVERSY

Readers may have noticed by now that I rarely use the term "pedophilia" in class. What can students possibly and *constructively* say about it? Instead, I focus on controversial issues that arise from the age difference and to which students can relate much better: sexual harassment, the student–teacher relationship, the athlete–coach relationship, pre-adolescent and geriatric sexuality, and the role of women. Sometimes I even continue the trouble on the final exam. Judith Levine contends: "Teens often seek out sex with older people, and they do so for understandable reasons: an older person makes them feel sexy and grown up, protected and special; often the sex is better than it would be with a peer who has as little skill as they do. For some teens, a romance with an older person can feel more like salvation than victimization" (2006: 105). Students are asked to analyze her claim, but true to our academic approach to controversy, only specific examples from the works we have read are allowed.

Are students more comfortable after such an approach? Probably not entirely, but is that really the goal of controversy? Students learn that dialogue can be difficult, that academic subjects can be troubling, and that (Platonic) love can be upsetting.

14

A World Away from Ours
Homoeroticism in the Classics Classroom[1]

WALTER DUVALL PENROSE, JR.

"IT'S FAGGOTS," a student once commented when I was explaining homeroticism in a *World History I* course. In this moment, perhaps the most difficult in my teaching career, I was caught off guard. I responded that the word was impolite and should not be used in the classroom, not knowing what else to do. To make it even worse, or so it seemed at that moment, I was being observed by a senior colleague in that very class! Luckily for me, my observer, Blanche Wiesen Cook, came to the class armed with forty years of teaching experience. She pulled me aside after the lesson and offered some sound advice. First, she said, ask the rest of the class what they think. Second, ask the student what the word "faggots" means to her. When this incident occurred again with the same student, a more effective strategy indeed turned out to be class discussion. The intense homophobia of the student-in-question was immediately tempered by the openness of

---

1. First and foremost, I would like to thank my students for their intellectual curiosity, generosity, and overall willingness to discuss the issues raised in this piece. Without them, this chapter could have never been written. Special thanks go out to Nancy Rabinowitz and Fiona McHardy for the hard work that has gone into editing this volume, to Nancy Rabinowitz and Susanna Braund for moderating the 2011 APA panel where this paper was first presented, and to my fellow panelists, Fiona McHardy, Page Dubois, and Barbara Gold for their enthusiasm and comments. I would also like to thank the administrators of SDSU and my fellow faculty members for allowing me to be myself in the classroom. Last, but certainly not least, I want to thank Blanche Wiesen Cook for her sage advice and enthusiastic friendship. None of these wonderful persons are responsible for any inaccuracies or errors contained herein. Translations are mine unless otherwise noted.

her peers. The Will and Grace generation present that day indeed had some feedback for her, helping to educate her on tolerance.

The above incident occurred while I was teaching at John Jay College of Criminal Justice in New York City. The students came from an inner-city background where homophobia and indeed other judgments, emotions, and feelings can sometimes be expressed very vocally. I am still teaching at a state university in San Diego, California, but I find that the student body is different. Rather than express homophobia verbally, some students tend to get wide-eyed and show their discomfort with the subject through body language. I still teach *World History I,* but now I also teach *Western Civilization I,* an upper-division *Ancient Greek History* class, and a graduate seminar, *Gender and Sexuality in Ancient Greece and Rome* at San Diego State University (SDSU). Whereas a number of students at SDSU seem to be open-minded and not shocked by issues of homoeroticism in general, their comfort level seems to decrease rapidly when one begins to address the age-differentiated sexuality of ancient Greece. Students may exhibit a real discomfort discussing ancient pederasty.[2] One can sometimes see shock on their faces. I might add here that I find myself feeling uncomfortable bringing up the subject as well, and I sometimes wonder if I am sensing my own discomfort as much as theirs.

There are moments, however, when such a lesson may actually serve to increase the comfort level of some students. One such student in a Greek history class later came to my office and told me how he had been beaten outside of a gay bar, and that his boyfriend had stood by and watched rather than defend him. I suspect my opening up the subject of homoeroticism in class made him feel comfortable enough to come my office, which is designated as a "safe zone" by a sign on the door. He was angry with the boyfriend and did not know where to turn for help. I consoled him as best I could, and referred him to one of our very capable counselors on campus who has a lot of experience with Lesbian, Gay, Bisexual, and Transgendered (LGBT) issues. While I am not a trained therapist, I have made it a point of attending LGBT mixers on campus where I was introduced to professionals who deal with LGBT student concerns. Attending such events is one way to learn more about available resources on your campus. Another option might be to contact the local LGBT student group, which will hopefully have suggestions on possible counselors. One might also try calling the counseling center itself and doing a brief interview with a psychologist before referring students to her or him. I would not send a student to an

---

2. See further Endres in this volume.

unknown counselor, as some may not be sensitive to, trained in, or sympathetic towards LGBT issues. Handling such issues requires care, whether on the psychotherapy couch or in the classroom.

In this chapter, I will present some general suggestions and guidelines on how to deal with homophobia in the classroom, then move on to more specifics on how to teach ancient Greek pederasty in a freshman survey or upper-division Greek history course. I will begin by presenting general ideas that could be used in teaching any discipline where homophobia might crop up while simultaneously debunking modern student assumptions about homosexuality and related issues. Next, I will suggest ways to demonstrate to students that age-differentiated relations between men and youths were in many respects different from what we today call pedophilia. In this sense, the sexual universe of ancient Greece was a world away from ours,[3] and I will suggest some other lesson plans that can be used to demonstrate this to students as well. Ancient Greek texts and images can be used to further reveal that male homoeroticism was associated with masculinity rather than effeminacy, and was integral rather than foreign to military organization. In a similar vein, female homoeroticism seems to have served a pedagogical purpose as well, and I will discuss the limited texts available to share with students on this account as well.

No word that can be directly translated as homosexuality exists in either Greek or Latin because the ancients did not understand sexual orientation as we do, but rather thought that most persons could experience attractions towards either sex. Hence, I have used the term homoeroticism to think about same-sex sexual desire in the remote past. In order to begin to teach about homoeroticism in the ancient world, however, one needs to first create a bridge from the present to the past. Modern homophobia stems from our contemporary conception of homosexuality, and disarming student prejudice is the first step in such pedagogy.

UNDERSTANDING HATE, TEACHING TERMINOLOGY

Generating discussion is ultimately the most important tool to deal with homophobia, but knowing the right questions to ask and the best way to use the Socratic Method is key to success in such conversations. An instructor can generate discussion by posing questions such as: What connotations does the word "faggot" hold? Why is it perhaps offensive to others? Is

---

3. See further Halperin (2002: 17).

homosexuality a disease, or in other words, is homosexual behavior "sick"? Is sexuality visible? How can one's intolerant statements hurt other students? Is discrimination based upon sexual orientation illegal in the United States, and if so, specifically in which states? Regarding issues of modern religion, I am careful to tell my students, "It is not my job to tell you what to believe. It is my job to explain to you how to think critically and analytically like an historian."

Analysis of the terminology of the modern world seems as good a place as any to begin this task in the classroom. Etymology is a useful tool to help students understand the hateful connotations of the word "faggot," for example. The English derogatory term "faggot" was ultimately derived from the French *fagot*. The *Oxford English Dictionary* defines a faggot as "a bundle of sticks, twigs, or small branches of trees bound together for use as fuel."[4] In medieval England, France, and Italy, faggots were used to burn sodomites and other heretics at the stake, and hence the word presents us with a history of hate crimes.[5] The second definition in the *OED* reads "With special reference to the practice of burning heretics alive, *esp.* in phrase fire and faggot; †to fry a faggot, to be burnt alive; also, to bear a faggot, to carry a faggot, as those did who renounced heresy. Hence *fig.* the punishment itself." One can compare these types of sanctioned murders to the hanging of African Americans by the Klu Klux Klan in the late nineteenth- and twentieth-century United States. Perhaps students' opinions regarding Ku Klux Klan murders could then be juxtaposed to the following question, "So, if we are going to argue that Ku Klux Klan murders are hate crimes and morally wrong, can an ethical comparison be made to the burning of sodomites at the stake?"

The term "faggot" may conjure up student notions that are quite different from associations made with race or gender, however. Some students today continue to think of homosexuality as a form of sickness. It should be stressed in class that homosexuality was removed from the register of mental illnesses published by the American Psychiatric Association in 1973, and is no longer considered a psychological disorder today.[6] While calling homosexuality an illness might be seen as offensive by many today, the term homosexuality was initially invented as a psychiatric diagnosis

---

4 *Oxford English Dictionary,* online s. v. "faggot|fagot" accessed February 5, 2014, http:// www.oed.com/.

5. See further Bailey (1955: 142–3); Blansher (1981: 1–30); Greenberg (1988: 298); Fone (2000: 143–44); cf. Dynes et al. (1990) s.v. faggot.

6. Bayer (1981: passim but esp. 3). I am grateful to Charles Silverstein for this reference.

in 1869 by a Swiss doctor named Karoly Maria Benkert.[7] During the last thirty years of the nineteenth century, liberal physicians such as Richard von Krafft-Ebing began to treat what they called "deviant nonprocreative sexual acts" as symptoms of mental illness, rather than as sins or crimes.[8] From its onset, the medicalization of homosexuality was imbued with associations of gender deviance.

The nineteenth-century heteronormative ideology of sexuality understood desire for women to be a male trait, and desire for men to be a female trait. Any sexual attraction outside of this strictly heterosexual paradigm was seen as an inversion of the proper order, and hence as illness. It is important for students to understand that this idea is a social construction. Biology, in contrast, strongly suggests that same-sex sexual behaviors are normal. Among the bonobos, the closest relatives to humans, homoerotic behavior is common and frequent. "[I]f bonobo behavior provides any hints, very few human sexual practices can be dismissed as 'unnatural.'"[9]

Students, clearly a product of the culture that produces them, tend to assume that gay men are effeminate, and that lesbians are masculine. It is useful to point out to pupils that effeminacy was attached to male "inverts" in nineteenth-century psychology, and became a part of the modern conception of male homosexuality as it evolved. By the same token, women "inverts," lesbians, were manly. The heteronormative psychology of the latter nineteenth and early twentieth centuries did not allow for any other possibilities.[10] Male homoerotic behavior and relationships in ancient Greece, however, were actually associated with masculinity and the military. These ideas about same-sex eroticism stand at polar opposites, and demonstrate keenly how very different our culture is from the remote Greek past—a world away.[11]

Another assumption that students tend to make is that either persons are gay or straight. Little leeway seems to be left to think about bisexuality. If a guy sleeps with another guy, he is automatically assumed to be gay despite having interests in women as well. The Janus Report, published in 1993, is telling in its attitude towards what defines homosexuality. Through interviews of the public, the authors of the report found that 22 percent of

---

7. Weeks (1977: 3).
8. Oosterhuis (2002: 275).
9. de Waal and Lanting (1997: 4–5). On p. 4, de Waal and Lanting further note that "Bonobos engage in sex in virtually every partner combination: male-male, male-female, female-female, male-juvenile, female-juvenile, and so on."
10. Ellis (1925: 75–263).
11. As Blanshard (2010: xii) notes, "the Classical world exists in dynamic tension with the modern."

men and 17 percent of women had had homosexual experiences. Whereas only 4 percent of the population self-identified as homosexual, 5 percent as bisexual, and the rest as heterosexual, the authors offer the following analysis:

> Although the figure of 4% is generally used to indicate the number of male homosexuals (gay groups use the figure 9% to 10%), does this mean that anyone who has ever had a homosexual experience is to be classified as a homosexual? If so, then the correct statistic would be . . . 22% for men and 17% for women—much larger than most estimates. On the other hand, if we use the category of ongoing, then we have a much lower finding.[12]

This ambiguity reflects a societal position taken that one homosexual act makes a man gay. The authors ultimately decide that this is not so, but still decide to include men who self-identify as "bisexual" (5 percent of their study) in their overall count of "homosexual" men, thus making the total 9 percent. Simply put, the gay/straight divide is an artificial construct of our own modern society that largely fails to recognize bisexuality. Bringing this to the attention of students can help them to bridge the gap between our universe and that of the ancient Greeks.

Perhaps the most common assumption students tend to make is that ancient pederasty is the same thing as modern pedophilia. While I will argue below that there is a distinction between these different practices, students may not even recognize that there is a difference between the compulsive disorder of a pedophile who seeks out sex with young children and an adolescent choosing to have sex with another adolescent or even an adult today.[13] In the popular U.S. media, "pedophilia" is defined as "any kind of sexual behavior between an adult and a legally underage person."[14] According to Jay R. Feierman, M.D., however, the scientific definition of "pedophilia" is "sexual attraction to prepubertal children," whereas sexual attraction to adolescents is rather called "ephebophilia" or "hebephilia."[15] It is the latter practice which seems to fit better with the Greek custom of pederasty, even though the words pederasty and pedophilia are both derived

---

12. Janus and Janus (1993: 70).
13. According to Garland and Dougher (1990: 502), "There is a consensus that threats of force greatly enhance the traumatic aspects of a child's or an adolescent's sexual interaction with an adult."
14. Feierman (1990: 3).
15. Ibid. While some pedophiles may be homosexual, the assumption that "all homosexuals are pedophiles" is also completely misguided, but sadly still with us in the minds of some members of our society. Pedophilia is not homosexuality, and pedophiles are not necessarily homosexuals. It is important to stress the distinction between pedophilia and homosexuality with students.

from the same word root *pais*. Although the literal translation of this word is "boy" or child the term was used by the Greeks to refer to teens as well as slaves. One can hence how see that in students' minds there is a slippage between the terms pedophilia and pederasty—they sound alike and evoke similarities in terms of etymology.

TEACHING ANCIENT PEDERASTY

Given students' associations between pedophilia and pederasty, as well as the opprobrium of homosexuality felt by some students due to religious or other causes, it might just be easier to never mention either subject. Indeed, when I was discussing the theme of this book, how to teach uncomfortable subjects in the Classics classroom, with a colleague, she said to me, "My contribution to such a volume would consist of two words, 'Avoid them.'" But can one teach ancient Greek political history without discussing pederasty? It would be almost impossible, as the "tyrannicide" of the famous lovers Harmodius and Aristogeiton was integrally linked in Athenian thought to democratic reform in Athens, just as the relationship between Lysander and Agesilaus is so important to our understanding of the peak and decline of Spartan hegemony in Greece and Asia Minor. In the former case, a juicy story of a love triangle and murder is just the kind of thing an instructor can use to get students involved in the development of democracy. In the latter case, the allure of power is sexy, especially when sex is used to get it. To ignore the complexities of these famous male-male relationships would leave lessons that are filled with tension, drama, and intrigue (the kinds of things that students find most interesting) rather flat.

The ultimate overthrow of the Athenian tyranny in the sixth century BCE was attributed to the actions of Harmodius and Aristogeiton (Hdt. 5.55–6; Thuc. 1.20; 6.54–5).[16] Hipparchus, a younger son of Pisistratus and brother of the tyrant Hippias, lusted after Harmodius, an Olympic victor and youth of a prominent family. Thucydides writes that "Harmodius was then a most beautiful young man in the flower of his youth, and he was loved and possessed by Aristogeiton, a citizen who belonged to the middle class." Aristogeiton was very much in love and was afraid that Hipparchus, a far more powerful man than himself, would take Harmodius away from him. Hence he began to plot to overthrow the tyranny due

---

16. A complete list of sources on the tyrannicides can be found in Taylor (1991: 99–109).

to private, not public concerns.¹⁷ When Harmodius refused Hipparchus' unwanted advances yet again, his sister was removed by the tyrants from being the *kanēphora* or basket-bearer in the annual Panathenaic Procession (Thuc. 6.55). It was imperative that the *kanēphora* be a virgin, and removing Harmodius' sister from the post was a means of indicating that she was unchaste, a slander not only to the girl but to her entire family. So Harmodius plotted with his older lover Aristogeiton and others to kill Hippias and overthrow the tyranny. On that fateful day of the Panathenaic festival, Harmodius and Aristogeiton panicked when they saw one of their fellow conspirators conversing with Hippias. Thinking that their plot had been revealed, they rushed instead upon Hipparchus and killed him. Hippias' paranoia after this attempt on his life led to a reign of terror, and finally to a democratic uprising four years later (Hdt. 5.56).

I use several techniques to teach this story. First, I act out the drama, playing each of the characters myself. When I do so, eyes drift away from laptops and towards the front of the room, exactly what an instructor wants. Once I have the students engaged, I turn to analysis, association, and discussion. First of all, the relationship between Harmodius and Aristogeiton was seen as leading to the later democratic glory of Athens, even though the motives of the couple were private. Thucydides (1. 20) tells us that many Athenians mistakenly believed that Aristogeiton and Harmodius had actually killed the tyrant himself, because they thought that Hipparchus was the tyrant rather than Hippias. In any event, Harmodius' youthful role as *erōmenos* was not a cause of concern to the ancients. Furthermore, the actions of these male lovers were seen as heroic and masculine. They had taken revenge on Hipparchus. Aristotle implied that the taking of revenge was an important part of ancient Greek manhood. Indeed, he advised that taking vengeance on one's enemies was nobler than reconciling with them (*Rh.* 1367a).¹⁸ In Herodotus (6.109), the glorious memory of the tyrannicides is used to spur the Athenians into courageous action in the defense of freedom during the later Persian wars. Against the towering threat of the Persians, the ancient "GI Joe" model of a soldier was not necessarily heterosexual, but rather involved in homoeroticism.

Next, I ask the students whether we should call these heroes gay. At this point, I emphasize the bisexuality of Aristogeiton. In addition to being in love with Harmodius, Aristogeiton was evidently also involved with a woman at the same time, Leaena (Polyaenus 45; Pliny the Elder *NH*

---

17. Monoson (2000: 23).
18. See further Nisters (2000: 63).

7.23.87).¹⁹ Leaena was arrested and tortured by Hippias to make her reveal the names of the co-conspirators of the plot. When she could stand the torment no more, she bit off her tongue in order to avoid condemning the other revolutionaries, and the Athenians commemorated her action with a gold statue of a tongue-less lioness afterwards, as *leaina* means "lioness" in Greek. While students might want to label Aristogeiton as "gay," his relationship with Laeana points to a different understanding of sexuality in ancient Greece as opposed to any modern, Western conception.

Perhaps the most important point of the lesson, however, is that there was a relationship between pederasty and politics in ancient Greece. While Thucydides (6.54.2) suggests that Harmodius was an aristocrat (he is described as *lampros,* an adjective commonly used to describe the aristocracy), he asserts that Aristogeiton was of the "middling sort" (*mesos*). Thucydides draws attention to this fact because Aristogeiton was a personage with whom the entire *demos* of Athens could identify, an "average" (if we dare call him that) citizen who refused the *hubris* of tyranny and attempted to overthrow its yoke. Never mind that it was technically the Spartans who ended the tyranny several years later—the story of Harmodius and Aristogeiton was seen by Athenians as a "foundation myth" of democracy.²⁰ Statues of the tyrannicides were erected in the *Agora,* their deeds were praised in hymns, and sacrifices were offered to the god Eros alongside those of Athena at Plato's Academy, because it was deemed that the Athenians had obtained their freedom from Eros (Athen. 13.561d–e). The central location of the statues of the tyrannicides politicized pederasty, "announcing that the liberation could not have come to pass without it," thus placing "the homoerotic bond at the core of Athenian political freedom" while asserting "that it and the manly virtues (*aretai*) of courage, boldness, and self-sacrifice that it generated were the only guarantors of that freedom's continued existence."²¹ The tale of the lovers became "the common currency of civic discourse about the character of the relations between the public and private lives of citizens of democratic Athens," and "worked economically to represent Athenian civic ideals, specifically unity and reciprocity."²²

In a similar light, pederasty "was seen as beneficial—even essential—to the polis" as it provided the *erōmenos* with "an education in civics." Through pederasty, the "door to education and to politics" was opened by

---

19. Athenaeus (596F) tells us that the *hetaira* Leaena was Harmodius' mistress.
20. Wohl (2002: 3).
21. Stewart (1997: 73).
22. Monoson (2000: 22).

the lover, the role model, to the beloved.²³ Such relationships were by no means unique to Athens, but rather seem to lie at the core of the Greek political and even military history. On this note, Plutarch's *Life of Agesilaus* and *Life of Lysander* stand out as important reading assignments in an ancient Greek history course. This combination of texts underscores the two-dimensional political relationship of the Spartan general Lysander and his *erōmenos* Agesilaus. Lysander had achieved tremendous fame by leading Sparta to victory in 404 BCE against the Athenians and their allies, hence ending the Great Peloponnesian War. A lesser known fact is that Lysander rose from poverty to the helm of antiquity's greatest fighting force (Plut. *Lys.* 2.3). He did this in part through his relationship with Agesilaus. As Agesilaus was a prince in one of the royal families, Lysander would have gained much on his journey to leadership through his association with the youth. This does not necessarily negate that the two had shared *erōs*, however, as Plutarch indicates that Agesilaus was attractive and had qualities that appealed to Lysander. Agesilaus had an impaired leg, but this did not stop him from completing the *agōgē*. "The youthful flowering of his body concealed the lameness of his leg, and he carried such [a burden] with ease and cheer, since he was the first to joke about it and mock himself, for his correction of his disability was not small, but made his ambition even more conspicuous, as he was dissuaded from neither hardship nor toil on account of his lameness . . . " (Plut. *Ages.* 2.3).²⁴

From a standpoint of Disability Studies, Plutarch writes the quintessential narrative of "overcoming" disability.²⁵ Nevertheless, Agesilaus was almost prevented from becoming king due to the ancient Greek treatment of deformity as a mark of disfavor of the gods. Plutarch (*Ages.* 3.6) further tells us that the respected soothsayer Diopeithes was opposed to the appointment of a lame king because an oracle foretold that disability would bring disaster to Sparta:²⁶

> Consider, Sparta, for indeed you are proud
> For from you of swift feet a lame kingship may shoot forth
> And unexpected anguish, lingering, will tear you apart
> While rolling destruction will make war [on you] in waves.

---

23. Ludwig (2002: 30).

24. On Agesilaus and disability in ancient Greece, see Penrose (2006: 47–60).

25. Linton (1998) writes that "The popular phrase *overcoming a disability* is used most often to describe someone who seems competent and successful in some way. . . . " An "implication of the phrase is that the person has risen above society's expectation for someone with those characteristics. Because it is physically impossible to overcome a disability, it seems that what is overcome is the social stigma of having a disability."

26. See Trentin in this volume.

Agesilaus was courageous and seemingly well liked by the Spartans, but he was ultimately only able to overcome the adversity that he faced and become king with the assistance of his lover Lysander (Plut. *Lys.* 22). Using his prominence as a victorious commander Lysander argued that the lameness mentioned in the oracle referred to the illegitimacy of Agesilaus' rival, Leotychidas, who was the illegitimate child of a Spartan queen and the Athenian Alcibiades, even though his alleged Spartan father, Agesilaus' brother King Agis had proclaimed Leotychides his own son on his deathbed (Xen. *Hell.* 3.3.3; Plut. *Ages.* 3). (He had initially refused to claim him.) Having been persuaded by Lysander, the Spartiates thus decided to proclaim Agesilaus king in 398 BCE.[27] Lysander's support of Agesilaus stemmed of course from his role as Agesilaus' *erastēs,* but was also self-serving—Lysander hoped to regain supreme command of the Spartan and allied troops through his association with Agesilaus, although he ultimately failed to do so. In any event, the relationship of Lysander and Agesilaus extended long beyond Agesilaus' youth. In 398, he was more than forty years old, and his *erastēs,* Lysander, still came to his rescue.[28]

Furthermore, Agesilaus' early success as a king of Sparta is attributed to his catering to the concerns of the ephors, whereas other Spartan kings were usually at odds with them (Plut. *Ag.* 4). Plutarch (*Lys.* 2.3) also tells us that Lysander was "subservient to men of power and influence, beyond what was usual in a Spartan, and content to endure an arrogant authority for the sake of gaining his ends, a trait which some hold to be no small part of political ability." An intertextual reading suggests that Agesilaus learned to be respectful of and even seemingly subservient to the ephors from Lysander, his *erastēs* and hence role model, and that this "civic virtue" was a recipe for success.

PEDERASTY, NOT PEDOPHILIA?

The example of Agesilaus and Lysander illustrates that ancient pederasty could ultimately serve to nurture rather than harm a youth, and that the benefits of such a relationship might continue into adulthood, even for the younger partner. The ideal of pederasty then stands in stark contrast to modern pedophilia, which is the coercion of a child into sex by an adult *without* the knowledge of the child's parents (unless one or both of the

---

27. Hamilton (1991: xvii).
28. Cartledge (1987: 8), suggests an approximate date of 445 "or perhaps a little later," for Agesilaus' birth. On other pederastic relationships that extended long beyond youth in ancient Greek texts, see further Endres in this volume.

parents is/are the pedophile(s)). As a point of comparison, in this volume Sharon James equates the pedophilia that occurred recently at Penn State with rape. Ancient Greek pederasty, on the other hand, when it conformed to cultural norms, was controlled, involved education of the youth by his older lover, and in some cases may not have been sexual at all.[29] This is not to say that there was no rape of boys or male youths in antiquity, but rather to understand that pederasty was meant to be something very different, and steps were taken within such an ancient context to assure that rape of the youth did not occur.

Even if there may be some overlap in terms of age structure between pederasty and pedophilia, there are major differences that an instructor can point out. First of all, while pedophilia can and does refer to sex between an adult and a young child, visual evidence (vase paintings, in particular) can be used to demonstrate to students that the "boy" in a Greek pederastic relationship was "often a youth who had attained full height."[30] A poem written by Strato of Sardis (*P. A.* 12.4), used by Cantarella as evidence on this account, suggests that the socially-sanctioned age of an *erōmenos* was somewhere between 12 and 17. In another poem, however, Strato (*P.A.* 12.228.1–2) asserts that "If an immature boy makes an error before he has reason, it brings a greater disgrace to the friend who persuades him. . . . "[31] This data is that it is derived from Roman-era Greek-speaking Asia Minor. Strato apparently lived during the reign of Hadrian, although little else is known about him.

It is even harder to affix an age to the *erōmenos* [beloved] in the Classical era of Greek history. Nevertheless, texts from the Classical period can be read with students to demonstrate that parental or guardian consent was necessary to pursue a pederastic relationship in ancient Greece, and, furthermore, that a chaperone might be present at meetings of an *erastes*

---

29. See further Davidson (2007: esp. 482). Davidson argues, in contrast to the "Dover model," that Athenian boys under the age of 18 were prevented from intimacy with older youths or men through the institution of the *paidagogoi* "who escorted the wealthier boys around." This is of interest and reinforces my point that chaperones were required for underage youths, yet this tells us little about the lower classes at Athens. Were they less protected? Furthermore, Davidson argues that "in antiquity puberty seems to have arrived four years later than it does now."

30. Dover (1989: 16). Lear (2008: 71) astutely notes that most Greek vase paintings known to us today were not found in Greece; rather a large percentage of them come from either "Greek cities in Sicily or from the territory of the Etruscans in central Italy." This fact raises the question of whether Greek vase painting reflects the tastes of Etruscans, to whom many were exported. "Our knowledge of Etruscan homosexual relations is poor," Lear notes, and asserts that we end up speculating when we try to answer such questions. The fact that some of the pots were found in Greek Sicily suggests that at least some aspect of Greek taste is evident in the iconography.

31. See further Cantarella (2008: 4–5).

and *erōmenos*. In Xenophon's *Symposium* (1.2), for example, Callias courts a boy (*pais*) named Autolycus, who has just won a victory in the pancratium. The pancratium was an athletic contest involving "a fierce combination of boxing, wrestling, and kick-boxing."[32] There were apparently separate events open to men and boys.[33] Callias courts Autolycus by inviting both the youth and his father to dinner. Xenophon asserts that Callias "happened to be in love" [*erōn etugchanen*] with Autolycus. We do not know the exact age of Autolycus, though he was clearly old enough to compete in the pancratium, but most likely in the boys' rather than the men's class. Xenophon elaborates on the relationship later in the dialogue, noting that the entire city of Athens knew that Callias was in love with Autolycus, and that it was a noble, spiritual love rather than a carnal one. Of most interest to students, Xenophon notes that Callias always included Autolycus' father in their meetings, and asserts that the virtuous lover does not keep his intentions concealed from his beloved's father. Aeschines (*Against Timarchus* 1.16) states that "if an Athenian commits *hubris* against a freeborn boy, the *kurios* [legal guardian] of the boy must enter an action before the *thesmothetai* requesting a punishment." Cantarella notes that *hubris* is a broad term that can include sexual as well as other types of violence.[34] While the nature of the act is vague here, this law suggests that some form of parental consent was necessary for a man to have sex with a youth who was still under the thumb of a guardian,[35] in tandem with Xenophon's assessment in the *Symposium*.

The text of Ephorus (*FGrH* 70 F 149, apud. Strabo 10.21.4) presents a Cretan form of parental guidance that students find bizarre yet intriguing. Ephorus tells us that after passing through puberty, a Cretan youth was ritually captured by an older *erastes*, who then took his new *erōmenos* into the wilderness and taught him to be a warrior. A strange form of parental consent was built into this practice. At least three days prior to his "attack," the suitor would warn the family of his objective of capturing the youth. If the family of the youth liked the suitor and thought he would be good to their boy, they put up little resistance when the *erastes* came to "capture" the youth. If they did not approve of the suitor, they would fight him off with

---

32. Scanlon (2002: 11).
33. See further Miller (2004: 60).
34. Cantarella (2008: 5).
35. Cohen (1991: 179–80) argues that "the consent of a boy younger than a certain age would not negate the charge of *hubris*." See also Cantarella (2008: 5). Cantarella argues that "the minimum age is around twelve or thirteen years of age, but the sanction that applies to those who don't respect that are entirely social." In point of fact, it seems as though the consent of the *kurios*, or guardian, was perhaps necessary.

fierce intensity, indicating that he was not to come back. This custom seems very similar to the Spartan idea of heterosexual marriage, where the bride was captured by her husband-to-be (Plut. *Lyc.* 15). Next, a "bridesmaid" would cut the bride's hair and dress her in a man's cloak and sandals after her capture, and then the groom would come to her to consummate the marriage. The latter text presents a transgendered moment in a heterosexual context that students find of particular interest. The ritual capture described by Ephorus was a rite of passage, where a boy became a warrior, and hence a man, just as Spartan marriage by capture was a rite of passage whereby a girl became a wife, and hence a woman.

A final point may help students to better understand not just pederasty but also the young age of marriage for women in the premodern period. The age conventions of both are related to the shorter life spans of human beings in the earlier periods, and hence to the history of childhood. Philippe Ariès has astutely argued that up until the mid-eighteenth century in Europe, the extended concept of childhood that we now recognize did not yet exist.[36] By the age of seven, a young person might be apprenticed as a cobbler or a scullery maid. By the age of fourteen s/he might be a parent, a soldier, a spouse, or even a king or queen; by the age of forty s/he would probably be dead.[37] In ancient Sparta, boys were in military training by the age of seven. They lived in barracks with other recruits and away from their parents. The parallel with Early Modern Europe is clear—there was not much of a concept of childhood in ancient Sparta either, at least not the prolonged "period of dependency and protection lasting into physical and social maturity" that we today call childhood and adolescence.[38] A youth at Sparta was expected to take a male lover during his adolescence. This was the norm, according to Xenophon, although he asserts that the relationships between "men and boys" at Sparta were not supposed to be based on lust:

> It seems to me that one must say something concerning the love of youths, as the matter is associated with education. On the one hand, among the other Greeks, such as the Boeotians, man and youth consort with one another as though they were a married couple. Among the Eleans, they seduce youths who are prime for plucking by means of favors. Others

---

36. Ariès (1994: esp. 33, 365–407).
37. Plumb (1975: 66); Levine (2002: xxvii).
38. Levine (2002: xxvii). Ariès (1994: 411) notes that "medieval civilization had forgotten the *paideia* of the ancients . . . " but the Spartans, by forcing boys to leave home at the age of seven, nevertheless did interrupt their "childhood."

altogether forbid the potential lover from having any such dealings with the youths. Lycurgus thought the opposite of all of these, for if someone adored a boy for his spirit and in order to be with him attempted to create a platonic friendship, he approved of this. But if someone appeared to be lusting after the body of the boy, he prohibited this as shameful, so that in Lacedaemon, the lover, not less than if he were the father or brother of the boy, would abstain from having sexual relations with him (ed. Marchant).

The men's "love of youths" was integrally connected with education: the *erastes-erōmenos* relationship was, in essence, a military apprenticeship. There is some indication that these relationships at Sparta may have been more sexual than Xenophon allows, however. The Greek verb *lakonizein* or "to Laconize, to act like a Lacedameonian (i.e., Spartan)" was used by Athenians to refer to anal intercourse.[39] Dover suggests that this was Athenian invective, but it at least stands to reason that some Spartans broke the Lycurgan rule.

HOMOEROTICISM, MASCULINITY, AND THE ANCIENT GREEK MILITARY

Another lesson plan that I have used with success in an ancient Greek history course lays out the military history of homoeroticism side-by-side with Greek intellectual history. Reading Plato's *Symposium* with students seems a good starting place for such a task.[40] Plato associates courage with men who experience desire for other men. Plato's character Aristophanes, in his well-known discourse on the origins of sexual desire, considers homoerotically-inclined men to be the "most courageous" [*andreiotatoi*] of all men, though he notes that others view such men as shameless (*Symp.* 192a). Courage and masculinity were part and parcel in ancient Greek thought—courage in battle was the most masculine of qualities and even courageous women were considered "masculine."[41] It is not shamelessness, but rather "confidence" [*tharros*], "manly courage" [*andreia*], and "manliness" [*arrenōpia*] that causes them to be attracted to their own kind.[42] In contrast, Plato's Aristophanes

---

39. Dover (1989: 187).
40. On teaching Plato *Symposium,* see further Endres in this volume.
41. Penrose (2006: esp. chs. 2 and 3).
42. In this context, a translation of *andreia* as "manliness" would make little sense, as *arrenōpia* clearly means "manliness." *LSJ* s.v. *arrenōpia.* Hence, I have translated *andreia* here as "manly courage." *LSJ* suppl. s.v. *andreia.*

does not describe men whose desires are strongly heterosexual as courageous or manly (*Symp.* 191d–e). These men, according to the myth, are reincarnated from the divided souls of beings who were once androgynes.

The masculinity associated with ancient Greek homoeroticism directly confronts student assumptions that gay men are effeminate. At this point, students begin to see that the norms, customs, and laws of the ancient Greeks were a far cry from our own. When I teach students the historian's craft, I try to impress upon them that we must begin by understanding an ancient culture through its own values, rather than ours. Richard Marius and Melvin Page offer the following advice to students of history: "Offering your own original ideas does not mean that you should choke your prose with your own emotions. . . . In writing about the past, you judge people and decide whether they were good or bad. The best way to convey these judgments is to tell what these people did or said. You don't have to prove that you are on the side of the angels. You should trust your readers. If characters you describe did terrible things, readers can see the evil if you give them the details. If characters did noble things, your readers can tell that too, without any emotional insistence on your part. Simply adopt the approach of good historians by trying to tell the truth about what happened."[43] This advice is applicable to the classroom as well. How can we judge a pagan people, such as the ancient Greeks, by Christian standards of morality, when Christianity did not exist in the fifth century BCE? If students find homosexuality to be wrong according to their own religious beliefs, it is still important for them to understand that the ancient Greeks did not share their opinions.

Up until recently, homosexuality was completely banned from the U.S. military, and it is here that we find one of the sharpest contrasts between ancient and modern ideologies. In the United States, gay men and lesbians were not allowed to serve in the military at all up until the early 1990s, when President Clinton tried to reverse the policy. When he met with stiff resistance from the higher ups in the U.S. military, Clinton compromised with them to institute the now notorious "Don't Ask, Don't Tell" Policy, which was passed by the U.S. Congress in 1993. This policy prohibited recruiters from asking about a recruit's sexual preferences, but at the same time kept gay military personnel in the closet by prohibiting their coming out while serving. The controversial "Don't Ask, Don't Tell" policy was finally repealed on September 11, 2011, but controversy still exists over gays and lesbians serving in the United States army.[44]

---

43. Marius and Page (2010: 18).
44. Gil Kaufman, "Don't Ask, Don't Tell Officially Over: Policy Requiring Gay and Lesbian

Students become very engaged when they learn that ancient Greek militaries were sometimes formed by pairing male lovers together on the battlefield. It was thought that they would then fight to the death nobly rather than be shamed as a coward or runaway in front of their lover or beloved. In Sparta, Elis, and Thebes, excellence and courage in military matters were associated with homoeroticism. In Plato's *Symposium* (178e–179a), Phaedrus asserts that the best military formations are made up of paired lovers and beloveds, because a soldier would be least likely to desert his post if his lover was watching. A comparison is here made to Alcestis, a mythological heroine who dies for true love, albeit a heterosexual love (179B). In Xenophon's *Symposium*, this argument is echoed. Socrates asserts that Pausanias, the lover of the famous poet Agathon, argues that the most valiant army would be recruited of lovers and their beloveds (8.32). Furthermore, Socrates tells us, such an arrangement is already employed by the Thebans and Eleans, where male lovers share a common bed and are posted next to one another in battle (8.34). The Theban Sacred Band, according to Plutarch, was composed of pairs of lovers and beloveds (*Pelopidas* 18–19).[45] This elite unit became the most invincible fighting force in Greece, and ultimately defeated the previously unbeatable Spartans at Tegyra in 375 BCE and Leuctra in 371 BCE. Plutarch believes that the unit was composed of lovers and their beloveds, and asserts that a man would be more anxious to earn the respect of a lover than of others (18).

SAPPHO AND "LESBIANISM"

While there is abundant evidence about Greek pederasty, far less data survives on female homoeroticism in ancient Greek contexts. The main exception to this is the poetry of Sappho. Students find Sappho to be of interest, in part because our word lesbian is derived from her place of origin. It is important to point out that Sappho may have been more of a Lesbian with a capital "L" (meaning that she came from the island of Lesbos) than an exclusive lesbian with a lowercase "l" in modern terms. The term Lesbian

---

Service Members to Keep Their Orientation Secret Was Officially Repealed Tuesday," *MTV News* (September 20, 2011) http://www.mtv.com/news/articles/1671028/dont-ask-dont-tell-repeal.jhtml Retrieved on November 18, 2011.

    45. The evidence provided in Xenophon's *Symposium* strongly suggests that the Theban Sacred Band did exist in the fourth century, even if it is not explicitly labeled as such. Leitao (2002) argues that if it had existed at that time, surely Xenophon would have mentioned it in his *Hellenica*. Xenophon may not mention the homoeroticism of the Theban Sacred Band because it was obvious to his readers.

was used by the Greeks to refer to a person from Lesbos, but Brooten asserts that we have no evidence of the term being used to refer to either masculine or homoerotically-inclined women until the medieval period.[46] A tenth-century CE commentator on Clement of Alexandria uses the term *Lesbiai* (Lesbians) to refer to "women erotically inclined toward other women."[47] There is a reference to a masculine, homoerotically-inclined woman who is called both a *hetairistria* and a "rich Lesbian" in the *Dialogues of the Courtesans* (5) by Lucian, but it is not clear that the term Lesbian here refers to any sort of homoerotic inclination, but rather simply may just be a place of origin.[48] The woman was born with the name Megilla, but prefers to call herself, or, perhaps better stated, himself Megillus. S/he has a shaved head, and, from a modern perspective is a female-to-male transgendered person.

In any event, reading Sappho's poetry with students alongside later Byzantine commentary (*Suida* s.v. Sappho) reveals that Sappho not only had erotic liaisons with other women, but that she was allegedly married and had a daughter named Cleis. Sappho clearly alludes to a homoerotic liaison in the following poem:

"I simply wish to die."
Tears running down her cheeks,
she left me, and said
"We've suffered terribly
Sappho I leave you against my will."
I answered, go happily
And remember me,
You know how we cared for you,
If not let me remind you
. . . the lovely times we shared.

Many crowns of violets,
Roses and crocuses
. . . together you set before me
And many scented wreaths
Made from blossoms

---

46. It should be noted here that in Classical Greek the verbs *lesbiazein* and *lesbizein* meant "to perform fellatio." Brooten (1996: 22); Dover (1989: 182).

47. Arethas scholion to *Paidagōgos* 3.3.21.3 (*Clemens Alexandrinus,* ed. Otto Stählin, vol. 1. p. 339); Brotten (1996: 5, 337); Cassio (1983: 296ff).

48. Dover (1989: 182–83). Dover notes that Lesbos, like Corinth, had a reputation in antiquity for sexual enterprise, and "if there is a significance in Lucian's choice of cities, this is probably it."

> Around your soft throat. . . .
> . . . with pure, sweet oil
> . . . you anointed me
> And on a soft, gentle bed . . .
> You quenched your desire . . .
> . . . no holy site . . .
> We left uncovered,
> No grove . . . dance
> . . . sound (no. 94, ed. Lobel and Page)[49]

While Sappho's place of origin is now attached to female homosexuality (lesbianism), she too may have experienced attraction to men as well as women, as another of her poems may suggest: "A handsome man is good to look at, but a good man will be attractive as well" (no. 50, ed. Lobel and Page). The first part of this verse deals with attraction, but the second part seems to be saying that one's attraction to a man can grow if he treats you well. It is of course possible that Sappho wrote this poem for a patron or performance, and it does not represent her own voice, but it is impossible for us to know for sure. Sappho may have written this in her role as teacher, if indeed she was one. Regardless, it is sound advice.[50] "Better to marry a man who is good to you, rather than one who is very handsome but beats you," might be one way to rephrase the message.

What we can say about Sappho is that she achieved incredible fame in antiquity, and obviously her attractions to women did not impede her renown. Sappho was revered by ancients as the greatest "poetess" of all time.[51] Antipater of Sidon, writing around 150 BCE, proclaimed Sappho to be a tenth muse: "Mnemosyne [Memory] was smitten with astonishment when she heard honey-voiced Sappho, wondering if mortals possess a tenth muse" (*Greek Anthology* 9.66). Most of Sappho's poetry was lost forever in the Middle Ages, except for a few fragments. Despite her pagan popularity, Sappho's works were publicly burned, at least according to legend, during the Middle Ages due to her immorality.[52]

Little other evidence of female homoeroticism comes down to us from Greek antiquity. Some poetry of the Hellenistic poet Nossis is homoerotic

---

49. Sappho translations based upon those by Rayor (1991).
50. On Sappho's role as a teacher of young women, and as the leader of a chorus of young girls, see Calame (2001: 210–14); cf. Blanshard (2010: 156).
51. Antipater of Thessalonica, ca. 10 BCE, wrote: "My name is Sappho, and I excelled all women in song as much as Maeonides excelled men." On Sappho's fame, see further Robinson (1963).
52. Johnson (1991: xvii–xviii); see also Penrose (forthcoming).

in character and still extant, and there are some homoerotic love spells from Egypt that are preserved in ancient Greek. Plutarch (*Lyc.* 18.4) asserts that women at Sparta courted girls in the same fashion that men courted youths, and that relationships of these types were "highly valued." The attraction of girls to one another at Sparta is confirmed in several poems of Alcman, and takes place in an educational setting.[53] The data gleaned from Sappho to Plutarch suggests that eroticism between persons of the same sex was perfectly acceptable during youth, but marriage was an expectation for both women and men.

CONCLUSION

In conclusion, there is a stark difference between twenty-first century American attitudes towards sexuality and those of the ancient Greeks. When a student vocalizes homophobia in the classroom, it is important to open up discussion with his/her peers, and to inquire as to what connotations derogatory terms such as "faggot" have to that student. Explaining the history of a term like faggot, which ultimately refers to the burning of sodomites at the stake, is a place to begin to help students realize that their own assumptions are not only culturally specific, but ultimately derive from a history of intolerance and hatred. Along the same lines, I have suggested that we as educators can help students understand how all of our understanding of sexuality—even our own—is culturally constructed. Ideas that all gay men are effeminate and lesbians are always masculine, as well as the insistence of some that homosexuality is sick, all stem from modern psychology. It is important for students to understand that homosexuality was removed from the list of psychological disorders by the American Psychological Association in 1973.

Another assumption made by students is that ancient pederasty is the same thing as modern pedophilia. An analysis of ancient texts, such as those of Xenophon and Ephorus, can be used to demonstrate to students that parental or guardian consent was necessary to engage in ancient Athenian or Cretan pederasty, whereas pedophilia is a coercion disorder in which children may be molested without their parents knowing anything about it. Pedophilia, by medical definition, refers to sex between an adult and a pre-pubescent youth. Visual evidence can be used to demonstrate that the beloved in an ancient Greek pederastic relationship was, at least in most cases, an adolescent.

---

53. Calame (2001: 7).

Additional lesson plans have been suggested to demonstrate to students that ancient male-male homoeroticism was associated with masculinity and hence found its place in the ancient military, and that ancient Greek female homoeroticism was also pederastic in nature, at least according to the limited evidence that we have. In a course focused on gender and sexuality, an instructor might be able to use a published reader to cover these lessons. I have used *Homosexuality in Greece and Rome: A Sourcebook of Basic Documents,* edited by Thomas Hubbard (2003), with success in my graduate seminar. Not all of the suggested sources in this article are in this collection, but with some supplementation, the reader worked well for my students' needs. In an *Ancient Greek History* course, a number of the texts mentioned above may already be assigned as primary sources in translation: Herodotus, Thucydides, Xenophon's *Hellenica,* and Plutarch's *Lives.* In addition to these sources, an instructor should consider assigning the *Symposia* of both Plato and Xenophon, homoerotic verses of Sappho and Alcman, and, of course should use images of ancient Greek artwork to supplement texts.[54] In terms of textbooks, *Ancient Greece: A Political, Social, and Cultural History* by Sarah B. Pomeroy, Stanley M. Burstein, Walter Donlan, Jennifer Tolbert Roberts, and David Tandy (2011) stands out as openly discussing homoeroticism and integrating it into the rest of Greek history. Alistair Blanshard's *Sex: Vice and Love from Antiquity to Modernity* (2010: 166–89) contains a very useful annotated bibliography of secondary sources on ancient sexuality, organized topically. Armed with the right tools, an instructor can help to lessen student discomfort with ancient Greek pederasty while opening up an avenue to understand the Greeks from their own perspective—not ours.

---

54. Excellent descriptions and citations of pertinent images can be found in Cantarella and Lear (2008), Rabinowitz (2002), Stewart (1997), Kilmer (1993), and Dover (1989).

15

Queering Catullus in the Classroom
The Ethics of Teaching Poem 63[1]

MAXINE LEWIS

"BUT IN THIS LINE is Attis a man, or a woman?!"
So asked my student angrily, one of many in the classroom who were frustrated and confused by the gender—and grammatical—vagaries of Catullus' poem 63. The text is a harrowing tale of Attis' self-castration, divine *furor*, and all-too-late repentance. When Attis wakes up after near-Bacchic revelry (post-castration) and *uidet sine quis* "sees what s/he is without" (v. 46), s/he laments and asks,

> ego nunc deum ministra et Cybeles famula ferar?
> ego Maenas, ego mei pars, ego uir sterilis ero?

> Shall I now be called slave-girl of the gods and hand-maiden of Cybele?
> Will I be a Maenad, a part of myself, will I be a barren man? (vv. 68–69)

---

1. The strategies that I discuss in this chapter were developed in the classroom across a series of courses. I am grateful to all my students for their thoughtful responses to a challenging topic. In particular, my graduate Latin students at the University of Auckland and the 3b class at the Sydney Latin Summer School provided stimulating discussion. In 2012 I presented versions of this paper at the U.K. Classical Association Annual Conference in Exeter and the University of Auckland's Department of Classics and Ancient History Seminar Series. I wish to thank the listeners, who provided thoughtful, engaged advice. I also wish to thank the anonymous readers for their feedback on this piece. Lastly, I am grateful to Dr Fiona McHardy and Professor Nancy Rabinowitz for their invitation to contribute to the present volume. I could not have asked for a more appropriate home for this topic.

The poem confronts the reader with the specter of gender identity in crisis,[2] and confronts instructor and student alike with a set of grammatical and political problems.[3] The difficulties with teaching poem 63 in an English speaking classroom arise because while Catullus depicts Attis moving between and beyond the binary poles of "male" and "female," standard English has no vocabulary to describe gender identities outside of these two supposed opposites. As the quote with which I began this paper suggests, Catullus' grammatical maneuver causes practical issues when teaching this poem, whether it is to Latinists who will nevertheless need to discuss the poem in English, or to students reading the material solely in English translation. It also poses an ethical dilemma. When discussing this poem, is the instructor making the classroom a safe and inclusive space for students who themselves possess gender or sex identities outside the limits of "male" and "female," because they are intersex, transgender, or genderqueer?[4] I consider this one of my responsibilities as an instructor.[5] Teaching poem 63 requires me to pursue this goal vigilantly because transphobia and intersex-phobia are more likely to be voiced in a classroom where students are learning about a character who castrates himself.

Because this poem thrusts the notion of gender instability in our very faces at the deepest linguistic level (the level of gendered terminations), and because (as I will show) our own language cannot render that gender instability accurately, it has pushed me into trying new approaches in the classroom. There are radical ways to express identity in English without defining a person's gender—this poem can push us to seek them out. There are ways to get students thinking outside the box of "he" versus "she," and this poem invites us to use them. In this chapter, I offer four strategies that I have used with students, to combat the various difficulties caused by Catullus' depiction of Attis.

---

2. On poem 63 as a text that challenges modern—and ancient—expectations of gender, see especially Skinner (1993), Nauta (2004) and Harrison (2004).

3. This is not the only Catullan poem to cause difficulty in the classroom; see Ancona and Hallett (2007) on the politics and practicalities of teaching a poet whose oeuvre includes graphic invective and homoerotic themes. See Garrison (2007) for practical strategies to teach Catullus' oeuvre.

4. On terms used in the various communities (e.g., intersex, transgender, genderqueer, transsexual, trans) see "Transgender Terminology" (2009) on the National Center for Transgender Equality website, accessed April 28, 2012, http://transequality.org/Resources/NCTE_TransTerminology.pdf. I use transgender in its inclusive sense as an umbrella term to include both people who are in transition from one gender to another and those who do not wish to transition but who possess a non-gendered or bi-gendered identity and/or gender expression; see Ekins and King (2006: 13–30).

5. Transphobia and gender discrimination in the Western world lead to legal, social and economic discrimination and disadvantage, violence, and even death; see Wilchins (2004: 153–54); Kailey (2005: 77–79). For those living beyond the gender binary, the issue of how gender is perceived, described, and named is not merely an academic matter, but is one of survival.

THE STRATEGIES

1. I initiate a classroom discussion about English's gendered language and pronouns. I provide background on historical attempts to replace "he" and "she" and invite students to try alternatives "they," "one" and "she" or "s/he" when translating and discussing poem 63.
2. I provide students with gender-neutral pronouns used by some transgendered people. I explain the history, background and purpose of such pronouns. I invite the students to use them when discussing Attis, discussing as a class where such pronouns might be relevant and where they might contradict the Latin.
3. I invite students to write about poem 63 and translate it using visual symbols of male and female gender. I initiate a discussion asking at what point gender manifests in our thought and whether symbols convey gender differently to the various pronouns we have used.
4. I ask students to interrogate the scholarship on this poem, identifying points where scholars' gender ideologies have shaped their textual, editorial, and translation choices.

In this chapter I explain how these strategies can work as tools that turn poem 63 from a problem into an opportunity. They can help students to think outside the linguistic constraints of their own language, and to better see how gender is constructed both in language and society, not only in antiquity but also in their own lives.

WHY POEM 63 IS TRICKY—THE PROBLEM WITH ENGLISH

Poem 63 describes the Greek youth Attis' journey from an unnamed *patria*, complete with *gymnasium*, wrestling, and hordes of admirers (vv. 64–67), to the wilds of Phrygia, where he castrates himself and becomes a *Gallus*, a priest of Cybele. The key event of poem 63 is the protracted gender transformation of the protagonist, a transformation which challenges readers' understanding of what it means to be male and female.[6] The transforma-

---

[6] Skinner (1993: 109). There are obviously other events occurring in the text and other themes in operation, many of which have received scholarly attention. See especially: Panoussi (2003) on the thematic relationship between cc.63–64; Takács (1996) on how c.63 relates to the worship of Cybele in antiquity; Nauta (2004) for the reception of the poem in its Roman socio-political context; Harrison (2004) on the relationship between Rome, Greece, and "The East" in c.63; Rubino (1974) which treats polarities in Roman thought reflected in the poem; and Oliensis (2009) on c.63 in terms of castration anxiety.

tion begins at line 5, where the hitherto masculine Attis (clearly defined as such by grammatical terminations) slices off his testicles, described rather coyly as "*pondera.*" In the following line the narrator explains that Attis sensed that the "members" remaining were *sine uiro*, without manhood or manliness. After this act, which will later be revealed as a monumental slip-up, Attis, frenzied, rushes into the woods to worship Cybele. During these introductory lines, Catullus uses the gender terminations of the participles to show Attis' gender shifting:[7]

> super alta uectus *[masc.]* Attis celeri rate maria,
> Phrygium ut nemus citato cupide pede tetigit *[masc.]*,
> adiitque *[masc. implied]* opaca siluis redimita loca deae,
> stimulatus *[masc.]* ibi furenti rabie, uagus *[masc.]* animis,
> deuolsit *[masc. implied]* ili acuto sibi pondera silice,   5
> itaque ut relicta sensit *[gender?]* sibi *[gender?]* membra sine uiro,
> etiam recente terrae sola sanguine maculans *[gender?]*,
> niueis citata *[fem.]* cepit *[fem.]* manibus leue typanum,
> typanum tuum, Cybebe, tua, mater initia,
> quatiensque *[gender?]* terga tauri teneris caua digitis   10
> canere haec suis adorta est *[fem.]* tremebunda *[fem.]* comitibus.

> Conveyed over the high seas, Attis, in a swift craft,
> as he eagerly arrived at the Phrygian grove with speedy foot
> and entered the shady places of the goddess wreathed with forests,
> goaded there by raging madness, he, bewildered in spirits,
> tore from himself the weights of his loins with the sharp flint.   5
> And so, as he/she sensed the members left for him/her were without manhood,
> still he/she spattering the soil of the earth with fresh blood,
> with snow-white hands she seized quickly the light timbrel,
> timbrel of yours, Cybebe, your initiation-rites, mother,
> and he/she shaking the hollow hide of the bull with slender fingers   10
> she tremulously began to sing these words to her companions.

The gendered adjectives *uectus, stimulatus,* and *uagus* in the masculine, followed by *citata, adorta* and *tremebunda,* in the feminine, are strewn among finite verbs. In an English rendering these finite verbs would nor-

---

7. Oliensis (2009: 111–12) notes how provocative this gender change would have been to Roman audiences; Romans did not consider eunuchs to be female.

mally be rendered by a third-person personal pronoun in the masculine or feminine gender, "he" or "she." In other Latin texts, the reader can take the gender of the protagonist as static and thus consistently translate finite verbs with either "he" or "she." Aeneas is always a man, Dido is always a woman.

Not so Attis, because in poem 63, the adjectives, pronouns, and relative pronouns applied to Attis are inconsistent, thus leading to our difficulty in translating the finite verbs. Further on in the poem we see the narrator apply feminine forms to Attis: *furibunda* (v. 31), *uaga* (v. 31), *ipsa* (v. 45), *allocuta* (v.49), *illa* (v. 90); but Cybele will refer to Attis as male in *hunc* (v. 78) and *qui* (v. 80).[8] The narrator also uses participial forms throughout that are ambiguous and could be masculine, feminine or neuter, such as *anhelans* (v. 31), *agens* (v. 31), and *uisens* (v. 48). Attis refers to him/herself as *miser* (v. 51) in the masculine but possibly *furibunda* (v. 54) in the feminine (more on *furibunda* later in the chapter). Catullus constructs Attis' gender through grammatical terminations as being fluid and even contestable—Cybele's determination that Attis is still male contradicts the narrator's use of feminine forms, while Attis' perspective on his/her own gender shifts back and forth. The unstable nature of Attis' gender suggested by the gender of the words is verified by the narrator's statement that Attis is *notha mulier* (v. 27), and Attis' own concern that s/he might be either a (female) maenad or a barren man—or perhaps both (vv. 68–69, above).

The matter of how to render—and even to understand—the finite verbs is made more complex by Catullus' inclusion of the paradoxes *notha mulier* and *uir sterilis,* and it was while discussing lines 68–9 that my student had her outburst. Her frustration was understandable in a society that is based on a binary gender system. Catullus confronts the reader with an Attis who moves between and beyond gender binaries, and at some points cannot be defined simply as either male or female (grammatically and conceptually).

The complexity of Catullus' play with gender here, usually observed by my students within minutes of first reading the poem, is belied by the technical vocabulary which English-speakers possess to describe an animate being in the third-person. In general, English is a less "gendered" language than say French or German, or Latin, for that matter.[9] English does not have gendered terminations for adjectives or verbs, gendered nouns such as "stewardess" or "actress" are less common than they used to be, and English

---

8. And as Skinner (1993: 127 n.47) notes, some of the poem's feminine forms such as *allocuta* and *adorta* are "metrically guaranteed" and could not have been masculine forms, while others (e.g., *ipsa* v.45, *excitam* v.42, *teneram* v.88 and *illa* v.89) have been emended to the feminine gender by later editors.

9. Wittig (1985: 3).

does not apply "the mark of gender" to its non-animate beings.[10] Yet, English *is* gendered as regards third-person personal pronouns, using "he," "she" or "it."[11] Indeed, Corbeill notes that "in English the only significant expression of gender that survives is in the third-person personal pronouns."[12] It is nearly impossible *not* to use gendered pronouns and possessive adjectives to describe an animate being in the third-person, as *either* "he" or "she." Thus at points in the poem where Attis is described with a mixture of masculine and feminine grammatical forms, or when forms that could be either gender are used, it becomes difficult to translate it into English, to discuss it in an English-speaking classroom, and for students to write their papers in English referring to Attis. How are they to refer to *her* (or is that *him?*) without obscuring the fluidity which is the subject of the work?

STRATEGY 1. PROBLEMATIZING ENGLISH'S GENDERED THIRD-PERSON PRONOUNS: "HE," "SHE," "IT"

When I teach poem 63, I take the opportunity to ask my students what alternatives to "he" or "she" they might use to describe Attis, to capture Attis' gender ambiguity. I ask my students to try out the following options, "they," "one," and "s/he." This generally generates a productive discussion.

As one recent style guide details, "they" is sometimes used as a gender-neutral substitute for "he" or "she" (gender-neutral words being "free of explicit or implicit reference to biological gender or sexual identity"[13]). My students, however, have usually agreed that "they" is unsatisfactory. Using a plural for a singular is ungrammatical and the problem is not just one of technical nicety. "They" is awkward because it can confuse the issue at hand, introducing the specter of a plural subject where there is none. This is relevant in poem 63, which features a singular leader of shifting grammatical gender and a plural band of female followers (her *comites,* the *Gallae*). It is thematically significant that Catullus calls Attis' comrades *Gallae,* using the feminine termination to denote male eunuchs (where usually the masculine is used).[14] Using "they" in English to describe Catullus' Galli obscures

---

10. Ibid.
11. *The American Heritage Guide to Contemporary Usage and Style,* s.v. "pronoun," accessed April 22, 2012, http://www.credoreference.com/entry/hmcontempusage/pronouns_personal.
12. Corbeill (2008: 78).
13. *The American Heritage Guide to Contemporary Usage and Style,* s.v. "gender neutral," accessed April 22, 2012, http://www.credoreference.com/entry/hmcontempusage/gender_neutral.
14. Always noted by commentators but Ellis (1889: 263); Fordyce (1961: 262, 264–5), and Kroll (1968: 132) are best on the history of the word in both Greek and Latin.

his play with gendered terminations, while simultaneously using "they" to describe Attis confuses the issue of who "they" is (or are)! "They," then, does not help. Likewise, "one" is not particularly useful, because in common usage it does duty as an impersonal first person pronoun ("one needs to go to the bathroom," she said archly). It is confusing in a poem that moves between direct speech and reported action.

For the sake of providing some political context for students, I raise the issue that gendered pronouns have come under attack from feminists and their allies in recent history. The use of the "generic he," that is, the use of the male pronoun to stand in for all people, can be considered sexist, akin to the use of "man" to stand for "human."[15] Hence some second-wave feminists fought for "she" to be used instead as the generic subject. The "generic she" foregrounds woman rather than man, thus redressing the former sexist imbalance inherent in language that assumes maleness for generic human subjects.[16] Arising somewhat later from the movement for political correctness is the substitution "s/he" for "he" and "him/her" for "him," etc. "S/he" and "him/her" allow for the possibility that the generic subject might be either woman or man. These examples are now in relatively common usage, and do indeed mitigate some of the effects of sexist language.[17] My students' attitudes to these terms tend to range widely, from whole-hearted acceptance of the language and the need for it, to rejection that such substitutions are necessary or desirable in a "post-feminist" world. Many are indifferent. Thus far in my experience, the spread of attitudes has not cut clearly across age, class, or sex lines.

Generating a discussion about these common alternatives to sexist language is useful because it allows me to point out (if none of the students do it themselves) that none of these politically-conscious and -motivated options are *gender-neutral*. Rather, they each presume a binary opposition between two genders. The substitution of "she" for "he" is a type of linguistic affirmative action designed to combat sexism, while "s/he" avoids sexism in that it does not preclude the subject being of either sex. Yet by using these alternatives to "he," whether by replacing man with woman ("she" for the "generic he") or by allowing woman to stand alongside man ("s/he" for "he"), we actually solidify the conviction that there are *two* genders/sexes. This is an example of a trap that the queer theorist Riki Wilchins

---

15. *The American Heritage Guide to Contemporary Usage and Style*, s.v. "he/she," accessed April 22, 2012 http://www.credoreference.com/entry/hmcontempusage/he_she.

16. See Wittig (1985: 5) on this imbalance.

17. As a woman I can testify that I notice (with pleasant surprise) when Classical scholars use "she" to represent the generic "reader"; see for example Skinner (2003).

has observed in feminism; by attempting to redress inequalities faced by women, it defines women as an ontological category and thus reifies the binary structures of "male/female and masculine/feminine."[18]

Substituting "she" for "he" is not really an adequate option for poem 63, where Catullus names a specific, not a generic subject. I do, however, ask the students to try it on for ideological "size," so to speak, that is, to "read" Attis as female throughout the poem. I do this because it emphasizes that Catullus is not in fact casting Attis simply as female (or male). In the context of a Latin class, the students generally become very uncomfortable with depicting Attis as "she" when they know that grammatically in that line, Attis is masculine. This reflects their concern with accurately capturing the sense of Catullus' Latin, in thought and then in word. Generally I find that students want to follow Catullus' often ambiguous lead, and are frustrated by their inability to do so when using English. Once I have explained Latin grammatical gender to students seeing the poem in translation, I find that they too are confused about whether they ought to talk about Attis as "he" or "she," and at what point—if any—"he" becomes "she."

DIGRESSION—
THE LINGUISTIC IS THE POLITICAL IS THE PERSONAL

Before outlining my second strategy (providing students with gender-neutral pronouns used in some sections of transgender communities), I need to emphasize the dually problematic nature of using "he" and "she" to refer to Catullus' Attis. So far, I have been stressing the practical questions generated in the classroom by the limitations of English, such as: how are our students to correctly describe Attis, in an essay, or an exam translation? How are they to convey that they understand Catullus' subtle play with gendered language—and gender expression—when "he" and "she" erase that very subtlety?

This practical problem, though important for grading and for the pure philology of it all, is academic in both senses of the word. There is a bigger issue. When we render Attis as he *or* she in a classroom setting, we—instructors and students alike—perpetuate a core Western assumption that there is an innate binary opposition between male/masculine and female/feminine. This idea, that humans are dimorphic, that there are only two

---
18. Wilchins (2004: 126). S/he would be more useful for the purpose of teaching poem 63 as it at least includes two genders—it cannot however be verbally expressed which makes it difficult in verbal discussions.

sexes, male and female, and only two genders which correspond to the two sexes—masculine and feminine, respectively—can be traced back to Plato, while its effect on our medical understanding of terminology is rooted in the Victorian era.[19] It is deeply pervasive.[20] It is also false, according to certain scientists, feminists, queer theorists and sociologists, and most importantly, according to many intersex, transgendered, and genderqueer people.[21]

It is a truism that when a baby is born, the first question asked by parents after "is it healthy?" is "is it a boy or a girl?" Yet the Intersex Society of North America estimates that one in approximately one thousand, six hundred and sixty-six babies are born intersex, that is, with chromosomes that are neither XX or XY.[22] That is, in every two thousand people, there is at least one who is neither exactly male or female. In its literature, the Intersex Society makes the point that "intersex" is a term that covers a multitude of conditions, a multiplicity of difference from the norm of male and female. Yet, in the Western world today, lack of belief in the multiplicity of biological sexes that exists among humans, in concert with societal expectation that there be only two sexes, still lead to genital surgery being performed without consent on infants, so that an intersex baby who is neither "he" or "she" can be made to fit the model of binary sex and gender.[23] Such operations have garnered recent media attention, thanks in large part to activism conducted by the intersex people themselves who have experienced such surgery and argue against it.[24] The existence of intersex people who bear a wide variety of different chromosomal conditions belies Western society's own notion that there are only two biological sexes.

Meanwhile, the existence of transsexual and transgendered people, as well as those who identify as genderqueer or gender outlaws, calls into question the related notion that along with the two sexes, female and male, come

---

19. Fausto-Sterling (2000: 19–20, 22).
20. Wilchins (2004: 145–46).
21. For the science, see Fausto-Sterling (1993: 19–21); Dreger (1998: 26); Ekins and King (2006: 24–27). Cf. the narratives—both political and personal—in Nestle, Howell, and Wilchins (2002); Bloom (2003: 3–47); Wilchins (2004); Kailey (2005).
22. "How common is intersex?" at http://www.isna.org/, accessed April 28, 2012. Fausto-Sterling (2000: 20) estimates even higher, at 17 in 1000.
23. Wilchins (2004: 72–78). The formerly widespread practice of performing such operations currently seems to be gradually diminishing, thanks in large part to pressure from intersex people who have had their gender assigned at birth via "corrective" surgery. See Dreger (1998); Fausto-Sterling (2000: 19–21).
24. See for instance the stated agenda of the Intersex Society of North America on their homepage http://www.isna.org.

two genders, feminine and masculine.²⁵ The National Centre for Transgender Equality in the United States, estimates that between 0.25 and 1% of the population is transgender.²⁶ Of these people, many will have medical treatments, including surgery, to alter their biological sex characteristics so as to better match their perceived gender.²⁷ However, not all transgender people choose to transition fully into the "opposite" sex,²⁸ while some are not able to for legal, social, or economic reasons.²⁹ Some trans-identifying people choose to (and are able to) "pass" as a natural or "cis" born member of the opposite sex, while others choose to occupy a liminal gender identity, between masculine and feminine.³⁰ As recent accounts by transgendered people themselves show, there is no single "transgender" experience, since culture, ethnicity, and class play determining roles in any individual's experience of his or her gender, legal, and social position, and access to medical, social, and legal support.³¹ Transgendered people in our community thus undermine the very notion that there are only two genders.

In short, there is a wide array of evidence that there are *more* than two sexes, and more than two genders. Yet in the Western world, there remains the widely-held belief that a binary opposition between man and woman reflects the only possible options of sex and gender presentation.³² Our use of the gendered third person personal pronouns "he" and "she" reflects (and is shaped by) this notion.

---

25. "Transsexual" and "transgender" are terms applied with some fluidity; "transgender" can be an umbrella term that overlaps with "genderqueer" and "gender outlaw" which both have radical political connotations; See Ekins and King (2006: 13–30) on the development of the terms "transsexual," "transgender," and "trans" and the range of possible meanings of each term; Kailey (2005: 3–5) explains why it is so difficult to define the boundaries between transsexual, transgender, and genderqueer experiences.

26. "Understanding Transgender" (2009) on the National Center for Transgender Equality website, accessed April 28, 2012, http://transequality.org/Resources/NCTE_UnderstandingTrans.pdf. The figures must be estimated because, as the authors of this resource note, no official agency currently collects data on how many people in the United States identify as transgender; cf. Bloom (2003: 33).

27. "Understanding Transgender" (2009: 3–5).

28. See Ekins and King (2006: 97–142) on stories of those who "oscillate" between genders, and (2006: 143–80) of those who "negate" some of their biological sex characteristics but do not adopt those of another sex.

29. Kailey (2005: 3–5). See the personal stories of transgender experiences in a variety of manifestations in: Nestle, Howell, and Wilchins (2002: 67–129); Bloom (2003: 10–11, 29–32).

30. Fausto-Sterling (2000: 22); Ekins and King (2006: 28–29); Kailey (2005: 3–5).

31. Nestle, Howell, and Wilchins (2002: 67–129, 238–62); Bloom (2003: 3–47); Kailey (2005); Ekins and King (2006: 43–220); and see the report "Injustice at every turn: a look at Black respondents in the national transgender discrimination survey" (2011) National Center for Transgender Equality website, accessed April 28, 2012, http://transequality.org/PDFs/BlackTransFactsheetFINAL_090811.pdf on discrimination against African-American transgendered people in the United States.

32. Fausto-Sterling (1993), Kailey (2005: 5–6).

How does this relate to the classroom, and to the teaching of poem 63 in particular?

As teachers who speak English in the classroom, we gender our students every day by using linguistic structures that define them as *either* male *or* female. We talk—and think—about our students in terms of a gender binary. "Did Hyun-Jin hand in his essay?" "Why isn't Rosa here—is she ill?" The process is not one-way—our students gender us, too. "I want to take that class. His lectures are so interesting!" Our language creates an educational environment and a classroom situation wherein everyone is identified as either he or she.

Yet given the statistics (a possible 1.7% of the population being intersex; between 0.25% and 1% of the population being transgendered), it is possible that trans-identifying or intersex students are in our courses. Thus in any classroom situation, our everyday use of gendered pronouns can silence and marginalize the identities and experience of transgender or intersex students. In a classroom where Catullus' poem 63 is being taught, discussed, and possibly translated, the silencing and marginalization can take on another dimension. The protagonist, Attis, is a man whose gender identity becomes de-stabilized, and whose existence thus admits the possibility (albeit one that Skinner shows is seen as horrific by the poet himself[33]) of a world beyond the gender binary. Yet in using "he" and/or "she" to label Attis, as English-speakers we may be undermining Attis' fluidity and thus (likely unwittingly or even unwillingly) further marginalizing any student who is not simply he or she. It is partly due to my desire to avoid marginalizing such students that I developed my second strategy, the use of gender-neutral pronouns commonly used within genderqueer communities. While the medical community has "yet to adopt a language that is capable of reflecting" the full scope and permutations of biological sex and gender,[34] many transgender people are already doing so.[35]

STRATEGY 2. MOVING BEYOND GENDER—ZIE, NU, AND HIR

In the classroom, I introduce the pronouns "zie," "nu," and "hir" after some discussion of the poem has already occurred. I find it useful to have already

---

33. Skinner (1993: 113–15).
34. Fausto-Sterling (2000: 22).
35. See for instance Ekins and King (2006: 158–61) on Christie Elan-Cane's use of "per" to describe per ungendered self; Kailey (2005: 165–66, 168); and Gibson (2010) who covered the transperson Norrie's fight to have hir sex defined as "not specified" on Australian legal documents.

initiated the discussion about "they," "one," and "s/he," and to have allowed the students to discover for themselves, by reading the poem, that there *is* a difficulty expressing Attis' gender in English. Then, I present the students with the information that there *are* pronouns in existence that have been created to combat the bi-gendered perspective embodied within the words "he" and "she." There are various pronouns created for use within some transgender communities such as "per," "nu," and "zie" (also spelt "ze") for the nominative and accusative cases, and "hir" and "per" for the possessive adjective.[36] In introducing these words to my students, I make sure to distinguish between non-*sexist* language like the use of "she" for "he," which aims to combat sexism (but not to eradicate the idea of two sexes) and non-*generist* language, which aims to do away with the polarity between two distinct genders/sexes and to express an experience of the self that is neither male nor female.

The existence of pronouns such as "nu," "zie," "ze," and "hir" comes as a shock to most students. I have not yet encountered a student who was familiar with any of the words. Even the concept of non-gendrist language is surprising to many, as it highlights the pervasive but often un-stated reality that our language *is* gendered. However, the introduction of "zie," "nu," and "hir" flows on somewhat naturally from our earlier discussions of alternatives to our common use of gendered pronouns. It also generally strikes a chord with the students, who by this point have mostly recognized that Attis' gender is subject to continual slippage and change.

Having named the pronouns and provided some background on their use in transgender communities, I ask students to apply them to Catullus' Attis. In my experience, the students are very hesitant at first. The words seem strange, "not natural," as one student of mine put it. They are aurally unfamiliar. They are also instantiations of an extremely unfamiliar concept, that it is possible for a person to be neither simply he nor she.

To make the terms more familiar, I use them when I speak about Attis to my classes, shifting between gendered and non-gendered pronouns. This felt strange at first, but I can now use zie and hir without pause in class, which I suspect normalizes things for the students. I ask them to "play" with these terms as we progress through our readings of and discussion about the poem, using the words when they feel appropriate. The bolder students will experiment with saying "zie" or "hir"; others indicate shyness or confusion. This holds true whether the students are discussing the poem broadly in a class taught in translation, or working through a line-by-line

---

36. Kailey (2005: 165–66, 168); Ekins and King (2006: 158–61).

reading in a Latin class. In the latter situation, I will ask a student to translate a given line that refers to Attis with all the possible options available for personal pronouns, re-reading the line for the class multiple times and switching between "they," "one," "he," "she," "zie," and "nu" each time. This can become tedious but ultimately proves fruitful, since we then discuss as a class which particular pronoun makes more sense. Often the grammar and context of the Latin will make it clear that some options are less preferable. An adjective like *quatiens* in line 10 can be more readily understood as "zie, shaking" than as either "he, shaking" or "she, shaking," since it can grammatically be either. In the opposite situation, where a Latin adjective or pronoun is clearly one gender or the other, students will argue that it ought to be translated with the corresponding gendered pronoun in English (and I agree, despite often playing devil's advocate). Yet, this seems to be a product of their desire to accurately translate the Latin rather than a hangover of bi-gendered ideology, since quite a few students do choose to use "zie," "ze," "nu," or "hir" in lines where Catullus has left Attis' gender ambiguous.

At these points in the discussion when a student uses gender-neutral language in the classroom, I am sometimes reminded of the French feminist critic Monique Wittig, who in her staunch attacks on gendered language argued that it is crucial "to consider how gender works in language, how gender works upon language, before considering *how it works from there upon its users.*"[37] It is this last phrase that I think of in the moments when my students and I deconstruct Attis' gender and sex as a counterfeit woman and a barren man, as a he, a she, and sometimes a zie. We are working gender back onto language, and questioning both as we go. Through self-consciously interrogating our own gendered language and through using new alternatives, we can become conscious that our role in naming Attis does more than name zie/her/him, it constructs nu/him/her.

What is Attis' identity here? And can it be said to be that of a trans-identifying or intersex person? These questions have been asked of me in class. The answer to the first, I think, is that Attis is, in the end, simply and only Attis. She is not a woman, and he is not a man. Zie is Catullus' warning to his readers that it is a tragedy for a man to stray outside his socially and biologically assigned gender role (in Roman terms, it is a tragedy when a boy does not become a man, with a man's position in society).[38]

The answer to the second question is, I think, a resounding "no." I feel compelled to stress to students that intersex conditions are biological;

---

37. Wittig (1985: 4); italics added.
38. Quinn (1972: 249–51); Skinner (1993: 113–15).

Attis' situation is not. Transgender people are often motivated to have surgery to realign their sex characteristics with their gender; Attis had no such desire. It is implied that like his companions, Attis too castrated himself "out of excessive hatred of Venus," *Veneris nimio odio* (v. 17), while other lines (such as vv. 64–7) suggest that his adolescent reluctance to fully take on the role of active, adult male led him to reject all the trappings of civilization by abandoning his urban homeland.[39] As Skinner puts it, in the Roman world Attis is a "psychosexual oxymoron," a sign of Roman anxiety about gender transgression.[40] If Attis could have fully become a woman, there would have been no tragedy in this story, or, in the Roman world, less of a tragedy. The point of the poem, the reason for Attis' lament and the narrator's fear-filled conclusion, is that gender *fluidity*, not gender transition, is terrifying in a world composed of a binary gender opposition.[41] Catullus did not cast Attis as an ancient transgendered or intersex person—those are modern epistemological categories (and indeed, in modern terms Attis seems like a trans-phobe stuck in a genderqueer body; zie is devastated that zie is now semi-female rather than all male). Thus, it may seem anachronistic to discuss Attis through the lens of contemporary queer theory.

However, the student feedback I have received from teaching this text with some context of modern gender theory has been positive. Students have indicated that they appreciated the greater sense of flexibility that knowing these pronouns gave them, and some have displayed interest in learning more about transgender and intersex experiences. Thus far, I have had no negative response to the strategy. I am aware that drawing students' attention to the existence of transgendered and intersex people could precipitate a trans- or intersex-phobic discussion or outburst which I would then have to mediate and moderate (compare Endres and Penrose on homophobia in the classroom, in this volume). As a cis-born woman-identifying-woman (that is, I am neither intersexed nor transgendered), I hesitate sometimes about raising this issue with a class for fear of precipitating such an outburst which might render a classroom unsafe.[42] However, on balance I believe

---

39. Skinner (1993: 115).
40. Skinner (1993: 114).
41. Cf. Skinner (1993: 114).
42. It is partly in anticipation of such an event that I have investigated local support centers for genderqueer, trans, and intersex people in an effort to gather information and resources, both to educate myself and to provide them to students if necessary. Some LGBTI organizations provide education workshops and/or web-based resources for nontranspeople who work with transgendered people, such as the Sydney-based organization Twenty10 which provides resources through its webpage http://www.twenty10.org.au/resources/gender, and the Gender Identity Project run through

that this strategy has three important benefits that make it worth persisting with.

At the most basic level, these tools are practical aids that allow students to use language in new ways. This can allow students to get closer to the sense of Catullus' text, whether they are working in Latin or in translation. At the next level, making such options available to all students may ease the marginalization experienced in the classroom by transgender, intersex, or genderqueer students. It allows them to use and to hear language in the classroom which might better reflect their non-binary experience of sex and gender and which is not generally known of outside a small community. Finally, ideally the process of experimenting with gender-neutral language allows all students in the room to expand their understanding of gender and sex, combating trans-, queer-, and intersex-phobia.

STRATEGY 3—BYPASSING LANGUAGE THROUGH SYMBOLS FOR GENDER ♂ ♀

In a classroom, the second strategy flows naturally from the first, and so too does the third follow easily on. The third strategy is to suggest that when writing about the poem, students can dispense with pronouns and use visual symbols. They can insert various visual symbols for gender, for instance next to Attis' name, an adjective, or the finite verb. This strategy was first suggested by a student in class[43] when we were discussing the difficulty of rendering in English the lines where Catullus has left Attis' gender ambiguous, such as v. 74. The visual device draws the reader's attention to the ambiguity of Attis' gender at these points. Indeed, using such symbols instead of pronouns throughout the piece could allow a visual representation of Attis' movement between and beyond gender binaries. To demonstrate that fluidity and ambiguity of Attis' gender at specific points, the male and female symbols could be placed next to each other, so that a translation of the opening lines would look something like this:

> Conveyed over the high seas, Attis ♂, in a swift craft,
> ♂ eagerly arrived at the Phrygian grove with speedy foot

The Center—The Lesbian, Gay, Bisexual & Transgender Center at http://www.gaycenter.org/gip. I have found it harder to find specific information on local support for people with intersex conditions in Australia and New Zealand. However, the website of the Intersex Society of North American at http://www.isna.org/ provides fairly comprehensive information and online resources.

43. I am indebted to Mr Anthony Gibbons for his extremely useful idea.

and entered the shady places of the goddess wreathed with forests,
goaded there by raging madness, bewildered in spirits,
tore from ♂ the weights of his loins with the sharp flint.   5
And so, as ♀♂ sensed the members left ♀♂ were without manhood,
still spattering the soil of the earth with fresh blood,
with snow-white hands ♀ seized quickly the light timbrel,
the timbrel of yours, Cybebe, your initiation-rites, mother,
and, ♀♂ shaking the hollow hide of the bull with slender fingers,   10
♀ tremulously ♀ began to sing these [words] to her companions.

The idea is that these visual cues, not generally being seen in text translation, jar the reader into consciously engaging with Attis' gender at a pre-verbal cognitive state. The visual image of both male and female symbols together suggest the complexity of Attis' gender, reminding us that it is fluid and not determined before we have a chance to formulate our normal verbal pattern of "he" *or* "she." This strategy is effective for working at the whiteboard and I encourage students to experiment with it in their written work; like "s/he" it is not, obviously, useful during a verbal discussion.

STRATEGY 4—DECONSTRUCTING THE SCHOLARSHIP

My final strategy has been to draw my students' attention to the way that their resources on this text—their commentaries, scholarly articles, and translations—reflect the constraints of English's gender pronouns and Western ideas of a simple gender binary. I invite the students to reflect on which scholars refer to Attis as "he" or "she" and at what points in the text. At the same time, I ask the students to consider whether the scholars' textual or interpretative decisions might be shaped by their society's ideas on gender, or whether their interpretations of the text do in fact extend beyond a false binary of male *or* female, but the limitations of our language have prevented them from fully expressing that interpretation. This can be done either in class as a group discussion, or as a research-based piece of assessment.

There are a number of points in the text where one can perform this analysis along with students. I have found line 54 to be extremely useful.[44]

---

44. V. 58 is another important example where what one decides the line means depends in part on how one reads Attis' gender, with the scholarship providing evidence of changing views. Briefly, in v.58 *remota* can be feminine singular agreeing with *ego* (thus indicating Attis' self-conception of hir future gender to be feminine) or neuter plural with *nemora* (which leaves Attis' gender ambiguous in the line). Fordyce (1961), Kroll (1968), and Thomson (1997) provide differing arguments

It has generated discussion in a series of commentaries over the last century and a half, so it provides a good representative sample on views on gendered language, and thus gender itself.

The difficulty in line 54 is in deciding what to do with *furibunda*, "raging," given the context of the surrounding lines:

> 'patria o mei creatrix, patria o mea genetrix,   50
> ego quam miser *[masc.]* relinquens, dominos ut erifugae
> famuli solent, ad Idae tetuli nemora pedem,
> ut aput niuem et ferarum gelida stabula forem,
> et earum omnia adirem furibunda *[fem. sg. nom. OR neut. pl. nom. acc.]*
>   latibula'

Grammatically, it can be feminine nominative, singular, agreeing with the here unnamed subject, Attis, meaning "raging" or "wild." Or, it can be neuter accusative plural, agreeing with *latibula*, "dens." Comments by critics as diverse in space and time as Ellis (1889), Fordyce (1961), Skinner (1993), and Thomson (1997), show that the grammatical role of *furibunda* depends not on objective lexical criteria, but on how one is already "reading" Attis' gender.

In the late 1800s, Ellis (1889) took *furibunda* as neuter plural with *latibula*, writing "the dens are *furibunda* as sheltering lions and other fierce beasts of prey."[45] His reasoning was that Catullus had called Attis *miser*, "wretched" in line 51, using the masculine form of the adjective and thus rendering him male once more. Ellis thought that a shift back to the feminine form in line 54 would be "impossible" and thus took *furibunda* as neuter plural.[46] This decision suppressed the possibly feminine, nominative identification of *furibunda* because the critic had already "read" Attis' gender here as masculine, stable, static. The implication is that Attis was never really the "she" that the feminine adjectives of earlier lines suggested. The textual decision reflects Ellis's beliefs about gender, as well as grammar.

---

which Latin students can—and must—dissect to decide what their own interpretation of the grammar will be. The different views can also be seen by comparing published translations. Green (2005: 131) gives "Ah, am I doomed to these alien forests, far from what's home, what's familiar" which suggests to me that he has taken *remota* with *ego;* Godwin (1995: 49) has "am I to take myself into these glades, far removed from my home?" where in English "far from" could refer either to the "I" or the "glades" and thus maintains the semantic uncertainty present in the Latin. Lee (1990: 79) writes of "these forests far distant from my home" which indicates that he takes *remota* with *nemora*. Encouraging students of Latin to widely consult English translations has proved useful in my teaching of this particular poem, as it demonstrates how one's reading of Attis' gender effects what one actually makes the poem "mean" in English.

45. Ellis (1889: 270).
46. Ibid.

In the 1990s Thomson was comfortable instead taking *furibunda* to refer to a female Attis, following Fordyce's tentative suggestion three decades before, that the grammatical form was "probably feminine singular as in [line] 31."[47] Here we have an alternative interpretation of the line based on an alternative reading of Attis' gender. Thomson notes that *miser*, "wretched," had appeared in line 51 in the masculine form. But, he argues that there is no contradiction with a feminine nominative reading of *furibunda*, because with *miser* Attis was referring to hir prior, and hence male, self. It seems that for Thomson, once Attis has been castrated and referred to with *some* feminine adjectives, zie must remain both grammatically and conceptually female.

Ellis's, Fordyce's, and Thomson's readings of the grammar in line 54 were each based at least in part on a conviction that movement between the binary poles of male/masculine and female/feminine, can only go one-way. At the opposite end of the spectrum, Skinner took *furibunda* as feminine, seeing the shift from the masculine *miser* as an indication of how Attis' self-castration destabilized the "conceptual category of the masculine."[48] In her interpretation, Catullus was inviting us to read Attis, who is referring to hirself in these lines, as confused in hir own mind about hir gender. Skinner's reading is based in a modern feminist ideology that sees gender as more fluid, constructable, shifting, allowing her to see the same beliefs at work in Catullus' text.

In my experience, when students analyze the scholarly reception of this line, they develop a sense of how gendered language is inextricably linked with gender ideology in the modern world. This then allows them to reflect back on Catullus' own play with gender from a more sophisticated perspective. It also gives them a sense of the fluidity of scholarship itself—how our readings of another language are contingent on our own historical setting and our mother-tongue.[49]

CONCLUSIONS

I believe that this exercise, combined with giving students verbal and iconographic alternatives to translating the gendered English pronouns "he" and "she," has encouraged my students to move beyond the limitations of our gendered language. At a practical level, I have found that these strategies

---

47. Fordyce (1961: 268); Thomson (1997: 382).
48. Skinner (1993: 114).
49. In connection with this idea it is useful to point out that some feminine forms in the poem are the result of emendations; see Skinner (1993: 127 n. 47).

help my students to understand the poem better. They enable Latin students to better grasp the subtleties of Catullus' usage, and they allow students reading the poet in translation better access to the original's "flavor." They allow the student asking "what *is* Attis here?" to consider conceptual as well as grammatical manifestations of gender, and to interrogate how they themselves construct gender through language. At an ethical level, I believe that these strategies have made my classroom a more inclusive space for intersex, transgender, and genderqueer students, in part by challenging and expanding the entire class's understanding of gender and sex in our own society.

BIBLIOGRAPHY

Adams, J. N. (1982) *The Latin Sexual Vocabulary.* London: Duckworth.

Adams, R. (2001) *Sideshow USA. Freaks and the American Cultural Imagination.* Chicago: University of Chicago Press.

Agger, I. (1994) *The Blue Room: Trauma and Testimony among Refugee Women. A Psycho-Social Exploration.* London: Zed Books.

Alexiou, M. (2002) *The Ritual Lament in Greek Tradition,* 2nd ed., rev. by D. Yatromanolakis and P. Roilos. Lanham, MD: Rowman and Littlefield.

U.S. Army (2014) "America's Army," http://www.americasarmy.com.

Amy-Chinn, D. (2006) "Making it Safe to Think Differently about Sex in the Academy." *Discourse: Learning and Teaching in Philosophical and Religious Studies* 6: 189–209.

Ancona, R. and Hallett, J. P. (2007) "Catullus in the Secondary School Curriculum." In M. B. Skinner (ed.) *A Companion to Catullus.* Malden, MA: Blackwell: 481–502.

Anderson, B. (2006) *Imagined Communities,* rev. ed. London: Verso.

Andreescu, L. (2008) "Academic Freedom and Religiously-Affiliated Universities." *Journal for the Study of Religions and Ideologies* 7.19: 162–83.

Ariès, P. (1975) *Western Attitudes toward Death: From the Middle Ages to the Present,* translated by P. Ranum. Baltimore: Johns Hopkins University Press.

——— (1994) *Centuries to Childhood: A Social History of Family.* New York: Vintage Books.

Arieti, J. A. (1997) "Rape and Livy's View of Roman History." In S. Deacy and K. F. Pierce (eds.) *Rape in Antiquity.* London: Duckworth: 209–29.

Ashcroft, R. E., Dawson, A., Draper, H., and McMillen, J. R. (eds.) (2007) *Principles of Health Care Ethics.* Chichester: Wiley-Blackwell.

Attwood, F. (2002) "Reading Porn: The Paradigm Shift in Pornography Research." *Sexualities* 5: 91–105.

AVA Project and Home Office (2010) "Teenage Relationship Abuse: A Teacher's Guide to Violence and Abuse in Teenage Relationships," http://www.homeoffice.gov.uk/publications/crime/teen-relationship-abuse/teen-abuse-teachers-guide.

Avalos, H., Melcher, S., and Schipper, J. (2007) *This Abled Body: Rethinking Disabilities in Biblical Studies.* Atlanta: Society of Biblical Literature.

Ayim, M. (1996) "Political Correctness: The Debate Continues." In A. Diller, B. Houston, K. P. Morgan, M. Ayim (eds.) *The Gender Question in Education: Theory, Pedagogy, and Politics.* Boulder, CO: Westview Press.

Bailey, D. S. (1955) *Homosexuality and the Western Christian Tradition.* London: Longmans, Green and Co.

Bakhtin, M. M. (1984) *Problems of Dostoevsky's Poetics,* edited and translated by C. Emerson. Manchester: Manchester University Press.

Bal, M. (1985) *Narratology: Introduction to the Theory of Narrative.* Toronto: University of Toronto Press.

Bales, K. and Trodd, Z. (eds.) (2008) *To Plead Our Own Cause: Personal Stories by Today's Slaves.* Ithaca, NY: Cornell University Press.

Balme, M. (trans.) (2001) *Menander. The Plays and Fragments.* Oxford: Oxford University Press.

Barrow, R. (2007) *An Introduction to Moral Philosophy and Moral Education.* London: Routledge.

Barter, C., McCarry, M., Berridge, D. and Evans, K. (2009) *Partner Exploitation and Violence in Teenage Intimate Relationships Executive Summary,* for NSPCC/University of Bristol.

Barton, D., and Crowder, M. K. (1975) "The Use of Role Playing Techniques as an Instructional Aid in Teaching about Dying, Death, and Bereavement." *Omega: Journal of Death and Dying* 6.3: 243–50.

Barton, D., Crowder, M. K., and Flexner, J. M. (1980) "Teaching about Death and Dying in a Multidisciplinary Student Group." *Omega: Journal of Death and Dying* 10.3: 265–70.

Baughan, E. P. (2009) "Lale Tepe: A Late Lydian Tumulus Near Sardis. 3. The Klinai." In N. D. Cahill (ed.) *Love for Lydia: A Sardis Anniversary Volume Presented to Crawford H. Greenewalt, Jr. Archaeological Exploration of Sardis; Report* 449–78. Cambridge, MA: Harvard University Press.

Bayer, R. (1981) *Homosexuality and American Psychiatry.* New York: Basic Books.

Bell, C. (1992) *Ritual Theory, Ritual Practice.* Oxford: Oxford University Press.

——— (1997) *Ritual, Perspectives, and Dimensions.* Oxford: Oxford University Press.

Ben-Moshe, L. and Colligan, S. (2010) "Regimes of Normalcy in the Academy: The Experiences of Disabled Faculty." In A. Nicolla, S. Best, and P. McLaren, (eds.) *Academic Repression: Reflections from the Academic Industrial Complex.* Edinburgh: AK Press.

Ben-Moshe, L., Cory, R., Feldbaum, M., and Sagendorf, K. (2005) *Building Pedagogical Curb Cuts: Incorporating Disability in the University Classroom and Curriculum.* Syracuse, NY: University of Syracuse Graduate School.

Benton, S. (2003) "Conflicts over Conflicts." *Pedagogy* 3: 245–49.

Berman, J. (2009) *Death in the Classroom: Writing about Love and Loss.* Albany: State University of New York Press.

Biers, W. (1992) *Art, Artefacts, and Chronology in Classical Archaeology.* London: Routledge.

Binford, L. R. (1971) "Mortuary Practices: Their Study and Their Potential." In J. A. Brown (ed.) *Approaches to the Social Dimensions of Mortuary Practices*. Memoirs of the Society for American Archaeology: 6–29.

Bisel S. C. and Angel, L. L. (1985) "Health and Nutrition in Mycenaean Greece." In N. Wilkie and W. Coulson (eds.) *Contributions to Aegean Archaeology*. Minneapolis: Kendall/Hunt Publishing Co: 197–210.

Blackmon, D. (2008) *Slavery by Another Name: The Re-Enslavement of Black Americans from the Civil War to World War II*. New York: Doubleday.

Blair, E. (2008) "In Ancient Dramas, Vital Words For Today's Warriors." *National Public Radio,* November 25, 2008, http://www.npr.org/templates/story/story.php?storyId=97413320.

Blanshard, A. (2010) *Sex, Vice, and Love from Antiquity to Modernity*. Chichester: Wiley Blackwell.

Blansher, S. R. (1981) "Criminal Law and Politics in Medieval Bologna." *Criminal Justice History: An International Journal* 2: 1–30.

Bloch, M. (1982) "Death, Women, and Power." In M. Bloch and J. Parry (eds.) *Death and the Regeneration of Life*. Cambridge: Cambridge University Press: 211–30.

Bloch, M. and Parry, J. (1982) "Introduction: Death and the Regeneration of Life." In M. Bloch and J. Parry (eds.) *Death and the Regeneration of Life*. Cambridge: Cambridge University Press: 1–44.

Bloom, A. (1987) *The Closing of the American Mind*. New York: Simon and Schuster.

——— (2003) *Normal: Transsexual CEOs, Crossdressing Cops and Hermaphrodites with Attitude*. New York: Bloomsbury Publishing.

Boardman, J. (1974) *Athenian Black Figure Vases*. London: Thames and Hudson.

——— (1978) *Eros in Greece*. London: John Murray.

——— (1985) *Greek Sculpture: The Archaic Period*. London: Thames and Hudson.

——— (1988) *Athenian Red Figure Vases: The Archaic Period*. London: Thames and Hudson.

——— (1989) *Athenian Red Figure Vases: The Classical Period*. London: Thames and Hudson.

——— (1998) *Early Greek Vase Painting*. London: Thames and Hudson.

Bohm, R. M. (1989) "The Effects of Classroom Instruction and Discussion on Death Penalty Opinions: A Teaching Note." *Journal of Criminal Justice* 17.2: 123–31.

Bold, M. (2006) "Use of Wikis in Graduate Course Work." *Journal of Interactive Learning Research* 17.1: 5–14.

Bradley, R. (1982) "The Destruction of Wealth in Later Prehistory." *Man* 17: 108–22.

——— (1984) *The Social Foundations of Prehistoric Britain*. London: Longman.

Brandon, D. and Hollingshead, A. B. (1999) "Collaborative Learning and Computer Supported Groups." *Communication Education* 48.2: 109–26.

Breck, J. (1998) *The Sacred Gift of Life: Orthodox Christianity and Bioethics*. Crestwood, NY: St. Vladimir's Seminary Press.

Brickley, M. (2000) *Defy Aging*. Columbus, OH: New Resources Press.

Bridges, G. (1986) "The Problem of Pederastic Love in Thomas Mann's *Death in Venice* and Plato's *Phaedrus*." *Selecta* 7: 39–46.

Brooks M. M. and Rumsey, C. (2007) "The Body in the Museum." In V. Cassman, N. Odegaard and J. Powell (eds.) *Human Remains: Guide for Museums and Academic Institutions.* Lanham, MD: AltaMira Press: 161–289.

Brooten, B. (1996) *Love between Women: Early Christian Responses to Female Homoeroticism.* Chicago: University of Chicago Press.

Brown J. A. (ed.) (1971) *Approaches to the Social Dimensions of Mortuary Practices.* Memoirs of the Society for American Archaeology.

Brown, L. (2010) "Wikis as an Alternative to Classroom Based Groupwork." *CEBE Transactions* 7.2: 26–36.

Brown, S. (1993) "Feminist Research in Archaeology: What Does It Mean? Why Is It Taking so Long?" In N. S. Rabinowitz and A. Richlin (eds.) *Feminist Theory and the Classics.* New York: Routledge: 238–71.

Bryson, N. (1986) "Two Narratives of Rape in the Visual Arts: Lucretia and the Sabine Women." In S. Tomaselli and R. Porter (eds.) *Rape.* Oxford: Oxford University Press: 152–73.

Burman, M. and Cartmen, F. (2005) "Young People's Attitudes towards Gendered Violence." NHS Scotland.

Cain, W. (ed.) (1994) *Teaching the Conflicts: Gerald Graff, Curricular Reform and the Culture Wars.* New York: Garland.

Calame, C. (2001) *Choruses of Young Women in Ancient Greece: Their Morphology, Religious Role, and Social Functions,* trans. D. Collins and J. Orion. Lanham, MD: Rowman and Littlefield.

Calhoon, C. G. (1997) "Lucretia, Savior and Scapegoat: The Dynamics of Sacrifice in Livy 1.57–59." *Helios* 24: 151–69.

Cannadine, D. (1981) "War and Death, Grief and Mourning in Modern Britain." In J. Whaley (ed.) *Mirrors of Mortality.* Europa Press: 187–242.

Cannon, A. (1989) "The Historical Dimension in Mortuary Expressions of Status and Sentiment." *Current Anthropology* 30: 437–58.

Cantarella, E. (2008) "Textual Evidence." In A. Lear and E. Cantarella (eds.) *Images of Ancient Greek Pederasty: Boys Were Their Gods,* London: Routledge.

Carpenter, T. H. (1991) *Art and Myth in Ancient Greece.* London: Thames and Hudson.

Cartledge, P. (1987) *Agesilaos and the Crisis of Sparta.* London: Duckworth and Co.

Cartledge, P. (1998) "Classics: From Discipline in Crisis to (Multi)-Cultural Capital." In Y. L. Too and N. Livingstone (eds.) *Pedagogy and Power: Rhetorics of Classical Learning.* Cambridge: Cambridge University Press: 16–28.

Cassio, A. C. (1983) "Post-Classical *Lesbiai.*" *CQ* 33: 296–97.

Chamberlain, A. (2006) *Demography in Archaeology.* Cambridge: Cambridge University Press.

Chapman, G. A. (1985) *Women in Early Greek Comedy: Fact, Fantasy and Feminism.* Durban, Pietermaritzburg: University of Natal Press.

Chapman, R. W. and Randsborg, K. (1981) "Approaches to the Archaeology of Death." In R. Chapman, I. Kinnes, and K. Randsborg (eds.) *The Archaeology of Death.* Cambridge: Cambridge University Press: 1–24.

Charlier, P. (2008) "The Value of Paleoteratology and Forensic Pathology for the Comprehension of Atypical Burials: Two Mediterranean Examples from the Field." In E. M. Murphy (ed.) *Deviant Burial in the Archaeological Record.* Oxford: Oxbow Books: 57–70.

Charmatz, K., Howarth, G., and Kellehear, A. (eds.) (1997) *The Unknown Country: Death in Australia, Britain, and the USA.* Basingstoke: Palgrave Macmillan.

Chew, K. (1997) "What Does *E Pluribus Unum* Mean?: Reading the Classics and Multicultural Literature Together." *CJ* 93: 55–81.

Childe, V. G. (1945) "Directional Changes in Funerary Practices during 50,000 Years." *Man* 45: 13–19.

Clark, P. (1998) "Women, Slaves, and the Hierarchies of Domestic Violence.: The Family of Saint Augustine." In S. Murnaghan and S. R. Joshel (eds.) *Women and Slaves in Greco-Roman Culture.* London: Routledge: 109–29.

Claassen, J.-M. (1998) "The Familiar Other: The Pivotal Role of Women in Livy's Narrative of Political Development in Early Rome." *AClass* 41: 71–103.

Clegg, S. and David, M. E. (2008) "Power, Pedagogy and Personalisation in Global Higher Education: The Erasure of Feminism?" *Discourse: Studies in the Cultural Politics of Education* 29: 483–98.

Cohen, A. (1985) *The Symbolic Construction of Community.* London: Routledge.

Cohen, D. (1991) *Laws, Sexuality, and Society: The Enforcement of Morals in Classical Athens.* Cambridge: Cambridge University Press.

Cook, W. W. and Tatum, J. (2010) *African American Writers and Classical Tradition.* Chicago: University of Chicago Press.

Corbeill, A. (2008) "Genus quid est? Roman Scholars on Grammatical Gender and Biological Sex." *TAPA* 138.1: 75–105.

——— (2010) "The Republican Body." In N. Rosenstein, and R. Morstein-Marx (eds.) *A Companion to the Roman Republic.* Oxford: Blackwell Publishing: 439–56.

Creighton, S., Alderson, J., Brown S., and Minto, C. L. (2002) "Medical Photography: Ethics, Consent and the Intersex Patient." *British Journal of Urology International* 89: 67–72.

Culham, P., and Edmunds, L. (eds.) (1989) *Classics: A Discipline and Profession in Crisis?* Lanham, MD: University Press of America.

Cullen, L. T. (2007) *Remember Me: A Lively Tour of the New American Way of Death.* New York: Harper Collins.

Cullinan, A. L. (1990) "Teachers' Death Anxiety, Ability to Cope with Death, and Perceived Ability to Aid Bereaved Students." *Death Studies* 14.2: 147–60.

Curl, J. S. (1972) *The Victorian Celebration of Death.* Detroit: Partridge Press.

Curran, L. (1984) "Rape and Rape Victims in the *Metamorphoses*." In J. Peradotto and J. P. Sullivan (eds.) *Women in the Ancient World: The Arethusa Papers,* SUNY, 263–86.

Curren, R. R. (2000) *Aristotle on the Necessity of Public Education.* Lanham, MD: Rowman and Littlefield.

Curry, R. (1996) "Media Scholars Teaching Pornography: Stepping Across Broadway." *Jump Cut* 40: 114–18.

Dahl, R. (1979) *My Uncle Oswald.* London: Michael Joseph.

Dasen, V. (1993) *Dwarfs in Ancient Egypt and Greece.* Oxford: Oxford University Press.

Davidson, J. (2007) *The Greeks and Greek Love: A Radical Reappraisal of Homosexuality in Ancient Greece.* London: Weidenfeld and Nicolson.

Davies, D. (2002) *Death, Ritual and Belief: The Rhetoric of Funerary Rites,* 2nd ed. London: Continuum.

Davis, L. (2005) "Why Disability Studies Matters." *Inside Higher Education* 1.

de Bono, E. (1976) *Teaching Thinking.* London: Temple Smith.

de Jong, I. J. F. (1987) *Narrators and Focalizers: The Presentation of the Story in the* Iliad. London: Bristol Classical Press.

de Marre, M. (2001) "Aristophanes on Bawds in the Boardroom: Comedy as a Guideline to Gender Relations in Antiquity." *Social Identities* 7: 37–65.

de Waal, F., and Lanting, F. (1997) *Bonobo: The Forgotten Ape.* Berkeley and Los Angeles: University of California Press.

Deacy, S. (1997) "The Vulnerability of Athena: Parthenoi and Rape in Greek Myth." In S. Deacy and K. Pierce (eds.) *Rape in Antiquity.* Swansea: Duckworth/Classical Press of Wales.

——— (2013) "'A Flowery Tale': Young Women and Heroic Rape." *Arethusa* 46.3: 395–413.

Deacy, S. and McHardy, F. (forthcoming) *Gender and Violence in Ancient Greece.* London: Bloomsbury.

Deacy, S., and Pierce, L. (eds.) (1997) *Rape in Antiquity.* Swansea: Duckworth and Classical Press of Wales.

Dean-Jones, L. (1994) *Women's Bodies in Classical Greek Science.* Oxford: Clarendon Press.

Deleuze, G. (1992) [1983] *Cinema 1: The Movement-Image,* trans. H. Tomlinson and B. Habberjam. London: Continuum.

Demand, N. (1994) *Birth, Death, and Motherhood in Classical Greece.* Baltimore: Johns Hopkins University Press.

Dempsey, D. K. (1975) *The Way We Die: An Investigation of Death and Dying in America Today.* New York: McGraw-Hill.

Denvir, D. (2010) "$12 Million Army Video Game Recruitment Center to Close." *The Huffington Post,* June 20, 2010, http://www.huffingtonpost.com/.../12-million-army-videogam_b_618783.html.

DeSpelder, L. A. and Strickland, A. L. (2008) *The Last Dance: Encountering Death and Dying,* 8th ed. New York: McGraw Hill.

Doblhofer, G. (1994) *Vergewaltigung in der Antike.* Stuttgart: B. G. Teubner.

Donaldson, I. (1982) *The Rapes of Lucretia: A Myth and Its Transformations.* Oxford: Oxford University Press.

Dossey, L. (2008) "Wife-beating and Manliness in Late Antiquity." *Past and Present* 199: 3–40.

Douglas, L. C. (1929) *Magnificent Obsession.* New York: Houghton Mifflin.

——— (1942) *The Robe.* New York: Houghton Mifflin.

Douglas, M. (1966) *Purity and Danger: An Analysis of the Concepts of Pollution and Taboo.* London: Routledge.

Dove, R. (1989) *Grace Notes.* New York: W. W. Norton and Co.

Dover, K. (1989) *Greek Homosexuality.* Cambridge, MA: Harvard University Press.

Dreger, A. D. (1998) "'Ambiguous Sex'—or Ambivalent Medicine?" *The Hastings Center Report* 28.3: 24–35.

Driver, S. (2004) "Pornographic Pedagogies? The Risks of Teaching 'Dirrty' Popular Cultures." *M/C Journal* 7, http://journal.media-culture.org.au/0410/03_teaching.php.

D'Souza, D. (1991) *Illiberal Education: The Politics of Race and Sex on Campus.* New York: Free Press.

Du Preez, M. (2003) *Pale Native: Memories of a Renegade Reporter.* Cape Town: Zebra Press.

duBois, P. (1991) *Torture and Truth.* London and New York: Routledge.

——— (2001) *Trojan Horses: Saving the Classics from Conservatives.* New York: New York University Press.

——— (2003) *Slaves and Other Objects.* Chicago: University of Chicago Press.

——— (2010)a *Out of Athens: The New Ancient Greeks.* Cambridge, MA: Harvard University Press.

——— (2010)b *Slavery: Antiquity and Its Legacy.* London and New York: I. B. Tauris and Oxford University Press.

Ducate, L., Anderson, L. L., and Moreno, N. (2011) "Wading Through the World of Wikis: An Analysis of Three Wiki Projects." *Foreign Language Annals* 44.3: 495–524.

Duckworth, G. E. (1952) *The Nature of Roman Comedy: A Study in Popular Entertainment.* Princeton: Princeton University Press.

Dunbabin, K. M. D. (1986) "Sic erimus cunti. . . . . The Skeleton in Graeco-Roman Art." *Jahrbuch des Deutschen Archäologischen Instituts* 101: 185–255.

——— (1994) "Review of Dasen, *Dwarfs in Ancient Egypt and Greece.*" *Bryn Mawr Classical Review,* http://bmcr.brynmawr.edu/1994/94.09.07.html.

Durkheim, E. (1995) *The Elementary Forms of Religious Life,* translated by K. Fields. New York: Free Press.

Dynes, W. R., Johansson, W., Percy, W. A. and Donaldson, S. (1990) *The Encyclopedia of Homosexuality.* New York: Garland.

Eaton, M. A. (2001) "The Cultural Capital of Imaginary versus Pedagogical Canons." *Pedagogy* 1: 305–15.

Edelstein, L. (1943) *The Hippocratic Oath: Text, Translation, and Interpretation.* Baltimore: John Hopkins University Press.

Edwards, T. (2006) *Cultures of Masculinity.* London and New York: Routledge.

Ekins, R. and King, D. (2006) *The Transgender Phenomenon.* London: Sage Publications.

Ellis, H. (1925) "Sexual Inversion in Men," and "Sexual Inversion in Women." In *Studies in the Psychology of Sex* vol. 2; 3rd rev. ed. Philadelphia: F. A. Davis Company: 75–263.

Ellis, R. (1889) *A Commentary on Catullus,* 2nd ed. Oxford: Clarendon Press.

Endres, N. (2009) "Worlds of Difference? Gay and Lesbian Texts across Cultures." In D. Damrosch (ed.) *Teaching World Literature.* New York: MLA: 317–30.

Engstrom, M. E. and Jewett, D. (2005) "Collaborative Learning the Wiki Way." *TechTrends* 49.6: 12–68.

Faculty Handbook 18th ed. (June 2011) Western Kentucky University, http://www.wku.edu/academicaffairs/documents/wku_faculty_handbook_18thed.pdf.

Farr, M. (2012) "Confronting Asperger's in the Classroom." *University Affairs* 53.2: 18–22.

Farrell, J. J. (1980) *Inventing the American Way of Death, 1830–1920.* Philadelphia: Temple University Press.

Fausto-Sterling, A. (1993) "The Five Sexes: Why Male and Female are not Enough." *The Sciences* 33.2: 20–25.

——— (2000) "The Five Sexes, Revisited." *The Sciences* 40.4: 18–23.

Fedak, J. (1990) *Monumental Tombs of the Hellenistic Age.* Toronto: University of Toronto Press.

Feierman, J. R. (1990) "Introduction." In J. R. Feierman (ed.) *Pedophilia: Biosocial Dimensions.* New York: Springer-Verlag.

Feldherr, A. (1998) *Spectacle and Society in Livy's History.* Berkeley: University of California Press.

Fisher, B., Cullen, F., and Turner, M. (2000) "The Sexual Victimization of College Women." USDOJ: 182369, https://www.ncjrs.gov/pdffiles1/nij/182369.pdf.

Fitzgerald, W. (2000) *Slavery and the Roman Literary Imagination.* Cambridge: Cambridge University Press.

Flatley, J., Kershaw, C., Smith, K., Chaplin, R. and Moon, D. (2010) "Crime in England and Wales 2009/10: Findings from the British Crime Survey and Police Recorded Crime," http://webarchive.nationalarchives.gov.uk/20110218135832/rds.homeoffice.gov.uk/rds/pdfs10/hosb1210.pdf.

Flemming, R. (2000) *Medicine and the Making of Roman Women: Gender, Nature, and Authority from Celsus to Galen.* Oxford: Clarendon Press.

Foley, H. P. (1982) "The 'Female Intruder' Reconsidered: Women in Aristophanes' *Lysistrata* and *Ecclesiazusae.*" *Classical Philology* 77: 1–21.

Fone, B. (2000) *Homophobia: A History,* New York: Metropolitan Books.

Fordyce, C. J. (1961) *Catullus: A Commentary.* Oxford University Press.

Forster, E. M. (1921) *Howards End.* New York: A. A. Knopf.

Foubert, J. (2011) *Ending Rape through Peer Education: The Men's and Women's Programs.* New York, London: Routledge.

Foucault, M. (1990) *The History of Sexuality: The Use of Pleasure,* vol. 2, translated by R. Hurley. New York: Vintage.

Frederiksen, R. (1999) "From Death to Life: The Cemetery of Fusco and the Reconstruction of Early Colonial Society." In G. Tsetskhladze (ed.) *Ancient Greeks West and East.* Leiden: Brill: 229–52.

Freire, P. (1970) *Pedagogy of the Oppressed,* translated by M. B. Ramos. New York: Seabury.

Gaffney, D. A. (1988) "Death in the Classroom: A Lesson in Life." *Holistic Nursing Practice* 2.2: 20–27.

Gagarin M. and MacDowell D. M. (trans.) (1998) *Antiphon and Andocides.* Austin: University of Texas Press.

Garland, R. (2001) *The Greek Way of Death,* 2nd ed. Ithaca: Cornell University Press.

——— (2007) *Religion and the Greeks.* London: Bristol Classical Press.

——— (2010) *The Eye of the Beholder. Deformity and Disability in the Graeco-Roman World,* 2nd ed. London: Bristol Classical Press.

Garland, R. J., and Dougher, M. J. (1990) "The Abused/Abuser Hypothesis of Child Sexual Abuse." In *Pedophilia: Biosocial Dimensions.* New York: Springer-Verlag.

Garland-Thomson, R. (2002) "The Politics of Staring: Visual Rhetoric of Disability in Popular Photography." In L. Snyder, B. Brueggemann, and R. Garland-Thomson (eds.) *Disability Studies: Enabling the Humanities.* New York: MLA Press: 55–75.

Garrison, D. H. (2007) "Catullus in the College Classroom." In M. B. Skinner (ed.) *A Companion to Catullus*. Malden, MA: Blackwell: 503–19.

Geertz, C. (1974) *The Interpretation of Cultures*. New York: Basic Books.

Gennette, G. (1980) *Narrative Discourse: An Essay in Method*. Ithaca, NY: Cornell University Press.

Gibson, J. (2010) "Sexless in the City: A Gender Revolution." *Sydney Morning Herald*, March 10th, 2010, accessed April 28th, 2012, http://www.smh.com.au/nsw/sexless-in-the-city-a-gender-revolution-20100311-q1i2.html.

Gibson, L. R. and Zaidman, L. M. (1991) "Death in Children's Literature: Taboo or Not Taboo?" *Children's Literature Association Quarterly* 16.4: 232–34.

Gibson, R. (1996) "*Vade mecum* in Wantonness: The *Ars Amatoria* and its Translators." *Joint Association of Classical Teachers Review* 19: 3–5.

Gide, A. (2000) *The Immoralist*, translated by David Watson. Harmondsworth: Penguin.

Gil, V., and Anderson, A. F. (1999) "Case Study of Rape in Contemporary China: A Cultural-Historical Analysis of Gender and Power Differentials." *Journal of Interpersonal Violence* 14: 1151–71.

Gilbert, S. M. (2006) *Death's Door: Modern Dying and the Way We Grieve*. New York: W. W. Norton and Co.

Giroux, H. (1992) "Dreaming about Democracy." In D. J. Gless and B. H. Smith (eds.) *The Politics of Liberal Education*. Durham and London: Duke University Press: 119–44.

Godwin, J. (ed.) (1995) *Catullus: Poems 61–68*. Warminster: Aris and Phillips.

Godwin-Jones, B. (2003) "Blogs and Wikis: Environments for On-line Collaboration." *Language, Learning and Technology* 7.2: 12–16.

Goff, B. (2005) *Classics and Colonialism*. London: Duckworth.

Goff, B. and Simpson, M. (2007) *Crossroads in the Black Aegean: Oedipus, Antigone, and Dramas of the African Diaspora*. Oxford: Oxford University Press.

Gold, B. K. (1994) "Humor in Juvenal's Sixth Satire: Is it Funny?" In S. Jäkel and A. Timonen (eds.) *Laughter Down the Centuries*, vol. I. Turku, Finland: Turun Yliopisto: 95–111.

——— (1998) "'Vested Interests' in Plautus' *Casina*: Cross-Dressing in Roman Comedy." *Helios* 25: 17–29.

Goldberg, S. M. (2005) *Constructing Literature in the Roman Republic: Poetry and Its Reception*. Cambridge: Cambridge University Press.

Goody, J. R. (1962) *Death, Property, and the Ancestors*. Stanford, CA: Stanford University Press.

Gorer, G. (1965) *Death, Grief and Mourning in Contemporary Britain*. London: Cresset Press.

——— (1970) *Poetic Statement and Critical Dogma*. Evanston: Northwestern University Press.

Graff, G. (1992) *Beyond the Culture Wars: How Teaching the Conflicts Can Revitalize American Education*. New York: Norton.

Grainger, H. (2005) *Death Redesigned: British Crematoria: History, Architecture and Landscape*. Reading: Spire Books.

Grant, M. (1975) *Erotic Art in Pompeii*. London: Octopus.

Green, J. W. (2008) *Beyond the Good Death. The Anthropology of Modern Dying*. Philadelphia: University of Pennsylvania Press.

Green, P. (1967, 1974) *Juvenal: The Sixteen Satires.* New York: Penguin.

——— (2005) *The Poems of Catullus: A Bilingual Edition.* Berkeley: University of California Press.

Greenberg, D. F. (1988) *The Construction of Homosexuality.* Chicago: University of Chicago Press.

Greene, E. (1999) "Travesties of Love: Violence and Voyeurism in Ovid *Amores* I.7." *CW* 92: 409–18.

Greenwood, E. (2009) "Re-rooting the Classical Tradition: New Directions in Black Classicism." *Classical Receptions Journal* 1: 87–103.

——— (2010) *Afro-Greeks: Dialogue between Anglophone Caribbean Literature and Classics in the Twentieth Century.* Oxford: Oxford University Press.

Groce, N. E. (1988) *Everyone Here Spoke Sign Language: Hereditary Deafness in Martha's Vineyard.* Cambridge, MA: Harvard University Press.

Gubar, S. and Kamholtz, J. (1993) "Introduction." In S. Gubar and J. Kamholtz (eds.) *English Inside and Out: The Places of Literary Criticism.* New York: Routledge: 1–8.

Habenstein, R. W. and Lamers, W. M. (1990) *The History of American Funeral Directing.* Detroit, MI: Omnigraphics, Inc.

Hagopian, P. (2000) "Voices from Vietnam: Veterans' Oral Histories in the Classroom." *The Journal of American History* 87.2: 593–601.

Haley, S. P. (1989) "Classics and Minorities." In P. Culham and L. Edmunds (eds.) *Classics: A Discipline and Profession in Crisis?* Lanham, MD: University Press of America: 333–38.

——— (1993) "Black Feminist Thought and Classics: Re-membering, Re-claiming, Re-empowering." In N. S. Rabinowitz and A. Richlin (eds.) *Feminist Theory and the Classics.* New York: Routledge: 23–43.

Hall, C. (2005) "Emotional Intelligence and Experiential Learning." In P. Jarvis and S. Parker (eds). *Human Learning: An Holistic Approach.* London: Routledge: 139–56.

Hallett, J. (1993) "Feminist Theory, Historical Periods, Literary Canons, and the Study of Graeco-Roman Antiquity." In N. S. Rabinowitz and A. Richlin (eds.) *Feminist Theory and the Classics.* New York: Routledge, 44–72.

Halperin, D. M. (1986) "Plato and Erotic Reciprocity." *ClAnt.* 5: 60–80.

——— (2002) *How to Do the History of Homosexuality,* Chicago: University of Chicago Press.

Hamilton, C. (1991) *Agesilaus and the Failure of the Spartan Hegemony.* Ithaca, NY: Cornell University Press.

Han, S. Y. and Hill, J. R. (2007) "Collaborate to Learn, Learn to Collaborate: Examining the Roles of Context, Community, and Cognition in Asynchronous Discussion." *Journal of Educational Computing Research* 36.1: 89–123.

Hanson, A. E. (1992) "Conception, Gestation, and the Origin of Female Nature in the Corpus Hippocraticum." *Helios* 19: 31–71.

——— (1994) "A Division of Labor: Roles for Men in Greek and Roman Births." *Thamyris* 1: 157–202.

Hardwick, L. and Gillespie, C. (eds.) (2007) *Classics in Post-Colonial Worlds.* Oxford: Oxford University Press.

Hardwick, L. and Stray, C. (2008) "Introduction." In L. Hardwick and C. Stray (eds.) *A Companion to Classical Receptions.* Oxford: Blackwell, 1–10.

Harlow, M. and Laurence, R. (2002) *Growing Up and Growing Old in Ancient Rome: A Life Course Approach*. London: Routledge.

——— (2007) *Age and Ageing in the Roman Empire*. Portsmouth: JRA Supplement.

Harris, E. M. (1990) "Did the Athenians Regard Seduction as a Worse Crime than Rape?" *CQ* 40: 370–77. Repr. with addendum, in Harris, E. M. (2006) *Democracy and the Rule of Law in Classical Athens*. Cambridge: Cambridge University Press: 283–94.

——— (1997) "Review Article: Review of Deacy and Pierce." *EMC/CV* 40(16): 483–96.

——— (2004) "Did Rape Exist in Classical Athens? Further Reflections on the Laws about Sexual Violence." *Dike* 7: 41–83. Repr. as Harris 2006.

——— (2006) "Did Rape Exist in Classical Athens? Further Reflections on the Laws about Sexual Violence." In E. M. Harris, *Democracy and the Rule of Law in Classical Athens*. Cambridge: Cambridge University Press: 297–332.

Harris, M. (2008) *Grave Matters: A Journey through the Modern Funeral Industry to a Natural Way of Burial*. New York: Scribner.

Harris, W. V. (1982) "The Theoretical Possibility of Extensive Infanticide in the Graeco-Roman World." *CQ* 32: 114–16.

——— (1994) "Child-Exposure in the Roman Empire." *JRS* 84: 1–22.

Harrison, S. (2004) "Altering Attis: Ethnicity, Gender and Genre in Catullus 63." *Mnemosyne* 57.5: 520–33.

Hartman, S. (2008) *Lose Your Mother: A Journey along the Atlantic Slave Route*. New York: Farrar, Straus and Giroux.

Heise, L., Moore, K., and Toubia, N. (1995) *Sexual Coercion and Reproductive Health: A Focus on Research*. New York: Population Council.

Hemker, J. (1985) "Rape and the Founding of Rome." *Helios* 12.1: 9–20.

Henagen, C. D. (1998) "False Claims of Sexual Harassment in Education: The Path to an Appropriate Remedy for the Wrongly Accused." *Washington University Law Quarterly* 76.4: 1431–54.

Henderson, J. (1975) *The Maculate Muse: Obscene Language in Attic Comedy*. New Haven: Yale University Press.

——— (1976) "The Cologne Epode and the Conventions of Early Greek Erotic Poetry." *Arethusa* 9: 159–79.

Hentoff, N. (1992) *Free Speech for Me—But Not for Thee: How the American Left and Right Relentlessly Censor Each Other*. New York: Harper Collins.

Hertz, R. (1960) *Death and the Right Hand*, translated by R. and C. Needham. Glencoe, IL: Free Press.

Higgins, C. (2011) "Classics at Risk at Royal Holloway, University of London." In *The Guardian UK*, http://www.theguardian.com/culture/charlottehigginsblog/2011/sep/15/educationdegreecourses-classics.

Higgins, L. A. and Silver, B. R. (eds.) (1991) *Rape and Representation*. New York: Columbia University Press.

Himmelmann, N. (1998) *Reading Greek Art*. Princeton: Princeton University Press.

HM Government (2010) "Call to End Violence against Women and Girls," http://www.homeoffice.gov.uk/publications/crime/call-end-violence-women-girls/vawg-paper.

———— (2011) "Call to End Violence against Women and Girls Action Plan," http://www.homeoffice.gov.uk/publications/crime/call-end-violence-women-girls/vawg-action-plan.

Hodder, I. (1979) "Economic and Social Stress and Material Culture." *American Antiquity* 44: 446–54.

Hoffman, M. (1994) "Death in the Classroom." *The Alan Review* 21.2: retrieved from http://scholar.lib.vt.edu/ejournals/ALAN/winter94/ on November 13, 2011.

Holwarth, G. (2007) *Death and Dying: A Sociological Introduction*. Malden, MA: Polity Press.

Hoover, P. (2000) "Contextual Learning and Latin Language Textbooks Author(s)." *The Classical World* 94: 56–60.

Houby-Nielsen, S. H. (1995) "'Burial Language' in Archaic and Classical Kerameikos." *Proceedings of the Danish Institute at Athens* 1: 128–91.

Howard, L. G. (2007) *The Sexual Harassment Handbook*. Franklin Lakes, NJ: Career Press.

Hubbard, T. (ed.) (2003) *Homosexuality in Greece and Rome: A Sourcebook of Basic Documents*. Berkeley: University of California Press.

Hughes, D. (1991) *Human Sacrifice in Ancient Greece*. London: Routledge.

Huntington, R. and Metcalf, P. (1991) *Celebrations of Death: The Anthropology of Mortuary Ritual*, 2nd ed. Cambridge: Cambridge University Press.

Hürmüzlü, B. (2004) "Burial Grounds at Klazomenai: Geometric through Hellenistic Periods." In A. Moustaka et al. (eds.) *Klazomenai, Teos and Abdera: Metropoleis and Colony*. Thessaloniki: University Studio Press: 77–95.

Iles Johnston, S. (1999) *Restless Dead: Encounters between the Living and the Dead in Ancient Greece*. University of California Press.

Incorporated Association of Assistant Masters in Secondary Schools (1961) *The Teaching of Classics*, 2nd ed. Cambridge: Cambridge University Press.

Intersex Society of North America (1993–2008) "How Common is Intersex?" http://www.isna.org/faq/frequency.

Jackson, K. T. (1989) *Silent Cities: The Evolution of the American Cemetery*. New York: Princeton Architectural Press.

James, S. L. (1997) "Slave-Rape and Female Silence in Ovid's Love Poetry." *Helios* 24.1: 60–76.

———— (1998) "From Boys to Men: Rape and Developing Masculinity in Terence's *Hecyra* and *Eunuchus*." *Helios* 25: 31–47.

———— (2008) "Feminist Pedagogy and Teaching Latin Literature." *Cloelia* 38.1: 11–14.

———— (2012) "Teaching Rape in Roman Love Elegy, Part II." In B. Gold (ed.) *A Companion to Roman Love Elegy*. Malden, MA: Wiley-Blackwell: 549–57.

Jansen, J. (2011) *We Need to Talk*. Northcliff: Bookstorm and Pan Macmillan.

Janus S. S. and Janus, C. L. (1993) *The Janus Report on Sexual Behavior: The First Broad-Scale Scientific National Survey since Kinsey*. New York: Wiley.

Jarvis, P. (ed.) (2004) *The Theory and Practice of Teaching*. London: Routledge Falmer.

———— (2005) "Human Learning: The Interrelationship of the Individual and the Social Structure," in P. Jarvis and S. Parker (eds.) *Human Learning: An Holistic Approach*. London: Routledge: 116–28.

Jaschik, S. (2010) "Disappearing Languages at Albany," October 4, 2010, http://www.insidehighered.com/news/2010/10/04/albany.

Jenkins, H. (2004) "Foreword: So You Want to Teach Pornography?" In P. Church Anderson, (ed.) *More Dirty Looks: Gender, Pornography and Power.* London: BFI Publishing: 1–8.

Jenkins, I. (2006) *Greek Architecture and Its Sculpture.* Cambridge, MA: Harvard University Press.

Jeppesen-Wigelsworth, A. (2011) "Pedagogical Issues in Classics: Editor's Introduction: Teaching Rape." *Cloelia* 1: 25–26.

Johns, C. (1989) *Sex or Symbol: Erotic Images of Greece and Rome.* London: British Museum Press.

Johnson, J. A. (1995) "Life after Death: Critical Pedagogy in an Urban Classroom." *Harvard Educational Review* 65.2: 213–30.

Johnson, J. E. (2009) *Gender Violence in Russia: The Politics of Feminist Intervention.* Bloomington, IN: Indiana University Press.

Johnson, W. R. (1991) "Preface" in *Sappho's Lyre,* translated by Diane Rayor. Berkeley and Los Angeles: University of California Press.

——— (1996) "The Rapes of Callisto." *CJ* 92.1: 9–24.

Johnston, S. I. (1999) *The Restless Dead.* Berkeley: University of California Press.

Joint United Nations Programme on HIV AIDS (UNAIDS) (2009) "Country Situation: South Africa," http://www.unaids.org/ctrysa/AFRZAF_en.pdf.

Jones, M. and Carlin, C. G. (2004) "Call this English Lit?" *The Guardian* 4 February, 2004, http://arts.guardian.co.uk/features/story/0,11710,1140881,00.html.

Jones, W. H. S. (1957) *Hippocrates.* Cambridge, MA and London: Harvard University Press and William Heinemann Ltd.

Jonker, G. (2009) "The Many Facets of Islam: Death, Dying and Disposal between Orthodox Rule and Historical Convention." In C. M. Parkes, P. Laungani, and B. Young (eds.) *Death and Bereavement Across Cultures.* Cambridge, MA: Harvard University Press: 147–65.

Joplin, P. K. (1990) "Ritual Work on Human Flesh: Livy's Lucretia and the Rape of the Body Politic." *Helios* 17: 51–70.

Jordan, T. G. (1984) *Texas Graveyards: A Cultural Legacy.* Austin: University of Texas Press.

Joshel, S. J. (1992) "The Body Female and the Body Politic: Livy's Lucretia and Verginia." In A. Richlin (ed.) *Pornography and Representation in Ancient Greece and Rome.* Oxford: Oxford University Press: 112–30.

Joshel, S., Malamud, M., and McGuire, D. T. (eds.) (2005) *Imperial Projections: Ancient Rome in Modern Popular Culture.* Baltimore: Johns Hopkins University Press.

Kahn, M. (2004) "'Why Are We Reading a Handbook on Rape?' Young Women Transform a Classic." *Pedagogy* 4.3: 438–59.

——— (2005) *Why Are We Reading Ovid's Handbook on Rape? Teaching and Learning at a Women's College,* Boulder: Paradigm.

Kailey, M. (2005) *Just Add Hormones: An Insider's Guide to the Transsexual Experience.* Boston: Beacon Press.

Kajanto, A. (1965) *The Latin Cognomina.* Helsinki: Finska vetenskaps societeten.

Kalu, W. J. (2004) "Violence against Women in Africa: Impact of Culture on Womanhood." In L. L. Adler and F. Denmark (eds.) *International Perspectives on Violence.* Westport, CT: Praeger: 185–207.

Kampen, N. (1996) *Sexuality in Ancient Art.* Cambridge: Cambridge University Press.

Kapparis, K. (2002) *Abortion in the Ancient World.* London: Duckworth.

Kaufman, S. R. (2005) *. . . and a time to die: How American Hospitals Shape the End of Life.* Chicago: University of Chicago Press.

Kearl, M. C. (1989) *Endings: A Sociology of Death and Dying.* Oxford: Oxford University Press.

Keith, C. R. and Ellis, D. (1978) "Reactions of Pupils and Teachers to Death in the Classroom." *School Counselor* 25.4: 228–34.

Kellehear, A. (2007) *A Social History of Dying.* Cambridge University Press.

Kelly, L. and Radford, J. (1998) "Sexual Violence against Women and Girls: An Approach to an International Overview." In R. E. Dobash and R. P. Dobash (eds.) *Rethinking Violence against Women.* London: Sage, 53–76.

Kennedy, R. (2007) "In-Class Debates: Fertile Ground for Active Learning and the Cultivation of Critical Thinking and Oral Communication Skills." *International Journal of Teaching and Learning in Higher Education* 19: 183–90.

Kilmer, M. (1982) "Genital Phobia and Depilation." *JHS* 102: 104–12.

——— (1993) *Greek Erotica on Red-Figure Vases.* London: Duckworth.

King, H. (1998) *Hippocrates' Woman: Reading the Female Body in Ancient Greece.* London: Routledge.

Kirkham, P. and Skeggs, B. (1996) "Pornographies, Pleasures and Pedagogies in U.K. and U.S." *Jump Cut* 40: 106–13.

Kleinhans, C. (1996) "Teaching Sexual Images: Some Pragmatics." *Jump Cut* 40: 119–22.

Knigge, U. (1991) *The Athenian Kerameikos: History, Monuments, Excavations.* Athens: Krene Editions.

Knoll, E. and Prull, R. W. (1976) "Death Education: Accountable to Whom? For What?" *Omega* 7.2: 177–81.

Knox, B. (1994a) *The Oldest Dead White European Males and Other Reflections on the Classics.* New York: W. W. Norton and Company.

——— (1994b) *Backing into the Future: The Classical Tradition and Its Renewal.* New York: W. W. Norton.

Konur, O. (2006) "Teaching Disabled Students in Higher Education." *Teaching in Higher Education* 11.3: 351–63.

Koster, S. (2011) "The Self-managed Heart: Teaching Gender and Doing Emotional Labour in a Higher Education Institution." *Pedagogy, Culture and Society* 19: 61–77.

Kroll, W. (ed.) (1968) *Catullus,* 5th ed. Stuttgart: Teubner.

Kubler-Ross, E. (1997) *On Death and Dying,* New York: Scribner.

Kurtz, D. C. and Boardman, J. (1971) *Greek Burial Customs.* London: Thames and Hudson.

La Roche C. J. and Blakey, M. L. (1997) "Seizing Intellectual Power: The Dialogue at the New York African Burial Ground." *Historical Archaeology* 31: 84–106.

Laderman, G. (1996) *The Sacred Remains: American Attitudes towards Death, 1789–1883.* Yale University Press.

Laes, C., Goodey, C., and Rose, M. (2013) *Disabilities in Roman Antiquity: Disparate Bodies* A Capite ad Calcem. Leiden: Brill.

Laidlaw, J. (2000) "A Free Gift Makes No Friends." *Journal of the Royal Anthropological Institute* 6: 617–34.

Lamb, B. (2004) "Wide Open Spaces: Wikis Ready or not." *Educause Review* 39: 36–48.

Lambert, D. (2006) *The Cemetery in a Garden: 150 Years of the City of London Cemetery and Crematorium.* City of London.

Lambert, M. (2011) *The Classics and South African Identities.* London: Bristol Classical Press.

Landau, P. M. and Steele, D. G. (1996) "Why Anthropologists Study Human Remains." *American Indian Quarterly* 20: 209–28.

Larson, J. L. (1995) *Greek Heroine Cults.* Madison: University of Wisconsin Press.

Laungani, P. (2009) "Death in a Hindu Family." In C. M. Parkes, P. Laungani, and B. Young (eds.) *Death and Bereavement Across Cultures.* Cambridge, MA: Harvard University Press: 52–72.

Lauriola, R. (2011) "The Shuttle of Their Voices: A Comment on Class-Response to an Assignment about Rape." *Cloelia* N. S. 1: 26–31.

Leach, E. R. (1954) *Political Systems of Highland Burma: A Study of Kachin Social Structure.* London: Athlone Press.

Leaney, J. (1989) "Ashes to Ashes: Cremation and the Celebration of Death in Nineteenth-Century Britain." In R. Houlbrooke (ed.) *Death, Ritual and Bereavement.* London and New York: Routledge: 118–35.

Lear, A. (2008) "Ideals/Idealization." In A. Lear and E. Cantarella (eds.) *Images of Ancient Greek Pederasty: Boys Were Their Gods.* London and New York: Routledge.

Leland, J. (2009) "Urban Tool in Recruiting by the Army: An Arcade." *The New York Times*, January 4, 2009, http://www.nytimes.com/2009/01/05/us/05army.html?pagewanted=all.

Lee, G. (trans.) (1990) *Catullus: The Complete Poems.* Oxford: Oxford University Press.

Lee, R. L. M. (2008) "Modernity, Mortality and Re-Enchantment: The Death Taboo Revisited." *Sociology* 42.4: 745–59.

Lehman, P. (2006) "Dirty Little Secret: Why Teach and Study Pornography?" In P. Lehman, (ed.) *Pornography: Film and Culture.* New Brunswick: Rutgers University Press: 1–21.

Leigh, M. (2004) *Comedy and the Rise of Rome.* Oxford: Oxford University Press.

Leitao, D. (2002) "The Legend of the Sacred Band." In M. C. Nussbaum and J. Sihvola (eds.) *The Sleep of Reason: Erotic Experience and Sexual Ethics in Ancient Greece and Rome.* Chicago: University of Chicago Press.

Leming, M. R. (2010) *Understanding Dying, Death, and Bereavement.* Belmont, CA: Wadsworth Publishing.

Lerner, J. C. (1975) "Changes in Attitude toward Death: The Widow in Great Britain in the Early 20th Century." In B. Schoenber, I. Gerber, A. Weiner, A. Kitscher, D. Peretz, and A. Carr (eds.) *Bereavement: Its Psychosocial Aspects.* New York: Columbia University Press: 91–118.

Leupp, G. L. (1995) *Male Colors: The Construction of Homosexuality in Tokugawa Japan.* Berkeley: University of California Press.

Levine, E. (2009) "Jewish Views and Customs on Death." In C. M. Parkes, P. Laungani, and B. Young (eds.) *Death and Bereavement Across Cultures.* Cambridge, MA: Harvard University Press: 98–130.

Levine, J. (2002) *Harmful to Minors.* Minneapolis: University of Minnesota Press.

——— (2006) "Harmful to Minors: The Perils of Protecting Children from Sex." In K. R. Wells (ed.) *Teenage Sexuality: Opposing Viewpoints.* Farmington Hills, MI: Greenhaven Press.

Lévi-Strauss, C. (1953) "Social structure." in A. L. Kroeber (ed.) *Anthropology Today.* Chicago: University of Chicago Press: 524–53.

Lin, H. and Kelsey, K. D. (2009) "Building a Networked Environment in Wikis: The Evolving Phases of Collaborative Learning in a Wikibook Project." *Journal of Educational Computing Research* 40.2: 145–69.

Linton, S. (1998) *Claiming Disability: Knowledge and Identity.* New York: New York University Press.

Lisman, C. D. (1989) "Yes, Holden Should Read These Books." *The English Journal* 78.4: 14–18.

Liveley, G. (2012) "Teaching Rape in Roman Elegy, Part I." In B. Gold (ed.) *A Companion to Roman Love Elegy.* Malden, MA: Wiley-Blackwell: 541–48.

Llewellyn-Jones, L. (2011) "Domestic Abuse and Violence against Women in Ancient Greece," in Lambert, S. (ed.) *A Sociable Man.* Swansea: Classical Press of Wales, 231–66.

Lloyd, G. E. R., Chadwick, J., and Mann, W. N. (1978) *Hippocratic Writings.* Hammondsworth: Penguin Press.

Lofland, L. H. (1978) *The Craft of Dying: The Modern Face of Death.* Beverly Hills: Sage.

Lombardi, A. (2010) "Measuring Faculty Attitudes and Perceptions towards Disability at a Four-Year University: A Validity Study." PhD Dissertation, University of Oregon.

Lonie, I. (1981) *The Hippocratic Treatises "On Generation," "On the Nature of the Child," "Diseases IV."* Berlin and New York: de Gruyter.

Loraux, N. (1986) *The Invention of Athens. The Funeral Oration in the Classical City.* New York: Zone Books.

Lou, Y., Abramin, P. C., and d'Apollonia, S. (2001) "Small Group and Individual Learning with Technology: A Meta-analysis." *Review of Educational Research* 71.3: 449–521.

Ludwig, P. (2002) *Eros and Polis: Desire and Community in Greek Political Theory.* Cambridge: Cambridge University Press.

Maboe, M. (1994) "Strategies to Tackle Rape and Violence against Women in South Africa." In Center for Women's Global Leadership. *Gender Violence and Women's Human Rights in Africa.* New Brunswick, NJ: The Center for Women's Global Leadership: 30–37.

MacBain, B. (1982) *Prodigy and Expiation. A Study in Religion and Politics in Republican Rome.* Brussels: Latomus.

McCarthy, K. (2000) *Slaves, Masters and the Art of Authority in Plautine Comedy.* Princeton: Princeton University Press.

McConnell, M. W. (1990) "Academic Freedom in Religious Colleges and Universities." *Law and Contemporary Problems* (Duke University School of Law) 53: 303–24.

McCoskey, D. (1999) "Answering the Multicultural Imperative: A Course on Race and Ethnicity in Antiquity." *CW* 92: 553–61.

——— (2012) *Race: Antiquity and Its Legacy.* Oxford: Oxford University Press.

Macdonald, A. and Sanchez-Casal, S. (eds.) (2002) *Twenty-First-Century Feminist Classrooms: Pedagogies of Identity and Difference.* New York: Palgrave Macmillan.

McEwen, S. (2003) "Using Diversity to Teach Classics." *CW* 96: 416–20.

McHardy, F. (2005) "From Treacherous Wives to Murderous Mothers: Filicide in Tragic Fragments." In F. McHardy, J. Robson and F. D. Harvey (eds.) *Lost Dramas of Classical Athens*. Exeter: University of Exeter Press, 129–50.

——— (2008a) *Revenge in Athenian Culture*, London: Ducksworth.

——— (2008b) "The Trial by Water in Greek Myth and Literature." *LICS* 7: 1–20.

McKee, A. (2009) "Social Scientists Don't Say 'Titwank.'" *Sexualities* 12: 629–46.

MacKenzie, C. (ed.) (2006) *Herman Charles Bosman: The Complete Oom Schalk Lourens Stories* (from the short story entitled "The Rooinek"). Cape Town, Pretoria: Human and Rousseau.

McLaren, A. (1990) *A History of Contraception: From Antiquity to the Present*. Oxford: Blackwell.

McNair, B. (2009) "Teaching Porn." *Sexualities* 12: 558–67.

McWilliams, M. (1998) "Violence against Women in Societies Under Stress," in R. E. Dobash and R. P. Dobash (eds.) *Rethinking Violence against Women*. London: Sage, 111–40.

Maher, F. and Tetreault, M. K. T. (2001) *The Feminist Classroom: Dynamics of Gender, Race, and Privilege*, 2nd ed. Lanham, MD: Rowman and Littlefield.

Mahon, M. M., Goldberg, R. L., and Washington, S. K. (1999) "Discussing Death in the Classroom: Beliefs and Experiences of Educators and Education Students." *Omega—Journal of Death and Dying* 39.2: 99–122.

Mandela, N. R. (1994) *Long Walk to Freedom*. London: Abacus.

Mann, T. (1994) *Death in Venice: A New Translation, Backgrounds and Contexts, Criticism*, trans. C. Koelb. New York: Norton.

Marius, R. and Page, M. E. (2010) *A Short Guide to Writing About History*, 7th ed. New York: Longman.

Marshall, C. W. (2006) *The Stagecraft and Performance of Roman Comedy*. Cambridge: Cambridge University Press.

Marson, E. L. (1979) *The Ascetic Artist: Prefigurations in Thomas Mann's Der Tod in Venedig*. Bern: Peter Lang.

Matthes, M. M. (2000) *The Rape of Lucretia and the Founding of Republics: Readings in Livy, Machiavelli, and Rousseau*. University Park: Penn State University Press.

Mauss, M. (1990) *The Gift: Forms and Functions of Exchange in Archaic Societies*. London: Routledge.

Mayor, A. (2000) *The First Fossil Hunters: Paleontology in Greek and Roman Times*. Princeton: Princeton University Press.

Meineck, P. (2009) "'These Are Men Whose Minds the Dead Have Ravished': Theater of War/The Philoctetes Project." *Arion* 17: 173–92.

Mellink, M. J. (1998) *Kızılbel: An Archaic Painted Tomb Chamber in Northern Lycia*. Philadelphia: University of Pennsylvania Museum.

Mellor, P. A. and Shilling, C. (1993) "Modernity, Self-Identity and the Sequestration of Death." *Sociology* 27: 411–31.

Merry, S. (2009) *Gender Violence: A Cultural Perspective*. London: Blackwell.

Metcalfe, G. and Hays, C. (2005) *Being Dead Is No Excuse: The Official Southern Ladies' Guide to Hosting the Perfect Funeral*. New York: Miramax.

Meyer, R. E. (1989) *Cemeteries and Gravemarkers: Voices of American Culture.* Logan, UT: Utah State University Press.

Miles, G. B. (1995) *Livy: Reconstructing Early Rome.* Ithaca, NY: Cornell University Press.

Miller, S. (1995) "*In loco parentis:* Addressing (the) Class." In J. Gallop (ed.) *Pedagogy,* Bloomington: Indiana University Press.

Miller, S. G. (2004) *Ancient Greek Athletics.* New Haven: Yale University Press.

Miller-Young, M. (2010) "The Pedagogy of Pornography: Teaching Hardcore Media in a Feminist Studies Classroom." *Signs Special Feature: Films for the Feminist Classroom* 2.2.

Minow, J. C. and Einolf, C. J. (2009) "Sorority Participation and Sexual Assault Risk." *Violence against Women* 15.7: 835–51.

Mishima, Y. (1999) *Forbidden Colors,* translated by A. H. Marks. New York: Vintage.

Mitford, J. (1963) *The American Way of Death.* New York: Simon and Schuster.

——— (2000) *The American Way of Death Revisited.* New York: Vintage.

Monoson, S. S. (2000) *Plato's Democratic Entanglements.* Princeton: Princeton University Press.

Mooney, J. (2000) *Gender, Violence and the Social Order.* Basingstoke: Macmillan.

Morris, I. (1987) *Burial and Ancient Society: The Rise of the Greek City-State.* Cambridge: Cambridge University Press.

——— (1992) *Death-ritual and Social Structure in Classical Antiquity.* Cambridge: Cambridge University Press.

——— (1994) "Everyman's Grave." In A. L. Boegehold and A. C. Scafuro (eds.) *Athenian Identity and Civic Ideology.* Baltimore: Johns Hopkins University Press: 67–101.

Muller, C. F. J. (1981) *Five Hundred Years: A History of South Africa.* Pretoria: Academica Publishers.

Murphy, E. M. (2008) "Introduction." In E. M. Murphy (ed.) *Deviant Burial in the Archaeological Record.* Oxford: Oxbow Books: xii–xviii.

Murray, J. (2009) "An African Thermopylae? The Battles of the Anglo-Zulu War, 1879." *Akroterion* 54: 51–68.

Naismith, L., Lee, B.-H. and Pilkington, R. M. (2011) "Collaborative Learning with a Wiki: Differences in Perceived Usefulness in Two Contexts of Use." *Journal of Computer Assisted Learning* 27.3: 228–42.

National Center for Transgender Equality website (2009) "Transgender Terminology," http://transequality.org/Resources/NCTE_TransTerminology.pdf.

——— (2009) "Understanding Transgender," http://transequality.org/Resources/NCTE_UnderstandingTrans.pdf.

——— (2011) "Injustice at Every Turn: A Look at Black Respondents in the National Transgender Discrimination Survey," http://transequality.org/PDFs/BlackTransFactsheetFINAL_090811.pdf.

National Resource Center (2006), http://www.difficultdialogues.org/.

Nauta, R. (2004) "Catullus 63 in a Roman Context." *Mnemosyne* 57.5: 596–628.

Nelson, L. (2012) "'Gainful' Comes to the Nonprofits: Obama Higher Education Plan Signals Policy Shift." *Inside Higher Ed* January 30, http://www.insidehighered.com/news/2012/01/30/obama-higher-education-plan-signals-policy-shift#ixzz1pqkGiLcu.

Nestle, J., Howell, C., and Wilchins, R. (eds.) (2002) *GenderQueer: Voices from beyond the Sexual Binary.* Los Angeles, CA: Alyson Books.

Nguyen, Hoang Tan (2010) "The Opening of Kobena, Cecilia, Robert, Bruce, Linda, Erica, Juana, Hoang and the Others." Paper presented at At the Limit: Pornography and the Humanities Conference, SUNY Buffalo, March 27.

Nicosia, F. (2009) "Ecology, Embodiment and Aesthetics of Death in Hurricane Katrina." *Mortality* 14.1: 1–18.

Nisbet, G. (2009) "'Dickus Maximus': Rome as pornotopia." In D. Lowe and K. Shahabudin (eds.) *Classics For All: Reworking Antiquity in Mass Culture.* Newcastle: Cambridge Scholars Publishing: 150–71.

Nisters, T. (2000) *Aristotle on Courage.* Frankfurt am Main: Peter Lang.

NSW Office of Communities "Change Your Ways: Australian Men Talk about Domestic Violence," http://www.communities.nsw.gov.au/publications/changeyourways.asp.

Nünlist, R. (2003) "The Homeric Scholia on Focalization." *Mnemosyne* 56: 61–71.

Nunokawa, J. (1992) "Homosexual Desire and the Effacement of the Self in *The Picture of Dorian Gray.*" *American Imago* 49: 311–21.

Nussbaum, M. C. (1986) *The Fragility of Goodness: Luck and Ethics in Greek Tragedy and Philosophy.* Cambridge: Cambridge University Press.

O'Shea, J. (1984) *Mortuary Variability.* Orlando: Academic Press.

Oakley, J. (2004) *Picturing Death in Classical Athens.* Cambridge: Cambridge University Press.

Oliensis, E. (2009) *Freud's Rome: Psychoanalysis and Latin Poetry.* Cambridge: Cambridge University Press.

Olivere, D. and Monroe, B. (eds.) (2004) *Death, Dying and Social Differences.* Oxford: Oxford University Press.

Olivier, L. (1999) "The Hochdorf 'Princely' Grave and the Question of the Nature of Archaeological Funerary Assemblages." In T. Murray (ed.) *Time and Archaeology.* London: Routledge: 109–38.

Olson, J. (1992) *Understanding Teaching: Beyond Expertise.* Milton Keynes: Open University Press.

Oosterhuis, H. (2002) "Richard von Krafft-Ebing's 'Step-Children of Nature': Psychiatry and the Making of the Homosexual Identity." In K. M. Phillips and B. Reay (eds.) *Sexualities in History: A Reader.* New York: Routledge.

Outside the Wire (2011) "Theater of War," http://www.outsidethewirellc.com/projects/theater-of-war/overview.

Packman, Z. M. (1993) "Call It Rape: A Motif in Roman Comedy and its Suppression in English-Speaking Publications." *Helios* 20: 42–55.

Pader, E.-J. (1982) *Symbolism, Social Relations and the Interpretation of Mortuary Remains. BAR Supplementary Series 130.* Oxford: Archaeopress.

——— (1982) *Symbolism, Social Relations and the Interpretation of Mortuary Remains.* Oxford: British Archaeological Reports.

Palavestra, A. (1998) "Landmarks of Power: Princely Tombs in the Central Balkan Iron Age." In D. Bailey (ed.) *The Archaeology of Value: Essays in Prestige and Processes of Valuations.* Oxford: British Archaeological Reports: 55–69.

Panoussi, V. (2003) "*Ego Maenas:* Maenadism, Marriage, and the Construction of Female Identity in Catullus 63 and 64." *Helios* 30.2: 101–26.

Papathanassiou, M., Hoskin, M., and Papadopoulou, H. (1992) "Orientations of Tombs in the Late-Minoan Cemetery at Armenoi, Crete." *Journal of History of Astronomy, Archaeoastronomy Supplement* 23.

Parca, M. G. (2002) "Violence by and against Women in Documentary Papyri from Ptolemaic and Roman Egypt." In Henri Melaerts and Leon Mooren (eds.) *Le rôle et le statut de la femme en Égypte hellénistique, romaine et byzantine.* Leuven: Peeters, 283–96.

Parker, H. N. (1989) "Crucially Funny or Tranio on the Couch: The *Servus Callidus* and Jokes about Torture." *TAPA* 119: 233–46.

Parker, R. (1983) *Miasma: Pollution and Purification in Early Greek Religion.* Oxford: Clarendon Press.

——— (1998) "Pleasing Thighs: Reciprocity in Greek Religion." In C. Gill, N. Postlethwaite, and R. Seaford (eds.) *Reciprocity in Ancient Greece.* Oxford: Clarendon Press: 105–25.

Parker Pearson, M. (1982) "Mortuary Practices, Society and Ideology: An Ethnoarchaeological Case Study." In I. Hodder (ed.) *Symbolic and Structural Archaeology.* Cambridge: Cambridge University Press: 99–113.

——— (1999) *The Archaeology of Death and Burial.* Phoenix Mill: Sutton Publishing Limited.

Parkes, C. M., Laungani, P., and Young, B. (eds.) (1997) *Death and Bereavement across Cultures.* London: Routledge.

Parrot, A. and Cummings, N. (2006) *Forsaken Females: The Global Brutalization of Women.* Lanham: Rowman and Littlefield.

Parsons, B. (2003) "The Funeral and the Funeral Industry in the United Kingdom." In C. D. Bryant (ed.) *Handbook of Death and Dying,* vol. 1. Thousand Oaks, CA: Sage: 611–18.

——— (2005) *Committed to the Cleansing Flame: The Development of Cremation in Nineteenth-century England.* Reading: Spire Books.

Pearcy, L. T. (2013) "Talfourd's *Ion:* Classical Reception and Gender in Nineteenth-Century Philadelphia." In D. Lateiner, B. K. Gold and J. Perkins (eds.) *Roman Literature, Gender and Reception: Domina Illustris.* New York: Routledge: 241–51.

Pedley, J. (2006) *Sanctuaries and the Sacred in the Ancient Greek World.* Cambridge: Cambridge University Press.

Peebles, C. S. and Kus, S. M. (1977) "Some Archaeological Correlates of Ranked Societies." *American Antiquity* 42.3: 421–48.

Pennebaker, J. W. (1997) "Writing about Emotional Experiences as a Therapeutic Process." *Psychological Science* 8: 162–66.

Penrose, W. D., Jr. (2006) "Bold with the Bow and Arrow: Amazons, Ethnicity, and the Ideology of Martial Prowess in Ancient Greek and Asian Culture." PhD Dissertation, City University of New York Graduate Center.

——— (forthcoming 2014) "Sappho's Shifting Fortunes from Antiquity to the Early Renaissance." *Journal of Lesbian Studies.*

Perkins, J. (2003) "The Angel of History." *CW* 96: 421–26.

Pestilli, L. (2005) "Disabled Bodies: The (Mis)representation of the Lame in Antiquity and their Reappearance in Early Christian and Medieval Art." In M. Wyke and A. Hopkins (eds.) *Roman Bodies. Antiquity to the Eighteenth Century.* London: British School at Rome: 85–97.

Peters, V. L. and Slotta, J. D. (2010) "Scaffolding Knowledge Communities in the Classroom: New Opportunities in the Web 2.0 Era." In M. J. Jacobson and P. Reimann (eds.) *Designs for Learning Environments of the Future*. New York: Springer: 205–32.

Petersen, L. H. (2006) *The Freedman in Roman Art and Art History*. Cambridge: Cambridge University Press.

——— (2010) *Cultural Interaction and Social Strategies on the Pontic Shores: Burials Customs in the Northern Black Sea Area c. 550–270 B.C.* Aarhus: Aarhus University Press.

Petronius (2000) *Satyricon*, translated by S. Ruden. Indianapolis: Hackett.

Pflugfelder, G. M. (1999) *Cartographies of Desire: Male-Male Sexuality in Japanese Discourse, 1600–1950*. Berkeley: University of California Press.

Plato (1989) *Symposium*, translated by A. Nehamas and P. Woodruff. Indianapolis: Hackett.

——— (1995) *Phaedrus*, translated by A. Nehamas and P. Woodruff. Indianapolis: Hackett.

Platter, C. (2007) *Aristophanes and the Carnival of Genres*. Baltimore: Johns Hopkins University Press.

Plumb, J. H. (1975) "The New World of Children in Eighteenth-Century England." *Past and Present* 67: 64–95.

——— (ed.) (1964) *Crisis in the Humanities*. Harmondsworth: Penguin.

Pomeroy, S. B., Burstein, S. M., Donlan, W., Roberts, J. T., and Tandy, D. (2011) *Ancient Greece: A Political, Social, and Cultural History*, 3rd ed. Oxford: Oxford University Press.

——— (1994) *Xenophon Oeconomicus: A Social and Historical Commentary, with a New English Translation*. Oxford: Clarendon Press.

——— (2007) *The Murder of Regilla: A Case of Domestic Violence in Antiquity*. Cambridge, MA: Harvard University Press.

Popham, M. R., Calligas, P. G., and Sackett, L. H. (eds.) (1993) *Lefkandi II: The Protogeometric Building at Toumba: Part 2, the Excavation, Architecture and Finds*. Oxford: The British School of Archaeology at Athens.

Porter, R. and Tomaselli, S. (eds.) (1986) *Rape: A Historical and Social Enquiry*. Oxford: Blackwell.

Posamentir, R. (2007) "Colonisation and Acculturation in the Early Necropolis of Chersonesos." In G. Erkut and S. Mitchell (eds.) *The Black Sea: Past, Present and Future*. London: British Institute at Ankara: 45–55.

——— (2011) *Chersonesan Studies I: The Polychrome Grave Stelai from the Early Hellenistic Necropolis*. Austin, TX: University of Texas Press.

Prince, C. K. (2009) "The Lioness and the Cheese-grater (Ar. *Lys.* 231–232)." *Studi Italiani di Filologia Classica* 7: 149–75.

Qian, Y. (2007) "Meaningful Learning with Wikis: Making a Connection." In C. Crawford et al. (eds.) *Proceedings of Society for Information Technology and Teacher Education International Conference 2007*, AACE: 2093–97.

Quinn, K. (1972) *Catullus: An Interpretation*. London: Batsford.

Rabinowitz, N. S. (1998) "Embodying Tragedy: The Sex of the Actor." *Intertexts* 2: 3–45.

——— (2002) "Excavating Women's Homoeroticism in Ancient Greece: The Evidence from Attic Vase Painting." In N. S. Rabinowitz and L. Auanger (eds.) *Among Women: From the Homosocial to the Homoerotic in the Ancient World*. Austin: University of Texas Press: 106–66.

Radcliffe-Brown, A. R. (1922) *The Andaman Islanders.* Cambridge: Cambridge University Press.

——— (1945) "Religion and Society." *The Journal of the Royal Anthropological Institute of Great Britain and Ireland* 75.1/2: 33–43.

Ragon, M. (1983) *The Space of Death: A Study of Funerary Architecture, Decoration, and Urbanism.* Charlottesville: University of Virginia Press.

Ramos Lira L., Koss, M. P., and Russo, N. F. (1999) "Mexican-American Women's Definitions of Rape and Sexual Abuse." *Hispanic Journal of Behavioral Sciences* 21: 236–65.

Rankine, P. (2006) *Ulysses in Black: Ralph Ellison, Classicism, and African American Literature.* Madison, WI: University of Wisconsin Press.

Rayor, D. trans. (1991) *Sappho's Lyre: Archaic Lyric and Women Poets of Ancient Greece.* Berkeley: University of California Press.

Reading, A. (2006) "Professing Porn or Obscene Browsing? On Proper Distance in the University Classroom." *Media, Culture and Society* 27: 123–30.

Rediker, M. (2007) *The Slave Ship: A Human History.* New York: Viking.

Regis, H. A. (1999) "Blackness and the Politics of Memory in the New Orleans Second Line." *Cultural Anthropology* 14.4: 472–504.

Rehm, R. (1994) *Marriage to Death: The Conflation of Wedding and Funeral Rituals in Greek Tragedy.* Princeton: Princeton University Press.

Renault, M. (1988) *The Persian Boy.* New York: Vintage.

Richards, J. D. (1988) "Style and Symbol: Explaining Variability in Anglo-Saxon Cremation Burials." In S. T. Driscoll and M. R. Nieke (eds.) *Power and Politics in Early Medieval Britain and Ireland.* Edinburgh: Edinburgh University Press: 145–61.

Richardson, N. (1986) "Apartheid, Heresy and the Church in South Africa." *The Journal of Religious Ethics* 14: 1–21.

Richardson, W. (2006) *Blogs, Wikis, Podcasts, and Other Powerful Web Tools for Classrooms.* Thousand Oaks, CA: Corwin Press.

Richlin, A. (1992a) "Reading Ovid's Rapes." In A. Richlin (ed.) *Pornography and Representation in Greece and Rome.* Oxford: Oxford University Press: 158–79.

——— (ed.) (1992b) *Pornography and Representation in Ancient Greece and Rome.* Oxford: Oxford University Press.

——— (1993) "The Ethnographer's Dilemma and the Dream of a Lost Golden Age,." In N. Rabinowitz and A. Richlin (eds.) *Feminist Theory and the Classics.* London and New York: Routledge: 272–303.

——— (trans.) (2005) *Rome and the Mysterious Orient: Three Plays by Plautus.* Berkeley: University of California Press.

——— (forthcoming) "Talking to Slaves in the Plautine Audience." *ClAnt.*

Rimmon-Kenan, S. (1983) *Narrative Fiction: Contemporary Poetics.* London: Methuen.

Riordan, R. (2006) *The Lightening Thief: Book 1, Percy Jackson and the Olympians.* Los Angeles: Disney-Hyperion.

Roberts, C. (2009) *Human Remains in Archaeology: A Handbook.* York: Council for British Archaeology.

Robinson, D. M. (1963) *Sappho and her Influence.* New York: Cooper Square Publishers.

Roller, M. B. (2006) *Dining Posture in Ancient Rome: Bodies, Values, and Status*. Princeton: Princeton University Press.

Ronnick, M. (2006) *The Works of William Sanders Scarborough: Black Classicist and Race Leader*. Oxford: Oxford University Press.

Rose, M. L. (1995) "Physical Disability in the Ancient Greek World." PhD Dissertation, University of Minnesota.

——— (1996) "Review of Garland, R. *The Eye of the Beholder. Deformity and Disability in the Graeco-Roman World*." In *Disability Studies Quarterly* 16: 36–37.

——— (1997a) "Constructions of Physical Disability in the Ancient Greek World: The Community Concept." In D. T. Mitchell and S. L. Snyder (eds.) *The Body and Physical Difference: Discourses of Disability*, Ann Arbor: University of Michigan Press: 35–50.

——— (1997b) "Let there be a Law that no Deformed Child shall be Reared: The Cultural Context of Deformity in the Ancient Greek World." *AHB* 10.3–4: 79–92.

——— (1997c) "Deaf and Dumb in Ancient Greece." In L. J. Davis (ed.) *The Disability Studies Reader*. New York: Routledge: 29–51.

——— (1998) "Women and Disability in Ancient Greece." *AncW* 29.1: 3–9.

——— (2003) *The Staff of Oedipus. Transforming Disability in Ancient Greece*. Ann Arbor: University of Michigan Press.

——— (2006) "History of Disability: Ancient West." In *Encyclopedia of Disability*, Thousand Oaks, CA: Sage.

Rose, P. (2001) "Teaching Classical Myth and Confronting in Contemporary Contemporary Myths." In M. Winkler (ed.) *Classical Myth and Culture in the Cinema*. Oxford: Oxford University Press: 291–318.

Roussinos, D. (2011) "Blended Collaborative Learning through a Wiki-Based Project: A Case Study on Students' Perceptions." *International Journal of Digital Literacy and Digital Competence* 2.3: 15–30.

Rowling, L. (1995) "The Disenfranchised Grief of Teachers." *Omega—Journal of Death and Dying* 31.4: 317–29.

Rozée, P. D. (1993) "Forbidden or Forgiven? Rape in Cross-Cultural Perspective." *Psychology of Women Quarterly* 17: 499–514.

Rubino, C. A. (1974) "Myth and Mediation in the Attis Poem of Catullus." *Ramus* 3.2: 152–75.

Rütten, T. (1996) "Receptions of the Hippocratic Oath in the Renaissance: The Prohibition of Abortion as a Case Study in Reception." *Journal of the History of Medicine and Allied Sciences* 51: 456–83.

Saxe, A. A. (1970) "Social Dimensions of Mortuary Practices." PhD Dissertation, University of Michigan.

Scafuro, A. (1990) "Discourses of Sexual Violation in Mythic Accounts and Dramatic Versions of 'The Girl's Tragedy.'" *Differences* 2: 126–59.

Scanlon, T. (2002) *Eros and Greek Athletics*. New York: Oxford University Press.

Scarre, C. and Scarre, G. (2006) *The Ethics of Archaeology: Philosophical Perspectives on Archaeological Practice*. Cambridge: Cambridge University Press.

Schaps, D. (2006) "Zeus the Wife-beater." *SCI* 25: 1–24.

Scharffenberger, E. (2002) "Aristophanes' *Thesmophoriazousai* and the Challenges of Comic Translation: The Case of William Arrowsmith's *Euripides Agonistes*." *AJP* 123: 429–63.

Schefold, K. (1992) *Gods and Heroes in Later Archaic Art*. Cambridge: Cambridge University Press.

Schein, S. (2008) "'Our Debt to Greece and Rome': Canon, Class and Ideology." In L. Hardwick and C. Stray (eds.) *A Companion to Classical Reception*. Oxford: Blackwell: 75–85.

Schepartz, L. A., Miller-Antonio, S., and Murphy, J. M. A. (2009) "Differential Health among the Mycenaeans of Messenia: Status, Sex, and Dental Health at Pylos." In L. A. Schepartz, S. C. Fox, and C. Bourbou (eds.) *New Directions in the Skeletal Biology of Greece*, Hesperia Supplement 43. Princeton: American School of Classical Studies: 155–74.

Schrecker, E. (2010) *The Lost Soul of Higher Education: Corporatization, the Assault on Academic Freedom, and the End of the American University*. New York and London: New Press.

Scodel, R. (1998) "The Captive's Dilemma: Sexual Acquiescence in Euripides' *Hecuba* and *Troades*." *HSCP* 98: 137–54.

Scott, J. C. (1990) *Domination and the Arts of Resistance: Hidden Transcripts*. New Haven: Yale University Press.

Sedgwick, E. (2003) *Touching Feeling: Affect, Pedagogy, Performativity*. Durham, NC: Duke University Press.

de Sélincourt, A. (2002) *Livy: The Early History of Rome, Books I–V*. London: Penguin.

Setswe, G. (2009) "The HIV and AIDS Epidemic in South Africa: Where Are We?" *AED* Workshop, 8 July 2009, Human Sciences Research Council, South Africa.

Shakespeare, W. (1991) *Complete Sonnets*. New York: Dover.

Shalhoub-Kevorkian, N. (1999) "Towards a Cultural Definition of Rape: Dilemmas in Dealing with Rape Victims in Palestinian Society." *Women's Studies International Forum* 22.2: 157–73.

——— (2000) "Blocking Her Exclusion: A Contextually Sensitive Model of Intervention for Handling Female Abuse." *The Social Service Review* 74.4: 620–34.

——— (2001) "Using the Dialogue Tent to Break Mental Chains: Listening and Being Heard." *Social Service Review* 75: 135–50.

——— (2003) "Reexamining Femicide: Breaking the Silence and Crossing 'Scientific' Borders." *Signs* 28.2: 581–608.

Shanks, M. and Tilley, C. (1982) "Ideology, Symbolic Power and Ritual Communication." In I. Hodder (ed.) *Symbolic and Structural Archaeology*. Cambridge: Cambridge University Press: 129–54.

Shaw, M. (1975) "The Female Intruder: Women in Fifth-century Drama." *CPh* 70: 255–66.

Shay, J. (1995) *Achilles in Vietnam: Combat Trauma and the Undoing of Character*. New York: Simon and Schuster.

——— (2003) *Odysseus in America: Combat Trauma and the Trials of Homecoming*. New York: Scribner.

Shennan, S. E. (1975) "The Social Organization at Branĉ." *Antiquity* 49: 279–88.

Shepherd, G. (2005) "Dead Men Tell No Tales: Ethnic Diversity in Sicilian Colonies and the Evidence of the Cemeteries." *Oxford Journal of Archaeology* 24: 115–36.

——— (2007) "Poor Little Rich Kids? Status and Selection in Archaic Western Greece." in S. Crawford and G. Shepherd (eds.) *Children, Childhood and Society,* BAR International Series *1696.* Oxford: Archaeopress: 93–106.

Shils, E. (1981) *Tradition,* Chicago: University of Chicago Press.

Skinner, M. B. (1993) *"Ego mulier:* The Construction of Male Sexuality in Catullus." *Helios* 20.2: 107–30.

——— (2003) *Catullus in Verona: A Reading of the Elegiac* libellus, *Poems 65–116.* Columbus: Ohio State University Press.

Sleeter, C. E. and McLaren, P. L. (eds.) (1995) *Multicultural Education, Critical Pedagogy, and the Politics of Difference.* New York: State University of New York Press.

Slocum, J. and Carlson, L. (2011) *Final Rights: Reclaiming the American Way of Death.* Hinesberg, VT: Upper Access, Inc.

Smith, C. (2009) "Pleasure and Distance: Exploring Sexual Cultures in the Classroom." *Sexualities* 12: 568–85.

Smith D. N. (1999) "Images, Education, and Paradox in Plato's *Republic." Apeiron* 32: 125–41.

Smith, L. P. (1994) "Audience Response to Rape: Chaerea in Terence's *Eunuchus." Helios* 21: 21–38.

Smith, S. E. (2010) *To Serve the Living: Funeral Directors and the African American Way of Death.* Cambridge, MA: Belknap Press of Harvard University Press.

Stahl, G. (2005) "Group Cognition in Computer-assisted Collaborative Learning." *Journal of Computer Assisted Learning* 21: 79–90.

——— (2006) *Group Cognition: Computer Support for Collaborative Knowledge Building.* Cambridge, MA: MIT Press.

Steiner, D. T. (2001) *Images in Mind: Statues in Archaic and Classical Greek Literature and Thought.* Princeton: Princeton University Press.

Stevenson, T. (2011) "Women of Early Rome as *Exempla* in Livy, *Ab urbe condita,* Book 1." *CW* 104: 175–89.

Stewart, A. (1997) *Art, Desire, and the Body in Ancient Greece.* Cambridge: Cambridge University Press.

Straus, M. (2004) "Prevalence of Violence against Dating Partners by Male and Female University Students Worldwide." *Violence against Women* 10: 790–811.

Stray, C. (1998) *Classics Transformed: Schools, Universities, and Society in England, 1830–1960.* Oxford: Oxford University Press.

Stroup, S. C. (2004) "Designing Women: Aristophanes' *Lysistrata* and the 'Hetairization' of the Greek Wife." *Arethusa* 37: 37–73.

Swain, H. (2007) *An Introduction to Museum Archaeology.* Cambridge: Cambridge University Press.

Synodinou K. (1987) "The Threats of Physical Abuse of Hera by Zeus in the *Iliad." WS* 100: 13–22.

Taaffe, L. K. (1993) *Aristophanes and Women.* London and New York: Routledge.

Tainter, J. R. (1978) "Mortuary Practices and the Study of Prehistoric Social Systems." In M. Schiffer (ed.) *Advances in Archaeological Method and Theory.* New York: Academic Press: 105–41.

Takács, S. A. (1996) "*Magna Deum Mater Idaea,* Cybele, and Catullus' *Attis.*" In E. N. Lane (ed.) *Cybele, Attis, and Related Cults: Essays in Memory of M. J. Vermaseren.* Leiden: Brill: 367–86.

Tang, I. (1999) *Pornography: The Secret History of Civilization.* London: Channel 4 Books.

Tarlow, S. A. (1999) *Bereavement and Commemoration: An Archaeology of Mortality.* Oxford: Wiley-Blackwell.

——— (2011) *Ritual, Belief and the Dead Body in Early Modern Britain and Ireland.* Cambridge: Cambridge University Press.

Tatum, J. (trans.) (1983) *Plautus: The Darker Comedies.* Baltimore: John Hopkins University Press.

Taylor, M. W. (1991) *The Tyrant Slayers: The Heroic Image in Fifth-Century* B.C. *Athenian Art and Politics,* second edition, Salem, NH: Ayer.

Thomson, D. F. S. (ed.) (1997) *Catullus.* Toronto: University of Toronto Press.

Thomson, R. G. (1996) *Freakery: Cultural Spectacles of the Extraordinary Body.* New York: New York University Press.

Tompkins, J. (1990) "The Pedagogy of the Distressed." *College English* 52: 653–60.

Too, Y. L. (1998) "Introduction." In Y. L. Too and N. Livingstone (eds.) *Pedagogy and Power: Rhetorics of Classical Learning.* Cambridge: Cambridge University Press: 1–15.

Trentin, L. (2009) "What's in a Hump? Re-examining the Hunchback in the Villa Albani-Torlonia." *CCJ* 55: 130–56.

——— (2011) "Deformity in the Roman Imperial Court." *G&R* 58.2: 195–208.

——— (2013a) "Disability in Class and Classics: Towards a More Nuanced Understanding of Ancient History." *Prandium: The Journal of Historical Studies* 2.1: 55–58.

——— (2013b) "Exploring Visual Impairment in Ancient Rome." In C. Laes, C. Goodey and M. Rose (eds.) *Disabilities in Roman Antiquity. Disparate Bodies* a Capite ad Calcem. Leiden: Brill: 89–114.

——— (forthcoming) *The Hunchback in Hellenistic and Roman Art.* London: Bloomsbury Academic.

Tsagarakis, O. (2000) *Studies in Odyssey 11.* Stuttgart: F. Steiner.

Tuchman, G. (2009) *Wannabe U: Inside the Corporate University.* Chicago: University of Chicago Press.

Turner, V. W. (1995) *The Ritual Process.* New York: De Gruyter.

Ucko, P. J. (1969) "Ethnography and the archaeological interpretation of funerary remains." *World Archaeology* 1: 262–90.

Ure P. N. (ed.) (1927) *Sixth and Fifth Century Pottery from Excavations Made at Rhitsona.* London: Oxford University Press.

——— (1934) *Aryballoi and Figurines from Rhitsona in Boeotia.* Cambridge: Cambridge University Press.

UVa Today website (31 March 2011) "Out of the Shadows: Event to Commemorate Kitty Foster and Canada Community," http://www.virginia.edu/uvatoday/newsRelease.php?id=14654.

Vallee, F. G. (1955) "Burial and Mourning Customs in a Hebridean Community." *The Journal of the Royal Anthropological Institute of Great Britain and Ireland* 85.1/2: 119–30.

van der Geest, S. (2000) "Funerals for the Living: Conversations with Elderly People in Kwahu, Ghana." *African Studies Review* 43: 103–29.

Van Gennep, A. (1960) *The Rites of Passage,* translated by M. Visedom and G. Caffee. Chicago: University of Chicago Press.

Van Rensburg, J. P. J. (1970) *Lusistrata: Aristophanes.* Cape Town, Pretoria: Human and Rousseau.

Van Zyl Smit, B. (2005) "Aristophanes in South Africa." *South African Theatre Journal* 19: 254–76.

Verbeke, G. (1990) *Moral Education in Aristotle.* Washington, D.C.: Catholic University of America.

Vermeule, E. D. T. (1965) "Painted Mycenaean Larnakes." *JHS* 85: 123–48.

Verstrate, B. C. and Provencal, V. (2005) *Same-Sex Desire and Love in Greco-Roman Antiquity and in the Classical Tradition of the West.* Special issue of *Journal of Homosexuality* 49: 3–4.

Vlahogiannis, N. (1998a) *Representations of Disability in the Ancient World.* London: Routledge.

——— (1998b) "Disabling Bodies." In D. Montserrat (ed.) *Changing Bodies, Changing Meanings: Studies in the Human Body in Antiquity.* London and New York: Routledge: 13–36.

——— (2005) "Curing Disability." In H. King (ed.) *Health in Antiquity.* London: Routledge: 180–91.

Wacquant, L. (2002) "From Slavery to Mass Incarceration: Rethinking the 'Race Question' in the US." *New Left Review* 13: 41–60.

Wallace, L. (1880) *Ben-Hur: A Tale of the Christ.* New York: Harper and Brothers.

Walter, T. (1991) "Modern Death: Taboo or not Taboo?" *Sociology* 25.2: 293–310.

——— (1995) "Natural Death and The Noble Savage." *Omega-Journal of Death and Dying* 30.4: 237–48.

Warner, J. H. (2009) *Dissection: Photographs of a Rite of Passage in American Medicine 1880–1930.* New York: Blast Books.

Warren, P. N. (1995) *The Front Runner.* Beverly Hills: Wildcat Press.

——— (2006) *The Lavender Locker Room: 3,000 Years of Great Athletes Whose Sexual Orientation was Different.* Beverly Hills: Wildcat Press.

Watson, R. S. (1990) "Remembering the Death: Graves and Politics in Southeastern China." In Watson and Rawski (eds.) *Death Ritual in Late Imperial and Modern China.* Berkeley: University of California Press: 203–27.

Weaver, M. A. (2000) "Gandhi's Daughters." *The New Yorker,* January 10, 2000: 50–61.

Weeks, J. (1977) *Coming Out: Homosexual Politics in Britain from the Nineteenth Century to the Present.* London: Quartet Books.

Weiler, K. (1988) *Women Teaching for Change: Gender, Class and Power.* South Hadley, MA: Bergin and Garvey.

Wheeler, S., Yeomans, P., and Wheeler, D. (2008) "The Good, the Bad, and the Wiki: Evaluating Student-generated Content for Collaborative Learning." *British Journal of Educational Technology* 39.6: 987–95.

Wicke, J. (2004) "Through a Gaze Darkly: Pornography's Academic Market." In P. Church Gibson (ed.) *More Dirty Looks: Gender, Pornography and Power.* London: British Film Institute: 176–87.

Widdows, D. (2011) "Teaching Classical Texts that Include Rape at an All-Male College." *Cloelia* 1: 31–32.

Wilchins, R. (2004) *Queer Theory, Gender Theory: An Instant Primer.* Los Angeles, CA: Alyson Books.

Wilde, O. (1999) *Collins Complete Works of Oscar Wilde,* centenary ed. Glasgow: Harper Collins.

Williams, L. (1999) *Hard Core: Power, Pleasure, and the 'Frenzy of the Visible.'* Berkeley and Los Angeles: University of California Press.

——— (2004) "Porn Studies: Proliferating Pornographies On/Scene: An Introduction." In L. Williams (ed.) *Porn Studies.* Durham, NC: Duke University Press: 1–23.

Wilson M. and Daly, M. (1998) "Lethal and Nonlethal Violence against Wives and the Evolutionary Psychology of Male Sexual Proprietariness." In R. E. Dobash and R. P. Dobash (eds.) *Rethinking Violence against Women.* London: Sage, 199–230.

Wiseman, T. P. (1983) "The Wife and Children of Romulus." *CQ* 33.2: 445–52.

Wittig, M. (1985) "The Mark of Gender." *Feminist Issues* 5.2: 3–12.

Wohl, V. (2002) *Love among the Ruins: The Erotics of Democracy in Classical Athens.* Princeton: Princeton University Press.

Women's Aid and HM Government (2010) "Expect Respect: A Toolkit for addressing Teenage Relationship Abuse," http://www.homeoffice.gov.uk/publications/crime/teen-relationship-abuse/teen-abuse-toolkit

Woodford, S. (1993) *The Trojan War in Ancient Art.* London: Duckworth and Co.

Wyke, M. (1997) *Projecting the Past: Ancient Rome, Cinema, and History.* New York: Routledge.

Yale Graduate Teaching Center (2008) "Teaching Controversial Subjects," http://www.procon.org/sourcefiles/TeachingControversialSubjects.pdf.

Yourcenar, M. (2005) *Memoirs of Hadrian,* translated by Grace Frick. New York: Farrar, Straus and Giroux.

Zumbach, J., Reimann, P., and Koch, S. (2006) "Monitoring Students' Collaboration in Computer-mediated Collaborative Problem-solving: Applied Feedback Approaches." *Journal of Educational Computing Research* 35.4: 399–424.

CONTRIBUTORS

PATRICIA BAKER is senior lecturer in Classical and Archaeological Studies at University of Kent, Canterbury, UK. Her publications include: *The Archaeology of Medicine in the Greco-Roman World* (2013); *Medicine and Space: Body, Buildings and Borders in the Classical and Medieval Traditions* (2012) co-edited with C. van't Land, and H. Nijdam; *Medical Care for the Roman Army on the Rhine, Danube and British Frontiers from the First through Third Centuries AD* (2004) and *Practitioners, Practices and Patients: New Approaches to Medical Archaeology and Anthropology* (2002) co-edited with G. Carr.

MARGARET E. BUTLER is assistant professor of Classical Studies at Tulane University, USA. She has published "The logic of opportunity: Philip II, Demosthenes, and the charismatic imagination," in *Syllecta Classica* 21 (2011).

SUSAN DEACY is principal lecturer in Classical Civilisation at the University of Roehampton, UK. Her publications include: *Athena* (2008); *Athena in the Classical World* (2001) co-edited with A. Villing; *Rape in Antiquity* (1997) co-edited with K. Pierce. Her *A Traitor to her Sex? Athena the Trickster* is forthcoming with Oxford University Press and she is currently co-authoring a volume on *Gender Violence in Ancient Greece* with Fiona McHardy.

PAGE DUBOIS is Distinguished Professor of Classics and Comparative Literature at the University of California at San Diego, USA. Her publications include: *A Million and One Gods* (2014); *Out of Athens: New Ancient Greeks* (2010); *Slavery: Antiquity and Its Legacy* (2009); *Slaves and Other Objects* (2008); *Trojan Horses: Saving the Classics from Conservatives* (2001); *Sappho Is Burning* (1997); *Torture and Truth* (1991); *Sowing the Body: Psychoanalysis and Ancient Representations of Women* (1988); *Centaurs and Amazons: Women and the Prehistory of the Great Chain of Being* (1982).

NIKOLAI ENDRES is associate professor of World Literature at Western Kentucky University, USA. He has published on Plato, Petronius, Gustave Flaubert, Oscar Wilde, E. M. Forster,

F. Scott Fitzgerald, Mary Renault, Gore Vidal, Patricia Nell Warren, and others. His next project is a "queer" reading of the myth and music of Richard Wagner. He is also working on a book-length study of Platonic love as a homoerotic code in the modern gay novel.

BARBARA K. GOLD is Edward North Professor of Classics at Hamilton College, USA. She is the author of *Literary Patronage in Greece and Rome* (1987); editor of *Literary and Artistic Patronage in Ancient Rome* (1982); and co-editor of *Sex and Gender in Medieval and Renaissance Texts: The Latin Tradition* (1997) and *Roman Dining* (2005). She has published widely on satire, lyric and elegy, feminist theory and late antiquity. Her *Blackwell Companion to Roman Love Elegy* was published in 2012 and a co-edited volume *Roman Literature, Gender and Reception: Domina Illustris* in 2013. Forthcoming is *Perpetua: a Martyr's Tale* (2015).

SHARON L. JAMES is associate professor of Classics at the University of North Carolina at Chapel Hill, USA. She is author of *Learned Girls and Male Persuasion: Gender and Reading in Roman Love Elegy* (2003) and with Sheila Dillon, she has co-edited Blackwell's *Companion to Women in the Ancient World* (2012). With Dorota Dutsch and David Konstan she has co-edited *Women in Roman Drama* (forthcoming). She is now completing a book entitled *Women in New Comedy*.

HELEN KING is professor of Classical Studies at The Open University, UK. Her publications include: *The One-Sex Body on Trial: The Classical and Early Modern Evidence* (2013); *Midwifery, Obstetrics and the Rise of Gynaecology: Users of a Sixteenth-Century Compendium* (2007); *The Disease of Virgins: Green Sickness, Chlorosis and the Problems of Puberty* (2004); *Hippocrates' Woman: Reading the Female Body in Ancient Greece* (1998), with Véronique Dasen, *La médecine dans l'Antiquité grecque et romaine* (2008).

MAXINE LEWIS is lecturer in the Department of Classics and Ancient History at the University of Auckland, New Zealand. She is the author of "Audience, Communication and Textuality in Catullus *Carmen 67*" in *Antichthon* 43 (2009) and is writing a book on *Catullus' Poetics of Place* for Oxford University Press.

GENEVIEVE LIVELEY is senior lecturer at the University of Bristol, UK. She is author of *A Reader's Guide to Ovid's Metamorphoses* (2012) and *Ovid: Love Songs* (2005); co-editor and contributor to *Latin Elegy and Narratology: Fragments of Story* (2008). Other publications include articles and essays on the classical tradition, cyborgs, and chaos theory.

FIONA MCHARDY is principal lecturer in Classical Civilisation at the University of Roehampton, UK. She is author of *Revenge in Ancient Greek Culture* (2008); and co-editor of *Lost Dramas of Classical* Athens (2005) and *Women's Influence on Classical Civilisation* (2004). She is currently working on *Gender Violence in Ancient Greece* with Susan Deacy for Bloomsbury.

WALTER DUVALL PENROSE, JR. is assistant professor of History at San Diego State University, USA. He specializes in the history of gender and sexuality. His forthcoming book, *Amazons, Ethnicity, and the Ideology of Courage in Ancient Greek, Asian, and African Cultures*, is under contract with Oxford University Press. He has published several essays on homoeroticism and gender in South Asian history, and has forthcoming publications on homoeroticism in the Tomb of the Diver paintings and the reception of Sappho from antiquity to the early Renaissance.

NANCY SORKIN RABINOWITZ is professor of comparative literature at Hamilton College. She is the author of *Anxiety Veiled: Euripides and the Traffic in Women* (1993) and *Greek Tragedy* (2008), co-editor of *Feminist Theory and the Classics* (1993), *Among Women: From the Homosocial to the Homoerotic in the Ancient World* (2002), and *Vision and Viewing in Ancient Greece*, a special issue of *Helios* 40.1 and 2 (2013), as well as co-editor and co-translator of *Women on The Edge: Four Plays by Euripides* (1999). Her more than thirty articles, on subjects ranging from tragedy to Greek vase painting, from teaching in prisons to contemporary fiction, have appeared in such journals as *Helios*, *Arethusa*, and *Theatre Studies*. New work on Electra appears in *Sex in Antiquity* (2014), a volume which she is also co-editing.

SUZANNE SHARLAND is senior lecturer in Classics at the University of KwaZulu-Natal in Durban, South Africa. She has published articles on Horace's *Satires* and on film studies and is the author of *Horace in Dialogue: Bakhtinian Readings in the Satires* (2010).

TYLER JO SMITH is associate professor of Classical Art and Archaeology at the University of Virginia, USA. She is author of *Komast Dancers in Archaic Greek Art* (2010) and co-editor of *A Companion to Greek Art* (2012). Her current book project concerns art and religion in ancient Greece.

POLYXENI STROLONGA is visiting assistant professor at Franklin and Marshall College, USA. Her publications include: "The Foundation of the Oracle at Delphi in the Homeric Hymn to Apollo" in *Greek, Roman and Byzantine Studies* 51 (2011).

CARRIE SULOSKY WEAVER is a Kenneth P. Dietrich School of Arts and Sciences postdoctoral fellow at the University of Pittsburgh, USA. She is a contributor to: "Funerary Feasting in Early Byzantine Sicily: New Evidence from Kaukana," in *American Journal of Archaeology* 115 (2011). Her book, *The Bioarchaeology of Classical Kamarina: Life and Death in Greek Sicily, ca. 5th to 3rd Century BCE*, will be published with the University Press of Florida in 2015.

SANJAYA THAKUR is assistant professor of Classics and former Co-Director of the Program in Feminist and Gender Studies at Colorado College, USA. He has published articles on Ovid and Virgil and is author of "Identity under Construction in Roman Athens" in *Negotiating the Past in the Past* (2007).

LAURENCE TOTELIN is a lecturer in Ancient History at the University of Cardiff, UK. She works on the history of ancient science and medicine, with a particular interest in gender issues. Her publications include *Hippocratic Recipes: Oral and Written Transmission of Pharmacological Recipes in Fifth- and Fourth-Century Greece* (2009).

LISA TRENTIN is lecturer in Classics in the Department of Historical Studies at the University of Toronto at Mississauga, Canada. Her book, *The Hunchback in Hellenistic and Roman Art*, is under contract with Bloomsbury. Her other publications include: "Exploring Visual Impairment in Ancient Rome," in *Disabilities in Roman Antiquity* (2013), "Deformity in the Roman Imperial Court," *Greece and Rome* 58.2 (2011) and "What's in a Hump? Re-examining the Hunchback in the Villa Albani-Torlonia," *Cambridge Classical Journal* 55 (2009).

INDEX

abduction, 15, 163–66. *See also* ritual capture

abortion, 2, 10–11, 64, 71–72, 74, 77–79, 85–91, 93, 96

Achilles, 17–18, 19, 44n6, 221

adolescence, 100, 226, 232, 240, 246, 261

adultery, 112, 119–20, 224

Aeschines, 239

Aeschylus, 117

afterlife, 24, 34, 41, 42, 45, 49

Agesilaus, 233, 236–37

Ajax, 18–19, 44, 50

Alcman, 246, 247

Andocides, 187–88

anger, 164, 205, 217; of students, 33, 90, 112–13, 175–76, 181, 185, 210, 228

anthropomorphism, 109–10

apartheid, 119, 121–22, 124, 127–28, 129n28, 132, 134, 135

Apollo, 17, 109, 120, 177

archaeology, 7, 11, 13–38, 39, 41, 45, 50, 54n4, 55, 61, 63, 70, 76, 79

Archilochus, 73, 108, 175, 181

Aristophanes, 2, 12, 73, 114–15, 117, 121, 129–33, 135–38, 194, 199, 206–7, 216, 241

Aristotle, 86, 111n11, 234

Ars Amatoria (Ovid), 143–44, 157, 163n20, 165, 168

art, 38, 45, 54, 55, 97, 139, 140, 151, 174, 191; Greek art, 16–26, 34; Roman art, 55, 61, 67, 70

Artemis, 17, 169n35

Asperger's Syndrome, 59

Astyanax, 19

athletes, 219–21, 226, 239

Attis, 12, 248–55, 258–66

baldness, 62, 65, 66

beauty, and love, 112, 221; female beauty, 163; male beauty, 215–16, 217, 220, 233

beatings: of a gay man, 228; of slaves, 197–98, 202, 210; of women and girls, 94, 180

Ben Hur, Judah, 189–90, 193, 196

bestiality, 142, 148

the Bible, 124, 128, 130, 192

biology, 70n19, 231; biological sex, 31, 256–58; biological gender, 253, 260

birth control, 71, 74

bisexuality, 225, 228–29, 231–32, 234, 261n42

blood, 18–19, 73n2, 78–79, 89, 97, 119n1, 192, 194, 251, 262

Braille, 57

burials, 13n1, 14–15, 20, 26–31, 34–35, 45, 50, 63; reburial, 37. *See also* cemeteries; graves

cancer, 40, 42

Catullus, 12, 142, 248–55, 258–66

cemeteries, 15, 20, 22, 30–31, 40–42, 45. *See also* burials; graves

censorship, 115, 127n22, 194

chastity, 111, 164, 234

child abuse, 214

childbirth, 30, 64, 79–80, 85, 89, 91, 222

Christianity, 15, 108–10, 116, 121–22, 123, 127–28, 130–36, 189–91, 192, 194, 196, 242

Cicero, 63, 66, 165n24

circumcision, 80–81

comedy, 76, 117, 129–31, 133, 136, 146, 177, 181, 194, 199–211. *See also* Aristophanes; Menander; Plautus; Terence

confidentiality, 58, 104, 156n9, 159

consent: age of, 214; forms for students, 148–49; in sexual relations, 155, 220n5, 238–39, 246; medical, 80, 256

conservatism, 2, 108, 111, 114–17, 121–23, 127–37

controlling behavior, 97–98, 100–101, 104, 167, 196, 204

corpses, 13, 16, 17–20, 24

counseling, 9, 12, 39, 102–5, 156n9, 159, 160n16, 161n18, 175, 178, 180n8, 182–85, 228–29

cremation, 15–16, 43

cross-dressing, 199–200

Cybele, 248, 250–52

Daphne, 109, 177

deafness, 62, 66, 67, 75, 85. *See also* microtia

death, 2, 9, 11, 13–52, 74–75, 85, 107, 111n10, 190, 221, 243; the death penalty, 42n4, 187, 214n3

Death in Venice (Mann), 213, 221–24

deformity, 57, 62–69, 88, 236

depression, 44, 85

disability, 5, 8, 11, 53–70, 75, 236

discomfort of students and staff, 10, 13, 26, 44, 51, 59, 61, 69, 73, 109, 115, 117, 144–47, 189, 199, 206, 208, 228, 247

discrimination, against disability, 54n2; gender, 249n5; race, 196–96; religion, 129n27; sex, 171; sexual orientation, 230; transgender, 257n31

disease, 31, 37, 40, 44, 65, 73, 85, 88, 120–21; homosexuality as a disease, 230; venereal disease, 74

disgust, 89, 145–46, 169n35,

dismemberment, 32

divorce, 117

domestic violence, 11, 92–106, 195

dwarfs, 67

dyslexia, 68, 85

embarrassment of instructors and students, 58, 73, 84, 121, 147, 207

embryotomy, 71, 89–90

emotional intelligence, 72, 91

emotional labor, 93, 106

emotions, 2, 16–17, 20, 26, 32, 34, 36, 38, 41, 46, 51–52, 55, 63, 64, 67, 72, 109, 158, 160, 162, 164, 183n14, 198, 218, 224, 228, 242 empathy, 24, 72, 104, 188

Ephorus, 239–40, 246

erotica, 142

ethical issues, 17, 37, 72–73, 75, 80, 84–86, 88–89, 141, 146, 150–51, 210, 230, 249, 266

ethnicity, 5, 6, 30, 55, 77, 94, 122n8, 176, 201, 203, 206n12, 208, 257. *See also* race

eulogies, 33–34

Eumolpus, 217

Euripides, 19, 32, 44, 117

euthanasia, 64, 71, 72, 87

evolution, 94, 196

fainting, 81

famine, 26, 44

Fasti (Ovid), 165n24, 167

feminism, 5–7, 255; Feminism and Classics conference, ix, 1, 152, 155, 171

Forbidden Colors (Mishima), 213, 224–25

freak shows, 68

Front Runner (Warren), 213n4, 219–21

funerals, 16–17, 20–22, 34, 40–41, 46, 221; funeral orations, 45

gender, 5, 6, 11, 27–28, 40, 53, 55, 69, 86, 89, 92–95, 102, 111, 116, 117, 131, 133, 135, 139, 141–47, 151, 152–70, 199–201, 206, 225, 228, 230–31, 247, 248–66

gender-neutral language, 250, 253–63

genitals, 73, 126n19, 129–30, 135, 142, 221; genital surgery, 256

Gladiator (Scott), 191, 193–94, 196

graves, 16–17, 21–2, 24, 26–31, 35, 37, 50. *See also* burials; cemeteries

grave goods, 30, 34, 38

Greek language, 6, 57, 62, 86, 117, 121, 129n30, 131, 146n19, 172, 187–89, 229

grieving, 11, 24, 33. *See also* mourning

Harmodius and Aristogeiton, 233–35

hate crimes, 230

health, 31, 37, 44, 64, 73–74, 85, 88, 256

Hector, 17–18

Herodotus, 97n14, 117, 233–34, 247

heterosexuality, 143–44, 221, 224, 231–32, 234, 240, 242–43

Hinduism, 16, 128n25

Hippocratic oath, 84, 86–89, 91

Hippolytus, 39, 44, 111

HIV/AIDS, 43, 74, 120–21

Homer, 15, 18n12, 19–21, 34, 110

homoeroticism, 153n2, 156, 213, 219, 221, 225, 227–47, 249n3

homophobia, 9, 11, 12, 194, 195, 214, 227–29, 246, 261

homosexuality, 77–78, 107, 112–14, 116, 121, 148, 204, 213–24, 229–33, 242, 245–47

honor, 215; and shame 44, 49; honor killing, 94–95

Horace, 141–42

hubris, 235, 239

hunchbacks, 62, 66, 67

human remains, 15, 17, 26, 31, 34–38. *See also* corpses; skeletons

human sacrifice, 18

humiliation, 66, 140, 142, 190

humor, 46, 55, 65–67, 75, 144, 199–200, 205. *See also* jokes

illegitimacy of children, 237

immaturity of students, 73, 79, 115, 134

infanticide, 10, 55, 63–65, 94

intersex, 249, 256, 258, 260–62, 266

intersexphobia, 249, 262

INDEX · 301

Islam, 15, 128n25, 132

Jesus, 111, 190–91
jokes, ancient, 75, 133, 200–202, 205, 207; inappropriate jokes, 61, 63, 66–67, 69. See also humor
Judaism, 15, 122n8, 128n25, 189–90

Ku Klux Klan, 192, 230

Laeana, 235
lameness, 62, 67, 75, 236–37
Latin language, 6, 62, 74, 142, 172, 185, 208n15, 229, 248–66
laws: at Athens, 188, 239, 242; at Rome, 63–64, 144; of Romulus, 63; on abortion, 87–88, 90; on rape, 176, 181
lawsuits, 148
learning difficulties, 60
lesbianism, 5, 9, 212, 221, 228, 231, 242, 243–46
Livy, 64, 155, 157, 159n13, 162–68
Lucretia, 162–64, 166–68, 174, 182
lust, 167–68, 240–41
Lysander, 233, 236–37
Lysias, 179n6
Lysistrata (Aristophanes), 74n3, 114n12, 121, 129–38, 199

marriage, 24, 114, 123, 134, 166, 179–80, 209n16, 214–15, 224, 240, 246; gay marriage, 220
masculinity, 192, 229, 231, 241–42, 247
masturbation, 131n31, 143, 148
mediating classroom discussion, 161, 261

medicine, 11, 55, 64, 71–91, 120
Menander, 199
Metamorphoses (Ovid), 119n1, 157, 161, 168n35, 172, 174, 176, 177, 181
microtia, 75
miscarriage in pregnancy, 86, 89
misogyny, 134, 171, 224–25
morality, 8, 63–65, 88, 107, 109–16, 127n22, 136, 191, 230, 242, 245
mortality, 11, 13, 31, 51
mourning, 13, 20, 22, 24–25, 46. See also grieving
multiculturalism, 3n4, 4–5, 8
murder, 15, 19, 94, 99, 112, 180, 192, 230, 233
museums, 15, 17, 31–39, 68, 141
mutilation, 96–97; mutilation of the Herms, 188

Niobe, 17
normalization of violence, 98–101
nudity, 145, 220

obesity, 62, 67
obituaries, 33–34, 42
obscenity, 108, 137, 141, 143, 145, 217
oral sex, 73, 143, 224n46
"othering," 143; "the Other," 61, 67, 113, 207
Ovid, 1, 119, 141–44, 151n30, 153, 157, 158n12, 161, 163n20, 165–69, 172, 174–79, 181, 184, 185

paganism, 30, 109, 130, 136, 190–91, 242, 245
Patroclus, 15, 17, 221
pederasty, 12, 51, 116, 148, 156, 160, 212–14, 217, 228–29, 232–41, 243, 246–47

pedophilia, 176, 214, 222, 226, 229, 232–33, 237–38, 246

Pentheus, 32

philosophy, 13, 39, 97, 173, 188–89, 223

Picture of Dorian Grey (Wilde), 213, 218–19

Plato, 12, 13n2, 45, 111–12, 117, 147n21, 212–16, 220, 223, 225, 235, 241, 243, 247, 256

Platonic love, 212–13, 216, 226

Plautus, 91, 179n6, 199, 202–3, 206–7, 210n20

Plutarch, 26n44, 65, 97n14, 165n24, 223, 236–37, 240, 243, 246–47

political correctness, 2, 9, 67, 254

polygamy, 111, 116

Pompeii, 121, 141–42

pornography, 12, 76n5, 78, 127n22, 139–51, 191

preconceptions of students, 73, 140, 142, 148, 155

pregnancy, 31, 75, 90, 97n14, 163

prejudices, 128, 148, 205, 229

Priam, 18–19, 26

prisoners of war, 96, 203

prostitutes, 142, 197, 199, 201, 209, 214, 217

post-traumatic stress disorder (PTSD), 44

queer studies, 212

race, 2, 5, 6n6, 8, 47, 53, 55, 69, 98, 107, 116, 119–20, 124n13, 146n21, 147, 199, 201, 206, 208, 230. *See also* ethnicity

racism, 119, 123, 127n22, 195, 206n12,

rape, 1–2, 6, 10, 11, 12, 51, 74, 93–96, 103–4, 115n14, 117n16, 120n5, 141–42, 148, 152–69, 171–86, 193, 195, 198, 199, 201, 204, 206–10, 214, 238

reception studies, 4, 141, 143, 151

religion, 8, 34, 39, 64, 98, 107, 109, 110 121, 133, 135, 230

religious beliefs of students, 10, 32, 107–117, 129–33, 242

revenge, 224, 234

ritual capture, 239–40. *See also* abduction

Romulus, 63, 163–64, 166

Sabine women, 155, 159n13, 162–68, 174

Sappho, 212n2, 243–46, 247

Satyricon (Petronius), 212n2, 213, 217–18

sculpture, 17, 22, 27

self-castration, 248, 265

sex (sexual intercourse), 2, 73–74, 96, 101, 109, 120n5, 121, 123, 133, 134, 137, 141–42, 145, 146, 148, 167, 209n16, 210, 214, 217–18, 223–26, 231–32, 233, 237, 238, 246. *See also* oral sex

sexism, 6, 9, 171, 195, 254, 259. *See also* discrimination

sex trafficking, 198

sexual abuse, 93, 97, 104, 176, 184, 214. *See also* rape

sexual desire, 169, 218, 223, 229, 241

sexual harassment, 148, 217–20, 226

sexual violence, 96, 100, 152–57, 160–67, 169, 174, 176, 189n11. *See also* rape

sexuality, 2, 12, 39–40, 69, 74, 97, 107, 121, 123n9, 130, 134, 141–51, 153n2, 156, 170, 201, 214n3, 224, 226, 228, 230–31, 235, 246–47

shock of students, 64, 73–74, 85, 89–90, 132, 137–38, 142, 144n15, 148–49, 179, 228, 259; shock tactics in the classroom, 73, 96

skeletons, 13, 26, 30–31, 34–38, 50, 70n19, 80. *See also* human remains

slavery, 10, 12, 39, 111, 124, 179, 187–98, 199, 201, 206–10, 222

Socrates, 2, 7, 13, 216, 219–20, 223, 243

Sophocles, 18, 44, 117

Soranus, 63, 86, 87

Spartacus, 190–96

Strato of Sardis, 238

suicide, 9, 15, 17–19, 30, 38, 44, 49–52

Symposium (Plato), 111–14, 116–17, 147n21, 212–16, 221, 225, 241, 243, 247

Tarquin, 167–68, 182

Terence, 177, 184, 199, 207–9

Thucydides, 233–35, 247

tolerance, 107, 115, 228, 246,

tombs, 27, 33

torture of slaves, 188–89, 197–98, 199, 207, 209

tragedy, 34, 45, 76, 149, 194, 205n10. *See also* Aeschylus; Euripides; Sophocles

training for staff, 8, 60, 93, 102–5, 153–54

transgender, 12, 228, 240, 244, 249–50, 255–59, 261–62, 266

transphobia, 249

underworld, 18, 26, 45, 110

U.S. military, 242

violence, 52, 78, 171, 239, 249n5; violence against women, 92, 152, 162, 169, 181, 209n16. *See also* domestic violence; sexual violence

virginity, 111

visual impairment, 57, 62, 65

voyeurism, 194, 218

Vulcan, 67

warfare, 19, 39, 43, 49, 52, 125–26, 134, 137, 190–92, 196, 202, 234, 236

warning students about difficult material, 46n8, 75, 78, 80, 89, 96, 117, 147–49, 160, 178, 182, 184

Warren cup, 141

whipping, 190, 204, 207

wikis, 17, 33, 41, 47–50

Women's Studies, 5, 140, 158, 209

Xenophon, 179n6, 239–41, 243, 246, 247

Zeus, 94, 97n14, 109, 110

www.ingramcontent.com/pod-product-compliance
Lightning Source LLC
Chambersburg PA
CBHW020638230426
43665CB00008B/229